ANNUAL EDITIONS

Health

07/08

Twenty-eighth Edition

EDITOR

Eileen L. Daniel

SUNY at Brockport

Eileen Daniel, a registered dietitian and licensed nutritionist, is a Professor in the Department of Health Science and Associate Dean of Professions at the State University of New York at Brockport. She received a B.S. in Nutrition and Dietetics from the Rochester Institute of Technology in 1977, an M.S. in Community Health Education from SUNY at Brockport in 1978, and a Ph.D. in Health Education from the University of Oregon in 1986. A member of the American Dietetics Association, and other professional and community organizations, Dr. Daniel has published more than 40 journal articles on issues of health, nutrition, and health education. She is the editor of *Taking Sides: Clashing Views on Controversial Issues in Health and Society, 6th edition,* (Contemporary Learning Series, 2004).

Contemporary Learning Series

2460 Kerper Blvd., Dubuque, IA 52001

Visit us on the Internet
http://www.mhcls.com

Credits

1. **Promoting Healthy Behavior Change**
   Unit photo— Keith Thomas Productions/Brand X Pictures/PictureQuest
2. **Stress and Mental Health**
   Unit photo—Ryan McVay/Getty Images.
3. **Nutritional Health**
   Unit photo—Corbis/Royalty-Free
4. **Exercise and Weight Management**
   Unit photo—Getty Images
5. **Drugs and Health**
   Unit photo—CORBIS Images/Jupiter Images
6. **Sexuality and Relationships**
   Unit photo—Alan Bailey/Getty Images
7. **Preventing and Fighting Disease**
   Unit photo—Courtesy of Tara McDermott
8. **Health Care and the Health Care System**
   Unit photo—Stockbyte/PunchStock
9. **Consumer Health**
   Unit photo—Nick Koudis/Getty Images
10. **Contemporary Health Hazards**
    Unit photo—U.S. Drug Enforcement Agency

Copyright

Cataloging in Publication Data
Main entry under title: Annual Editions: Health. 2007/2008.
1. Health—Periodicals. I. Daniel, Eileen L., *comp.* II. Title: Health.
ISBN-13 978-0-07-351621-9   ISBN-10 0-07-351621–X   658'.05   ISSN 0278–4653

Twenty-eighth Edition

Cover image Photos.com/PhotoLink/Getty Images
Printed in the United States of America   1234567890QPDQPD9876   Printed on Recycled Paper

Editors/Advisory Board

Members of the Advisory Board are instrumental in the final selection of articles for each edition of ANNUAL EDITIONS. Their review of articles for content, level, currentness, and appropriateness provides critical direction to the editor and staff. We think that you will find their careful consideration well reflected in this volume.

Preface

In publishing ANNUAL EDITIONS we recognize the enormous role played by the magazines, newspapers, and journals of the public press in providing current, first-rate educational information in a broad spectrum of interest areas. Many of these articles are appropriate for students, researchers, and professionals seeking accurate, current material to help bridge the gap between principles and theories and the real world. These articles, however, become more useful for study when those of lasting value are carefully collected, organized, indexed, and reproduced in a low-cost format, which provides easy and permanent access when the material is needed. That is the role played by ANNUAL EDITIONS.

America is in the midst of a revolution that is changing the way millions of Americans view their health. Traditionally, most people delegated responsibility for their health to their physicians and hoped that medical science would be able to cure whatever ailed them. This approach to health care emphasized the role of medical technology and funneled billions of dollars into medical research. The net result of all this spending is the most technically advanced and expensive health care system in the world. In an attempt to rein in health care costs, the health care delivery system has moved from privatized health care coverage to what is termed "managed care." While managed care has turned the tide regarding the rising cost of health care, it has done so by limiting reimbursement for many cutting edge technologies. Unfortunately many people also feel that it has lowered the overall quality of care that is being given. Perhaps the saving grace is that we live at a time in which chronic illnesses rather than acute illnesses are our number one health threat, and many of these illnesses can be prevented or controlled by our lifestyle choices. The net result of these changes has prompted millions of individuals to assume more personal responsibility for safeguarding their own health. Evidence of this change in attitude can be seen in the growing interest in nutrition, physical fitness, dietary supplements, and stress management. If we as a nation are to capitalize on this new health consciousness, we must devote more time and energy to educating Americans in the health sciences so that they will be better able to make informed choices about their health.

Health is a complex and dynamic subject, and it is practically impossible for anyone to stay abreast of all the current research findings. In the past, most of us have relied on books, newspapers, magazines, and television as our primary sources for medical/health information, but today, with the widespread use of personal computers connected to the World Wide Web, it is possible to access vast amounts of health information any time of the day without ever leaving one's home. Unfortunately, quantity and availability does not necessarily translate into quality, and this is particularly true in the area of medical/health information. Just as the Internet is a great source for reliable timely information, it is also a vehicle for the dissemination of misleading and fraudulent information. Currently there are no standards or regulations regarding the posting of health content on the Internet, and this has led to a plethora of misinformation and quackery in the medical/health arena. Given this vast amount of health information, our task as health educators is twofold: (1) to provide our students with the most up-to-date and accurate information available on major health issues of our time, and (2) to teach our students the skills that will enable them to sort out fact from fiction in order to become informed consumers. *Annual Editions: Health 07/08* was designed to aid in this task. It offers a sampling of quality articles that represent the latest thinking on a variety of health issues, and it also serves as a tool for developing critical thinking skills.

The articles in this volume were carefully chosen on the basis of their quality and timeliness. Because this book is revised and updated annually, it contains information that is not generally available in any standard textbook. As such, it serves as a valuable resource for both teachers and students. This edition of *Annual Editions: Health* has been updated to reflect the latest thinking on a variety of contemporary health issues. We hope that you find this edition to be a helpful learning tool filled with information and presented in a user-friendly format. The 10 topical areas presented in this edition mirror those that are normally covered in introductory health courses: Promoting Health Behavior Change, Stress and Mental Health, Nutritional Health, Exercise and Weight Control, Drugs and Health, Sexuality and Relationships, Preventing and Fighting Disease, Health Care and the Health Care System, Consumer Health, and Contemporary Health Hazards. Because of the interdependence of the various elements that constitute health, the articles selected were written by authors with diverse educational backgrounds and expertise including: naturalists, environmentalists, psychologists, economists, sociologists, nutritionists, consumer advocates, and traditional health practitioners.

Annual Editions: Health 07/08 was designed to be one of the most useful and up-to-date publications currently available in the area of health. Please let us know what you think of it by filling out and returning the postage paid *article rating form* on the last page of this book. Any anthology can be improved. This one will be—annually.

Eileen L. Daniel
Eileen L. Daniel
Editor

Contents

UNIT 1
Promoting Healthy Behavior Change

UNIT 2
Stress and Mental Health

The concepts in bold italics are developed in the article. For further expansion, please refer to the Topic Guide and the Index.

UNIT 3
Nutritional Health

The concepts in bold italics are developed in the article. For further expansion, please refer to the Topic Guide and the Index.

UNIT 4
Exercise and Weight Management

The concepts in bold italics are developed in the article. For further expansion, please refer to the Topic Guide and the Index.

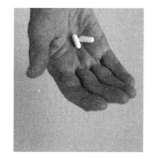

UNIT 5
Drugs and Health

UNIT 6
Sexuality and Relationships

The concepts in bold italics are developed in the article. For further expansion, please refer to the Topic Guide and the Index.

UNIT 7
Preventing and Fighting Disease

The concepts in bold italics are developed in the article. For further expansion, please refer to the Topic Guide and the Index.

UNIT 8
Health Care and the Health Care System

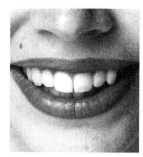

UNIT 9
Consumer Health

The concepts in bold italics are developed in the article. For further expansion, please refer to the Topic Guide and the Index.

UNIT 10
Contemporary Health Hazards

The concepts in bold italics are developed in the article. For further expansion, please refer to the Topic Guide and the Index.

The concepts in bold italics are developed in the article. For further expansion, please refer to the Topic Guide and the Index.

Topic Guide

This topic guide suggests how the selections in this book relate to the subjects covered in your course. You may want to use the topics listed on these pages to search the Web more easily.

On the following pages a number of Web sites have been gathered specifically for this book. They are arranged to reflect the units of this *Annual Edition*. You can link to these sites by going to the student online support site at *http://www.mhcls.com/online/*.

ALL THE ARTICLES THAT RELATE TO EACH TOPIC ARE LISTED BELOW THE BOLD-FACED TERM.

Internet References

The following internet sites have been carefully researched and selected to support the articles found in this reader. The easiest way to access these selected sites is to go to our student online support site at *http://www.mhcls.com/online/*.

AE: Health 07/08

The following sites were available at the time of publication. Visit our Web site—we update our student online support site regularly to reflect any changes.

General Sources

National Institute on Aging (NIA)
http://www.nia.nih.gov/

The NIA, one of the institutes of the U.S. National Institutes of Health, presents this home page to lead you to a variety of resources on health and lifestyle issues on aging.

U.S. Department of Agriculture (USDA)/Food and Nutrition Information Center (FNIC)
http://www.nal.usda.gov/fnic/

Use this site to find nutrition information provided by various USDA agencies, to find links to food and nutrition resources on the Internet, and to access FNIC publications and databases.

U.S. Department of Health and Human Services
http://www.os.dhhs.gov

This site has extensive links to information on such topics as the health benefits of exercise, weight control, and prudent lifestyle choices.

U.S. National Institutes of Health (NIH)
http://www.nih.gov

Consult this site for links to extensive health information and scientific resources. Comprising 24 separate institutes, centers, and divisions, the NIH is one of eight health agencies of the Public Health Service, which, in turn, is part of the U.S. Department of Health and Human Services.

U.S. National Library of Medicine
http://www.nlm.nih.gov

This huge site permits a search of a number of databases and electronic information sources such as MEDLINE. You can learn about research projects and programs and peruse the national network of medical libraries here.

World Health Organization
http://www.who.int/en

This home page of the World Health Organization will provide links to a wealth of statistical and analytical information about health around the world.

UNIT 1: Promoting Healthy Behavior Change

Ask Dr. Weil
http://www.drweil.com/u/Home/index.html

Dr. Weil, a Harvard-trained physician, is director of the Center for Integrative Medicine at the University of Arizona. He offers a comprehensive Web site that addresses alternative medicine. Look for research, FAQs, and links to related sites.

Columbia University's Go Ask Alice!
http://www.goaskalice.columbia.edu/index.html

This interactive site provides discussion and insight into a number of personal issues of interest to college-age people and those younger and older. Many questions about physical and emotional health and well-being are answered.

The Society of Behavioral Medicine
http://www.sbm.org/

This site provides listings of major, general health institutes and organizations as well as discipline-specific links and resources in medicine, psychology, and public health.

UNIT 2: Stress and Mental Health

The American Institute of Stress
http://www.stress.org

This site provides comprehensive information on stress: its dangers, the beliefs that build helpful techniques for overcoming stress, and so on. This easy-to-navigate site has good links to information on anxiety and related topics.

National Mental Health Association (NMHA)
http://www.nmha.org/index.html

The NMHA is a citizen volunteer advocacy organization that works to improve the mental health of all individuals. The site provides access to guidelines that individuals can use to reduce stress and improve their lives in small yet tangible ways.

Self-Help Magazine
http://www.selfhelpmagazine.com/index.html

Reach lots of links to self-help resources on the Net at this site, including resources on stress, anxiety, fears, and more.

UNIT 3: Nutritional Health

The American Dietetic Association
http://www.eatright.org

This organization, along with its National Center of Nutrition and Dietetics, promotes optimal nutrition, health, and well-being. This easy-to-navigate site presents FAQs about nutrition and dieting, nutrition resources, and career and member information.

Center for Science in the Public Interest (CSPI)
http://www.cspinet.org/

CSPI is a nonprofit education and advocacy organization that focuses on improving the safety and nutritional quality of our food supply and on reducing the health problems caused by alcohol. This agency also evaluates the nutritional composition of fast foods, movie popcorn, and chain restaurants. There are also good links to related sites.

Food and Nutrition Information Center
http://www.nalusda.gov/fnic/index.html

An official Agriculture Network Information Center web site. The FNIC is one of several information centers at the National Agriculture Library, the Agricultural Research Service, and the U.S. Department of Agriculture. The web site has information on nutrition-related publications, an index of food and nutrition-related Internet resources, and an on-line catalog of materials.

UNIT 4: Exercise and Weight Management

American Society of Exercise Physiologists (ASEP)
http://www.asep.org

The ASEP is devoted to promoting people's health and physical fitness. This extensive site provides links to publications related to exercise and career opportunities in exercise physiology.

Eating Disorders Awareness and Prevention, Inc.
http://www.edap.org

This site offers information on eating disorders, including suggestions for families and friends of sufferers, details for professionals, and general information on eating disorders for the interested public.

Cyberdiet
http://www.cyberdiet.com/reg/index.html

This site, maintained by a registred dietician, offers CyberDiet's interactive nutritional profile, food facts, menus and meal plans, and exercise and food-related sites.

Shape Up America!
http://www.shapeup.org

At the Shape Up America! Web site you will find the latest information about safe weight management, healthy eating, and physical fitness.

UNIT 5: Drugs and Health

Food and Drug Administration (FDA)
http://www.fda.gov/

This site includes FDA news, information on drugs, and drug toxicology facts.

National Institute on Drug Abuse (NIDA)
http://www.nida.nih.gov/

Use this site index for access to NIDA publications and communications, information on drugs of abuse, and links to other related Web sites.

Prescription Drugs: The Issue
http://www.opensecrets.org/news/drug/

This site offers information on a variety of prescription drugs, including interactions, side effects, and related material.

UNIT 6: Sexuality and Relationships

Planned Parenthood
http://www.plannedparenthood.org/

This home page provides links to information on contraceptives (including outercourse and abstinence) and to discussions of other topics related to sexual health.

Sexuality Information and Education Council of the United States (SIECUS)
http://www.siecus.org/

SIECUS is a nonprofit private advocacy group that affirms that sexuality is a natural and healthy part of living. This home page offers publications, what's new, descriptions of programs, and a listing of international sexuality education initiatives.

UNIT 7: Preventing and Fighting Disease

American Cancer Society
http://www.cancer.org

Open this site and its various links to learn the concerns and lifestyle advice of the American Cancer Society. It provides information on tobacco and alternative cancer therapies.

American Heart Association
http://www.amhrt.org

This award-winning comprehensive site of the American Heart Association offers information on heart disease, prevention, patient facts, eating plans, what's new, nutrition, smoking cessation, and FAQs.

National Institute of Allergy and Infectious Diseases (NIAID)
http://www3.niaid.nih.gov/

Open this site and its various links to learn the concerns and lifestyle advice of the National Institute of Allergy and Infectious Diseases.

American Diabetes Association Home Page
http://www.diabetes.org

This site offers information on diabetes including treatment, diet, and insulin therapy.

UNIT 8: Health Care and the Health Care System

American Medical Association (AMA)
http://www.ama-assn.org

The AMA offers this site to find up-to-date medical information, peer-review resources, discussions of such topics as HIV/AIDS and women's health, examination of issues related to managed care, and important publications.

MedScape: The Online Resource for Better Patient Care
http://www.medscape.com

For health professionals and interested consumers, this site offers peer-reviewed articles, self-assessment features, medical news, and annotated links to Internet resources. It also contains the *Morbidity & Mortality Weekly Report,*which is a publicatiobn of the Centers for Disease Control and Prevention.

UNIT 9: Consumer Health

FDA Consumer Magazine
http://www.fda.gov/fdac

This site offers articles and information that appears in the *FDA Consumer Magazine.*

Global Vaccine Awareness League
http://www.gval.com

This site addresses side effects related to vaccination. Its many links are geared to provide copious information.

UNIT 10: Contemporary Health Hazards

Centers for Disease Control: Flu
http://www.cdc.gov/flu

This CDC site provides updates, information, key facts, questions and answers, and ways to prevent influenza (the flu). Updated regularly during the flu season.

National Sleep Foundation
http://www.sleepfoundation.org

The National Sleep Foundation (NSF) is an independent nonprofit organization dedicated to improving public health and safety by achieving public understanding of sleep and sleep disorders.

Center for the Study of Autism
http://www.autism.org

This site provides resources for both professionals and family members of individuals with autism. The site includes interventions, family support, and stories of persons with the condition.

Food and Drug Administration Mad Cow Disease Page

http://www.fda.gov/oc/opacom/hottopics/bse.html

This Food and Drug Administration page includes information, articles, and updates about Bovine Spongiform Encephalopathy (BSE) also known as "Mad Cow Disease."

Environmental Protection Agency

http://www.epa.gov

Use this site to find environmental health information provided by various EPA agencies.

We highly recommend that you review our Web site for expanded information and our other product lines. We are continually updating and adding links to our Web site in order to offer you the most usable and useful information that will support and expand the value of your Annual Editions. You can reach us at: *http://www.mhcls.com/annualeditions/.*

UNIT 1
Promoting Healthy Behavior Change

Unit Selections

Key Points to Consider

- Why do you think that people continue to engage in negative health behaviors when they know that these behaviors will have a negative impact on their health? Have you ever done so? If so, why?

- What negative behaviors practiced by college students contribute to academic difficulties?

- What behaviors do you wish you could undo?

- What factors contribute to successful lifestyle change?

- What personal health behaviors would you like to improve? What prevents you from making these changes? How can you overcome these obstacles?

- Should companies charge employees more for health insurance if they continue to engage in unhealthy behaviors?

- What social and economic issues affect health behaviors?

Student Website
www.mhcls.com/online

Internet References
Further information regarding these websites may be found in this book's preface or online.

Ask Dr. Weil
http://www.drweil.com/u/Home/index.html

Columbia University's Go Ask Alice!
http://www.goaskalice.columbia.edu/index.html

The Society of Behavioral Medicine
http://www.sbm.org/

"Those of us who protect our health daily and those of us who put our health in constant jeopardy have exactly the same mortality: 100 percent. The difference, of course, is the timing." This quotation from Elizabeth M. Whelan, Sc.D., M.P.H., reminds us that we must all face the fact that we are going to die sometime. The question that is decided by our behavior is when and, to a certain extent, how. This book and especially this unit are designed to assist students in the development of cognitive skills and knowledge that when put to use help make the moment of our death come as late as possible in our lives and to maintain our health as long as possible. While we cannot control many of the things that happen to us, we must all strive to accept personal responsibility for, and make informed decisions about, things that we can control. This is no minor task, but it is one in which the potential reward is life itself.

Perhaps the best way to start this process is by educating ourselves on the relative risks associated with the various behaviors and lifestyle choices we make. To minimize all risk to life and health would be to significantly limit the quality of our lives, and while this might be a choice that some would make, it certainly is not the goal of health education. A more logical approach to risk reduction would be to educate the public on the relative risk associated with various behaviors and lifestyle choices so that they are capable of making informed decisions. While it may seem obvious that certain behaviors, such as smoking, entail a high level of risk, the significance of others such as toxic waste sites and food additives are frequently blown out of proportion to the actual risks involved. The net result of this type of distortion is that many Americans tend to minimize the dangers of known hazards such as tobacco and alcohol and focus attention, instead, on potentially minor health hazards over which they have little or no control.

Educating the public on the relative risk of various health behaviors is only part of the job that health educators must tackle in order to assist individuals in making informed choices regarding their health. They also must teach the skills that will enable people to evaluate the validity and significance of new information as it becomes available. Just how important informed decision making is in our daily lives is evidenced by the numerous health-related media announcements and articles that fill our newspapers, magazines, and television broadcasts. Rather than inform and enlighten the public on significant new medical discoveries, many of these announcements do little more than add to the level of confusion or exaggerate or sensationalize health issues. Why is this so? While there is no simple explanation, there appear to be at least two major factors that contribute to the confusion. The first has to do with the primary goals and objectives of the media itself. One only has to scan the headlines on the cover pages of magazines or newspapers to realize that the primary goal of these publications is to entice the potential reader into purchasing their product. How better to capture the readers' attention than to sensationalize and exaggerate scientific discoveries? This is not to blame the media but rather to remind the reader that given the economic realities of the competitive world in which we live, sometimes the methodical plodding of the scientific method takes second place to the marketing needs of a publisher.

Let's assume for a minute that the scientific community is in general agreement that certain behaviors clearly promote our health while others damage our health. Given this information, are you likely to make adjustments to your lifestyle to comply with the findings? Logic would suggest that of course you would, but experience has taught us that information alone isn't enough to bring about behavioral change in many people. Why is it that so many people continue to make bad choices regarding their health behaviors when they are fully aware of the risks involved? John Dorschner's article "Putting a Premium on Health," suggests that we can empower ourselves to change our behavior and benefit both physically and financially. We can vow to make changes to try and undo or minimize negative health behaviors of our past. While strategies such as these may work for those who feel they are at risk, how do we help those who do not feel that they are at risk or those who feel that it is too late in their lives for the changes to matter? In "The Perils of Higher Education," the author maintains that while college is a place to learn and grow, for many students it becomes four years of a bad diet, too little sleep, and too much alcohol. These negative health behaviors affect not the students' health, but may impact their grades.

Another viewpoint is demonstrated in Alexandra García's article which addresses whether or not health promotion is relevant across cultures and among different socioeconomic groups. The author maintains that health promoters should consider the social issues relevant to their patient's health and develop programs based on these issues.

While the goal of health education is to promote healthy behaviors that lead to healthy lifestyles, this objective will not be reached unless, or until, the public is armed with the knowledge and skills necessary to make informed decisions regarding their health. Even then, there is no guarantee that the information gleaned will serve as motivation. In a free society such as ours, the choice is, and must remain, up to the individual.

The Perils of Higher Education

Can't remember the difference between declensions and derivatives? Blame college. The undergrad life is a blast, but it may lead you to forget everything you learn.

STEVEN KOTLER

We go to college to learn, to soak up a dazzling array of information intended to prepare us for adult life. But college is not simply a data dump; it is also the end of parental supervision. For many students, that translates into four years of late nights, pizza banquets and boozy week ends that start on Wednesday. And while we know that bad habits are detrimental to cognition in general—think drunk driving—new studies show that the undergrad urges to eat, drink and be merry have devastating effects on learning and memory. It turns out that the exact place we go to get an education may in fact be one of the worst possible environments in which to retain anything we've learned.

Dude, I Haven't Slept in Three Days!

Normal human beings spend one-third of their lives asleep, but today's college students aren't normal. A recent survey of undergraduates and medical students at Stanford University found 80 percent of them qualified as sleep-deprived, and a poll taken by the National Sleep Foundation found that most young adults get only 6.8 hours a night.

All-night cramfests may seem to be the only option when the end of the semester looms, but in fact getting sleep—and a full dose of it—might be a better way to ace exams. Sleep is crucial to declarative memory, the hard, factual kind that helps us remember which year World War I began, or what room the French Lit class is in. It's also essential for procedural memory, the "know-how" memory we use when learning to drive a car or write a five-paragraph essay. "Practice makes perfect," says Harvard Medical School psychologist Matt Walker, "but having a night's rest after practicing might make you even better."

Walker taught 100 people to bang out a series of nonsense sequences on a keyboard—a standard procedural memory task. When asked to replay the sequence 12 hours later, they hadn't improved. But when one group of subjects was allowed to sleep overnight before being retested, their speed and accuracy improved by 20 to 30 percent. "It was bizarre," says Walker. "We were seeing people's skills improve just by sleeping."

For procedural memory, the deep slow-wave stages of sleep were the most important for improvement—particularly during the last two hours of the night. Declarative memory, by contrast, gets processed during the slow-wave stages that come in the first two hours of sleep. "This means that memory requires a full eight hours of sleep," says Walker. He also found that if someone goes without sleep for 24 hours after acquiring a new skill, a week later they will have lost it completely. So college students who pull all-nighters during exam week might do fine on their tests but may not remember any of the material by next semester.

Walker believes that the common practice of back-loading semesters with a blizzard of papers and exams needs a rethink. "Educators are just encouraging sleeplessness," says Walker. "This is just not an effective way to force information into the brain."

Who's Up For Pizza?

Walk into any college cafeteria and you'll find a smorgasbord of French fries, greasy pizza, burgers, potato chips and the like. On top of that, McDonald's, Burger King, Wendy's and other fast-food chains have been gobbling up campus real estate in recent years. With hectic schedules and skinny budgets, students find fast food an easy alternative. A recent Tufts University survey found that 50 percent of students eat too much fat, and 70 to 80 percent eat too much saturated fat.

But students who fuel their studies with fast food have something more serious than the "freshman 15" to worry about: They may literally be eating themselves stupid. Researchers have known since the late 1980s that bad eating habits contribute to the kind of cognitive decline found in diseases like Alzheimer's. Since then, they've been trying to find out exactly how a bad diet might be hard on the brain. Ann-Charlotte Granholm, director of the Center for Aging at the Medical University of South Carolina, has recently focused on trans fat, widely used in fast-food cooking because it extends the shelf life of foods. Trans fat is made by bubbling hydrogen through unsaturated fat, with copper or zinc added to speed the chemical reaction along. These metals are frequently found in the brains of people with Alzheimer's, which sparked Granholm's concern.

To investigate, she fed one group of rats a diet high in trans fat and compared them with another group fed a diet that was just as greasy but low in trans fat. Six weeks later, she tested the animals in a water maze, the rodent equivalent of a final exam in organic chemistry. "The trans-fat group made many more errors," says Granholm, especially when she used more difficult mazes.

When she examined the rats' brains, she found that trans-fat eaters had fewer proteins critical to healthy neurological function. She also saw inflammation in and around the hippocampus, the part of the brain responsible for learning and memory. "It was alarming," says Granholm. "These are the exact types of changes we normally see at the onset of Alzheimer's, but we saw them after six weeks," even though the rats were still young.

Students who fuel their studies with fast food have something serious to worry about: They may literally be eating themselves stupid.

Her work corresponds to a broader inquiry conducted by Veerendra Kumar Madala Halagaapa and Mark Mattson of the National Institute on Aging. The researchers fed four groups of mice different diets—normal, high-fat, high-sugar and high-fat/high-sugar. Each diet had the same caloric value, so that one group of mice wouldn't end up heavier. Four months later, the mice on the high-fat diets performed significantly worse than the other groups on a water maze test.

The researchers then exposed the animals to a neurotoxin that targets the hippocampus, to assess whether a high-fat diet made the mice less able to cope with brain damage. Back in the maze, all the animals performed worse than before, but the mice who had eaten the high-fat diets were most seriously compromised. "Based on our work," says Mattson, "we'd predict that people who eat high-fat diets and high-fat/high-sugar diets are not only damaging their ability to learn and remember new information, but also putting themselves at much greater risk for all sorts of neurodegenerative disorders like Alzheimer's."

Welcome to Margaritaville State University

It's widely recognized that heavy drinking doesn't exactly boost your intellect. But most people figure that their booze-induced foolishness wears off once the hangover is gone. Instead, it turns out that even limited stints of overindulgence may have long-term effects.

Less than 20 years ago, researchers began to realize that the adult brain wasn't just a static lump of cells. They found that stem cells in the brain are constantly churning out new neurons, particularly in the hippocampus. Alcoholism researchers, in turn, began to wonder if chronic alcoholics' memory problems had something to do with nerve cell birth and growth.

In 2000, Kimberly Nixon and Fulton Crews at the University of North Carolina's Bowles Center for Alcohol Studies subjected lab rats to four days of heavy alcohol intoxication. They gave the rats a week to shake off their hangovers, then tested them on and off during the next month in a water maze. "We didn't find anything at first," says Nixon. But on the 19th day, the rats who had been on the binge performed much worse. In 19 days, the cells born during the binge had grown to maturity—and clearly, the neurons born during the boozy period didn't work properly once they reached maturity. "[The timing] was almost too perfect," says Nixon.

While normal rats generated about 2,500 new brain cells in three weeks, the drinking rats produced only 1,400. A month later, the sober rats had lost about half of those new cells through normal die-off. But all of the new cells died in the brains of the binge drinkers. "This was startling," says Nixon. "It was the first time anyone had found that alcohol not only inhibits the birth of new cells but also inhibits the ones that survive." In further study, they found that a week's abstinence produced a twofold burst of neurogenesis, and a month off the sauce brought cognitive function back to normal.

What does this have to do with a weekend keg party? A number of recent studies show that college students consume far more alcohol than anyone previously suspected. Forty-four percent of today's collegiates drink enough to be classified as binge drinkers, according to a nationwide survey of 10,000 students done at Harvard University. The amount of alcohol consumed by Nixon's binging rats far exceeded intake at a typical keg party—but other research shows that the effects of alcohol work on a sliding scale. Students who follow a weekend of heavy drinking with a week of heavy studying might not forget everything they learn. They just may struggle come test time.

Can I Bum a Smoke?

If this ledger of campus menaces worries you, here's something you really won't like: Smoking cigarettes may actually have some cognitive benefits, thanks to the power of nicotine. The chemical improves mental focus, as scientists have known since the 1950s. Nicotine also aids concentration in people who have ADHD and may protect against Alzheimer's disease. Back in 2000, a nicotine-like drug under development by the pharmaceutical company Astra Arcus USA was shown to restore the ability to learn and remember in rats with brain lesions similar to those found in Alzheimer's patients. More recently Granholm, the scientist investigating trans fats and memory, found that nicotine enhances spatial memory in healthy rats. Other researchers have found that nicotine also boosts both emotional memory (the kind that helps us *not* put our hands back in the fire after we've been burned) and auditory memory.

There's a catch: Other studies show that nicotine encourages state-dependent learning. The idea is that if, for example, you study in blue sweats, it helps to take the exam in blue sweats. In other words, what you learn while smoking is best recalled while smoking. Since lighting up in an exam room might cause problems, cigarettes probably aren't the key to getting on the dean's list.

Nonetheless, while the number of cigarette smokers continues to drop nationwide, college students are still lighting up: As many as 30 percent smoke during their years of higher education. The smoking rate for young adults between the ages of 18 and 24 has actually risen in the past decade.

All this news makes you wonder how anyone's ever managed to get an education. Or what would happen to GPAs at a vegetarian university with a 10 P.M. curfew. But you might not need to go to such extremes. While Granholm agrees that the excesses of college can be "a perfect example of what you shouldn't do to yourself if you are trying to learn," she doesn't recommend abstinence. "Moderation," she counsels, "just like in everything else. Moderation is the key to collegiate success."

STEVEN KOTLER, based in Los Angeles, has written for *The New York Times Magazine, National Geographic, Details, Wired* and *Outside.*

Is Health Promotion Relevant Across Cultures and the Socioeconomic Spectrum?

Alexandra García, PhD, RN

Is health promotion a White middle-class phenomenon that people from other cultures and classes do not regard as important? When implementing health-promotion initiatives, are healthcare providers making assumptions that are not valid for other cultural or socioeconomic groups? How do people of various cultures and classes perceive health and health promotion? To explore these questions, this article reviews some of the relevant literature on culture and class in relation to health promotion, exploring issues foundational to the effectiveness of health-promotion programs and pertinent to delivering health-promotion interventions to ethnic, racial, and cultural minorities and poor populations. Health promoters are encouraged to consider the social determinants of their patients' health and tailor programs on the basis of their patients' motivations and resources.

The relevance of health promotion to heterogeneous populations is an important issue for healthcare practitioners, researchers, and policy makers who are interested in developing and delivering inclusive, culturally appropriate interventions and evaluating their outcomes. Researchers and providers have implemented health-promoting interventions for diverse groups of people for many years and have reported mixed degrees of success. They have also been aware that unequal distributions of disease and disability disproportionately affect racial and ethnic minorities and impoverished peoples.[1] These disproportionate impacts are called health disparities. To address these disparities, healthcare providers have been directed by the *Healthy People 2010* guidelines to increase the quality and years of healthy life by promoting health and preventing disease, disability, and premature death,[2] thereby attempting to eliminate health disparities.

In the purest sense, health promotion is associated with wanting to improve one's health via "behavior motivated by the desire to increase well-being and actualize human health potential."[3] Such behavior changes might include engaging in more physical activity or getting more sleep. Health promotion, consistent with the *Healthy People 2010* mandate, also includes health protection, or "behavior motivated by a desire to actively avoid illness, detect it early, or maintain functioning within the constraints of illness."[3(p7)] Health protection might include incorporating more hygienic or safer practices into daily routines, participating in disease screenings, or obtaining immunizations and vaccinations.

Sociocultural factors, such as ethnic or racial identity, culturally based practices, and socioeconomic standing, are acknowledged in several health-promotion models[3] but are viewed as relatively fixed and not amenable to healthcare providers' interventions. These factors deserve closer attention because they may be the key to improving health-promotion efforts and resolving health disparities.

We should not build on the assumption that health is a universal value that can be uniformly promoted to all populations because much of what healthcare deliverers assume about health promotion may not hold for many patients. The ineffectiveness of some health-promotion interventions may be the result of unarticulated incongruence of social and cultural assumptions between the health-promotion intervention deliverers and the targeted group. To explore questions related to issues of relevance that seem to be crucial to developing the next stage of health-promotion interventions, this article reviews literature on health promotion with respect to culture and social class.

Culture

Culture is a term that refers to the inherited set of implicit and explicit rules guiding how a group's members view, feel about, and interact with the world. Cultural expressions and, to a lesser extent, cultural values change over time and are influenced by others. Individual and group beliefs about personal control, individualism, collectivism, spirituality, familial roles, and communication patterns contribute to cultural expression.[4] Even so, cultures are heterogeneous so that there are few, if any, constants among all members.[5]

Most people belong to more than one culture based on their ethnicity or where they live and work. Healthcare professionals themselves comprise a particular culture.[6] The notion that healthcare providers and people outside the healthcare culture (including those who are ill or have a disability, live in rural or underserved areas, are of low education levels, or who are impoverished) may have differing beliefs, values, or perspectives on health, illness, and how to manage health has been well documented by medical anthropologists.[7,8] Ethnomedicine and emic approaches have been used to understand how people conceptualize their health, diseases, illnesses, treatments, and symptoms in the context of their culture and experience. For instance, Hunt and Arar[9] reported that though patients and physicians were usually compatible in their beliefs about the cause and course of diabetes, they differed strongly in their goals, strategies, and evaluations of care.

In fact, although researchers have focused on how people of various cultures define illness, they focus less often on how people define their health and maintain it according to their definition. Several studies have quantified behaviors believed by healthcare providers to promote health (eating a diet high in fiber and low in cholesterol, eg) but few have explored which behaviors people of other cultures (ie, minority, disabled, rural, underserved, chronically ill) consider important or the meanings ascribed to those behaviors. Arcury et al[10] explored these questions with rural-dwelling elderly Anglo-Americans, Blacks, and Native Americans and found agreement in several domains and themes of health-promoting behaviors across the groups. For instance, balance and moderation were themes common among members of all 3 ethnic groups.

On the basis of an awareness of the importance of culture, program developers have made considerable efforts to make interventions that are culturally relevant.[11] The following 5 questions arise from a concern for cultural relevance and health promotion.

First, is health promotion not relevant because of differences in cultural norms? For instance, is health promotion too individualistic for a member of a collectivist culture? Strong group or family-oriented values can create a predisposition not to engage in activities when they are for the exclusive benefit of an individual, especially when they interfere with that person's obligations.[12] Health-promotion efforts would be more successful if based on the understanding that for many participants personal fulfillment comes from satisfying group rather than individual needs.

Second, does the Anglo-American emphasis on efficiency create a barrier to people who are used to more personal healthcare systems? In Hispanic cultures, *personalismo*, characterized by a trusting close relationship, is an important element for Hispanics' interactions with their healthcare providers. Does *personalismo* have a counterpart in non-Hispanic cultures? Perhaps so, for even Anglo-Americans reminisce about the "good old days" when physicians made house calls and were intimate members of their patients' societies. Health-promotion programs might incorporate more *personalismo* in order to attract and retain Hispanic clients and others preferring friendly and intimate interactions.[12,13]

Third, if the culture is oriented more in the present than in the future, is a focus on disease prevention relevant? Is promoting health a goal for people who hold a fixed belief on their future health status? Some people seem governed by fatalism, which inhibits the seeking of medical help and possibly deters them from making lifestyle modifications.[12] For them, it can be extremely difficult to change from a sedentary lifestyle or a long accustomed harmful diet. As cited in Hunt and Arar,[9 (p356)] one Mexican American said, "Well I have diabetes, what the hell, I'm gonna die anyways."

Fourth, could a group's pervasive low self-esteem and depression be to blame for some participants' reluctance to engage in health-promotion activities? Hunt and Arar[9(p356)] quoted an Anglo-American physician's assistant working in South Texas who said, "*Mi cuerpo es jonque* [my body is junk] is a typical comment [from Mexican American patients]. Their houses and cars are junk, too, so they accept the same for their bodies.... They don't see much to live for, so they want to die happy, eating."

Finally, some cultural beliefs may be inconsistent with the requirement to be proactive. Holland and Courtney[14] suggested that Hispanic immigrants tend to expect the healthcare provider to cure their ailments and are not accustomed to an emphasis on health promotion, disease prevention, and self-responsibility. So, are differences in expectations about responsibility for health based on differences in culture? These questions and others like them should be explored for people of various cultural groups.

Social Class

Certainly, not all behaviors and beliefs can be explained by culture; many other factors may determine behaviors and beliefs. For instance, individual factors (such as age, gender, intelligence, education, and experience), socioeconomic factors (such as social class, occupation, and sources of social support systems), and environmental factors (including the natural and built environments and exposures) may influence behavior at various times.

Social classes, or "hierarchically arranged, socially meaningful groupings linked to the structure of society,"[15 (p377)] make up complex societies and have their own mores.[4] In the sociological literature, class relates to the economic and political power described by Marx. More commonly, social class is used interchangeably with socioeconomic status (SES),[16] referring to stratifications based on education, income, occupation, and property ownership.[15] As cited in 2 extensive reviews of patterns of SES and health,[15,17] many studies have demonstrated a clear relationship between SES and health during the latter half of the 20th century, reflecting rapid gains in health for those with high SES and worsening conditions for those with lower SES.

In general, health disparities are often attributed to low SES.[1,15] Higher levels of income and education are related to lower mortality rates.[18–22] Lower SES respondents were more likely to smoke cigarettes, not exercise or exercise less, and eat fewer fruits and vegetables. Furthermore, lower SES respondents were less likely to be future oriented, had lower expectations of longevity, and had stronger beliefs than higher SES respondents toward the importance of chance to health status.[23] These behaviors and beliefs begin in childhood. Children who have grown up in socially disadvantaged homes are less likely to have consistent daily mealtimes and bedtimes or eat lunch or dinner with their family.[24] Overall, people with lower SES die earlier than people with higher SES, partly because people with higher SES have healthier lifestyles.[25] Moreover, social inequalities lead to unequal exposures to environmental hazards.[26]

Although health-status differences between income groups are greater than differences between races, minority status is often used as a synonym for low SES in part because health indicators are rarely reported by income levels in the United States.[27] Poverty affects proportionately more women of color than White women and affects more women than men. Women are vulnerable because of their responsibilities as caretakers to children and elders. Minority women are affected more than White women because race is more likely than gender to influence quality of education, leaving a larger percentage of minority women ill prepared to earn a living wage.[28]

Long-term adherence to a healthy diet and exercise regimen is always challenging for patients in terms of motivation and self-control, but it is particularly challenging for the impoverished because of the necessary extra expenditures of money and the time needed. Health-promotion strategies, therefore, may not be effective for people with lower SES because of their bigger challenges to meet their basic needs, that is, to earn a living and provide a home for their family members. It is likely that some of what healthcare providers ask people to do for health promotion is not compatible with the essential demands upon their time and income, much less with their preferences for food or "leisure" activity. Furthermore, patients who are depressed (because of the effects of disease, poverty, or racism) may not feel they can make a significant difference or even begin to learn and practice new behaviors.

Access to, and quality of, medical care, though an important determinant of health status,[1,15] is not always readily available to low-SES persons. People who cannot get an appointment for illness care certainly will not try to make preventive or wellness visits.[29] This is unfortunate because when they do receive medical care that care seems to exert a greater impact on their health than on their more advantaged counterparts.[15] There is a definite need for creative health-promotion strategies to reach low-SES families.

For example, a low-SES Latina with diabetes could not justify time for medical visits, preparing healthy meals, or exercising because she worked 12 hours a day, 7 days a week, to care for her children. Only after her bilateral amputations when she could no longer work did she have the time (but not the income) to focus on her and her family's health.[30] Low-income Latinas declared that lack of time and money was a major barrier to attending preventive mental health programs[31] and health-promotion programs for new mothers and their families (B.S. Sterling et al, unpublished data).

Individuals identified as members of the middle-class described health as having "energy, positive attitudes, and the ability to cope well and be in control of one's life."[32 (p171)] Crawford argued that middle-class samples were more likely than working-class samples to relate health to a sense of personal control.[33] Freund et al posited that because working-class people have less control over their circumstances than do middle-class people, the concept of personal control may be remote or even inconceivable to them.[32] Accordingly, the amount of control people have may be the key determinant of their ability to be interested in wellness, its components, and aspects as well as their ability to follow healthcare recommendations. It stands to reason that those with some time to spare and interest in current affairs are likely to be the first to hear about the latest developments in healthcare. High-SES people also have the resources to put this information to work for them, whether in buying necessary products, changing routines or behaviors, or in accessing professional help.[34]

People with chronic illnesses may be viewed by the medical, government, and middle-class establishments as being in opposition to the model of a good citizen, that is, the citizen "who actively participates in social and economic life, makes rational choices and is independent, self-reliant and responsible."[35 (p107)] Those lower SES persons who are also burdened with chronic illness usually lack the resources to be so responsible. They are not likely to engage in an active approach to healthy living, which necessitates engaging in time-consuming or costly health-promoting activities, or even to abstaining from risky health behaviors, which may provide a feeling of pleasure. The ability to benefit from health promotion seems to be related to one's autonomy and self-determination; therefore, people who lack either or both are likely not to respond as well to health-promotion interventions.

Control over one's circumstances allows one to consider following health-promotion advice, like choosing a health-promoting diet and engaging in regular physical activity. This "choice" seems far more real for those who actually have the ability and control necessary to opt for healthier living. Those who do not follow health promoters' advice appear to be choosing a lifestyle that jeopardizes their well-being and are labeled as noncompliant.[36]

> No one wants to die of AIDS, lung cancer, cirrhosis of the liver, or injuries sustained in an automobile accident. The public policy debate is not over the desirability of avoiding illness, injury, or premature death, but over the individual and collective sacrifices we are willing to make to maximize our chances of living long and healthy lives. If those sacrifices were simply of a material nature, the personal and social dilemmas that life-style modification issues raise would be less intractable. The choice, however, is rarely limited to spending more or less money; it invariably involves allowing more or less personal freedom.[36(p249)]

Crossley[37] (building on Crawford[33]) explored the notion that health has become a moral phenomenon in that there is an expectation in Western society that people will do what is necessary to live long and well. She described a tension between the values of individual responsibility toward health and individual freedom for decision making. She suggested that the more extreme practices of actively resisting health messages by smoking, drinking more than modest quantities of alcohol, eating excessive amounts of fattening foods, and engaging in other risky health behaviors are a way for people to assert their rights, freedom, and independence from society at large and from what they perceive to be the government's interference in their personal lives.[38,39]

Her focus group participants expressed skepticism toward health-promotion messages and a distrust of the credibility of health-promotion authorities (scientists, government agencies, and healthcare providers) because of the frequent changing messages about particular health behaviors.[37] Rather, the participants embraced the popular philosophy that all things can be healthy in moderation and the notion that too strict a lifestyle is unhealthy, an echo of Williams's[40] explanation that lay beliefs embrace pleasure as part of being healthy. In a similar vein, Blaxter[41(p752)] noted that some working-class people "express[ed] scorn for those who need to engage in health-promoting activity [as] the mark of a self-indulgent life." For people of these opinions, Crossley's[39] solution was to engage them in a dialogue about the benefits of the suggested behaviors instead of giving them authoritative directives.

According to Blaxter,[41] members of the working class and middle class agreed that health depends on personal behaviors and that individuals are responsible for their own health. In fact, it seems that both classes have internalized the dominant Western cultural value of health as an individual's responsibility,[33,35,40] to the extent of blaming individuals for ill health. On the other hand, those in the middle class were more likely than those in the working class to attribute ill health to environmental and social causes.[41]

Most health-promotion messages seem to presume that lifestyles are controllable and disregard the possible effects of luck or chance and environmental circumstances.[42] Considering that most improvements in health and life expectancy have been the result of public health achievements, such as vaccinations, safer workplaces, motor vehicle safety, increased safety and improved nutritional content of food, family planning, safe-sex recommendations, and anti-smoking campaigns,[43] perhaps more health-promotion efforts should be aimed at the community level. By recognizing the multiple social determinants to health and safety, health-promotion strategies can be tailored according to the unique resources, circumstances, and concerns of the community.[44] Community-wide strategies that make health maintenance a normal way of living are of benefit to people of all cultures and classes and can make individual health messages more palatable to those who would benefit from behavioral changes.

Conclusion

Healthcare providers seem to be caught in the tension between the population's health perceptions and needs. In our Western society, health interventions are often targeted to individuals without taking into account important social determinants of their health status. Our current health-promotion model therefore is not necessarily relevant for people whose social determinants are so weighted against their health that they do not exercise control over their own behavior. Identification of these

people and their particular frames of reference can more effectively market health-promotion efforts.

There is however a risk of paying too much attention to "culture." We must be careful that identifying members of particular cultures does not label them with a finite set of determinants that leaves out individual beliefs, feelings, and experiences that may turn out to be important for the success of health-promotion interventions. Effective healthcare provision addresses both individually focused strategies and broad policies to improve the economic and social environment and can be tailored to address the problem at hand.

Practitioners realize that placing blame upon patients and labeling them as noncompliant is not helpful. Instead, health promoters must intervene at the individual level on health behavior because they can recognize the barriers to compliance, such as overwhelming poverty, and also try to find reasonable and viable alternatives. Individual providers cannot remedy either SES or the environment and must, therefore, work harder to adapt the plan to the circumstances.

The lifestyle choices people make depend on their individual characteristics, their personal health circumstances, as well as the biases assimilated from their culture. The challenge for health promoters is to deliver healthcare messages in a way that all kinds of people find relevant and to enable all patients to practice the advice they are given. To that end, health-promotion interventions need to be based on knowledge of cultural effects and be personalized and adapted to patients' situations and SES.

REFERENCES

1. Institute of Medicine. *Unequal Treatment: Confronting Racial and Ethnic Disparities in Healthcare.* Washington, DC: National Academies Press; 2003.

2. US Department of Health and Human Services. *Health People 2010: Understanding and Improving Health.* 2nd ed. Washington, DC: US Government Printing Office; 2000.

3. Pender NJ, Murdaugh CL, Parsons MA. *Health Promotion in Nursing Practice.* Upper Saddle River, NJ: Prentice Hall; 2002.

4. Kreuter MW, Lukwago SN, Bucholtz DC, Clark EM, Sanders-Thompson V. Achieving cultural appropriateness in health promotion programs: targeted and tailored approaches. *Health Education & Behavior.* 2002;30:133–145.

5. Helman CG. *Culture, Health, and Illness.* New York: Arnold Publishers; 2001.

6. Hahn RA. *Sickness and Healing: An Anthropological Perspective.* New Haven, CT: Yale University Press; 1995.

7. Kleinman A. Concepts and a model for the comparison of medical systems as cultural systems. *Social Science & Medicine.* 1978;12:85–93.

8. Kleinman A, Eisenberg L, Good B. Culture, illness, and care: clinical lessons from anthropologic and cross-cultural research. *Annals of Internal Medicine.* 1978;88:251–258.

9. Hunt LM, Arar NH. An analytical framework for contrasting patient and provider views of the process of chronic disease management. *Medical Anthropology Quarterly.* 2001;15:347–367.

10. Arcury TA, Quandt SA, Bell RA. Staying healthy: the salience and meaning of health maintenance behaviors among rural older adults in North Carolina. *Social Science & Medicine.* 2001;53:1541–1556.

11. Brown SA, Garcia AA, Winchell M. Reaching underserved populations and cultural competence in diabetes education. *Current Diabetes Reports*. 2002;2:166–176.

12. National Coalition of Hispanic Health and Human Services Organizations (COSSMHO). Meeting the health promotion needs of Hispanic communities. *American Journal of Health Promotion*. 1995;9:300–311.

13. Warda MR. Mexican Americans' perceptions of culturally competent care. *Western Journal of Nursing Research*. 2000;22:203–224.

14. Holland L, Courtney R. Increasing cultural competence with the Latino community. *Journal of Community Health Nursing*. 1998;15:45–53.

15. Williams DR, Collins C. US socioeconomic and racial differences in health: patterns and explanations. *Annual Review of Sociology*. 1995;21:349–386.

16. Kniepp SM, Drevdahl JJ. Problems with parsimony in research on socioeconomic determinants of health. *Advances in Nursing Science*. 2003;26:162–172.

17. Whitfield KE, Weidner G, Clark R, Anderson NB. Sociodemographic diversity and behavioral medicine. *Journal of Consulting and Clinical Psychology*. 2002;70:463–481.

18. Duleep HO. Measuring socioeconomic mortality differentials over time. *Demography*. 1989;26:345–351. Cited by: Williams DR, Collins C. US socioeconomic and racial differences in health: patterns and explanations. *Annual Review of Sociology*. 1995;21:349–386.

19. Feldman JJ, Makue DM, Kleinman JC, Coroni-Huntley J. National trends in educational differentials in mortality. *American Journal of Epidemiology*. 1989;129:919–933. Cited by: Williams DR, Collins C. US socioeconomic and racial differences in health: patterns and explanations. *Annual Review of Sociology*. 1995;21:349–386.

20. Haan M, Kaplan G, Camacho, T. Poverty and health: prospective evidence from the Alameda County Study. *American Journal of Epidemiology*. 1987;125:989–998. Cited by: Williams DR, Collins C. US socioeconomic and racial differences in health: patterns and explanations. *Annual Review of Sociology*. 1995;21:349–386.

21. Mare RD. Socio-economic careers and differential mortality among older men in the United States. In: Vallin J, D'Souza S, Palloni A, eds. *Measurement and Analysis of Mortality: New Approaches*. Oxford: Clarendon; 1990:362–387. Cited by: Williams DR, Collins C. US socioeconomic and racial differences in health: patterns and explanations. *Annual Review of Sociology*. 1995;21:349–386.

22. Pappas G, Queen S, Hadden W, Fisher, G. The increasing disparity in mortality between socioeconomic groups in the United States, 1960 and 1986. *The New England Journal of Medicine*. 1993;329:103–115. Cited by: Williams DR, Collins C. US socioeconomic and racial differences in health: patterns and explanations. *Annual Review of Sociology*. 1995;21:349–386.

23. Wardle J, Steptoe A. Socioeconomic differences in attitudes and beliefs about healthy lifestyles. *Journal of Epidemiology and Community Health*. 2003;57:440–443.

24. Flores G, Tomany-Korman SC, Olson L. Does disadvantage start at home? Racial and ethnic disparities in health-related early childhood home routines and safety practices. *Archives of Pediatrics & Adolescent Medicine*. 2005;159:158–165.

25. Isaacs SL, Schroeder SA. Class: the ignored determinant of the nation's health. *The New England Journal of Medicine*. 2004;351:1137–1142.

26. Schultz A, Northridge ME. Social determinants of health: implications for environmental health promotion. *Health Education & Behavior*. 2004;31:455–470.

27. Kawachi I, Daniels N, Robinson DE. Health disparities by race and class: why both matter. *Health Affairs*. 2005;24:343–352.

28. Starrels ME, Bould S, Nicholas LJ. The feminization of poverty in the United States: gender, race, ethnicity, and family factors. *The Journal of Family Issues*. 1994;15:590–607.

29. Elliott BA, Beattie K, Kaitfors SE. Health needs of people living below poverty level. *Family Medicine*. 2001;33:361–366.

30. García AA. *Diabetes Symptom Self-Care of Mexican Americans* [dissertation]. Austin: The University of Texas; 2002.

31. Mann A, Garcia AA. Characteristics of community interventions for Latinas with depression. *Hispanic Health Care International*. 2005;3:87–93.

32. Freund PES, McGuire MB, Podhurst LS. *Health, Illness, and the Social Body: A Critical Sociology*. Upper Saddle River, NJ: Prentice Hall; 2003.

33. Crawford R. A cultural account of "health": control, release and the social body. In: McKinlay JB, ed. *Issues in the Political Economy of Health Care*. London: Tavistock; 1984:60–103.

34. Syme SL. Control and health: a personal perspective. *Advances*. 1991;7:16–27. Cited by: Williams DR, Collins C. US socioeconomic and racial differences in health: patterns and explanations. *Annual Review of Sociology*. 1995;21:349–386.

35. Galvin R. Disturbing notions of chronic illness and individual responsibility: towards a genealogy of morals. *Health*. 2002;6:1007–1037.

36. Leichter HM. *Free to be Foolish: Politics and Health Promotion in the United States and Great Britain*. Princeton: Princeton University Press; 1991.

37. Crossley ML. "Would you consider yourself a healthy person?" Using focus groups to explore health as a moral phenomenon. *Journal of Health Psychology*. 2003;8:501–514.

38. Crossley M. Resistance and health promotion. *Health Education Journal*. 2001;60:197–204.

39. Crossley M. Health resistance: the limits of contemporary health promotion. *Health Education Journal*. 2002;61:101–112.

40. Williams S. Health as a moral performance: ritual, transgression, and taboo. *Health*. 1998;2:435–457.

41. Blaxter M. Whose fault is it? People's own conceptions of the reasons for health inequalities. *Social Science & Medicine*. 1997;44:747–756.

42. Davison C, Frankel S, Davey Smith G. The limits of lifestyle: re-assessing "fatalism" in the popular culture of illness prevention. In: Sidell M, Jones L, Katz J, Peberdy A, Douglas J, eds. *Debates and Dilemmas in Promoting Health: A Reader*. Houndmills, Great Britain: Palgrave MacMillan; 2003:84–93.

43. Centers for Disease Control and Prevention. Ten great public health achievements: United States, 1900–1999. *MMWR Morbidity and Mortality Weekly Report*. 1999;48:241–243.

44. Institute of Medicine. *Improving Health in the Community: A Role for Performance Monitoring*. Washington, DC: National Academies Press; 1997.

Putting a Premium on Health

Employers are looking to cut healthcare costs by charging less for those who maintain a healthy lifestyle—and charge more for those who don't

JOHN DORSCHNER

As healthcare costs soar, some experts are now asking tough questions: Should fat people pay more for health insurance? What about smokers? Should healthy people who go regularly to the gym pay less?

"We believe people should be given the tools to improve their health," says Howard Gruverman, a Fort Lauderdale consultant with Chapman Schewe who advises companies on their health plans. "To the extent they follow the tools, they shouldn't pay more. But if they don't take advantage of [the tools], then they *should* pay more."

Some major South Florida employers—Baptist Health, Ryder System, the University of Miami— already require smokers to pay more for health coverage. But that may be just the beginning.

"The relationship between employer and employee is going to change in the next five years," says Bruce Shanefield, a Miami healthcare specialist with Aon Consulting.

Some consumer advocates are wary.

"This is an area worthy of exploration, but it has to be done with great care," says Ron Pollack of Families USA. Charging smokers more "makes eminent sense, but there are other areas that could be questionable."

A few companies nationally, like Weyco in Michigan, have fired smokers and warned they will do random tests for nicotine, but large employers here are taking a more complex approach which, at least to begin with, involves more carrot than stick.

Would smokers pay more?

"The main point is to get people healthy," says Maribeth Rouseff, who handles Baptist Health's wellness program. "We have to get away from the notion of a pill to fix everything."

"Our system is based on illness, not wellness, and frankly we need to change that paradigm," says Andy Scibelli of Florida Power & Light. "There is no other place to go with shifting healthcare costs."

Surveys

What's happening is a multistep process. Many employers start with health-assessment surveys—a basic measure of an employee's health, including weight, blood pressure, and chronic conditions, such as diabetes.

Many consultants would like to see all employees who want health insurance be forced to complete the surveys, but those employers using the survey locally have made them voluntary. "We believe the carrot is stronger than the stick right now," says Pam Rothstein at Ryder.

Employees at the transportation company are invited to fill out a survey on the Internet about health status and "lifestyle choices" that is then analyzed by an independent third party that will not show the data to Ryder, says Pam Rothstein, who handles health benefits. About 20 percent of employees have done the survey in the several months that the program has been available.

As a reward, the employees who complete the survey get their names entered in a drawing, and 10 end up with six months of free health insurance.

Baptist Health offers free health screenings twice a year that include tests to measure for cholesterol, blood sugar, body fat and osteoporosis. About a third of Baptist employees have participated, says Rouseff, and 20 percent go on to complete the health assessment survey. Their reward: A $10,000 death benefit paid to the survivor.

At Florida Power & Light, about 30 percent fill out the survey. They're rewarded by getting their names entered in raffles for items like digital cameras and iPods.

Employers say that answers on the surveys will have no repercussions in the workplace, and they're assuming employee honesty in filling them out. But how many employees want to be honest about their penchant for Big Macs or Pinot Noir?

"A big question is how far you go before it's an invasion of privacy," says Pollack, the consumer advocate. "And how does it get monitored."

Step two: Giving employees advice based on the surveys. Those overweight may get pamphlets on diet and exercise. Diabetics can be instructed on the importance of having blood sugar levels measured regularly. Smokers can be told about a variety of programs to help them stop.

This advice is naturally linked to employers' growing use of wellness programs. Baptist Health and Ryder, for example, have free on-site gyms.

Florida Power & Light offers gyms at small monthly fees, and it gives extra raffle entries for those who make such health-driven steps.

Wellness Coaches

Baptist also has "wellness coaches" who are sometimes stationed outside employee parking garages during shift changes, to chat with employees and pass out brochures on healthy lifestyles. "The coach hopes to look hundreds of employees in the eyes," says Rouseff.

Baptist Health started the emphasis on this wellness program in 2001, after the 10,500-employee organization went mostly to self-insurance. Rouseff says the program has paid off. Instead of annual increases "in the mid-double digits" for healthcare expense, the five-hospital organization now sees changes of 6.5-8 percent annually—a noteable achievement.

FPL reports it has averaged 5 percent annual increases the past two years, but attributes that to a wide range of factors designed to make employees more careful consumers of healthcare. Hewitt Associates says the average increase in Florida runs about 12 percent.

Eventually, consultants believe employers need to use the stick: If your cholesterol is too high, start lowering it with statins or diets. If you're too overweight, sign in at the gym three times a week.

And if you don't take those steps, says Gruverman, then employers should have a right to raise your insurance rates, because the history of healthcare indicates you're likely to be costing your employer more.

Right now, the stick is seen only with smokers, and it's a minimal one. The University of Miami and Ryder charge smokers $10 a month more.

Baptist Health charges $10 per biweekly pay period, though Rouseff says studies show smokers really cost an employer an average of $1,200 to $1,500 a year more in health expenses.

UM was an early starter in the smoking field, beginning its surcharge more than a decade ago. "We had about 1,800 acknowledged smokers in 1992," of its 9,000 employees, says benefits manager Bill Walsh, "and now we're down to 600 or 700."

He says that "every dollar" of the extra money from smokers "is dedicated to assist employees who want to break the habit." That includes paying for stop-smoking classes and nicotine patches.

The issue of overweight persons paying extra is more problematic. Tommy Thompson, secretary of Health and Human Services in the first George W. Bush administration, suggested in 2003 that group health plans should be rewarded if they maintained a healthy weight.

Local employers, however, are concerned that weight issues could be what Walsh calls "a black hole."

He and other benefits managers point to complex issues: Is obesity a disease or a lifestyle choice?

What's the right borderline for obesity? What happens if a person slips from normal to obese during the year, or goes from obese to normal?

Exercise

"I'm all for promoting a healthier lifestyle," says Pollack, the consumer advocate. "Promoting more exercise, free membership in gyms. But when you start penalizing people and possibly invading their privacy, that could be a very questionable practice."

Walsh at UM doubts obesity will ever become an issue in premium payments. "I don't see this coming down the pike."

But many other things may be. Scibelli says FPL is considering contributing dollars to employees tax-free health accounts depending on how many steps employees take toward a health lifestyle.

As Shanefield of Aon Consulting says, "You're just seeing the beginning."

Fix Your Worst Health Habits—Fast

Eating everything in sight? Smoking again?
Here, speedy ways to clean up your act—and lower your cancer risk.

HALLIE LEVINE

Almost everyone has at least one not-so-stellar health habit: Maybe you've smoked like a chimney since high school, gotten one too many sunburns in your mid-20s, or sworn off milk since the seventh grade. Now you're ready to clean up your act but don't want to slave away at it. We've got good news for you: Believe it or not, you can undo much of the damage caused by the most common health slip-ups in just two weeks—and with minimal effort. Follow our doable fast-fix plan, and you'll be well on your way to reclaiming your health and warding off the scariest diseases out there.

Health Slip-Up #1:

Splurging

Fix-it time: Two to four weeks You've returned from a ten-day vacation sporting some extra pounds. Don't let the weight sit; you may up your risk for developing breast cancer, among other diseases. (Fat triggers an increase in the production of a form of estrogen that promotes rapid cell division.) The good news: You can burn off those pounds quickly. "If you gain three to five pounds during a ten-day vacation, you'll need about a month to take it off," says Kathy McManus, R.D., director of the department of nutrition at Brigham and Women's Hospital in Boston. Here's how:

Step #1: Don't diet! You're much more likely to stick to a sensible eating plan if you focus on the idea of eating healthy, rather than dieting. In a study at the University of Toronto, researchers found that people who were told they'd start a diet the next week actually consumed more food than non-dieters. "Just the thought of deprivation can make you fall off the healthy-eating bandwagon," says McManus.

Step #2: Avoid eating on the run. Set aside at least 20 minutes for each meal, so you can sit down and savor each bite. When researchers asked women to chew thoroughly and to stop eating once their food no longer tasted as good as the first bite, they found that their subjects lost an average of eight and a half pounds over a four-week period (as opposed to the control group, which *gained* three). "Your body monitors how many nutrients it needs and will dampen your taste buds once you've

had enough," says study author John Poothullil, M.D., of the Brazosport Memorial Hospital in Lake Jackson, Texas.

Step #3: Skip the starch. For a week or two, avoid simple carbs (e.g., pasta, white bread, and sugary cereals) and instead focus on fruits, veggies, whole grains, and lean sources of protein, such as fish, chicken, and low-fat dairy. "Starch and processed sugar increase your body's insulin levels, which in turn stimulates your appetite," explains Pamela Peeke, M.D., author of *Fight Fat After Forty*. Simple carbs also cause your body to retain water, so when you stop eating them, you may drop up to five pounds of water weight.

Step #4: Don't be fats-phobic. It sounds counterintuitive, but eating some fat at every meal may help you stick to a healthy-eating plan. In a study of 101 people at Brigham and Women's Hospital, researchers found that after a year, those on a low-fat diet (20 percent of daily calories from fat) actually gained six pounds, while those on a moderate-fat diet (35 percent, mostly heart-healthy fat) lost ten pounds. "People on extremely low-fat diets tend to not feel full, so they end up consuming more calories," says McManus, who was lead researcher on the study. A few good ideas: Drizzle olive oil on steamed veggies, snack on a handful of walnuts, and eat a fatty fish, like salmon or tuna, on a regular basis.

Step #5: Get your moo juice. When women consumed low-fat dairy (such as skim milk, nonfat yogurt, and low-fat cheese) three to four times a day, they reduced their body fat by up to 70 percent, shows a study at the University of Tennessee in Knoxville. "Calcium serves as a switch that tells your body to burn excess fat faster," explains study author Michael Zemel, Ph.D., director of the university's Nutrition Institute. And no, you won't get the same results if you drink calcium-fortified beverages such as orange juice: Research shows that you get the best results from dairy.

Health Slip-Up #2:

Becoming a Couch Potato

Fix-it time: Visible results within two weeks Inactivity is linked to heart disease and certain kinds of cancer, but it doesn't take much to whip your body into shape. "If you make weight-training part of your regimen, you'll see results within two weeks of starting an exercise program," says Wayne Westcott, Ph.D., fitness director of the South Shore YMCA in Quincy, Massachusetts. After two weeks, you'll gain strength; after six weeks, you'll reap cardiovascular benefits.

"Avoid eating simple carbs and you may drop up to 5 pounds of water weight."

Step #1: Pick a consistent time to work out, preferably early in the day. A study at the Mollen Clinic in Phoenix found that 75 percent of morning exercisers stayed faithful to their workout routines, compared with only 25 percent of evening exercisers. If you're not an early bird, don't worry: It's more important to find a time that you can stick to, even if it's in the p.m. Can't manage working out for a whole half hour? Schedule two smaller sessions (for example, a 15-minute weight-lifting session in the morning, and a 15-minute walk during your lunch hour). Breaking up your sweat sessions allows your metabolism to kick into overdrive all day, burning additional calories for up to eight hours after your workout.

Step #2: Hit the weights. When starting a workout program, your first instinct may be to lace up your sneakers and head out for a jog. Better idea: Combine cardio with weight-training. In a study at Ohio State University, researchers found that muscles respond to weight-training in as little as two weeks. A study at the University of Athens in Greece found that people who combined strength-training and cardio were twice as aerobically fit as those who concentrated only on cardio.

Step #3: Shake up your routine. If you let your old workout slide because you were bored with it, find new activities that will keep you interested. One option: Reenergize your routine with interval-training, in which you add bursts of high-intensity moves into your workout, suggests Westcott. For example, if you usually jog a ten-minute mile, add a 30-second sprint or a one-minute incline every five minutes.

Step #4: Don't overdo it. When you haven't hit the gym in six months, it's tempting to push yourself—but don't. "Since you haven't exercised in a while, your muscles are more susceptible to injury," says Richard Cotton, spokesperson for the American Council on Exercise. In the first week, aim for 20 to 30 minutes of moderate-intensity cardio. Then increase your exercise time by about 10 percent each week.

Health Slip-Up #3:

Smoking

Fix-it time: Recovery begins two weeks after you stop If you think it's too late to undo the damage from smoking, consider this: Two weeks after that last cigarette, the hairs in your trachea responsible for keeping out viruses and bacteria, which had been killed off by smoking, start to regenerate; within one month your ability to smell and taste is enhanced; and within

two weeks your lung function increases by up to 10 percent. After a year your risk of heart attack is cut to half that of a smoker. After 10 years, your risk of dying of lung cancer is half that of a smoker. Inspired? Here's how to wean yourself off nicotine.

Step #1: Set an official "quit day." Mark your calendar to give yourself time to formulate a plan, says Edwin Fisher, Ph.D., a professor of psychology at Washington University in St. Louis and coauthor of *How to Quit Smoking Without Gaining Weight*. Reschedule your quit day if it falls right before your period. Research suggests that it's easier to stop smoking after your period, possibly because symptoms of nicotine withdrawal—depression, irritability, fatigue—mimic those of PMS.

Step #2: See your doc. Make an appointment a couple of weeks before your quit day to discuss smoking-cessation methods. Your doctor may suggest nicotine gum or prescribe Zyban. Studies show that some nicotine-replacement therapies double your chances of quitting; Zyban may even increase it threefold.

Step #3: Start exercising. Researchers at Brown University found that quitters who worked out were twice as likely to stay cigarette-free for at least one year after quitting as those who didn't exercise. The suspected reason? Spiked endorphin levels help counteract the symptoms of nicotine withdrawal, says Bess Marcus, Ph.D., a professor of psychiatry at Brown University School of Medicine. It may also help limit weight gain: On average, quitters who don't exercise pack on about 12 pounds, says Marcus, probably because their metabolism slows slightly once they stop smoking.

Step #4: Be prepared. The first few days are the worst because symptoms are more acute. Nicotine-replacement therapy or Zyban will help curb cravings, but keep a "survival kit" (with sugarless gum, a squeeze ball, and rubber bands) around to keep your hands and mouth busy. And enlist a buddy. In a study at St. George's Hospital Medical School, University of London, researchers found that quitters who seek social support can have more than twice the success rate of those who try to stop smoking solo. Log on to QuitNet (quitnet.com) to sign up for a quit buddy.

Health Slip-Up #4:

Sun-Fried Skin

Fix-it time: Three to six months Is there anything you can do to reverse all those sunburns? Yes. "Since most of the damage occurs on the superficial layers of the skin," notes Bruce Katz, M.D., director of the JUVA Skin & Laser Center in New York City and associate clinical professor of dermatology at Columbia Presbyterian Medical Center, "you can reverse up to 90 percent of all sun-damaged cells." Start following the advice below now, and you'll see results by the summer—and lower your skin cancer risk.

Step #1: Slap on sunscreen. Opt for the broad-spectrum kind that contains titanium or zinc oxide (such as Ultra Rich Neutrogena UVA/UVB Sunblock Lotion SPF 30 or Olay Complete Plus Moisture Lotion UVA/UVB Protection). Not only will it prevent further damage, it may help reverse minor damage, says Debra Jaliman, M.D., a New York City dermatologist.

Step #2: Use retinoids. These antiaging forms of vitamin A help your skin renew itself by increasing collagen production, reversing the effects of sun damage. If you've got only a few brown spots, try an over-the-counter retinol product (like Neutrogena Healthy Skin Anti-Wrinkle Cream). If the damage is more advanced (hint: skin feels rough and sandpapery, plus you've got fine lines and discoloration), go for a prescription retinoid, such as Retin-A, Retin-A Micro, or Renova for drier skin.

Step #3: Consider chemical peels. If you see signs of sun damage (rough patches and discoloration), ask your dermatologist about a chemical peel. A peel usually contains 20 to 40 percent glycolic acid, so you'll have some dryness or peeling afterward. But if you've had several bad burns or grew up in a sunny climate, ask your dermatologist about a medium-depth peel that penetrates beyond the skin's superficial layers, stimulating your skin to create new collagen. One option: A peel that combines alpha hydroxy acids and 5-FU, a chemotherapy agent normally used to treat premalignant skin cancer. Katz's research has found that a series of six to eight peels can result in as high as a 90 percent reduction in precancers, since "you're essentially taking away all the sun-damaged cells that can lead to skin cancer and premature aging," explains Katz. Cost: $150 to $225 per treatment. The procedure takes about an hour.

Step #4: Consider laser therapy. If you're in your late 30s, you may want to look into lasers instead of chemical peels, since lasers can get rid of more signs of sun damage and aging. Try one of the newer nonablative lasers: These are gentler than older lasers because they don't break the skin. "Essentially, the laser stimulates your skin to create collagen," says Jaliman. You can anticipate about a 20 to 30 percent improvement. Your skin will look more even and smoother and lines will be less visible. Cost: $350 to $500 a session (most people require three to four sessions, which take about an hour).

Health Slip-Up #5:
Missing Out on Calcium

Fix-it time: Immediately You've dissed dairy since the seventh grade, and now you're convinced that you haven't done enough to protect your bones. No need to panic. There's still plenty that you can do to maintain your bone density, says Bess Dawson-Hughes, M.D., a professor of medicine at Tufts University.

Step #1: Get at least 1,000 milligrams of calcium daily. Three servings a day of calcium-rich foods (like nonfat cheese and skim milk) and calcium-enriched juices and cereals will do the trick. Or try a supplement. For the best absorption, break the pill in half (for two 500 mg. doses) and take one half in the morning and the other at night—and make sure the supplement contains vitamin D.

Step #2: Get five servings a day of fruits and veggies. They're rich in potassium and magnesium, which help maintain bone-mineral density. Get your protein, too. Research by Dawson-Hughes found that bone-mineral density increased in people whose diets included high levels of protein as well as calcium.

Step #3: Work out regularly. Aim for at least a half hour each of aerobics and strength-training three times a week, recommends Miriam Nelson, Ph.D., director of the John Hancock Center for Physical Activity and Nutrition at Tufts. For optimal results, concentrate on high-impact activities, such as jogging, which put the most pressure on bones, making them stronger.

Step #4: Detox. Why avoid cigarettes and too much alcohol (more than one or two drinks a day)? They cause you to lose calcium through your urine. Another tip: Find a stress-buster. When you're stressed, your body pumps out stress hormones (such as cortisol), which stimulate osteoclasts, the cells that break down bone, explains Lisa Callahan, M.D., medical director of the Women's Sports Medicine Center at the Hospital for Special Surgery in New York City. So for your bones' sake, kick back and relax on a regular basis.

UNIT 2
Stress and Mental Health

Unit Selections

Key Points to Consider

- How have humankind's stressors changed over the last 5,000 years?

- What are the major stressors in your life? How do you manage your stress?

- What role do religion, love, and spirituality play in the progress of disease?

- Give examples that demonstrate the interaction between mental health and physical health.

- Explain how worry can be both a positive and a negative force in shaping one's life.

Student Website

www.mhcls.com/online

Internet References

Further information regarding these websites may be found in this book's preface or online.

The American Institute of Stress
http://www.stress.org
National Mental Health Association (NMHA)
http://www.nmha.org/index.html
Self-Help Magazine
http://www.selfhelpmagazine.com/index.html

The brain is the one organ that still mystifies and baffles the scientific community. While more has been learned about this organ in the last decade than in all the rest of recorded history, our understanding of the brain is still in its infancy. What has been learned, however, has spawned exciting new research and has contributed to the establishment of new disciplines such as psychophysiology and psychoneuroimmunology (PNI).

Traditionally, the medical community has viewed health problems as either physical or mental, treating each type separately. This dichotomy between the psyche (mind) and soma (body) is fading in light of scientific data that reveal profound physiological changes associated with mood shifts. Just what are the physiological changes associated with stress? Hans Selye, the father of stress research, described stress as a nonspecific physiological response to anything that challenges the body. He demonstrated that this response could be elicited by both mental and physical stimuli. Stress researchers have come to regard this response pattern as the "flight or fight" response, perhaps an adaptive throwback to our primitive ancestors. Researchers now believe that repeated and prolonged activation of this response can trigger destructive changes in our bodies and contribute to the development of several chronic diseases. So profound is the impact of emotional stress on the body that current estimates suggest that approximately 90 percent of all doctor visits are for stress-related disorders. If emotional stress elicits a generalized physiological response, why are there so many different diseases associated with it? Many experts believe that the answer may best be explained by what has been termed "the weak-organ theory." According to this theory, every individual has one organ system that is most susceptible to the damaging effects of prolonged stress.

Mental illness, which is generally regarded as a major dysfunction of normal thought processes, has no single identifiable etiology. One may speculate that this is due to the complex nature of the organ system involved. There is also mounting evidence to suggest an organic component to traditional forms of mental illness such as schizophrenia, chronic depression, and manic depression. The fact that certain mental illnesses tend to occur within families has divided the mental health community into two camps: those who believe there is a genetic factor operating and those who see the family tendency as more of a learned behavior. In either case, the evidence supports mental illness as another example of the weak-organ theory.

The reason a person is more susceptible to the damaging effects of stress may not be altogether clear, but evidence is mounting that one's perception or attitude plays a key role in the stress equation. A prime example demonstrating this relationship comes from research linking cardiovascular disease to stress. The realization that our attitude has such a significant impact on our health has led to a burgeoning new movement in psychology termed "positive psychology." Dr. Martin Seligman, professor of psychology at the University of Pennsylvania and father of the positive psychology movement, believes that optimism is a key factor in maintaining not only our mental health but our physical health as well. Dr. Seligman notes that while some people are naturally more optimistic than others, optimism can be learned.

One area in particular that appears to be influenced by the "positive psychology movement" is the area of stress management. Traditionally stress management programs have focused on the elimination of stress, but that is starting to change as new strategies approach stress as an essential component of life and a potential source of health. It is worth noting that this concept, of stress serving as a positive force in a person's life, was presented by Dr. Hans Selye in 1974 in his book *Stress Without Distress.* Dr. Selye felt that there were three types of stress: negative stress (distress), normal stress, and positive stress (eustress). He maintained that positive stress not only increases a person's self-esteem but serves to inoculate the person against the damaging effects of distress. Only time will tell if this change of focus in the area of stress management makes any real difference in patient outcome.

Researchers have made significant strides in their understanding of the mechanisms linking emotional stress to physical ailments, but they are less clear on the mechanisms by which positive emotions bolster one's health. One area in particular that is both difficult to study and appears to be getting increased scientific scrutiny is the area of humor and stress. While medical experts have known for years that hostility induces physiological changes that promote cardiovascular disease and appear to weaken the immune system, they are only beginning to explore the potential healing of mindfulness and spirituality. Stress and loneliness may also be responsible for the higher rates of heart disease, stroke, cancer, asthma, and diabetes.

Although significant gains have been made in our understanding of the relationship between body and mind, much remains to be learned. What is known points to perception and one's attitude as the key elements in shaping our responses to stressors.

Love Is Real Medicine

Loneliness fosters cardiovascular disease. Fortunately, there's an antidote.

DEAN ORNISH, M.D.

People who survive a heart attack often describe it as a wake-up call. But for a 61-year-old executive I met recently, it was more than that. This man was in the midst of a divorce when he was stricken last spring, and he had fallen out of touch with friends and family members. The executive's doctor, unaware of the strife in his life, counseled him to change his diet, start exercising and quit smoking. He also prescribed drugs to lower cholesterol and blood pressure. It was sound advice, but in combing the medical literature, the patient discovered that he needed to do more. Studies suggested that his risk of dying within six months would be four times greater if he remained depressed and lonely. So he joined a support group and reordered his priorities, placing relationships at the top of the list instead of the bottom. His health has improved steadily since then, and so has his outlook on life. In fact he now describes his heart attack as the best thing that ever happened to him. "Yes, my arteries are more open," he says. "But even more important, *I'm* more open."

Medicine today focuses primarily on drugs and surgery, genes and germs, microbes and molecules. Yet love and intimacy are at the root of what makes us sick and what makes us well. If a new medication had the same impact, failure to prescribe it would be malpractice. Connections with other people affect not only the quality of our lives but also our survival. Study after study find that people who feel lonely are many times more likely to get cardiovascular disease than those who have a strong sense of connection and community. I'm not aware of any other factor in medicine—not diet, not smoking, not exercise, not genetics, not drugs, not surgery—that has a greater impact on our quality of life, incidence of illness and premature death.

In part, this is because people who are lonely are more likely to engage in self-destructive behaviors. Getting through the day becomes more important than living a long life when you have no one else to live for. As one patient told me, "I've got 20 friends in this pack of cigarettes. They're always there for me. You want to take away my 20 friends? What are you going to give me instead?" Other patients take refuge in food, alcohol or drugs: "When I feel lonely, I eat a lot of fat—it coats my nerves and numbs the pain." But loneliness is not just a barrier to fitness. Even when you eat right, exercise and avoid smoking, it increases your risk of early death.

Fortunately, love protects your heart in ways that we don't completely understand. In one study at Yale, men and women who felt the most loved and supported had substantially less blockage in their coronary arteries. Similarly, researchers from Case Western Reserve University studied almost 10,000 married men and found that those who answered "yes" to this simple question—"Does your wife show you her love?"—had significantly less angina (chest pain). And when researchers at Duke surveyed men and women with heart disease, those who were single and lacked confidants were three times as likely to have died after five years. In all three studies, the protective effects of love were independent of other risk factors.

Awareness is the first step in healing. When we understand the connection between how we live and how long we live, it's easier to make different choices. Instead of viewing the time we spend with friends and family as luxuries, we can see that these relationships are among the most powerful determinants of our well-being and survival. We are hard-wired to help each other. Science is documenting the healing values of love, intimacy, community, compassion, forgiveness, altruism and service—values that are part of almost all spiritual traditions as well as many secular ones. Seen in this context, being unselfish may be the most self-serving approach to life, for it helps free both the giver and recipient from suffering, disease and premature death. Rediscovering the wisdom of love and compassion may help us survive at a time when an increasingly balkanized world so badly needs it.

ORNISH, a clinical professor of medicine at the University of California, San Francisco, is founder and president of the Preventive Medicine Research Institute. His books include "Love and Survival" and "Dr. Dean Ornish's Program for Reversing Heart Disease." For more information, go to pmri.org or ornish.com.

Enough to Make You Sick?

In America's rundown urban neighborhoods, the diseases associated with old age are afflicting the young. Could it be that simply living there is...

HELEN EPSTEIN

everly Blagmon lives in the School Street housing projects in southwest Yonkers, a once-vibrant manufacturing area just north of New York City long mired in unemployment and poverty. Beverly has asthma, diabetes, high blood pressure, rheumatoid arthritis, gout and an enlarged heart, and her blood has a dangerous tendency to clot spontaneously. She is 48, and she had her first heart attack in her late 20's. One of her brothers died of heart failure at 50, and another died of kidney failure at 45, as did a sister who was 35. A young cousin recently died of cancer. In the past three years, at least 11 young people she knows have died, most of them not from gunshot wounds or drug overdoses, but from disease.

Monica, who asked that her last name not be used, moved to the Crown Heights section of Brooklyn from School Street a year ago. She has diabetes, arthritis and asthma. She is overweight, and the pain from a back injury that occurred four years ago makes it hard for her to walk or even bend over a stove. Her elaborately braided hair is tinged with gray. In the past year, six of her friends have died, all of them younger than she is. When asked simple questions about her life—when she was born, where she grew up, when her three children were born—Monica answers in short phrases, wiping tears from her eyes. She is 36.

One researcher calls the grinding everyday stress of living in poverty in America 'weathering,' a condition not unlike the effect of exposure to wind and rain on houses.

Ebony Fasion, 22, and her friend Dominique Faulk, 17, both former residents of School Street, have asthma. Dominique's cousin Jo-Scama Wontong, 19, still lives in the School Street projects. Jo-Scama has lost so many people she loved to disease and accident recently that whenever she thinks about it, she is stricken with panic. "My heart beats so fast, and I can't breathe, and there's just death going through my mind the whole time."

Something is killing America's urban poor, but this is no ordinary epidemic. When diseases like AIDS, measles and polio strike, everyone's symptoms look more or less the same, but not in this case. It is as if the aging process in people like Beverly and Monica were accelerated. Even teenagers are afflicted with numerous health problems, including asthma, diabetes and high blood pressure. Poor urban blacks have the worst health of any ethnic group in America, with the possible exception of Native Americans. Some poor urban Hispanics suffer disproportionately from many health problems, too, although the groups that arrived most recently, like Dominicans, seem to be healthier, on average, than Puerto Ricans who have lived in the United States for many years. It makes you wonder whether there is something deadly in the American experience of urban poverty itself.

The neighborhoods where Beverly, Monica, Ebony, Dominique and Jo-Scama live look like poor urban areas all across the country, with bricked-up abandoned buildings, vacant storefronts, broken sidewalks and empty lots with mangy grass overgrowing the ruins of old cars, machine parts and heaps of garbage. Young men in black nylon skullcaps lurk around the pay-phones on street corners. These neighborhoods are as segregated from the more affluent, white sections of metropolitan New York as any township in South Africa under apartheid. Living in such neighborhoods as southwest Yonkers, central and East Harlem, central Brooklyn and the South Bronx is assumed to predispose the poor to a number of social ills, including drug abuse, truancy and the persistent joblessness that draws young people into a long cycle of crime and incarceration. Now it turns out these neighborhoods could be destroying people's health as well.

There are many different types of disadvantaged neighborhoods in America, but poor urban minority neighborhoods seem to be especially unhealthy. Some of these neighborhoods have the highest mortality rates in the country, but this is not, as many believe, mainly because of drug overdoses and gunshot wounds. It is because of chronic diseases—mainly diseases of adulthood that are probably not caused by viruses, bacteria or other infections and that include stroke, diabetes, kidney disease, high blood pressure and certain types of cancer.

The problems start at birth. The black infant death rate in Westchester County is almost three times as high as the rate for the county as a whole. Black youths in Harlem, central Detroit, the South Side of Chicago and Watts have about the same probability of dying by age 45 as whites nationwide do by age 65, and most of this premature death is due not to violence, but to illness. A third of poor black 16-year-old girls in urban areas will not reach their 65th birthdays. Four times as many people die of diabetes in the largely black area of central Brooklyn as on the predominantly white Upper East Side of Manhattan, and one in three adults in Harlem report having high blood pressure. In 1990, two New York doctors found that so many poor African-Americans in Harlem were dying young from heart disease, cancer and cirrhosis of the liver that men there were less likely to reach age 65 than men in Bangladesh.

Since the time of slavery, physicians have noted that the health of impoverished blacks is, in general, worse than that of whites. Racist doctors proposed that the reasons were genetic, and that blacks were intrinsically inferior and physically weaker than whites. But there is very little evidence that poor blacks or Hispanics are genetically predisposed to the vast majority of the afflictions from which they disproportionately suffer. As the living conditions of blacks have improved over the past century, their health improved in step; when conditions deteriorated, health deteriorated, too. This has helped support the contention among researchers that much chronic disease among minority groups is caused not by genes, but by something else.

That something else may come down to geography. Ana Diez-Roux, an epidemiologist at the University of Michigan, has shown that people who live in disadvantaged neighborhoods are more likely to have heart attacks than people who live in middle-class neighborhoods, even taking income differences into account. Researchers from the Rand Corporation found that neighborhoods where many buildings are boarded up and abandoned have higher rates of early death from cancer and diabetes than neighborhoods with similar poverty rates and similar proportions of uninsured people, but intact housing. Abandoned buildings do not in themselves cause disease, of course, but they are an indicator of neighborhood deprivation and neglect—and this does seem to be associated with poor health, though we don't know why.

In some ways, our public health institutions are in the same position they were in 150 years ago. In the mid-19th century, public health boards were established to fight the great killers of the day—cholera and tuberculosis. The poor were more susceptible to these diseases then, just as they are more susceptible to chronic diseases now. And then, as now, the reasons were unknown. Some believed diseases were acts of God and the poor got what they deserved. If they would only drink less, go to church and stay out of brothels, they wouldn't get sick. Others maintained that the afflictions of poverty were environmental. A stinking mass of invisible vapor, referred to as "miasma," hung in the air over the slums, they claimed, and sickened those who inhaled it.

It was not until the early 1880's, when the German scientist Robert Koch looked down his microscope at swirling cholera and tuberculosis bacteria, that everyone finally agreed about what was going on. The water the poor drank was full of sewage and contained deadly cholera germs; in overcrowded tenements, the poor breathed clouds of tuberculosis bacteria. Malnourished alcoholics tended to be more susceptible to these diseases, but immoral behavior was not their primary cause. Nor was miasma. The primary cause was germs.

We don't have a germ theory for chronic diseases like stroke, heart disease, diabetes and cancer. We know something about what can aggravate these diseases—diet, smoking and so on—but not enough about why they are so much more common among people who live in certain neighborhoods, or what makes, for example, a poor person who smokes the same number of cigarettes a day as a rich person more likely to get lung cancer. Or why several research studies show that smoking, eating, drinking and exercise habits do not fully account for why rich people are healthier than poor people. Even lack of health care cannot entirely explain the afflictions of the poor. Many poor people lack health insurance, and those who have it are often at the mercy of overworked doctors and nurses who provide indifferent care, but inadequate health care cannot explain why so many of them get so sick in the first place.

'You wake up stressed, you go to sleep stressed, you see all the garbage and the dealers … you say, "What's the use of doing anything?" '

Most poor minority neighborhoods "are less healthy," says Adam M. Karpati, who works in the Brooklyn office of the New York City Department of Health and Mental Hygiene. "You walk down the street and you know it. But what is that thing that you know is going on? What's at play there? That thing you can't name? We don't know that."

Clearly we need to examine this miasma with a different kind of microscope. The best we have at the moment are theories that fall into two main schools of thought. One school holds that the problem has mainly to do with stress; the other holds actual deprivation responsible. These two factors are often intertwined, but the emphasis is important. "There are so many fists in the face of poor African-Americans," says Arline Geronimus, a professor of public health at the University of Michigan who leans toward the stress school, and she proceeded to list them for me. They have enormous family obligations, she explained, and while the middle class are able to purchase child care and care for elderly relatives, the poor cannot. The experience of racism and discrimination in everyday life is also still very real, and very stressful. She says that blacks are faced with a society that institutionalizes the idea "that you are a menace—and that demeans you," she says. Nancy Krieger, a Harvard researcher, found that working-class African-Americans who said they accepted unfair treatment as a fact of life had higher blood pressure than those who challenged it.

Geronimus calls the grinding everyday stress of being poor and marginalized in America "weathering," a condition not unlike the effect of exposure to wind and rain on houses. Listening to Geronimus describe "weathering," I found it hard not to wonder whether anyone really knows what it is. Stress is subjective, a feeling, and it means different things to different people.

Philip Alcabes, associate professor of urban public health at Hunter College, says that stress is like the miasma that was once thought to cause cholera in 19th-century slums. "You can't see it, you can't really measure it, but it floats over certain people, especially the poor, and makes them sick."

The people I met who left the troubled neighborhoods of southwest Yonkers felt better, and moving appeared to have made all the difference.

If "weathering" and stress have their modern day Robert Koch, he is probably Bruce McEwen, a neuroendocrinologist at Rockefeller University in New York. McEwen argues that stress hormones threaten the health of poor people, especially blacks and the Hispanic poor. Stress hormones are produced by the adrenal glands in response to signals from the brain. When people feel frustrated, frightened or angry, stress hormones travel through the bloodstream and instruct different parts of the body to prepare for an emergency. They speed up the heart rate and narrow the arteries so that blood gets to the tissues faster; blood sugar rises, so that energy rushes to the muscles and other organs; and some bodily functions, like digestion and the mechanisms that maintain the strength of the bones and other tissues, are inhibited. But not all stress is the same. Occasional periods of intense stress, like what you feel during a near miss in a car, do no harm. However, McEwen's research suggests that constant exposure to stress hormones impairs the immune system and damages the brain and other organs.

Chronic stress also signals the body to accumulate abdominal fat around the waistline, which is more dangerous than fat that lies under the skin, or subcutaneous fat. Abdominal fat worsens many chronic health problems, including diabetes and heart disease, whereas subcutaneous fat does not. It's as if stress hormones were like lye, powerful stuff that in small amounts is useful for cleaning the stove, but that in large amounts will eat right through the floor.

Not everyone believes that stress is a major contributor to the health crisis among the poor. George Davey Smith, a professor of clinical epidemiology at the University of Bristol in England, agrees that the poor live very stressful lives, and that racism is an everyday reality for many people. However, in his view—the second school of thought on the matter—the health crisis among the poor has more to do with living in a deprived environment.

The experience of poverty in America has changed a great deal since the 19th century; the poor now have safe drinking water and live in less crowded dwellings, and many have cars and TV's. However, it's also true that many poor people eat unhealthful food, smoke and abuse drugs. Americans hear a great deal about the importance of making healthy choices in their lives; warnings about cigarettes and high-fat foods issue frequently from the surgeon general's office and fill the pages of magazines and best-selling advice books. There are plenty of

people who feel little sympathy for overweight diabetic people, poor or not, who eat regularly at McDonald's. But while there is considerable controversy about the ideal lifestyle regimen, you don't need to know much about impoverished neighborhoods to see the absurdity of choosing to go Atkins or macrobiotic for a person like Beverly Blagmon, who subsists on disability payments. Poor people are more likely to have unhealthy habits because fast food and cigarettes are abundant and cheap in their neighborhoods, and healthy alternatives tend to be limited.

A recent survey conducted in four regions of the United States found that there were three times as many bars in poor neighborhoods as in rich ones, and four times as many supermarkets in white neighborhoods as in black ones. There are fewer parks in poor neighborhoods as well, so it is more difficult to find open spaces in which to exercise, and many of them are dangerous. Forty-one percent of New York's public elementary schools have no consistent physical education program. As Mary T. Bassett, a New York City deputy health commissioner, said to me, public health campaigns that tell people to "just say no" to smoking, or to change their diets and start exercising, can be cruel if they are indifferent to neighborhood circumstances.

Davey Smith also points out that many of the poor black people who are sick today grew up in the 40's, 50's and 60's, when many black people lived in overcrowded dwellings, and were more prone than affluent whites to childhood infections. Some of these infections may have long-term effects on health. Helicobacter pylori, a bacterium that has been associated with both ulcers and stomach cancer in adulthood, is most often acquired in childhood, and this may explain why poor blacks in particular have relatively high rates of both diseases. Adults who were poor as children, even if they are not poor now, are also more prone to stroke, kidney disease and hypertensive heart disease.

I wondered about these alternatives. Presumably both stress and material disadvantage are important causes of ill health among the poor. But which is more important? And what would be the best way to address these problems? If stress is a major cause of ill health, interventions to alleviate it—counseling, antidepressants, even yoga—might be beneficial. A recent article in The British Medical Journal suggested that building self-esteem actually helped a group of Native Americans manage their obesity and diabetes better than did conventional counseling about diet and exercise. On the other hand, if material disadvantage is a major cause of ill health among the poor, then extensive changes in the environment in which the poor live—for example, cleaner buildings and more parks—are needed.

PERHAPS BEVERLY BLAGMON, who lives in the midst of such problems, could help resolve this matter. I asked her what she thought the health crisis in southwest Yonkers was caused by, and she answered without missing a beat. "Racism." We went on to talk about the lack of jobs in the area and the dilapidated state of the housing. I also learned that if stress is a killer, there is plenty of it on School Street, but yoga classes and motivational seminars are not likely to be of much help.

Beverly raised 10 children, eight orphaned nieces and nephews in addition to her own son and daughter. The kids were desperate for attention from the overextended Beverly. "It was hard," she said. "You had to deal with 10 different personalities." All the kids are grown now, and all but two have left home. Now she worries because some of them can't find jobs. When she was young, Yonkers was full of factories that hired many young people. But not anymore.

Then last year, disaster struck. Beverly's 21-year-old daughter was killed in a car accident; shortly thereafter, her nephew was shot and killed right outside her building. "I was totally out of it," she said. "People don't know how much a death can take from you. I went into the hospital right after my daughter's funeral. They didn't know if I'd had a mild stroke or not."

"Life is taken stupidly" all the time around School Street, Beverly said, but this doesn't make it easier to handle. Beverly struggles with these losses, and said her family, friends and even officials from the local Housing Authority have been supportive. But when Beverly talked about life on School Street, what she said is underscored with tension—the constant strain of "us versus them." She sees the police in particular as a constant source of grief. "Some of them are very prejudiced, even now," she told me. She claimed that a few officers harassed children and teenagers, and have even been known to swear at kids and shove them. She recalled, as if it were yesterday, a 1997 fight at School Street. Someone called Beverly to come outside, which she did, along with a visiting friend. Police officers were on the street, some of them shouting, and in the chaos that ensued, she said, a policeman knocked down Beverly's friend, a older woman who is legally blind. "I was freaked out," Beverly said. "The main witnesses were drug dealers, and they couldn't say anything." (The Yonkers police confirmed that the woman later filed a complaint, but said an internal investigation found no wrongdoing.) Beverly said she was infuriated when, shortly after the incident, she saw the mayor of Yonkers praise the police in a televised speech.

People who are not poor often casually ascribe their aches, pains and even more serious afflictions to "stress," but stress, if it is a killer, is a far more serious problem for people like Beverly. When middle-class people feel the police or other authorities treat them unfairly, they often have the resources to hire a lawyer and even effect change. But all too often poor blacks feel ignored when they complain about discrimination and abuse.

How might painful experiences like Beverly's be imprinted on the body? Laboratory animals suffer when stressed with electric shocks or when kept in isolated cages away from their peers, and they sometimes do develop symptoms that resemble human chronic diseases. But how does mouse stress compare to Beverly's stress? Or mine? Or yours? George Davey Smith would argue that it is entirely possible that the afflictions of poor people like Beverly are not due to stress, at all, but to old-fashioned deprivation: crowding, poor nutrition, lack of exercise and exposure to dirty air, germs and vermin. For a while, Beverly's family of 11 crowded into a two-bedroom apartment, until they were eventually moved into a six-room place. Once, money was so short that she begged the welfare office for food stamps. There is nowhere around School Street for kids to run

around, Beverly says, except a concrete playground with a set of monkey bars. "Why can't they put up some swings or build a basketball court? You see kids using garbage cans as basketball nets around here." Until two years ago, an incinerator in the building spewed forth horrible fumes that may have contributed to the high rates of asthma on School Street. "When you got ready to polish the furniture, it was black with dust," Beverly recalled. "Every day. Now, how much of that was getting in our lungs? I've been in the hospital every year with acute asthma." The incinerator has been replaced by a compactor, but as a result, life is a constant battle against roaches and mice, whose droppings also worsen asthma. Beverly told me that she recently caught three mice in one day. "I put them on the maintenance people's desk," she said. The elevators are always breaking down, which is hard on the elderly. Once she saw human feces in the hallway.

AFTER TALKING to Beverly, I could only conclude that her life was full of many sorts of trouble, any or all of which might be harmful to health. If only it were possible to devise an experiment that would examine the effects of stress and deprived living conditions on the health of the poor. For nearly 10 years, the U.S. Department of Housing and Urban Development has been conducting an experiment called Moving to Opportunity that seems to be doing just that. HUD researchers wanted to see what happens to poor urban families who move out of neighborhoods like Harlem in New York, Roxbury in Boston or the South Side of Chicago and settle in better neighborhoods. They wanted to know whether moving would help children do better in school, and escape being drawn into crime when they reached adolescence. They also wanted to know whether their parents would climb out of poverty.

HUD did find that people's lives improved in some ways. For example, the children who moved to better neighborhoods in Baltimore did better on standardized tests, and adults there were more likely to get off welfare. But HUD's most remarkable early findings had to do with health. In Boston, poor children who moved to low-poverty neighborhoods were less likely to experience severe asthma attacks. Adults in New York who moved were less likely to suffer from symptoms of depression and anxiety than those who stayed behind, and adults in Boston were more likely to report that they felt "calm and peaceful." The HUD researchers who devised the experiment had not set out to study health, but their findings were so striking that they decided to expand their study to determine whether moving out of poor neighborhoods affected other aspects of health that they did not measure in the first round, including blood pressure, obesity and other factors associated with such chronic afflictions as heart disease, cancer and stroke, like smoking. Those results aren't available yet, but when I heard about the earlier study, I decided to conduct a small experiment of my own.

I wanted to talk to families, like those who had participated in the IIUD program, who had recently moved out of the slums. Did the move affect their health? And if so, why? Did people experience less stress? Did they eat better food? Breathe better air? What might their experiences tell me about the mysterious miasma of contemporary poverty?

Staying indoors keeps kids safe from crime but puts them 'at the intersection of the asthma and obesity epidemics,' according to one researcher at Columbia.

My investigation led me to Jerrold M. Levy, the general counsel of the Enhanced Section 8 Outreach Program, or ESOP, which helps low-income families move out of depressed, dangerous inner-city neighborhoods in Yonkers into middle-class areas. ESOP wasn't conducting any studies of these people, of course, but Levy was willing to put me in touch with 10 of the families he'd helped move. He had noticed that the people who moved out of dangerous neighborhoods seemed happier. "A few weeks after they've moved," he says of his clients, who are mostly single mothers, "they come into my office, and it's like one of those programs on late-night TV where they do the makeovers, you know? They have their hair done nicely, they're wearing high heels and makeup, it's like they're transformed. They have a new sense of self-worth and dignity. But will you see changes in their health? I don't think so." Depression and anxiety are major health problems that affect large numbers of poor people, so I thought I would be satisfied just to find people whose mental health improved. And I did find such people. But I also found that most people who moved gained far more than high spirits.

Of the 10 families I met, 9 had at least one member who suffered from a serious health problem before the move that required either medication or hospitalization. Of the 16 people in these families who had health problems, 12 told me that they felt better in significant ways—either their symptoms were less severe so that they no longer required hospitalization, or they were taking less medication. Their health problems included severe asthma, diabetes, high blood pressure, liver cirrhosis and eczema. Emergency-room visits for the asthmatic kids virtually stopped, and some adults with high blood pressure or diabetes reduced the doses of their medications. This was hardly a rigorous scientific experiment. There was no control group, and I was not able to check medical records. Nevertheless, I was stunned by what people told me. These people felt better, and moving appeared to have made all the difference. If moving out of southwest Yonkers were a drug, I would bottle it, patent it and go on cable TV and sell it.

Juanita Moody is now 52. In the summer of 2001, she and her husband, William, moved to a middle-class section of Yonkers from a low-income housing complex on Nepperhan Avenue, where they lived for nearly 30 years. Juanita was crippled by polio when she was a teenager, and during an operation to adjust her spine, she was given a blood transfusion that contained hepatitis C. The virus lay dormant for many years. But two and a half years ago, Juanita's doctor told her that her liver was showing signs of damage and advised her to take inter-

feron, a prescription drug for viral infections. When Juanita found out about the possible side effects, however, she refused. Today Juanita's liver tests are almost normal, suggesting that her hepatitis is not progressing rapidly. "The doctor said I was fantastic, in terms of enzymes," Juanita told me. I did not speak to Juanita's doctor myself, so I could not confirm her diagnosis, but Juanita seemed energetic, and other doctors confirmed that it is possible for hepatitis to slow its progression. In addition, Juanita says that since she moved, her blood pressure has fallen from 140/90, which is considered high, to 130/78, which is almost normal, and the dose of blood-pressure pills she takes has been reduced by half.

Juanita, a born-again Christian, attributes her improved health to prayer and to the new regimen she has maintained since she moved. She has become a health-food nut. Before she moved, her daughter told me, "everything was fried, fried, fried. Before she'd eat at McDonald's and stuff, but not now." Now she drinks fruit and vegetable juices, and her kitchen cabinets are full of natural remedies: vitamins C and E, zinc, magnesium, calcium, alpha lipoic acid and milk thistle, which she says is excellent for the liver.

Juanita says she began focusing more on her health after she moved. When she lived on Nepperhan, there were too many other things to worry about, including frequent robberies and killings in and around the complex itself. The building managers put up a fence to keep drug dealers out, "but the crackheads living inside the building gave the dealers the keys." The elevators were often broken, which meant that someone would have to carry Juanita and her wheelchair up and down three flights of stairs.

Juanita's new apartment is not in a luxury building. It's on a busy road, near two gas stations and a shopping mall, and has few amenities. But it is safe and has nice, leafy views. On Nepperhan, "it was stressful just to walk out of that place. You were always scared for the kids.... You wake up stressed, go to sleep stressed, you see all the garbage and the dealers. That is depressing. In a bad environment like that you say, 'What's the use of doing anything?'" Living in her new apartment building gives her a very different feeling. "It inspires you to do all you can—spiritually, healthwise, any kind of way."

It is well known that junk food can make anxious people feel better. Researchers from the University of California recently discovered one possible reason. In response to constant stress, the brain makes a hormone called corticotropin-releasing factor, which instructs the adrenal glands to manufacture stress hormones, including adrenaline and cortisol. These hormones cause a range of physiological changes that over long periods can be harmful. When people with high levels of cortisol eat sugary, fatty foods, fat is deposited in the abdomen. The researchers theorize that these abdominal fat cells can temporarily inhibit the brain from making corticotropin-releasing factor, reducing feelings of stress and anxiety. If this theory is correct, it could explain how the stress of poverty creates a biological urge to overeat, thus putting poor people at greater risk of obesity and its consequences—diabetes, heart disease, stroke and certain types of cancer. Perhaps this explained why Juanita found it easier to change her diet once she moved out of the stressful atmosphere of

Nepperhan Avenue. She admitted that doctors had been telling her over the years that she should consume less fattening food. "But they can tell you, and you don't do it," Juanita said.

Noemi, 31, moved with her two teenage children and her 76-year-old aunt, Raimunda, from Burnham Street in Yonkers to a better neighborhood in northwest Yonkers only three months before I met her in August. Noemi, who asked that her last name not be used, has had diabetes since childhood. Shortly after she moved, her doctor reduced her dose of insulin by three units. Noemi thinks it's because she feels less stressed in the new neighborhood. "Stress affects your blood sugar," she explained. "It makes your sugar go up so you need more insulin." She drove me from her new neighborhood of neatly mowed lawns, bushy trees and two-car garages to the place she used to live. "Look at the neighborhood here," she said, as we drove by industrial garages, boarded-up buildings and vacant lots. An enormous, dented, wheezing Lincoln car screeched by. "I had to be worried all the time, you know. Are the children gonna get hit by a car? Is something gonna happen? We've lived in neighborhoods with a lot of drugs, a lot of people getting killed. You'd read about it in the paper the next day and think: Oh, God! That's only two blocks from here."

Noemi's aunt Raimunda speaks no English, although she has lived in the United States for more than 15 years. She has high blood pressure and heart disease. I asked Noemi to ask Raimunda how she was feeling these days. "She says her thing with the head is gone," Noemi translated. "Before she used to get dizzy, but not anymore. Not for the past couple of months." When I asked Raimunda why she thought the dizzy spells went away, she, unlike Noemi and Juanita, did not mention stress. Instead, she said she thought the improvement had something to do with diet. "She thinks the chicken is better here—easier to digest," Noemi said. "But what she doesn't know is that since we moved, I still buy the chicken in the same place."

After meeting Noemi, Raimunda and Juanita, I began to see more clearly what Arline Geronimus, the University of Michigan researcher, was talking about. Perhaps the miasma that is killing the poor really is stress after all. Then I spoke to the mothers of six children who had severe asthma. Every one of them had significantly fewer and less severe attacks after the families moved out of southwest Yonkers. Reduced stress could be partly responsible—stress can worsen asthma—but it seemed clear to me a cleaner environment was also responsible. The children ranged in age from 3 to 16; they all moved out of southwest Yonkers and settled in different parts of Westchester. The mothers, who asked that their last names not be used, saw astonishing changes, and hearing their stories convinced me that the only way to deal with the staggering epidemic of asthma that afflicts 30 percent of children in some New York City neighborhoods is to clean up the rundown, roach-infested buildings where so many of these children live.

Carmen and her 4-year-old son moved to a middle-class section of Westchester in the spring of 2002. In Yonkers, her son would have severe asthma attacks every month and would have to sit for hours every day breathing through a nebulizer. Since they moved, she says he has needed the nebulizer only twice. Two years ago, Monique, her 3-year-old son and 8-year-old daughter moved from Cedar Street in Yonkers to Peekskill. When they lived on Cedar Street, her son's severe asthma came complete with projectile vomiting. The attacks started just a few months after he was born, and they terrified Monique. She blames her former landlord. "There was no hot water for two weeks once, there were leaks in the roof, so it was damp all the time. Sometimes there was water coming through the roof, and mice playing in the living room," she says. "There were cockroaches everywhere, even in the refrigerator. The landlord did nothing until I called the health department. It was stressful having all those roaches around. You didn't know if they were crawling all over you at night." As soon as the family moved up to Peekskill, the boy's attacks became less severe. Although he is still on medication, the violent attacks and the vomiting have stopped.

Cockroaches and vermin do worsen asthma, and this might explain why Monique's son was so sick. But there could be another reason that so many children in poor neighborhoods have asthma, and why they get better when they move. In the past decade, rates of childhood asthma, as well as obesity and diabetes, have soared in the very neighborhoods that were worst affected by the crime waves of the 70's, 80's and 90's. One possible explanation, says Daniel Kass, a research scientist for the New York City health department, "is that asthma follows the crime epidemic, because it goes wherever people spend a lot of time indoors."

Poor parents, terrified that their kids will be killed on the street, tend to keep them inside, with the windows shut and the TV on, where they are constantly exposed to contaminants in indoor air, which some researchers believe can be as damaging as industrial pollution. Not only are sedentary, overweight kids more at risk for asthma, but kids with severe asthma tend to exercise less and are thus prone to obesity. Mothers trying to protect their kids from crime may not realize they are putting their future health at risk. As Mindy Fullilove, professor of clinical psychiatry and public health at Columbia University explained, "The best parents—the people who are the most upright, the churchgoers, the most protective mothers—keep their kids inside, and they are at the intersection of the asthma and obesity epidemics."

I thought of Trevor Jackson Jr., a 14-year-old boy with serious eczema who moved from southwest Yonkers up to Cortland Manor in northern Westchester two years ago. "This is a much better atmosphere," his mother, Dawn, told me. Their new apartment is in a large house with a wide sloping lawn surrounded by trees. "The kids can just go outside anytime. The little one wouldn't go to sleep when we first got here." He wanted to be outside all the time. In Cortland Manor, "kids have a better chance to grow," Trevor's father, Trevor Sr., says. "We see deer in the yard, woodchucks, otters, frogs. There's just life up here."

I WAS BEGINNING to see that the problems of stress and material deprivation were inseparable parts of the contemporary miasma of poverty. But how did these neighborhoods become so unhealthy? New York City is one of the most segregated metropolitan areas in the country. Blacks, whites and other ethnic groups interact every day, but to a large extent they live separately. At the same time, the city has also become more segregated by wealth, so that many black and Hispanic neighborhoods are also the poorest.

The Harvard sociologist William Julius Wilson has described how, thanks to the civil rights movement of the 60's, many middle-class blacks have been able to find jobs and housing outside traditional black areas, leaving behind the most impoverished, poorly educated people. This concentration of disadvantage—racial, social and economic—combined with the loss of many unskilled manufacturing jobs, is what Wilson says contributed to the many social problems associated with poverty today, including drug abuse, crime and single motherhood. Mindy Fullilove says that these trends contributed to widening health inequalities as well. As racial and economic segregation increased, health problems became concentrated in the most deprived areas, as if the miasma were condensing over them. Indeed, I wondered if the miasma might not turn out to be segregation itself.

In order to understand the health crisis among America's urban poor, Fullilove explains, you can't just consider what's going on now. "You have to look at the history of these neighborhoods" and think about the people who live there and what has happened to them in the past. "The history of each neighborhood will determine its pattern of disease. A city like New York suffers from an overlay of epidemics."

In the 70's, 80's and 90's, poor minority neighborhoods throughout the country experienced a protean health crisis. Rates of some chronic and infectious diseases began increasing for the first time since World War II. Even older blacks who made it into their 60's, and who once had as good a chance of reaching their 75th birthdays as 60-year-old whites, began dying at higher rates.

Fullilove says that urban-renewal projects that helped create concentrated poverty, along with redlining—discrimination by banks and insurance companies—and public-service cuts in poor neighborhoods led to catastrophic changes in the way the poor lived, and destroyed the foundation that made poverty endurable. The migrancy of poor people, displaced by fires, evictions and other calamities, destroyed informal community mechanisms for caring for children and controlling the behavior of adolescents and young adults, and this made it harder than ever for the poor to cope. "It was like a massive refugee situation," Fullilove says.

At the same time, as the middle class increasingly campaigned for restrictions on cigarette and alcohol advertising, those companies spent more of their marketing dollars in poor neighborhoods. As Rodrick and Deborah Wallace wrote in their book "A Plague on Your Houses," politicians looked the other way when companies posted huge, colorful billboards—depicting exuberant black people smoking cigarettes and drinking beer—outside schools and churches in Harlem, Brooklyn and the South Bronx. Construction on central Harlem's first full-size supermarket did not begin until 2002, but in the 90's there were more than a hundred places where a child under 18 could buy cigarettes, including individual "loosies," which are cheap but illegal.

The wave of crime and drugs of the 80's and 90's has subsided considerably, and some once-grim urban neighborhoods are even prospering. But poverty has risen in many suburban minority enclaves, and the health problems of the poor have not gone away.

Much has been written about how such social problems as joblessness and drug abuse worsen health problems, but it is also possible that the converse is true. Both Beverly and Monica have lost jobs as a result of illness, and many sick people fall into poverty. Anne Case, a Princeton University economist, has shown that unhealthy young people are far less likely to succeed in school and find good jobs later on. Thus, illness can trap poor families in cycles of disease, death and poverty for generations.

Adam Karpati of the New York City health department says that even though we don't know what the miasma is, there is still a great deal we can do to improve the well-being of the poor. In the 19th century, it was not the discovery of germs that led to the greatest advances in public health, but a series of profound changes in the way the poor lived—a virtual social revolution. Then, as now, health and poverty were inseparable from each other, and better housing, sewers, decent wages, better working conditions and improved nutrition saved millions of lives. Today much could be done to improve the environment and make life less stressful for the poor. The health department is working to reduce mold and roach infestation in public housing, as well as encouraging doctors and community organizations to address such problems as obesity, asthma and diabetes. These admirable programs, however, are modest in scale, and in the current fiscal climate, their financing is far from secure.

More ambitious changes are needed, but at present, our government is permitting matters to get even worse. Since 2000, millions of jobs have been lost, and nearly three million people have joined the ranks of the poor, who now account for more than 12 percent of the U.S. population and 24 percent of African-Americans. This means fewer families will be able to move out of poor neighborhoods on their own. For now, the federal Section 8 program—which provides subsidies for people to pay for private housing—is the only hope most people have of getting out of these neighborhoods, but even its future is in doubt. Possible budget cuts could mean thousands of Section 8 recipients will lose their vouchers next year, and in the longer term, Republicans in Congress hope to devolve the program to the states. This will almost certainly mean the program will shrink. Last month, moreover, HUD also suspended rental supplements that Jerrold Levy says have made programs like ESOP possible. "This will reinforce the ghettoization of poor people," Levy says.

Rising unemployment and budget cuts will not only harm people's health. They will also cost Americans money. Take diabetes and asthma as examples. Around one million people succumb to Type 2 diabetes each year, with African-Americans, Hispanics and Native Americans most at risk. The bill for treating the nation's 11 million known diabetics comes to $92 billion for medications and doctors' visits plus $40 billion in lost productivity due to absences from work and premature death. The yearly bill for the nation's asthma epidemic is $14 billion. As

Beverly pointed out to me, shortsighted cuts, amounting to a few hundred million dollars, from the HUD budget mean programs to refurbish public housing, organize recreation for children and build playgrounds have been halted. The exterminator teams that used to come every month now come once every two months, and the roaches are flourishing as never before.

Whatever the miasma is that afflicts America's minority poor, it is at least partly a legacy of the segregation of America's cities. These neighborhoods, by concentrating the poor, also concentrate the mysterious, as yet poorly understood, factors that make them sick. You'd almost think this new miasma was caused by some sort of infection, because of the way it seems to strike certain neighborhoods and certain types of people. I re-cently came across a research article by Angus Deaton of Princeton University, reporting that white people who live in cities with large black populations have higher death rates than whites with the same income who live in cities with smaller black populations. It made me wonder whether the deprived, polluted, roach-infested, stressful conditions in which poor blacks live aren't affecting all of us, to some degree. And even if we never find out what the miasma is, this possibility should scare us into treating this as the health emergency it is—if nothing else will.

HELEN EPSTEIN writes frequently about public health for The New York Review of Books. This is her first article for the magazine.

Are You OK?

It's easy to minimize the emotional symptoms that can interfere with your health and well-being. Here's how to check yourself and where to seek help.

I f you have a persistent cough or a sore that won't heal, you're likely to seek prompt medical attention. But when it comes to persistent emotional symptoms, such as tension, worry, gloom, and discouragement, Americans are notoriously reluctant to seek help. That's unfortunate, because treatment can often make a profound difference in your level of happiness and, indeed, your overall health. Emotional problems cannot only interfere with recovery from disease, but new research also shows they can increase your risk of heart disease, diabetes, dementia, and other disorders.

Negative emotions are, of course, a normal part of life for most people, especially those coping with illnesses or recovering from accidents or other trauma. Most of the time bad moods are fleeting, even if the underlying situations that cause them are not. Sometimes, however, bad moods become continuous and disabling, and it's not always obvious when to seek help. The percentage of U.S. adults reporting "frequent mental distress" is on the rise, from 8.4 percent in 1993 to 10.1 percent in 2001, according to an October 2004 report by the federal Centers for Disease Control and Prevention. Unfortunately, only a third of the 44 million Americans a year who are beset by anxiety, depression, or other psychological disorders get the help they need.

That is particularly unfortunate for those whose emotional symptoms are related to a physical disease. Certain medications, including beta-blockers and corticosteroids, and illnesses, such as thyroid disease, diabetes, and cancer, can also cause depressive symptoms. And it's now well established that emotional problems can complicate the treatment of and delay recovery from many diseases, including some that are life-threatening. Individuals who become depressed in the wake of a heart attack, for example, typically take longer to recover. Arthritis sufferers who become depressed tend to experience greater disability than do similar patients who stay upbeat. Depression also seems to delay the knitting of broken bones and to speed the progression from HIV to AIDS.

Evidence is mounting that emotional problems can cause as well as exacerbate physical illness. A 2003 report from the National Institute of Mental Health found depression to be just as significant a risk factor for cardiovascular disease as high blood pressure and elevated cholesterol. And research suggests that

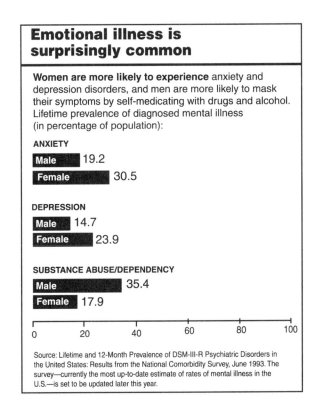

Emotional illness is surprisingly common

Women are more likely to experience anxiety and depression disorders, and men are more likely to mask their symptoms by self-medicating with drugs and alcohol. Lifetime prevalence of diagnosed mental illness (in percentage of population):

ANXIETY
Male 19.2
Female 30.5

DEPRESSION
Male 14.7
Female 23.9

SUBSTANCE ABUSE/DEPENDENCY
Male 35.4
Female 17.9

0   20   40   60   80   100

Source: Lifetime and 12-Month Prevalence of DSM-III-R Psychiatric Disorders in the United States: Results from the National Comorbidity Survey, June 1993. The survey—currently the most up-to-date estimate of rates of mental illness in the U.S.—is set to be updated later this year.

depression and possibly anxiety as well may raise the risk of developing osteoporosis and even Alzheimer's disease. A study of almost 2,000 people has also found that depression doubles the likelihood of developing diabetes.

"Antidepressants work for a large majority of people, but they're not wonder drugs. Side effects include loss of libido."

"Depression is an illness that has profound physiological effects all over the body," says Steven P. Roose, M.D., professor of clinical psychiatry at Columbia University's College of Phy-

Self-check for Emotional Symptoms

Emotional distress is a common response to negative life events. If symptoms are persistent, however, they may not resolve on their own. Do you frequently experience any of the following? Check all that apply:

___Feeling restless and on edge.
___Desire but inability to cut back on drinking alcohol.
___Lack of interest in things you used to enjoy.
___Moods that go from extreme highs to extreme lows.
___Reckless, foolish, or risky behavior.
___Inability to stop worrying.
___Muscle pains, headaches, or stomach problems with no physical cause.
___Nightmares or flashbacks to unpleasant events.
___Irritability; shouting at people and starting arguments.
___Sad, blue, or hopeless feelings.
___Emotional numbness.
___Drinking so much you forget what happened.

Results: Any of the above symptoms could signal a significant emotional problem or psychiatric disorder that could benefit from treatment. Seek an evaluation if you frequently experience even one of those symptoms and find that it interferes with your ability to function and enjoy your life.

Source: Adapted from the online screening programs of Screening for Mental Health Inc., Wellesley Hills, Mass. (**www.mentalhealthscreening.org**)

sicians and Surgeons in New York City. For example, depression impairs circulation by making platelets "stickier." And in people with anxiety or depression, the body secretes extra cortisol, a stress hormone that can damage the blood vessels. Ominously, these physiological changes can occur even in the absence of full-blown mental illness. Says Roose, "Risk increases proportionally to the severity of your symptoms."

Protecting Emotional Health

One strategy for keeping emotional distress in check is to be reflective about your moods and relationships. "That means observing negative patterns in your life and understanding the things that control you and hold you back," says Gail Saltz, M.D., associate professor of psychiatry at Weill-Cornell School of Medical Sciences in New York City. "If you can become aware of the patterns, you can direct them so that you can be your own pilot and not be driven by them."

The self-check questions for emotional symptoms is designed to alert you to symptoms that need evaluation. And the table treatment strategies for emotional disorders summarizes symptoms and treatments for the most common forms of emotional disorders. Here are some ways to find the right treatment.

Overcoming Barriers to Treatment

Many Americans view an emotional problem as a personal weakness rather than a medical problem, Saltz says. "We'll spend tons of money on a great haircut but won't do what's needed to evolve into someone who is more aware of emotional issues and therefore better able to get what we really want out of life," she adds.

Some people are so fearful of being labeled mentally ill that they deny the problem exists. Others deny that the problem is severe enough to warrant treatment. Financial barriers to treatment can also be significant. A single session with a psychiatrist can easily cost $100, and the cost of many antidepressants can run several dollars a pill. So those without insurance may find it difficult to afford help.

Another force that discourages treatment is the fear that unauthorized release of a person's medical records might jeopardize his or her employment or insurability. Despite prohibitions against this practice, violations continue. "Unauthorized disclosure of sensitive mental-health information can be devastating," says Ron Honberg, legal director of the National Alliance for the Mentally Ill. "It's a major concern."

Physicians who are too quick to offer drug treatment as the only option may be another barrier. Those who wish to avoid drug treatment should know that many studies have shown that various types of counseling and talk therapy can effectively relieve a range of emotional disorders. Talk therapy may take longer to have an impact than prescription drugs, but it also causes fewer side effects and can be a reasonable alternative when symptoms are not severe.

Best Therapy Options

Modern antidepressants, including selective serotonin reuptake inhibitors (SSRIs) like fluoxetine (*Prozac*) and sertraline (*Zoloft*), are often prescribed for depression and anxiety disorders. "They do work for a large majority of people," says Eric J. Nestler, M.D., Ph.D., chairman of the department of psychiatry at the University of Texas Southwestern Medical Center in Dallas, though they're not "wonder drugs." Side effects include weight gain and loss of libido, and recent evidence suggests that they may raise the risk of suicidal behavior in the first few weeks of treatment. A change in prescription can sometimes diminish side effects, and Nestler encourages people who could benefit from antidepressants not to be afraid of them.

A Consumer Reports survey of 3,079 readers with depression or anxiety found that **drug therapy** relieved symptoms faster than talk therapy. The majority of people who described their therapy as "mostly medication" had good outcomes. But it took trial and error to find the right medication. And the rates of adverse drug effects were much higher than those noted on the medications' package inserts.

Talk therapy rivaled drug therapy in effectiveness. Respondents who said their therapy was "mostly talk" and lasted at least 13 sessions had better outcomes than those whose therapy was "mostly medication." Therapy delivered by psychologists and clinical social workers was perceived as being just as effec-

Treatment Strategies for Emotional Disorders

Disorder, symptoms	Drug treatment	Best talk therapy
Alcohol dependency: Inability to cut back on drinking, strain on work or home life, resulting medical problems.	Acamprosate (*Campral*), disulfiram (*Antabuse*), or naltrexone (*ReVia*).	Counseling by physician, Alcoholics Anonymous or similar program.
Anxiety disorder (generalized): Persistent and uncontrollable worrying, trembling, headaches, insomnia, stomach trouble.	SSRI antidepressant, such as escitalopram (*Lexapro*) or paroxetine (*Paxil*) benzodiazepine sedatives, such as alprazolam (*Xanax*) or lorazepam (*Ativan*).	Cognitive-behavioral therapy, relaxation therapy.
Bipolar disorder: Boundless energy, sleeplessness, impulsive or reckless behavior regarding money, sexuality, and other areas.	Lithium (*Eskalith*), lamotrigine (*Lamictal*), or valproic acid (*Depakene*).	Psychotherapy, support groups.
Depression: Sadness, hopelessness, changes in appetite, weight, or sleep patterns.	SSRI antidepressant, such as citalopram (*Celexa*) or fluoxetine (*Prozac*), bupropion (*Wellbutrin*); possibly dietary supplement St. John's wort or SAM-e for mild-to-moderate symptoms.	Cognitive-behavioral therapy, interpersonal therapy.
Obsessive-compulsive disorder: Recurrent thoughts, repetitive and irrational behaviors.	SSRI antidepressant, such as fluoxetine (*Prozac*) or sertraline (*Zoloft*).	Cognitive-behavioral therapy
Panic disorder: Heart palpitations, profuse sweating, shortness of breath, avoidance of situations that induce panic.	SSRI antidepressant, such as fluoxetine (*Prozac*) or sertraline (*Zoloft*); tricyclic antidepressant, such as desipramine (*Norpramin*); MAOIs, such as pheneizine (*Nardil*) or tranylcpromine (*Parnate*).	Cognitive-behavioral therapy
Post-traumatic stress disorder: Reliving a trauma through flashbacks or nightmares, avoiding things pertaining to the trauma, feeling emotionally numb, feeling irritable, trouble sleeping or concentrating.	SSRI antidepressant, such as paroxetine (*Paxil*) or sertraline (*Zoloft*), tricyclic antidepressant, such as imipramine (*Tofranil*); MAOIs, such as pheneizine (*Nardil*) or tranylcpromine (*Parnate*).	Cognitive-behavioral therapy, interpersonal therapy; possibly "critical incident debriefing."
Social phobia: Avoidance of social gatherings because of heart palpitations, trembling, sweating, or blushing.	SSRI antidepressant, such as paroxetine (*Paxil*) or sertraline (*Zoloft*); beta-blocker, such as propranoiol (*Inderal*).	Cognitive-behavioral therapy

tive as that given by psychiatrists. Other professionals who offer therapy include psychoanalysts, psychiatric nurses, and marriage and family counselors.

If you need therapy, don't just pick a name from an ad or the Yellow Pages. Difficult as it may be when you're in distress, try to approach therapy as an active consumer. Ask your doctor and friends for referrals, and speak to potential therapists over the phone or in the office. (Many will meet with you briefly without charge.) Even a brief interview should tell you if you'd be comfortable sharing your most intimate thoughts and feelings.

No one type of therapy is best for all people. Many therapists favor a particular theoretical approach, although they often use a combination. Clinical trials have proved that two types of therapy are most consistently effective: cognitive behavioral therapy and interpersonal therapy. Both are designed to produce a meaningful improvement within 15 to 20 sessions. Both teach people to manage their moods—to think and behave their way to better mental health.

Cognitive behavioral therapy focuses on training patients to identify and consciously correct the distorted thought patterns associated with anxiety or depression. Anxious people tend to overestimate the likelihood of a catastrophe, while depressed people tend to react to setbacks or disappointments with extreme self-criticism and a feeling of hopelessness out of proportion to the situation. The therapy typically involves specific "homework" assignments. For instance, a depressed person might be assigned to arrange an enjoyable social activity or become more assertive on the job. Or an anxious person might be assigned to take steps to confront a feared situation.

Interpersonal therapy, used primarily for depression, focuses more on the patient's relationship problems with others, such as spouses, children, or co-workers. It can be especially effective when depression results from a major life transition, such as the birth of a child, divorce, loss of a job, or bereavement. Therapy typically involves learning to change one's manner of dealing with family and friends, adapting to changed life circumstances, or building up one's social skills.

What You Can Do

• Avoid unhealthy situations that can trigger negative emotions. These include chronic stress, unacknowledged anger, poor sleep habits, and lack of exercise.

• Monitor moods. As a general rule, it's time to consult your doctor if emotional problems persist beyond two weeks or interfere significantly with everyday life. In cases of bereavement and other severe loss, however, several months of depressed feelings are not unusual.

• Listen to a friend. Emotional problems can blunt your powers of observation and judgment, so you may not recognize symptoms that are obvious to others. If someone you trust voices concern or observes that you seem unusually sad or tired, don't be quick to dismiss his or her viewpoint.

• Comparison shop for a therapist. Referrals from health professionals and friends are a good starting point. Consider whether you have preferences regarding your therapist's gender, academic background, therapeutic approach, or other characteristics. Interview prospective therapists until you find someone you feel is a good fit.

Attention Deficit Disorder: Old Questions, New Answers

Despite persistent skepticism, the most common childhood psychiatric disorder is increasingly understood to be a brain malfunction. Different forms of the disorder may have different biological roots. New versions of older drugs are being introduced, and new drugs are being considered. Old and new concerns about the risks of drugs are raised, and there is now some evidence for alternative treatments. National, regional, and racial disparities in diagnosis and treatment persist and raise difficult questions.

Discoveries in neuroscience are reinforcing a growing consensus that attention-deficit/hyperactivity disorder (ADHD), as it is officially known, is not just a set of behavior problems but a biologically based disorder of brain function. The symptoms of impulsiveness, inattentiveness, and hyperactivity arise, this research suggests, because misfiring of the brain's executive function—its management system—make it difficult to stay still, concentrate, and exercise forethought and self-control.

ADHD is known to have a strong genetic component—one of the highest among psychiatric disorders—and several genetic markers are known. Similar symptoms have also been found in children with autism and fetal alcohol syndrome and even those exposed to nicotine in the womb. In recent studies, ADHD-like symptoms appeared in 15 of 29 children who had strokes, and in 16% of children admitted to trauma centers after a head injury.

Executive function involves so many brain pathways that its specific locations are not easy to tease out. But there's evidence that in children with ADHD, the disturbance occurs in a circuit that runs between the frontal cortex, a seat of judgment and planning, and the basal ganglia, which control habitual actions and convey reward signals. In one study, brain scans of 10 children with ADHD indicated that they did not engage this network normally but used other parts of the brain when performing certain experimental tasks.

Some experts regard the problem as inefficient reception of signals for delayed rewards. That causes impulsiveness, which in turn causes parents and teachers with high expectations to criticize and punish the child. After a while, the child stops trying to undertake projects that require long-range planning and never learns the necessary skills. So the motivation problem becomes a problem of executive function.

Stimulants

According to the National Survey on Children's Health, about 8% of children and adolescents ages 4–17 (a total of 4.4 million) have a diagnosis of ADHD, and about 50% of them are taking stimulant medications. The most important recent development

---

Resources

Children and Adults with Attention-Deficit/ Hyperactivity Disorder
800-233-4050
www.chadd.org
This support and educational organization for individuals with ADHD and parents of children with ADHD sponsors lectures, maintains support groups, publishes information, and refers patients for treatment.

National Institute of Mental Health
www.nimh.nih.gov/oybkucat/adhd.cfm
Provides information on symptoms, publicans, research, treatment, clinical trials, and how to get services.

---

in the drug treatment of ADHD is increased use of new formulations of these stimulants. There are nearly two dozen versions of methylphenidate and dextroamphetamine, under the old brand names Ritalin and Dexedrine and the more recent ones Concerta, Metadate, Focalin, Methylin, Adderall, and DextroStat. Added labels like LA (long-acting) and XR or ER (extended-release) refer to gradual or staged rather than immediate release of the drug into the bloodstream.

The long-acting and extended-release forms, which last 8–12 instead of 4–6 hours, have conquered the market because both children and parents prefer them. Users avoid the ups and downs produced by shorter-acting versions. Children taking the long-acting forms don't suffer the inconvenience of taking the drug three or four times a day or the embarrassment of taking it in school. Studies show that they are less likely to quit than those taking short-acting forms. The most widely used brand in late 2005 is Concerta, a type of extended-release methylphenidate with effects that last 12 hours.

Stimulant Risks

Meanwhile, spurred partly by reports of suicidal thinking and heart problems in children taking antidepressants, concern has grown about the risks of stimulants. In 2005, Canada temporarily suspended marketing of Adderall XR (a long-acting version of dextroamphetamine) after reports of sudden cardiac death in child and adult patients taking the drug. But the FDA has not concluded that stimulants raise the risk of cardiovascular problems for people without a heart condition.

Some recent animal experiments raise questions about long-term stimulant effects. Rats given daily injections of methylphenidate at ages equivalent to human childhood and adolescence became more sensitive to stress and less responsive to natural rewards like sugar water as adults. Interpreting these findings is not simple, because rats don't absorb drugs exactly as humans do, and injection directly into the abdominal cavity does not have the same effect as swallowing a pill. Studies on monkeys might clarify some of these issues.

The Addiction Question

Dextroamphetamine and methylphenidate can be addictive. In their mode of action and effects, they are similar to cocaine and the latest illicit drug scourge, methamphetamine. And stimulants are being used to enhance performance—by college students to win grades, by professional athletes to win games. But these users usually take the drugs orally, so they pass into and out of the brain too slowly to produce the highs and lows of addiction. The risk of addiction is even less when the drug is packaged for gradual or staged absorption. One reason for the popularity of Concerta is that it must be swallowed whole; it cannot be broken up into a powder and snorted or injected.

One recent review suggests that ADHD drugs actually lower the risk of later addiction. This research is not based on controlled studies, and correlation should not be confused with cause. Animal experiments have given conflicting results. There is no reliable evidence that taking ADHD medications affects the rate of addiction in later life.

Other Drugs

The search for alternative drugs will continue as long as 30% of children with ADHD do not respond to stimulants or cannot tolerate their side effects. In 2002, for the first time in many years, the FDA approved a new treatment for ADHD. Atomoxetine (Strattera) (See *Mental Health Letter,* December 2005) is apparently not addictive and is therefore uniquely approved for adults as well as children. The FDA has issued a warning about possible liver failure after two cases were reported (both recovered). The FDA is also requiring a warning about suicidal thinking on prescription labels. This caution is based on limited evidence from clinical trials.

Other potential drug treatments, all experimental, include the alpha-2 adrenergic agonists clonidine and guanfacine; modafinil (Provigil); and the antidepressants venlafaxine (Effexor), bupropion (Wellbutrin), imipramine (Tofranil), and de-sipramine (Norpramin). All these drugs, like atomoxetine and stimulants, increase the activity of norepinephrine or dopamine or both—neurotransmitters that act in the brain pathways thought to be affected by ADHD.

In 2005, magnesium pemoline (Cylert), which was rarely used and already carrying warnings about liver failure, lost its FDA approval and was removed from the market.

Last year's review of 146 studies conducted at the Oregon Evidence-Based Practice Center concluded that little is known about the comparative effectiveness or side effects of different versions of methylphenidate, dextroamphetamine, and atomoxetine and even less about the alternative drug treatments. Individual genetic differences probably affect responses to the drugs, and they may differ in their effects on specific symptoms of attention deficit disorder—a hint that more precisely targeted drug treatments could be developed.

Other Approaches

Children diagnosed with ADHD often receive little more than medications—not even further guidance from a physician. The American Academy of Pediatrics guidelines recommend that families stay in frequent contact with a doctor until the dose is adjusted and every few months after that. But in one survey, the average was one follow-up visit in six months.

It's not just that nondrug treatments are more expensive and time-consuming. The trouble is that behavior therapy and psychotherapy have been disappointing in controlled trials (See *Mental Health Letter*, January 2005). Still, many parents and professionals remain skeptical about medications because of concern about their long-term effects, and many children and adolescents do not want to take drugs. So the interest in alternatives persists. And there is preliminary evidence that psychosocial treatment may be helpful if it continues long enough. Extending an earlier program to two years, researchers found that parent training, school intervention, and a special summer day camp program reduced and occasionally eliminated the need for stimulant drugs in five- and six-year-old children with ADHD.

Clarification

In the article "The prevalence and treatment of mental illness in America today" (November 2005, p. 5), we cited a survey showing that "other mental health professionals" (apart from psychiatrists) provided services to 16% of people with psychiatric disorders, while "counselors or spiritual advisers" served 8%. Readers have pointed out that this description is incomplete and could be confusing. The counsellors grouped with spiritual advisers in the survey are human service providers working outside of specialized mental health settings. Licensed mental health counselors are included among the "other mental health professionals."

Is Television Bad and Green Good for ADHD?

The American Academy of Pediatrics says that children should watch no more than one hour a day of slow-paced programming before age six. But according to parents, the average is 3½ hours a day by age four, much of it consisting of fast-paced cartoons. It's been suggested that exposure to hours of rapid image and scene changes makes non-virtual life seem boring by comparison and may even slow or divert brain development. But cause and effect are not clear. Preoccupied or neglectful parents might let children watch too much television, and children who love television too much may also be more susceptible, for genetic or social reasons, to hyperactivity and distraction.

Not only less exposure to television but more exposure to nature might be good for children with attention problems. Several studies have found that impulse control and other ADHD symptoms improved when children had more access to trees and grass. This evidence, like the evidence for damaging effects of television, is limited, and its practical significance might be doubted. Still, it can't hurt any child to spend less time as a couch potato and more time outdoors in parks and playgrounds, woods and fields

The Persistence of ADHD

Probably the most important recent change in the understanding of ADHD is the growing recognition that people don't always grow out of it. The number of adults receiving drug treatment for ADHD more than doubled from 2001 to 2005 alone. The symptoms may even interfere with daily life more in adults than in children because adults have to exercise more self-control and do more planning.

In 2003, adult ADHD was included in a national survey for the first time; 4.4% of adults age 18–44 received the diagnosis, about half the rate in children. The only childhood risk factor for persistence into adulthood was the severity of the symptoms. ADHD is much more common in boys than girls, but adult women are now using ADHD drugs just as much as men the same age. Some think the symptoms are recognized more often in boys because their behavior is more troublesome, and less often in adult men because they don't seek help.

It's been said that identifying ADHD in adults can be like finding a missing jigsaw piece that solves the puzzle of behavior that looked like laziness, a character flaw, or a learning disability. Medications, group social skills training, individual psychotherapy, vocational counseling, and coaching may be helpful for adults with ADHD. The first controlled study of cognitive behavioral therapy for adult ADHD, published in 2005, found improvements in anxiety, depression, and attention.

Cultural Issues

The diagnosis and treatment for ADHD still depend on who you are and where you live. In some countries the disorder is rarely diagnosed. The rate of stimulant use, for example, is as much as 10 times higher in the United States than in Great Britain. Within the U.S., there is a great deal of regional variation, and blacks and Hispanics are less likely to receive the diagnosis than whites. A 2005 study found that African American parents regard the problem chiefly as misbehavior and do not like to seek help outside the family. They may mistrust the medical system or fear the stigma of a diagnosis.

National, racial, and regional variations in the diagnosis may raise unsettling questions about whether ADHD is a legitimate psychiatric or brain disorder, but most experts believe it occurs all over the world in a similar pattern. One review confirms this by showing that the disorder looks the same in every way in Brazil and the United States. There may be room for cultural variation, though, as long as the diagnosis is made only if symptoms occur in more than one setting and interfere seriously with personal life, work, or school.

References

Brown TE. *Attention Deficit Disorder: The Unfocused Mind in Children and Adults.* Yale University Press, 2005.

Bush G, et al. "Functional Neuroimaging of Attention-Deficit/Hyperactivity Disorder: A Review and Suggested Future Directions," *Biological Psychiatry* (June 1, 2005): Vol. 57, No. 11, pp. 1273–84.

Chacko A, et al. "Stimulant Medication Effects in a Summer Treatment Program among Young Children with Attention-Deficit/Hyperactivity Disorder," *Journal of the American Academy of Child and Adolescent Psychiatry* (March 2005): Vol. 44, No. 2, pp. 249–57.

Kuo FE, et al. "A Potential Natural Treatment for Attention-Deficit/Hyperactivity Disorder: Evidence from a National Study," *American Journal of Public Health* (September 2004): Vol. 94, No. 9, pp. 1580–86.

Ramsay JR, et al. "Adapting Psychotherapy to Meet the Needs of Adults with Attention-Deficit/Hyperactivity Disorder," *Psychotherapy: Theory, Research, Practice, Training* (Spring 2005): Vol. 42, No. 1, pp. 72–84.

Sonuga-Barke EJS. "Causal Models of Attention-Deficit/Hyperactivity Disorder: From Common Simple Deficits to Multiple Developmental Pathways," *Biological Psychiatry* (June 1, 2005): Vol. 57, No. 11, pp. 1231–38.

For more references, please see **www.health.harvard.edu/mentalextra**.

From *Harvard Mental Health Letter*, February 2006, pp. 3-6. Copyright © 2006 by Harvard Health Publications Group. Reprinted by permission.

Dealing with Demons

Seen as a public health problem, suicide is preventable—at least that's an approach several states are starting to take.

CHRISTOPHER CONTE

In the mid-1990s, the United States Air Force was hit by a deadly epidemic: Every year between 1991 and 1996, about 60 airmen took their own lives, making suicide the second leading cause of death among the service's 350,000 members.

Eager to reduce the terrible toll, the service conducted "psychological autopsies" of the victims. These linked most of the suicides to problems airmen were having with the law, finances, intimate relationships, mental health, job performance and alcohol and drugs. The study also found most of the airmen were socially isolated and lacked the skills needed to cope with stress.

With these findings in hand, the service launched a counterattack. Top Air Force officials began urging airmen to seek assistance when they encountered personal difficulties, assuring them that doing so would not hurt their chances of promotion. The service also started training all its members in suicide risk-awareness and prevention, and it established "stress management" teams to help airmen and their families deal with potentially traumatic events.

These and other efforts worked. The suicide rate, which had been 14.1 per 100,000 active-duty service members from 1991 to 1996, fell to 9.1 per 100,000 from 1997 to 2002. Air Force officials attribute the improvement to the breadth of the program. "Suicide prevention," says one service manual, "is everyone's business."

The Air Force experience is getting a lot of attention these days in state capitols. At least 20 states have adopted suicide-prevention plans, most of them in the past few years, and many other states are working on the issue, too. Their efforts are driven by the belief that public health strategies, which involve looking for patterns that may point to the sources of disease and launching broad-based public information campaigns to encourage healthier living among the population at large, may hold the key to reducing suicide—just as they have been used to reduce heart attacks, strokes and lung cancer.

Public health campaigns to discourage smoking, bad diet or unsafe sexual practices have become a familiar and remarkably successful part of American life, but the use of such strategies against a psychological disorder represents a significant new departure. If successful, it could usher in one of the most fundamental shifts in thinking about the role of state mental health programs in decades— one in which mental health agencies increasingly offer their services to the entire population rather than to the small group of people diagnosed as having severe mental illness.

"We have been missing opportunities to use public health promotion and prevention in the mental health sector," notes Alan Radke, who, as medical director for the adult mental health division of Hawaii's Department of Health, has been spearheading a broad review of prevention strategies for the National Association of State Mental Health Program Directors. "If we can demonstrate that the use of health promotion and prevention strategies works with suicide, from those learnings we can address any number of other conditions."

An Ounce of Prevention

That's a big "if." The overall suicide rate has been stuck between 10 and 13 per 100,000 people annually for the past 50 years, and despite a handful of promising signs such as the Air Force program, there is no conclusive evidence that any strategy to reduce it will work. Indeed, suicide-prevention advocates sometimes seem to be acting more on faith than scientific proof. "When I started, I worried that this is too hard to fix and too big to understand," concedes Jerry Reed, executive director of the Suicide Prevention Action Network—USA, a lobby group that represents "suicide survivors," as family members of suicide victims call themselves. "But sometimes you have to act like a little bird, and hope when you leave the nest that you'll sprout wings before you hit the ground."

Although the prospects for success seem uncertain, advocates can offer some compelling reasons to tackle the problem. Suicide is the 11th leading cause of death in the United States, accounting for about 30,000 deaths a year. That's more than die from homicide (about 20,000 annually) or AIDS (14,000 a year). Moreover, researchers estimate that as many as 25 people attempt suicide for every one who actually kills himself. In 2002, some 250,000 people required medical treatment following suicide attempts, according to the Centers for Disease Control and Prevention. And surveys by the CDC show that 20 percent of

TRAIL OF ANGUISH

State-by-state suicide death rates, 2001

BETWEEN 14 AND 23 DEATHS
PER 100,000 PEOPLE

- Alaska
- Arizona
- Arkansas
- Colorado
- Florida
- Idaho
- Montana
- Nevada
- New Mexico
- Oklahoma
- Oregon
- West Virginia
- Wyoming

BETWEEN 12 AND 14 DEATHS
PER 100,000 PEOPLE

- Delaware
- Kentucky
- Maine
- Missouri
- New Hampshire
- North Carolina
- North Dakota
- South Dakota
- Tennessee
- Utah

BETWEEN 11 AND 12 DEATHS
PER 100,000 PEOPLE

- Alabama
- Georgia
- Hawaii
- Indiana
- Mississippi
- South Carolina
- Vermont
- Virginia
- Washington
- Wisconsin

BETWEEN 6 AND 11 DEATHS
PER 100,000 PEOPLE

- California
- Connecticut
- Illinois
- Iowa
- Kansas
- Louisiana
- Maryland
- Massachusetts
- Michigan
- Minnesota
- Nebraska
- New Jersey
- New York
- Ohio
- Pennsylvania
- Rhode Island
- Texas

Source: Suicide Prevention Action Network Inc.

teenagers have seriously considered killing themselves. (Much of the current push to combat suicide stems from a tripling of the rate among people aged 15 to 24 between 1950 and 1993, even though it has since leveled off.)

Suicide survivors have played a central role in planting the idea that suicide is a community problem, rather than a private, individual matter. That is no small step, because suicide has long carried a stigma. "It took me a couple of years before I could even talk about it," says Massachusetts state Senator Robert Antonioni, who lost a brother to suicide and has since persuaded the Massachusetts legislature to spend close to $1 million on suicide-prevention efforts over the past several years.

The important point, adds Kentucky state Senator Tom Buford, who steered a suicide-prevention bill through his state legislature this year partly in honor of his father who killed himself years ago, is that although "you feel you're living in sinful territory because somebody in your family committed suicide, after a while you see it's just an illness that needs to be treated."

Because the majority of people who are suicidal go undiagnosed until it's too late to treat the illness, researchers say the only effective strategy may be to stress prevention in messages aimed at the entire population. "By reducing the risk for a lot of people, you get more bang for your buck than concentrating on the few who are at high risk," explains Kerry Knox, an assistant professor of preventive medicine at the University of Rochester.

The idea that broad strategies work more effectively than narrow ones against a hidden enemy is a fundamental tenet of public health. Epidemiologists liken society's approach to suicide today to its understanding of cardiovascular disease 30 years ago. Then, strokes, heart attacks and high blood pressure were treated largely on a case-by-case basis. The results were far from satisfactory because, as with suicide, these afflictions often went undetected until victims suffered crippling or fatal symptoms. But research in the 1970s and '80s showed that public information campaigns designed to promote low-cholesterol diets, exercise and screening for high blood pressure among the population at large were an effective way to prevent cardiovascular disease—even though many of the people who hear such warnings probably face little risk.

At first blush, suicide seems different because it isn't a medical disease. But the latest research suggests that it may not be so different. Like cardiovascular disease, it apparently results from both biological and environmental causes. People who commit suicide or attempt it have abnormalities in the prefrontal cortex area of their brains, which controls "inhibitory" functioning. Because of this biological condition, "they are less able to restrain themselves and more likely to have strong feelings," observes J. John Mann, chief of neuroscience at the New York State Psychiatric Institute. "When they get depressed, they get more depressed than most people." He concludes that suicide may be the product of "stress-diathesis"—that is, a confluence of "stressors" arising from the environment and a "diathesis," or predisposition for suicidal behavior.

Knox and Mann both serve on a suicide-prevention working group convened by the New York State Office of Mental Health (the Psychiatric Institute, considered one of the foremost research institutions in its field, is part of the state agency). Although they come from a public health and a neurobiological background, respectively, they agree that, as Mann puts it, "You need a combination of strategies to have an impact on the suicide rate." While he believes the day isn't far off when doctors will be able to detect people who have suicidal proclivities by reading their brain scans, the technology will be of little value unless people are willing to seek help for themselves or recognize when people they know need it. "You need to educate the public to understand there are such things as psychiatric illnesses, and that they can lead to suicide," he says. "That requires the involvement of government."

The CPR Method

Most states have started their suicide-prevention efforts with broad-based educational campaigns. This spring, for instance, New York State issued "SPEAK," which stands for Suicide Prevention Education Awareness Kits—packets of materials that explain the connections between depression and suicide and encourage help-seeking among teens, men, women and older people. Some states also offer advice to the news media on how to report on suicide. Guidelines adopted by Maine, for instance, seek to minimize the danger of "suicide contagion" by encouraging the press to refrain from describing how a person killed himself, glorifying a suicide and using such phrases as "successful suicide."

Some states have gone beyond educational programs to concentrate on strengthening the bonds that make for more supportive communities. In Alaska, where religious disillusionment and social breakdown are believed to lie behind high suicide rates among some native peoples, the state provides funds for village elders to teach children about their heritage. "This builds pride and relationships, so that if a kid gets in trouble later, he'll have somebody to turn to," explains Susan Soule, Alaska's program coordinator for suicide prevention and rural human services.

In the lower 48, suicide-prevention programs seek to accomplish the same objective by training "gatekeepers"—clergy, doctors, teachers, social workers and others—who might come into contact with people who are suicidal. Paul Quinnett, president and chief executive of the QPR Institute in Spokane, Washington, believes that doctors, psychologists and social workers should be required to receive suicide-prevention training as a condition of being licensed. QPR, a deliberate take-off on the familiar emergency treatment CPR, stands for "Question, Persuade and Refer," a simple methodology for detecting people at risk of suicide and helping them get professional assistance.

North Dakota has provided its own version of suicide-prevention training to 28,000 people since 2000 on a budget of just $75,000 a year. The program seeks official gatekeepers as well as informal leaders—people who tend to pull communities together by force of personality rather than official position. "We go into schools and ask, 'Who is the person who makes things happen?'" says Mark Lomurray, the state's suicide-prevention project leader. "That's who we train." While Lomurray can't prove a causal connection, he notes that the number of suicide deaths in North Dakota has fallen by almost half since the program began.

A Broad Reach

It is too early to say if all the efforts surrounding suicide prevention will pay off, but if they do, state mental health programs may well need more money. "Right now, we do a good job identifying people who are suicidal, and we can refer them for services if there's a crisis," notes Cheryl DiCara, director of Maine's Youth Suicide Prevention Program. But for people who are troubled and haven't reached the crisis point, she says, "there's not a lot we can do."

Prevention advocates say that public health strategies may save money in the long run by reducing the need for acute care. But that implies new methods of serving people who don't need institutionalization. New York State offers some clues about where this more expansive orientation might lead. Traditionally, the Office of Mental Health has focused exclusively on helping people with severe mental disorders. After the September 2001 terrorist attacks, however, the department, with funding from the Federal Emergency Management Agency, began offering post-trauma counseling to the entire population of New York City and 10 surrounding counties. In two years, more than a million people availed themselves of these free counseling and educational services.

"We're reaching out to a much broader constituency than we ever did previously," notes Sharon Carpinello, New York's mental health commissioner. She expects the agency to become involved in a variety of new public health endeavors. In addition to suicide prevention, the agency is developing a disaster preparedness and "resiliency" campaign for the entire state and a separate campaign aimed at combating eating disorders in young women.

John Allen, who serves as the office's liaison with outside groups, says the new public health focus has brought enormous changes to his job. In the past, he mainly worked with a few small groups that represented patients in mental hospitals. But the post-9/11 project took him into the mainstream. One of his most important partnerships was with the New York State Thruway Authority, which helped the office distribute brochures to commuters. And the suicide-prevention program is bringing him into contact with major employers, local civic organizations and chambers of commerce.

As the department increasingly operates in a bigger arena, some prevention advocates hope it will start asserting itself on matters that previously have been beyond its ability to influence—including proposals to require insurance companies to offer the same coverage for mental illness treatments as they provide for medical care. The idea, of course, is very controversial because of the possible costs, but it's nothing compared with another issue that some prevention advocates have in their sights: gun control.

At the moment, there is no consensus even among suicide experts that stricter gun control would reduce the suicide rate over the long run. The best evidence is that making the leading instrument of suicide less available might have an impact for a while but that the improvement might dissipate over time as people switch to alternative methods to kill themselves. But the simple fact that the idea is even being discussed is a measure of how optimistic the mental health community is about the potential of public health strategies.

"I think we have to stay away from the more controversial strategies until society changes a little bit, but I don't feel totally hopeless," says Madelyn Gould, a research scientist at the New York State Psychiatric Institute who has participated in the state's suicide-prevention working group. "After all, who would have thought a couple of decades ago that anti-smoking campaigns would be so successful that today you can't even smoke anymore in bars in New York City?"

CHRISTOPHER CONTE can be reached at crconte@earthlink.net

Too Young To Be Stressed

Aparna Bagdi

"For children, the pressures are beginning to tell."
"Required: Stress busters for smart kids." "Shrinks
called in as exam fever turns into epidemic."

The above headlines are not a sampling from sensationalized items on a television news show; instead, they led off articles that appeared in a mainstream national newspaper from India. Over the past few years, the *Times of India* has published many articles and editorials on the topic of childhood stress. According to Ramanathan (2002), a recent study conducted by the All India Institute of Medical Sciences reveals that nearly 35 percent of children ages 8-14, especially in urban areas, are stressed enough to need clinical attention. What is startling about such findings are the sheer numbers of children under stress, the early onset of their symptoms, and the extreme measures to which some children will go to cope (negatively) with their stress. This article explores some of the circumstances affecting the lives of children in India and some of the possible reasons for heightened childhood stress levels in a culture where, traditionally, the young are adored and indulged.

A recent study conducted by the All India Institute of Medical Sciences reveals that nearly 35 percent of children ages 8-14, especially in urban areas, are stressed enough to need clinical attention.

Cultural Context

Culture is a way of life shared by members of a certain population. The definition of culture encompasses the thoughts, emotions, behaviors, and customs shared by the people, as well as their social, economic, political, and religious institutions. As children grow and mature, they absorb the mindset, behaviors, and customs of the society in which they develop, and they begin to gain an understanding of their culture. Parents and other child-rearing agents consciously, or unconsciously, promote the competencies required to absorb cultural values and perform cultural tasks through culturally standardized techniques for raising children that have been developed over time and passed down from generation to generation. Children learn the ways of people in their culture by participating in cultural tasks and activities (Ogbu, 1988). The family is the primary unit through which customs, beliefs, habits, values, and modes of behavior are transmitted from one generation to the next through the process of socialization (Saraswathi & Dutta, 1988; Tandon, 1981). Therefore, while studying any aspect of child development, it is essential to examine it from within the child's cultural context (Ogbu, 1988).

Bronfenbrenner's (1979) social ecological theory has significance for studying how children cope with stress. According to this theory, children grow up in a dynamic world wherein they influence the environment around them and, in turn, are influenced by the environment. This reciprocity involves a process of mutual accommodation between children and their environment. The immediate setting, as well as the larger context of the setting, influences a child's development. Consequently, children's reactions to stress can be influenced by their immediate family and friends, and by the community in which they live. Several global considerations also may affect family functioning and child development. Examples of influential factors range from the home and school to the political climate of the country, international laws, and different social systems.

For an Indian child, the family's subculture (i.e., the community and society in which the child is born and brought up) determines the family's status in society, which acts as a filter in providing the child with his/her first role models, informal and formal education, and experiences within the culture. Traditionally, families in India have been classified as extended or joint in nature. Joint families consist of one or more married couples residing with their children and other close relatives, such as grandparents, aunts, and uncles, all in one home. A nuclear family structure, which is becoming increasingly common, constitutes a single married couple and their children (Ahuja, 1993; Bisht & Sinha, 1981; Muttalib, 1990). The structural differences between the joint family and the nuclear family lead to different interaction patterns among members of the two family types. Children in joint families are often indulged and overprotected, which encourages the child's dependence on the mother and other family members. In nuclear families, the child is in more direct contact with his or her parents, and the number of adult role models decreases. As compared to children from joint families, children from nuclear families are encouraged to function in an individualized manner, take initiative, and act independently. Fathers play an important role in nuclear families since they are often more approachable and psychologically available to their children (Bisht & Sinha, 1981). Thus, children's experiences growing up in such a complex society can be unique.

Stress in the Indian Context

While it is true that most parents in India look forward eagerly to the birth to their child, many start worrying about the child's future and the pressures of caring for him/her even before the child is born. The joy in anticipating the arrival of the child is often replaced with perturbation and anxiety (Sethi, 1996). Many factors contribute to augmented parental anxiety, including, but not limited to, the pressures of providing a good family and school life for the child, ensuring the child's academic success (and later in life as well), and trying to find a balance between a busy family life and a demanding work routine. In general, parents in India set very high expectations for their children to do well in school, in extracurricular activities as well as in studies, and these high expectations often lead to worried children and anxious parents (Adhyaru & Nandakumar, 2003).

For most Indian children, formal education starts at the preschool level. Literacy data from the 1991 census reveal that the literacy rate for girls is lower by nearly 20 points as compared to that of boys. The rate of increase in literacy during the last decade also has been slower for females (Guba, 1996). Government and nongovernment agencies are attempting to provide education incentives for children, in the form of free textbooks, uniforms, and meals. However, children face tremendous pressure and competition to gain admission into preschools. Each successive academic year adds to children's emotional strain. The stress reaches monumental proportions by the time students reach grades 10 through 12, performance in which determines the student's career and future success (Saraswathi & Pai, 1997).

Children as young as 3 are faced with pressure at home and in school. The rising number of applicants and the limited number of available seats in nursery schools have resulted in cramped, overcrowded classrooms. An even more difficult issue concerns admission to primary schools, which is based on child interviews. Consequently, good nursery schools are now expected to train young children for primary school admission interviews. During these interviews, children are forced to sit still and answer questions regarding colors, pictures, and fruits, and to recognize and write the alphabet. Many children are rejected because they are too young and therefore unprepared for these tasks. However, getting admission into good schools is considered crucial in order to ensure exposure to a scholarly environment and a good academic career. Parents therefore feel compelled to force their children to perform, even if a child is not developmentally ready. The demands on parents to prepare their children for rigorous entrance interviews have resulted in increased stress levels for both parents and children (Sharan, 1991; Times News Network, 2002). Even kindergartners have demonstrated feelings of inadequacy after being rejected during the interview process (Matthews, 1991).

Once in school, young children face enormous pressure from parents and teachers to work hard and do well. The child's worth is measured in terms of school grades. Children as young as 4 are overburdened with homework, tuition (coaching) classes, and scholarship exams. Although the government has banned classes meeting after 7:00 p.m., some schools begin the school day as early as 6:30 a.m. and operate well into the night (Ramanathan, 2002). A factorial study about the sources of academic stress among high school boys, conducted by Rajendran and Kaliappan (1991), revealed four major factors that contributed to high stress levels: personal inadequacy (e.g., difficulty in keeping up with class work); fear of failure (e.g., fear of failing class tests or exams); interpersonal difficulties (e.g., receiving criticism from teachers); and inadequate study facilities (e.g., time taken to travel to school).

Consequently, school is no longer merely challenging, but distressing, competitive, and anxiety-provoking. For many children, examinations symbolize emotional trauma and anxiety. The stringent ranking system used by several schools also influences children negatively. For older children, every point they receive can influence their chance of getting into a good school and ensuring their place in a shrinking job market. Being labeled as "average" or "below average" may overwhelm the child and cause low self-esteem. At this level, competition becomes unhealthy. Teamwork is considered to be unimportant, so the tendency to become more individualistic increases; moreover, tolerance toward peers decreases. Playing with friends is replaced by watching television, playing computer games, or reading books that are restricted to topics of general knowledge or education. As a result, the positive aspects of play—relaxing, coping with fear, giving vent to aggression, dealing with competition, learning social rules, cooperating, and learning to handle difficult situations—are lost (Jain, 1996; Matthews, 1991).

Extremely high parental expectations can greatly augment children's anxiety levels. According to Saksena (2002), some parents put unrealistic expectations on their child just so they can brag about their child's "smartness." Pushy and overenthusiastic parents may consciously or unconsciously hinder their children's development and make them more prone to early burnout and mental fatigue. Child psychologists warn that tremendously high parental expectations cause children to feel even more pressure than they do from examinations. The Times News Network (February 23, 2003) quotes Sumit Chandra, a child psychologist based in the city of Lucknow, India, as saying, "Parents often tell me that suddenly their child has been acting strange and has not been concentrating on his studies. But none of them understand that this is an obvious fallout of the expectation pressure they put their child through. Every year I see kids buckle under tremendous anxiety to perform well in their exams." Additionally, parents sometimes give their children subtle messages that they have failed them by not doing well in school. Children often react by becoming depressed and uninterested in school activities (Abraham & Neogi, 1997; Jain, 1996; Matthews, 1991; Saksena, 2002).

Some mental health experts believe that parents need to be counseled as much as children do. Many parents respond to high stress situations (such as board examinations) with extreme nervousness, which is then transferred to their child.

When all means of recreation are blocked in favor of a constant routine of studying for exams, and children's time to play and talk with friends is minimized, the result is that children's ability to effectively cope with exam stress is compromised (Mukherjee, 2003).

Factors such as competition, changing family patterns, and unhealthful lifestyles (such as a poor diet, excessive exposure to television, and limited exercise) contribute to the physical manifestations of stress (Singh, 2002). Major Indian metropolitan cities, such as Bombay and Calcutta, are plagued by problems of overcrowding and pollution. High incidences of physical and psychological symptoms in response to the crowding and noise have been observed (Lam & Palsane, 1997). In addition, such social problems as parental alcohol abuse, parental depression, and poverty also add to tension at home and the inability of children to keep up with academic activities. And then there is the ongoing problem of homeless children. For children living on street corners, education is not a part of their everyday lives. Instead, miserable working and living conditions, violence, crime, and drugs are a reality. Along with having few resources, poor children are also faced with lack of a support system and good role models (Abraham & Neogi, 1997; Sethi, 1996).

The age of clients visiting psychiatrists in cities such as Bombay is falling steadily. The number of children requiring treatment in the form of medications and/or counseling is increasing (Abraham & Neogi, 1997). Mental turmoil and resulting stress on children leads to physical manifestations, including stuttering, giddiness, fainting, palpitations, migraines, gastro-intestinal complaints, and bed-wetting. Stress-related maladies such as depression, hysterical behavior, abdominal pains, peptic ulcers, hypertension, and asthma have begun to affect children as young as 7. Children unable to cope with psychological tensions may suffer from severe headaches, insomnia, recurring nightmares, and moodiness; often, they do not want to go to school. Adolescent girls who are unable to cope with academic pressures may compensate by trying to be trendy, and trying to imitate fashion models and actresses. As a result, the rate of anorexia nervosa in girls older than 12 is rising. Higher incidences of dropping out of school, running away from home, and suicide attempts can also be the unfortunate result of extreme stress and inability to cope with it (Abraham & Neogi, 1997; Jain, 1996; Matthews, 1991; Sharan, 1991, Singh, 2002).

Despite the abundant newspaper coverage of these behaviors, little research-based literature regarding childhood stress and coping in the Indian cultural context can be found. One recent multi-method study was conducted with 8- to 11-year-olds in Bombay. Information for this childhood stress-coping study was gathered through questionnaires and small focus group sessions. Children were asked to talk about situations that make them feel sad, bad, upset, nervous, or anxious. Children also were asked to talk about what they did in order to help themselves feel better. The results of the study indicated that children are very willing and, indeed, capable of discussing their feelings and talking about things that upset them. The findings reveal that both girls and boys reported feeling stressed in several different aspects of their lives. The results also clearly indicate the need for significant adults, such as parents and teachers, to assist children in learning effective ways of coping with stress (Bagdi, 1998).

Credible efforts to address these important issues are being pursued. The South Point School in Calcutta has organized a six-day-long Art of Living workshop called Art Excel (or All-Round Training in Excellence) (Roy, 2003). The workshop is customized for children ages 9-15 and focuses on such coping mechanisms as breathing techniques and asanas (yoga exercises), as well as simple interactive games to improve physical agility, memory, and concentration. Programs such as Art Excel instill positive coping mechanisms and help children deal effectively with everyday stressors.

Conclusion

It is paradoxical that a culture that believes in adoring and indulging their young ones (Kakar, 1979) should also have inherent social mechanisms that create high levels of stress and anxiety in children. Although the social and educational systems of Indian society try to support and nurture the growth and development of children, it is evident that academic and career success comes at a high price for many children in India.

The goals of high academic achievement and a successful career are laudable. After all, many Indian children do grow up to be successful scientists, researchers, doctors, and educators. To ensure that success, however, it is critical that children and parents receive appropriate supportive structures and learn the crucial life skills of positive coping. Children in India appear to be growing up much too stressed, much too soon. We, as responsible adults, need to figure out a way to give their childhood back to them.

References

Abraham, M., & Neogi, S. (1997). The tension is killing. *The Week, 15*(7), 16–20.

Adhyaru, P., & Nandakumar, P. (2003, February 27). *Shrinks called in as exam fever turns to epidemic. The Times of India.* Retrieved July 18, 2003, from http://timesofindia.indiatimes.com/cms.dll/html/uncomp/articleshow?msid=38703643

Ahuja, R. (1993). *Indian social system.* New Delhi: Rajwat Publications.

Bagdi, A. (1998). *Children's perceptions of stressful events and how they cope with them: An Indian experience.* Unpublished doctoral dissertation, Syracuse University.

Bisht, S., & Sinha, D. (1981). Socialization, family, and psychological differentiation. In D. Sinha (Ed.), *Socialization of the Indian child* (pp. 41–54). New Delhi, India: Concept Publishing.

Bronfenbrenner, U. (1979). *The ecology of human development: Experiments by nature and design.* Cambridge, MA: Harvard University Press.

Guha, S. (1996). The girl child is not a lesser child. In J. P. Singh (Ed.), *The Indian woman: Myth and reality* (pp. 88–109). New Delhi, India: Gyan Publishing House.

Jain, M. (1996). The adult child. *India Today, 21*(7), 92–97.

Kakar, S. (1979). Childhood in India: Traditional ideals and contemporary reality. *International Social Science Journal, 31,* 444–456.

Lam, D. J., & Palsane, M. N. (1997). Research on stress and coping: Contemporary Asian approaches. In H. S. R. Rao & D. Sinha (Eds.), *Asian perspectives on psychology* (pp. 74–92). New Delhi, India: Sage.

Matthews, V. (1991, April 14). Do exams pass the test? *The Sunday Times of India.*

Mukherjee, A. (2003, March 02). Parents don't fret, have faith. *The Times of India.* Retrieved July 18, 2003, from http:// timesofindia.indiatimes.com/cms.dll/html/uncomp/ articleshow?msid=39001479

Muttalib, M. A. (1990). *Child development: A study of health culture of low income urban settlement.* New Delhi, India: Sterling Publishers.

Ogbu, J. U. (1988). Cultural diversity and human development. *New Directions for Child Development, 42,* 11–28.

Rajendran, R., & Kaliappan, K. V. (1991). A factorial study of sources of student academic stress. *Journal of Psychological Researches, 35,* 53–57.

Ramanathan, G. (2002, December 03). Stress gets the children. *The Times of India.* Retrieved July 18, 2003, fro http:// timesofindia.indiatimes.com/cms.dll/html/uncomp/ articleshow?msid=30113530

Roy, B. (2003, June 3). Stress buster yoga for kids. *The Times of India.* Retrieved July 18, 2003, from http://timesofindia.indiatimes.com/ cms.dll/html/uncomp/articleshow?msid=2803

Saksena, I. (2002, August 28). Required: Stress busters for smart kids. *The Times of India.* Retrieved July 18, 2003, from http:// timesofindia.indiatimes.com/cms.dll/html/uncomp/ articleshow?msid=20495256

Saraswathi, T. S., & Dutta, R. (1988). Invisible boundaries: Grooming for adult roles. *A descriptive study of socialization in a poor rural and urban slum setting in Gujarat.* New Delhi, India: Northern Book Centre.

Saraswathi, T. S., & Pai, S. (1997). Socialization in the Indian context. In H. S. R. Kao & D. Sinha (Eds.), *Asian perspectives on psychology* (pp. 74–92). New Delhi, India: Sage.

Sethi, H. (1996). Comment: Seeking a lost childhood. *Seminar, 443,* 46–47.

Sharan, A. (1991, April 2). The overburdened child. *The Independent Journal of Politics and Business*, p. 17.

Singh, H. (2002, April, 22). For children, the pressures are beginning to tell. *The Times of India.* Retrieved July 18, 2003, from http:// timesofindia.indiatimes.com/cms.dll/html/uncomp/ articleshow?msid=7697271

Tandon, T. (1981). Process of transmission of values in the Indian child. In D. Sinha (Ed.), *Socialization of the Indian child* (pp. 11–30). New Delhi, India: Concept Publishing.

Times News Network. (2002, August 16). NCERT module for preschool. *The Times of India.* Retrieved July 18, 2003, from http://timesofindia.indiatimes.com/cms.dll/html/uncomp/ articleshow?msid=19299179

Times News Network. (2003, February 23). Great expectations. *The Times of India.* Retrieved July 18, 2003, from http:// timesofindia.indiatimes.com/cms.dll/html/uncomp/ articleshow?msid=38332456

APARNA BAGDI is Assistant Professor, Department of Individual and Family Studies, University of Delaware, Newark.

UNIT 3
Nutritional Health

Unit Selections

Key Points to Consider

- Why are some fats healthier than others?

- What foods are considered healthy? Unhealthy?

- What dietary changes could you make to improve your diet? What is keeping you from making those changes?

- Do you think that fast food restaurants should be forced to limit the amount of fat and sodium in the food items they sell? Why or why not?

- Why do healthy foods cost more than unhealthy foods?

- Should you consider buying the more expensive organic foods?

Student Website
www.mhcls.com/online

Internet References
Further information regarding these websites may be found in this book's preface or online.

The American Dietetic Association
http://www.eatright.org

Center for Science in the Public Interest (CSPI)
http://www.cspinet.org/

Food and Nutrition Information Center
http://www.nalusda.gov/fnic/index.html

For years, the majority of Americans paid little attention to nutrition, other than to eat three meals a day and, perhaps, take a vitamin supplement. While this dietary style was generally adequate for the prevention of major nutritional deficiencies, medical evidence began to accumulate linking the American diet to a variety of chronic illnesses. In an effort to guide Americans in their dietary choices, the U.S. Department of Agriculture and the U.S. Public Health Service review and publish Dietary Guidelines every 5 years. The year 2000 Dietary Guidelines' recommendations are no longer limited to food choices; they include advice on the importance of maintaining a healthy weight and engaging in daily exercise. In addition to the Dietary Guidelines, the Department of Agriculture developed the *Food Guide Pyramid* to show the relative importance of food groups.

Despite an apparent ever-changing array of dietary recommendations from the scientific community, five recommendations remain constant: 1) eat a diet low in saturated fat, 2) eat whole grain foods, 3) drink plenty of fresh water daily, 4) limit your daily intake of sugar and salt, and 5) eat a diet rich in fruits and vegetables. These recommendations, while general in nature, are seldom heeded, and in fact many Americans don't eat enough fruits and vegetables and eat too much sugar and saturated fat.

Of all the nutritional findings, the link between dietary fat and coronary heart disease remains the most consistent throughout the literature. The article "What Does Science Say You Should Eat?" addresses recent research on fat in the diet. It discusses trans fatty acids, a type of saturated fat. These fats occur naturally in limited amounts in some meats and dairy products. The majority of these fats, however, enter the diet via a process known as hydrogenation. Hydrogenation causes liquid oils to harden into products such as vegetable shortening and margarine. In addition to these products, trans fats are found in many commercially prepared and restaurant foods. Current recommendations suggest that the types of fats consumed may play a much greater role in disease processes than the total amount of fat consumed. As it currently stands, most experts agree that it is prudent to limit our intake of trans fat, which appears to raise LDLs, the bad cholesterol, and lower HDLs, the good cholesterol, and thus increases the risk of heart disease. There's also evidence that trans fats increase the risk of diabetes.

While the basic advice on eating healthy remains fairly constant, many Americans are still confused over exactly what to eat. Should their diet be low carbohydrate, high protein, or low fat? When people turn to standards such as the *Food Guide Pyramid*, even here there is some confusion. The *Pyramid*, designed by the Department of Agriculture over 20 years ago, recommends a diet based on grains, fruits and vegetables with several servings of meats and dairy products. It also restricts the consumption of fats, oils and sweets. Researchers such as Walter Willett from the Harvard School of Public Health disagree with the basic tenets of the Pyramid and he has actually designed his own version in "What Does Science Say You Should Eat?" Willett's version draws a distinction between good and bad fats, between whole-grain and refined carbohydrates, and between healthy and less sources of protein. He also moves potatoes into the starch as opposed to the vegetable category.

While the public continues to be confused over which foods are healthy, the media often contributes to the confusion. In "Food News Blues", Barbara Kantrowitz and Claudia Kalb address the many conflicting articles and how to make sense of the media hype surrounding nutritional recommendations. One of those controversies is whether organic food is worth the increased price. In "When It Pays to Buy Organic", the benefits of eating organic is discussed and which foods are better for you if they're grown organically.

Of all the topic areas in health, food and nutrition is certainly one of the most interesting, if for no other reason than the rate at which dietary recommendations change. Despite all the controversy and conflict, the one message that seems to remain constant is the importance of balance and moderation in everything we eat.

Diet and Genes

It isn't just what you eat that can kill you, and it isn't just your DNA that can save you—it's how they interact.

ANNE UNDERWOOD AND JERRY ADLER

Jose Ordovas has glimpsed the future of medicine, and there's good news for anyone who has just paid $4 for a pint of pomegranate juice. Ordovas, director of the Nutrition and Genomics Laboratory at Tufts University, believes the era of sweeping dietary recommendations for the whole population—also sometimes known as fads—may be coming to an end. Red wine may be better for your arteries than ice cream, but you can't create a diet that's optimal for everyone, Ordovas says—or, to put it another way, even Frenchmen get heart attacks sometimes. Within a decade, though, doctors will be able to take genetic profiles of their patients, identify specific diseases for which they are at risk and create customized nutrition plans accordingly. Some people will be advised to eat broccoli, while others will be told to eat … even more broccoli.

GREEN TEA
helps silence genes that fuel breast cancer in some women.
ONE EXAMPLE:
- **Name of gene:** HER-2
- **Function of gene:** Triggers growth signals in cells
- **Long-term effect:** Slows HER-2 signaling in aggressive breast tumors

Maybe you have to be a nutritionist to appreciate the beauty of that scheme. The promise of nutritional genomics—a field that barely existed five years ago—is not to overturn a century's worth of dietary advice but to understand on the most basic level how health is determined by the interplay of nutrients and genes. The old paradigm was of a one-way process, in which "bad" foods gave you heart disease or cancer unless "good" genes intervened to protect you. New research suggests a continual interaction, in which certain foods enhance the action of protective (or harmful) genes, while others tend to suppress them. This supports what we know from observation, that some individuals are better adapted than others to survive a morning commute past a dozen doughnut shops. Pima Indians in the Southwest get type 2 diabetes at eight times the rate of white Americans. Individuals have widely varying responses to high- or low-fat diets, wine, salt, even exercise. Overwhelmingly, though, researchers expect that conventional dietary wisdom will hold for most people. So keep that vegetable steamer handy.

The model for nutritional genomics is the work that has already been done on drug-gene interactions. Researchers are starting to unravel the mystery of why a drug may be a lifesaver for one person while causing a fatal reaction in another, and in a third has no effect at all. Why do a third of patients fail to respond to the antidepressants known as SSRIs, including Prozac, Paxil and Zoloft? The drugs are meant to increase levels of the neurotransmitter serotonin by blocking its "reuptake," or clearance from the brain. Obviously, they can work only if serotonin is being produced in the first place. Last month researchers at Duke University discovered that some people have a variant gene which reduces the production of serotonin by 80 percent—making them both susceptible to major depression and resistant to treatment with SSRIs.

BROCCOLI
boosts genes that protect against heart disease.
ONE EXAMPLE:
- **Name of gene:** GST
- **Function of gene:** Produces the body's master antioxidants, glutathione
- **Long-term effect:** The additional glutathione helps keep arteries healthy

But food interactions are usually far more complicated. "Normally, you take one drug at a time and for a limited amount of time," says Dr. Muin Khoury, director of the Office of Genomics and Disease Prevention at the Centers for Disease Control and Prevention. "If you have a certain genetic variant, you stay away from a particular drug or take a different dose." But nutrients come in bulk, you consume them for a lifetime and you can get them without a prescription, even the Trucker's Pancake Special. Metabolism involves huge numbers of genes interacting in uncountable ways. There are at least 150 gene variants that can give rise to type 2 diabetes, 300 or more that are associated with obesity. Ordovas at Tufts compares the situation to an electrical panel: "We know about certain switches and how to turn them on and off. But in some people, you turn the switch but the light doesn't come on, because there are other switches upstream and downstream that we don't know about yet." It will be years before researchers have a good diagram of the circuit. That hasn't prevented the growth of a fledgling industry in personalized nutritional supplements to treat everything from osteoporosis to obsessive-compulsive disorder. At least one company will even profile your genes to take the guesswork out of choosing makeup.

SOYBEANS
affect 123 genes involved in prostate cancer.
ONE EXAMPLE:
- **Name of gene:** p53
- **Function of gene:** Kills mutant cells
- **Long-term effect:** A compound in soy increases activity of the p53 gene, helping to block tumor formation

But pieces of the diagram are beginning to emerge. Green tea contains potent antioxidants known to help prevent heart disease and certain cancers, but only some women seem to show a reduction in breast cancer from drinking it. A study at the University of Southern California suggests that part of the reason lies in a gene that produces an enzyme called COMT that inactivates the cancer-suppressing compounds; women with the gene variant that produces a less active form of COMT showed the most benefit from tea.

One interaction that has been studied in detail involves two categories of enzymes known as phase 1 and phase 2. These work in sequence to eliminate certain toxins from the body, such as heterocyclic amines—potent carcinogens that form, infuriatingly, in the tasty crust on broiled meat. Actually, the amines are not inherently harmful; they are dangerous only after the phase 1 enzymes have begun metabolizing them, and before the phase 2s can finish the job. So, obviously, it is desirable to have a balance of the two enzymes. But some people have a variant gene that speeds up the phase 1 enzymes, so they form carcinogens faster than the phase 2s can get rid of them. This gene is found in 28 percent of white Americans, but roughly 40 percent of African-Americans and Hispanics and nearly 70 percent of Japanese-Americans (who, as it happens, have a high rate of stomach cancer). But there are ways to tweak the system: garlic contains nutrients that slow down the phase 1 enzymes, and a substance known as sulforaphane boosts levels of the phase 2s. And sulforaphane is easy to obtain. You get it from broccoli.

TURMERIC
suppresses genes that ratchet up inflammation.
ONE EXAMPLE:
- **Name of gene:** Cox-2
- **Function of gene:** Makes inflammatory compounds
- **Long-term effect:** Could help ward off colon cancer and Alzheimer's

"You can see where we're headed. We're starting to take the guesswork out of the things we eat," says Raymond Rodriguez, who heads the Center of Excellence in Nutritional Genomics at the University of California, Davis. One notable case is the gene for a protein known as Apo E, which plays a major role in regulating cholesterol. It has three major variants (or "alleles"), designated E2, E3 and E4, of which E3 is the most common. People with one or two copies of the E2 allele generally have lower-than-average cholesterol, but the E4 variety—an estimated 15 to 30 percent of the population has at least one copy of the allele—is potentially lethal. It increases the risk of diabetes, it raises total cholesterol and it reverses the usual protective effects of moderate drinking. And it vastly increases the risks of smoking. "Smoking is bad for everybody," says Ordovas, "but in a person with E4 it's a total killer. We're not talking about probabilities. It's almost certain you'll get heart disease." But, he adds, E4 is extremely susceptible to environment. The increased diabetes risk is found only in people who are overweight. If you stop smoking, give up alcohol, exercise and eat a diet low in saturated fat, "you can remove *all* the genetic predisposition for heart disease that comes with E4"—not just some, but all of it.

Patients at risk for Alzheimer's may not want to know.

On the face of it, you could make a case for universal screening for the Apo E gene. But we don't do it, and the reasons shed light on the ethical complexities of the field. One reason is peculiar to the Apo E4 allele, which also doubles the risk of developing Alzheimer's. Since there's not much that can be done to prevent it, many doctors are reluctant to give patients this news, and many patients don't want to know it themselves. More generally, there is the danger that insurance companies will discriminate against people with risk factors in their genome. Ruth DeBusk, author of "Genetics: The Nutrition Connection," thinks this concern is overblown, because by and large the risks are spread across the population. "We all have some susceptibilities," she says. "It's not as if one group has all the bad genes and the rest of us are perfect." Susceptibilities, moreover, don't necessarily amount to destiny; perhaps we can figure out what people with the E4 gene should eat to forestall dementia. But

Jim Kaput, who founded a genomics-research company, wonders about people who get the correct nutritional advice for their genotype and then refuse to follow it. "Should the insurance company be obliged to pay for their health care, too?"

And—one might ask—what's the point of testing for something if the inevitable advice that comes out of it is to exercise and eat a healthy diet? Didn't we know that already? The answer lies in the "Churchill effect," people's natural inclination to believe that if Winston Churchill lived to 90 on a diet of marrow bones, champagne and cigars, why not them? "People always think the warnings don't apply to them," DeBusk says. "We hope if we can tell them 'Here's what *you're* at risk for,' it will hit home." Conversely, cardiologists now routinely put people on a low-salt diet to control high blood pressure, knowing it doesn't work for as much as half the population. Even if it doesn't work, it can't hurt, and the doctor, after all, isn't the one giving up hot dogs. But, as Dr. Victoria Herrera of Boston University says, telling patients to do something that doesn't work "makes liars out of doctors. We need to make a diagnosis based on genotype, so we can go beyond trial and error."

Not all research in the field is aimed at identifying alleles that differ among individuals. The broader purpose is to understand the interplay of nutrition and genetics. What protects Asians (at least the ones who still live in Asia and eat a traditional soy-based diet) from hormone-sensitive breast and prostate tumors? The most common explanation is that soy contains compounds that bind to estrogen receptors on cells, making them unavailable to more potent hormones. But Rodriguez has identified a soy constituent called lunasin that increases, by his count, the activity of 123 different genes in prostate cells. Among them are genes that suppress tumor growth, initiate the repair of damaged DNA and promote apoptosis, the programmed "suicide" of damaged cells

before they begin to multiply. He hasn't been looking for different alleles of these genes, although it's likely they exist and may subtly affect how individuals respond to lunasin. The genetic factors predisposing men to prostate cancer can, in principle, eventually be identified and calculated for each individual. When all is said and done, though, the recommendation will probably stay the same: eat more soy. (And more fresh fruits and vegetables, and less saturated fat … and so on.)

Another compound getting a lot of study is curcumin, the yellow pigment in turmeric, an ingredient in curry spice. Curcumin reduces the action of a number of genes that promote inflammation, which is linked to heart disease, colon cancer and Alzheimer's. "It's probably no coincidence that India has the lowest incidence of Alzheimer's in the world," says Sally Frautschy, a professor of neurology at UCLA, who studies turmeric together with her husband and colleague, Greg Cole. "What I hear from the pharmaceutical industry," says Cole, "is 'What are you trying to do, ruin us?'"

Some people seem immune to the effects of salt on blood pressure.

There's not much chance of that, of course. More likely, nutritional genomics will create opportunities for drug companies to isolate, concentrate, synthesize and improve on the compounds in nature, which they've been doing for a hundred years. What Cole and his colleagues seek is to shed light on the mystery of how the human body has evolved the miraculous ability to overcome, once in a while, the threat posed by the consequences of its own appetites.

When It Pays to Buy Organic

Which apple? The decision doesn't end once you've figured out whether to buy, say, the McIntosh or the Red Delicious. In many food stores across the country, you're also faced with the more vexing question of buying organic or conventional, and not just at the apple bin. All kinds of organic fruits, vegetables, meats, poultry, eggs, cooking oils, even cosmetics are crowding store shelves.

For many shoppers, the decision often comes down to money. On average, you'll pay 50 percent extra for organic food, but you can easily end up shelling out 100 percent more, especially for milk and meat. Nevertheless, organic products are one of the fastest-growing categories in the food business. Nearly two-thirds of U.S. consumers bought organic foods and beverages in 2005, up from about half in 2004. While some buy organic to support its producers' environmentally friendly practices, most are trying to cut their exposure to chemicals in the foods they eat.

Critics argue that we're wasting our money because there's no proof that conventially produced foods pose significant health risks. Now, however, there are many new reasons to buy organic. First, a growing body of research shows that pesticides and other contaminants are more prevalent in the foods we eat, in our bodies, and in the environment than we thought. And studies show that by eating organic foods, you can reduce your exposure to the potential health risks associated with those chemicals.

Second, we found many ways to add more organic products to your shopping list without busting your budget. For one thing, you don't have to buy organic across the board. The truth is, not all organic-labeled products offer added health value. We found, for example, that it's worth paying more for organic apples, peaches, spinach, milk, and beef to avoid chemicals found in the conventionally produced versions of those items. But you can skip organic asparagus and broccoli because conventional varieties generally have undetectable pesticide levels. You can also pass on organic seafood and shampoo, which have labels that are often misleading. (See ShopSmart)

Moreover, we found that you need not pay a premium for organic foods if you know where to shop. See our tips for ways to cut your organic-food tab.

But you should also be aware that as more consumers are turning to organic products, some of the country's largest food producers are trying to chip away at what organic labels promise to deliver.

CR Quick Take

Nearly two-thirds of consumers bought organic products in the past year, despite higher prices.

- The good news: New studies show that by eating organic food, you can greatly reduce your exposure to chemicals found in conventionally produced food.
- More good news: You don't have to clean out your wallet to buy organic foods if you know which ones to buy and where.
- The bad news: As more big players enter the organic market, government standards have come under attack. So it's more important than ever to understand food labeling and what's behind it.

Organic Food Fight

If the organic label conjures up images of cackling chickens running free in a field and pristine vegetables without a trace of pesticides, keep reading. While the organic label indicates that a product meets certain government standards, those standards are coming under pressure as big companies cash in on the growing demand for organic foods. H. Lee Scott Jr., chief executive of Wal-Mart Stores, has described organic as "one of the fastest-growing categories in all of food and in Wal-Mart."

During the past decade, U.S. organic sales have grown 20 percent or more annually. Organic food and beverage sales are estimated to have topped $15 billion in 2004, up from $3.5 billion in 1997. Sales are projected to more than double by 2009.

"Consumer spending on organic has grown so much that we've attracted big players who want to bend the rules so that they can brand their products as organic without incurring the expenses involved in truly living up to organic standards," says Ronnie Cummins, national director of the Organic Consumers Association, an advocacy group based in Finland, Minn.

Lobbying by large food companies to weaken organic rules started when the U.S. Department of Agriculture fully implemented organic labeling standards in October 2002. Food producers immediately fought the new rules. A Georgia chicken producer was ultimately able to persuade one of his state's congressional representatives to slip through a federal legislative amendment in a 2003 appropriations bill to cut its costs. The amendment stated that if the price of organic feed was more than twice the cost of regular feed—which can contain heavy metals, pesticides, and animal by-products—then livestock producers

did you know?
Food Labels Can Be Misleading

Organic-sounding labels can be confusing, or even meaningless. Below are examples of labels that are meaningful because there are government standards to back them up. You'll also find a couple of examples of meaningless labels. For more information on food labels, go to **www.eco-labels.**

Meaningful

"100% Organic." No synthetic ingredients are allowed by law. Also, production process must meet federal organic standards and must have been independently verified by accredited inspectors.

"Organic." At least 95 percent of ingredients are organically produced. The remainder can be nonorganic or synthetic ingredients. One exception: Organic labels on seafood are meaningless because the U.S. Department of Agriculture has no standards to back them up.

"Made with Organic Ingredients." At least 70 percent of ingredients are organic. The remaining 30 percent must come from the USDA's approval list.

Meaningless

"Free-range" or "free-roaming." Stamped on eggs, chicken, and other meat, this label suggests that an animal has spent a good portion of its life outdoors. But U.S. government standards are weak. The rule for the label's use on poultry products, for example, is merely that outdoor access be made available for "an undetermined period of each day." In other words, if a coop door was open for just 5 minutes a day, regardless of whether the chicken went outside, the animals' meat and eggs could legally be labeled "free-range."

"Natural" or "All Natural." This label does not mean organic. Their reason is that no standard definition for this term exists except when it's applied to meat and poultry products, which the USDA defines as not containing any artificial flavoring, colors, chemical preservatives, or synthetic ingredients. And the claim is not verified. The producer or manufacturer alone decides whether to use it.

could feed their animals less costly, nonorganic feed but still label their products organic.

That bizarre change in standards was repealed in April 2003 after consumers and organic producers protested, but the fight to maintain the integrity of organic labeling continues. In October 2005, Congress weakened the organic-labeling law despite protests from more than 325,000 consumers and 250 organic-food companies. The law overturns a recent court ruling that barred the use of synthetic ingredients in "organic" foods. It mostly affects processed products such as canned soups and frozen pizza.

shopsmart

Know when it pays to buy organic food products to reduce your exposure to pesticides and other additives, when it might sometimes pay, and when it's a waste of your money. Use this section the next time you're making a grocery list.

Buy these items organic as often as possible

WHAT Apples, bell peppers, celery, cherries, imported grapes, nectarines, peaches, pears, potatoes, red raspberries, spinach, and strawberries.

WHY The U.S. Department of Agriculture's own lab testing reveals that even after washing, some fruits and vegetables consistently carry much higher levels of pesticide residue than others. Based on an analysis of more than 100,000 U.S. government pesticide test results, researchers at the Environmental Working Group (EWG), a research and advocacy organization based in Washington, D.C., have developed the "dirty dozen" fruits and vegetables, above, that they say you should always buy organic if possible because their conventionally grown counterparts tend to be laden with pesticides. Among fruits, nectarines had the highest percentage testing positive for pesticide residue. Peaches and red raspberries had the most pesticides (nine) on a single sample. Among vegetables, celery and spinach most often carried pesticides, with spinach having the highest number (10) on a single sample. (For more information on pesticide levels for other types of produce, go to **www.foodnews.org.**)

WHAT YOU'LL PAY About 50 percent more on average for organic produce, but prices vary based on the item and the time of year. A CONSUMER REPORTS price survey conducted in the New York City area in October 2005 found a premium of 24 percent on organic strawberries and 33 percent on grapes and spinach. Organic Idaho potatoes cost 101 percent more than conventional. When you buy organic produce in season at a farmer's market or directly from local providers, however, you might avoid paying a premium at all.

WHAT Meat, poultry, eggs, and dairy.

WHY You greatly reduce the risk of exposure to the agent believed to cause mad cow disease and minimize exposure to other potential toxins in nonorganic feed. You also avoid the results of production methods that use daily supplemental hormones and antibiotics, which have been linked to increased antibacterial resistance in humans.

WHAT Baby food.

WHY Children's developing bodies are especially vulnerable to toxins and they may be at risk of higher exposure. Baby food is often made up of condensed fruits or vegetables, potentially concentrating pesticide residues. Michelle Faist, a spokeswoman for Del Monte, says that even though its baby foods are not organic, pesticides and heavy metals are kept below government-recommended levels.

WHAT YOU'LL PAY Varies widely by store.

Buy these items organic if price is no object

WHAT Asparagus, avocados, bananas, broccoli, cauliflower, sweet corn, kiwi, mangos, onions, papaya, pineapples, and sweet peas.

WHY Multiple pesticide residues are, in general, rarely found on conventionally grown versions of these fruits and vegetables, according to research by the EWG. So if you're buying organic only for health reasons, you may not want to pay 22 percent extra for organic bananas, let alone more than 150 percent for organic asparagus—the premiums we found in our price survey of several New York City area supermarkets.

WHAT Breads, oils, potato chips, pasta, cereals, and other packaged foods, such as canned or dried fruit and vegetables.

WHY Although these processed products may have lower levels of contaminants in them, they offer limited health value because processing tends to wash away important nutrients. The process of milling organic whole grains into flour, for example, eliminates fiber and vitamins, though they are sometimes added back in. The more a food is processed, the less health value its organic version offers, especially in products such as cereals and pastas with labels that say "made with organic ingredients." Read the list of ingredients and you might find that while the flour is organic, the eggs aren't. The processed foods with the most added value are labeled "100% Organic" and "USDA organic." Price premiums vary. In our survey, organic Heinz ketchup cost 25 percent more than the conventional product; organic minestrone soup was only 8 percent more.

Don't bother buying these items organic

WHAT Seafood.

WHY Whether caught in the wild or farmed, fish can be labeled organic, despite the presence of contaminants such as mercury and PCBs. Some wild fish such as bluefish are very high in PCBs, and tuna and swordfish are laced with mercury. The USDA has not yet developed organic certification standards for seafood. In the meantime, producers are allowed to make their own organic claims as long as they don't use "USDA" or "certified organic" logos. California, however, recently passed a law that prohibits the use of any organic labeling on fish and other seafood until either state or federal certification standards are established.

WHAT Cosmetics.

WHY Unless a personal-care product consists primarily of organic agricultural ingredients, such as aloe vera gel, it's pointless to buy organic in this category. Most cosmetics contain a mix of ingredients, and USDA regulations allow shampoos and body lotions to carry an organic label if their main ingredient is "organic hydrosol," which is simply water in which something organic, such as a lavender leaf, has been soaked. While the USDA claims that organic labeled-cosmetics follow the same standards as food, we have found indiscriminate use of synthetic ingredients and violations of food-labeling standards. "Many of the ingredients in personal-care products didn't grow out of the ground but in test tubes—they're chemicals," says Lauren Sucher, director of public affairs at the EWG. Just because a product has the word "organic" or "natural" in its name doesn't necessarily mean it's safer. Only 11 percent of ingredients found in personal-care products, organic or not, have ever been screened for safety. In fact, when the EWG conducted its own safety rating of these products (available at **www.ewg.org**), scoring them on a scale of 0, for those posing lowest level of concern, to 5, for the highest concern due to potentially unsafe ingredients, those with scores of 4 or more included benign-sounding Naturessence All Day Moisture Cream.

The Massachusetts-based Organic Trade Association (OTA), which represents large and small food producers including corporate giants such as Kraft Foods and Archer Daniels Midland Co., supported the amendment. "The issue is whether processed products could use a list of benign synthetic ingredients already approved by the National Organic Standards Board," says Katherine DiMatteo, executive director of the OTA, "and we do not believe standards will be weakened at all."

Not all organic producers agree, however. Executives at Earthbound Farm, which has been in the organic business for more than 20 years and is the nation's leading supplier of specialty organic salad greens, were startled to find their company's name on an OTA letter supporting the amendment. Earthbound objects to built-in "emergency exemptions" that would allow nonorganic ingredients in organically labeled food if the organic alternative is considered "commercially unavailable." As with the Georgia chicken-feed case, if organic corn is expensive because it's in short supply, a soup maker might argue that it is commercially unavailable and get an exemption to use nonorganic corn.

"This presents a risk to the integrity of the organic label that we would have preferred not to see," says Charles Sweat, chief operating officer at Earthbound Farm.

Other changes in the organic industry are occurring more quietly in the farm fields. Wal-Mart alone gobbles up so much of the organic dairy supply that some producers that have his-

torically accounted for the bulk of organic products on the market haven't been able to meet the new demand. Suppliers filling the gap are doing so in part by exploiting loopholes in the organic rules, some consumer advocates say.

Organic Valley, a Wisconsin-based national cooperative of farmers that had been one of Wal-Mart's primary suppliers of organic milk, ended that direct relationship at the end of 2004. "When the first U.S. case of mad cow was discovered in a dairy cow at the end of 2003," says Theresa Marquez, chief marketing executive at Organic Valley, "demand for organic milk spiked and we've been in a short-supply situation ever since, with demand growing at 25 percent annually and supply growing at only 10 percent."

With supplies limited, Marquez says, the company decided to "stay true to our mission" and give top priority to filling orders from natural-food markets, its oldest customers, leaving it to Horizon Organic and other large competitors to "duke it out figuring out how to service Wal-Mart."

Horizon Organic is an organic dairy company that was acquired in 2003 by Dean Foods, the leading U.S. dairy processor. Its operations range in size from a 12-cow farm in Vermont to a 4,000-cow operation in Idaho, where animals may be confined in outdoor corrals and given organic feed, grasses, and hay. They graze in open pastures only on a rotating basis instead of primarily grazing in open pastures, as cows are required to do on farms that supply Organic Valley.

Current federal regulations state that organically raised animals must have access to pasture and may be "temporarily confined only for reasons of health, safety, the animal's stage of production, or to protect soil or water quality." But that vague language allows large producers to cut corners and compromise on what consumers expect from organic food, consumer advocates say.

The regulations also leave open questions about whether dairy animals could have been treated with antibiotics or consumed feed containing genetically modified grain or animal byproducts prior to becoming part of an organic dairy farm.

Horizon says it uses no antibiotics or growth hormones in its organic herd, though it can't control what animals eat before they arrive there. And the company says it plans to upgrade its Idaho farm to offer more pasture by 2007. In the meantime, Horizon says, its cows are being kept in good health and treated humanely. "We permit cows to exercise and exhibit natural behaviors," says Kelly Shea, director of government and industry relations at Horizon. "We would never support lowering the standards."

What's in the Food

So what can you count on when you buy organic? No animals, except dairy cows prior to being moved to organic farms, can be given antibiotics, growth hormones, or feed made from animal byproducts, which can transmit mad cow disease. No genetic modification or irradiation is permitted, nor is fertilizer made with sewage sludge or synthetic ingredients, all of which are allowed in most conventional food production.

Organically raised animals must also have access to the outdoors, though it might simply mean that cattle are cooped up in outdoor pens. The rules governing poultry are even less stringent than for other livestock. Some "organic" chickens, for example, spend their short lives confined in coops with screen windows.

Healthwise

Chemical Health Risks of Conventionally Produced Foods

Here's what we know about those pesticides, hormones, antibiotics, and other chemicals used in the production of conventional meats, vegetables, and other foods:

Pesticides. More than a dozen formerly widely used pesticides have been banned, restricted, or voluntarily withdrawn by manufacturers since 1996, when a new federal law required pesticides to meet safety standards for children, whose developing immune, central-nervous, and hormonal systems are especially vulnerable to damage from toxic chemicals. Under that law, more pesticides are being investigated each year and banned or are undergoing lowering of limits on what can safely be tolerated, but consumers can still easily consume small amounts of more than 30 pesticides daily when eating a healthful variety of foods.

New evidence also shows that contrary to previous scientific belief, pesticides in a woman's bloodstream can be passed to a fetus in the womb. A study released in 2005 in which umbilical-cord blood of 10 children was collected by the Red Cross and tested for pollutants showed that 21 pesticides crossed the placenta.

Eating an organic diet can limit further exposure, however. A study supported by the Environmental Protection Agency and published in 2005 measured pesticide levels in the urine of 23 children in Washington State before and after a switch to an organic diet. Researchers found that after just five consecutive days on the new diet, specific markers for commonly used pesticides decreased to undetectable levels, and remained that way until conventional diets were reintroduced. The study's conclusion: "An organic diet provides a dramatic and immediate protective effect" against such pesticide exposure.

"A lot of these pesticides are toxic to the brain," says Philip Landrigan, M.D., a professor of pediatrics and preventative medicine at Mount Sinai School of Medicine in New York City. "We have very good evidence that exposure of the fetus to organophosphorus pesticides produces babies with small head circumference, which is a risk factor for reduced intelligence and behavioral disturbances."

Hormones. Studies suggest that synthetic growth hormones may be carcinogenic and that exposure to them may be linked to the precocious onset of puberty in girls. The USDA bans the use of such hormones in all poultry (organic or not), but when it comes to hogs, beef, or dairy cattle, only organic producers are legally bound not to use them.

Antibiotics. Farmers' widespread use of antibiotics to speed up animals' growth and to deal with health issues that crop up from keeping animals in overcrowded and unsanitary pens has helped spawn antibiotic-resistant bacteria. This resistance increases the odds that a drug that might have saved your life if you were to be hit by, say, a life-threatening case of food poisoning will now do you no good.

Other toxins. Nonorganic foods can expose you to a range of other contaminants with potential health risks. Conventionally raised chicken, for example, eat feed that can contain neurotoxins, such as arsenic or heavy metals. And the animals' feet may be dipped in motor oil as a treatment for an ailment known as scaly leg mite.

Organic fruits and vegetables are farmed with botanical or primarily nonsynthetic pest controls quickly broken down by sunlight and oxygen, instead of long-lasting synthetic chemicals. Organic produce sometimes carries chemical residues because of pesticides that are now pervasive in groundwater and rain, but their chemical load is much lower.

According to the Environmental Working Group (EWG), a research and advocacy organization in Washington, D.C., eating the 12 most contaminated fruits and vegetables exposes you to about 20 pesticides a day on average. If you eat the 12 least contaminated, you're exposed to about two pesticides a day.

Joseph Rosen, a professor of food science at Rutgers University, says that when it comes to pesticide exposure, "the amount in conventional foods is so low that it's not a health threat." Richard Wiles, senior vice president at the EWG, on the other hand, says that the cumulative effect of even low-level multiple pesticide exposures is both worrisome and little studied at this point.

Buying Organic on the Cheap

If you decide that you'd prefer fewer chemicals and other addititives in your food, the choice isn't an easy one. Organic sticker shock can hit the most stalwart of organic shoppers. The fact is that organic farmers produce more labor-intensive products and don't enjoy the economies of scale or government subsidies that their big brothers in agribusiness do. But we found many ways to save on the cost of organic products.

Comparison shop. Do a price check among local grocery stores for often purchased organic items and shop where you find the lowest prices. In the New York City area, for example, we found a 4-ounce jar of Earth's Best organic baby food for as little as 69 cents and as much as $1.29. When it comes to fresh produce, remember that you'll save by buying it in season.

Go local. You can find organic growers at most farmer's markets, and a USDA study in 2002 found that about 40 percent of those farmers don't charge a premium. For listings of local farmer's markets and other sources, go to **www.ams.usda.gov/farmersmarkets** and **www.localharvest.org.**

Join the farm team. Buy a share in a community-supported organic farm and you'll get a weekly supply of produce from spring until fall. The cost to feed a family of four generally ranges from $300 to $500 for the season. (Some farms also require you to work a few hours a month distributing or picking produce.) The savings can be substantial. A price study by a community-supported farm in the Northeast showed that the average $10 weekly cost for a shareholder's produce supply almost always beat farmer's market organic prices and often cost less than the same nonorganic items at a supermarket. Go to **www.sare.org** for a list of community-supported farms.

Order by mail. National providers will ship items such as organic beef (**www.mynaturalbeef.com**). Some local businesses, such as FreshDirect (**www.freshdirect.com**) in the New York City area and Pioneer Organics (**www.pioneerorganics.com**) in the Pacific Northwest, offer home deliveries. Other helpful sites are at **www.eatwellguide.org** and **www.theorganicpages.com**.

Be a supermarket spy. Make sure you get what you pay for by watching where produce sits on shelves. All grocers are legally required to stack organic fruits and vegetables where they won't be exposed to water runoff from the misting of conventional produce, which could contaminate organic items with pesticide residue. If a store is not following that rule, you may be wasting your money by buying organic produce there.

The Future of Foods?

Hawaiian farmers were in trouble. In the mid-1990s, an insect-borne virus—the papaya ring spot virus (PRSV)—threatened to decimate Hawaii's second-largest fruit crop. Plant breeders scrambled to produce a virus-resistant papaya. When traditional plant breeding methods failed, researchers turned to genetic engineering.

LINDA BREN

Years of research were finally met with success, and by spring of 1998, Hawaiian farmers were planting the seeds of PRSV-resistant papaya.

"The results were dramatic," says Dennis Gonsalves, Ph.D., a Cornell University plant pathologist who led the researchers' efforts to save the tropical delicacy and the livelihood of Hawaii's growers. "It was not a matter of increasing the yield, but a matter of whether they could grow it or not grow it."

Gonsalves' team of researchers from academia, industry, and government had isolated and copied a virus gene, then used a device called a gene gun to "shoot" the gene into the cells of the papaya plant. The virus gene in the plant works somewhat like immunization, but the mechanism of resistance is different, says Gonsalves, now director of the U.S. Department of Agriculture's Pacific Basin Agricultural Research Center in Hilo, Hawaii. "By integrating this virus gene into the chromosomes of the papaya, this made the papaya and subsequent generations resistant to the virus."

The rescue of the Hawaiian papaya industry is "a really satisfying story," says Gonsalves, and one that shows the difference that genetic engineering can make in people's lives.

But not all share Gonsalves' enthusiasm for genetically engineered foods. Although the newness of these foods may be wearing off, public concern about the safety and environmental impact of genetically engineered foods remains.

Some consumers and advocacy groups urge mandatory labeling that discloses the use of genetic engineering. Others advocate more stringent testing of these products before marketing. Still others want a ban on all genetically engineered foods.

"The Food and Drug Administration is confident that the genetically engineered food products on the U.S. market today are as safe as their conventionally bred counterparts, and the agency is prepared to meet the safety and regulatory challenges presented by new products as they emerge from the laboratory," says Commissioner of Food and Drugs Mark B. McClellan, M.D., Ph.D. "Genetically engineered foods must adhere to the same high standards of safety under the Federal Food, Drug, and Cosmetic Act that apply to more traditional food products," McClellan adds.

What are Genetically Engineered Foods?

Genetically engineered foods are produced from crops whose genetic makeup has been altered through a process called recombinant DNA, or gene splicing, to give the plant a desirable trait. Genetically engineered foods are also known as biotech, bioengineered, and genetically modified, although "genetically modified" can also refer to foods from plants altered through other breeding methods, says James Maryanski, Ph.D., the FDA's food biotechnology coordinator. "Scientists and farmers have been genetically modifying plants for hundreds of years," he says. Hybrid corn and tangelos (hybrid of a tangerine and grapefruit), for example, are the result of genetic modification through traditional methods of plant breeding. And the many varieties of apples we eat today were produced through genetic modification.

Using traditional genetic modification methods, such as cross-fertilization, scientists can produce a desired trait, such as a hardier plant. But in doing so, they mix thousands of genes from several plants, requiring many attempts over many years to weed out the unwanted traits that occur.

Newer methods of genetic modification, in the form of genetic engineering, are more precise and predictable—and faster. By controlling the insertion of one or two genes into a plant, scientists can give it a specific new characteristic without transferring undesirable traits.

What Are We Eating?

The first genetically engineered whole product—a tomato—went on the market in 1994. The FDA determined that the new tomato, which could be shipped vine-ripened without rotting rapidly, was as safe as other commercial tomatoes. Since then, more than 50 other genetically engineered foods have been determined by the agency to be as safe as their conventional counterparts.

A Look Into the Biotech Laboratory

Scientists are developing new varieties of crops that can withstand harsh growing conditions.

Ray Wu, Ph.D., a genetic engineering pioneer and molecular biologist at Cornell University in Ithaca, N.Y., has added two genes from the *E. coli* bacteria to rice plants, making them tolerant to drought, cold temperatures and salty soil. The genes produce trehalose, a naturally occurring sugar found in a variety of organisms, including bacteria, that protects them from environmental stresses.

The rice plants grew successfully in the greenhouse and are ready for field testing, says Wu. He predicts that in about five years, the plants can be growing in farmers' fields.

Wu explains that the two *E. coli* genes in the rice will not harm consumers. "*E. coli* contains thousands of genes," says Wu. "We are only taking two particular genes that we know will not produce toxic products." As an added precaution, Wu used a "promoter" to control the expression of the *E. coli* genes to direct the plant to make trehalose in specific parts, such as the non-edible leaf. Also tested was a second promoter, which serves as an "on-off switch" so that trehalose is made only in response to an environmental stress.

Although rice is a relatively minor crop in the United States, it is a staple in many developing parts of the world, says Wu. And scientists can use the same procedure of inserting genes and a promoter to create biotech wheat, corn and other cereal plants that can withstand harsh conditions. "The world population continues to increase at an explosive rate, our arable land is deteriorating, fresh water is becoming scarce, and increasing environmental stresses will pose ever more serious threats to global agricultural production and food security in future years," says Wu. "Anything we can do to help crop plants cope with environmental stresses will also raise the quality and quantity of food for those who need it most."

* * *

One concern about genetic engineering is that scientists might unknowingly create or enhance a food allergen. But researchers are hoping that this powerful technology can be used to eliminate or reduce allergens, such as those found in peanuts, wheat and soy.

Experts estimate that 8 percent of children 6 years old and younger and 1 to 2 percent of adults have food allergies, which can cause severe, and sometimes life-threatening, reactions.

Early attempts to eliminate a food allergen have yielded promising results. In 2002, researchers genetically engineered soy to eliminate expression of a common soy protein. Soy allergies are particularly common in infants and young children, according to the National Institute of Allergy and Infectious Diseases. It's difficult to avoid eating soy because of its wide use in many processed foods, including infant formula, cereals, and salad dressings.

Using a "gene silencing" technique, researchers were able to "knock out" a gene that makes a protein called P34, which is thought to trigger most allergic reactions to soy. Tests on blood from people allergic to soy showed no antibody response to the plant with the knocked-out gene, indicating that the allergen could not be detected. The plant's characteristics were also analyzed. "We see no change in the pattern of growth, productivity, or protein composition," says Eliot Herman, Ph.D., lead researcher on this project and molecular biologist at the U.S. Department of Agriculture's Agricultural Research Service.

The work is not done yet, cautions Herman. "There are up to 15 different proteins in soybeans that people are allergic to," he says. "The major one, P34, is responsible for 75 percent of the allergic reactions. How much do you have to get rid of to not trigger an allergic response at all? This is what we need to find out."

Herman sees the benefit of genetically engineered soy in both human food and animal feed. "Baby pigs are similar to baby humans in their reaction to soybeans," he says. "They have gastric distress too." Herman's team is studying the reaction of piglets to the genetically engineered soy, and these studies may pave the way to human clinical trials.

The Grocery Manufacturers of America estimates that between 70 percent and 75 percent of all processed foods available in U.S. grocery stores may contain ingredients from genetically engineered plants. Breads, cereal, frozen pizzas, hot dogs and soda are just a few of them.

Soybean oil, cottonseed oil and corn syrup are ingredients used extensively in processed foods. Soybeans, cotton and corn dominate the 100 million acres of genetically engineered crops that were planted in the United States in 2003, according to the U.S. Department of Agriculture (USDA). Through genetic engineering, these plants have been made to ward off pests and to tolerate herbicides used to kill weeds. Other crops, such as squash, potatoes, and papaya, have been engineered to resist plant diseases.

Safety of Genetically Engineered Foods

Genetically engineered plants are regulated by three government agencies: the FDA, the USDA, and the Environmental Protection Agency (EPA). The FDA ensures that foods made from these plants are safe for humans and animals to eat, the USDA makes sure the plants are safe to grow, and the EPA ensures that pesticides introduced into the plants are safe for human and animal consumption and for the environment. While these agencies act independently, they have a close working relationship since many products come under the review of all three.

The Federal Food, Drug, and Cosmetic Act (FD&C Act) gives the FDA authority to regulate foods for humans and ani-

More than 50 biotech food products have been evaluated by the FDA and found to be as safe as conventional foods, including:

- Canola oil
- Corn
- Cottonseed oil
- Papaya
- Potatoes
- Soybeans
- Squash
- Sugar beets
- Sweet corn
- Tomatoes

Sources: Council for Biotechnology Information and Food and Drug Administration

mals, including foods derived from bioengineered plants. Under the act, companies have a legal obligation to ensure that any food they sell meets the safety standards of the law. The safety standards apply equally to conventional food and genetically engineered food. If a food does not meet the safety standards, the FDA has the authority to take it off the market.

Bioengineered foods do not pose any risks for consumers that are different from conventional foods, says Maryanski. "We make sure there are no hazards, such as an unexpected allergen or poisonous substance in the food, or that the food is not changed in some way that would affect its nutritional value."

The FDA's efforts to ensure the safety of bioengineered foods include publishing rigorous safety testing guidelines, establishing a consultation process with industry, and seeking the expertise of scientists outside the agency.

In 1992, the FDA published a policy statement and testing guidelines for foods developed using all methods of plant breeding, including the use of genetic engineering. These guidelines explain the types of food safety questions that developers should address in evaluating the safety of all plant-derived foods.

In 1994, the FDA set up a consultation process to assist developers in meeting the safety standards set forth in its guidelines. FDA scientists advise companies on the tests needed to assess the safety of new foods. After testing is completed, companies send safety and nutritional information to the FDA for the agency's scientific evaluation.

Although consultation is voluntary on the part of developers, the legal requirements that the foods have to meet are not. Some consumer advocates and scientists have urged the FDA to make the consultation process mandatory, but the agency believes that companies are cooperating within the voluntary system.

"This current process is working very well and fully protects public health," says McClellan. "To the best of our knowledge, all bioengineered foods on the market have been evaluated by FDA through the current consultation process." This includes genetically engineered foods produced by companies outside the United States and marketed here.

In July 2003, the Codex Alimentarius Commission adopted international guidelines for biotech food safety that are consistent with the FDA's approach. Codex, an entity established by the World Health Organization and the Food and Agriculture Organization of the United Nations, is the highest international body on food standards.

Several private and government organizations have studied the safety of genetically engineered foods. In a study released in 2000, a committee of the National Academy of Sciences (NAS) concluded, "The committee is not aware of any evidence that foods on the market are unsafe to eat as a result of genetic modification." This conclusion was echoed in a report published by the Government Accounting Office in 2002. On the animal side, the international Organization for Economic Cooperation and Development published a consensus document in 2003. It noted that there is no evidence to date from animal feeding studies with bioengineered plants that the performance of animals differed in any respect from those fed the non-bioengineered counterpart.

Labeling

The FDA has received many inquiries about the labeling of genetically engineered foods. Some consumer advocates and organizations, such as the Union of Concerned Scientists, urge the FDA to require labeling to identify which foods are genetically engineered.

Under the FD&C Act, Congress has provided the FDA a limited basis on which to require labeling. Generally, there must be something tangibly different about the food product—not the process by which it's made—for the FDA to require labeling.

"The FDA has no information that the use of biotechnology creates a class of food that is different in quality, safety or any other attribute from food developed using conventional breeding techniques," says Maryanski. He adds that disclosure of genetic engineering techniques is not required on the label, just as identification of conventional breeding techniques is not required—for example, "hybrid corn" can just be called "corn."

Any significant differences between the bioengineered food and its conventional counterpart do have to be disclosed in labeling. These would include differences in nutritional properties, the presence of an allergen that consumers would not expect in the food, or any property that would require different handling, storage, cooking or preservation. For example, when a manufacturer produced a line of soybeans whose oil had higher levels of oleic acid than found in conventional soybean oil, the FDA agreed to naming the product "high-oleic soybean oil" to distinguish it from traditional soybean oil. The high-oleic oil can be used in frying without the need for the chemical process of hydrogenation, which produces *trans* fat.

Food processors may voluntarily label either the presence or absence of a genetically engineered food in their products as long as the information is truthful and not misleading to consumers. The FDA has produced guidance to the industry for this type of labeling.

Future Foods and Regulatory Challenges

The first generation of genetically engineered crops was developed primarily to benefit the growers. Plants were created to re-

'Pharm' Factories of the Future

Plants may become miniature "factories" for pharmaceuticals through genetic engineering. Scientists are growing plants that produce antibodies to help fight cancer, heart disease and tooth decay. And researchers are experimenting with growing fruits and vegetables that contain vaccines for measles, hepatitis B, Norwalk virus, diarrhea, cholera and more.

These edible vaccines could be pureed into an applesauce-like consistency and fed to children and adults alike. They could be produced in larger quantities and at less expense than current vaccines, although they will have to be grown and handled under strict conditions imposed by the U.S. Department of Agriculture (USDA) aimed at ensuring that they do not inadvertently enter the food supply.

The Food and Drug Administration regulates pharmaceuticals, whether they are manufactured in traditional factories or in crops in the field, to ensure their safety, purity and potency. The FDA and the USDA have jointly published draft guidance specifically addressing the use of bioengineered plants to produce pharmaceutical products.

The FDA is also part of a White House National Economic Council working group that is addressing the regulation of genetically engineered crops to ensure there are no gaps in protecting human health and the environment.

sist pests and diseases and to tolerate herbicides used to kill weeds. Scientists see the next generation of genetically engineered products benefiting consumers directly. They are adding nutrients to foods to help prevent diseases, reducing allergens and toxins, and making foods tastier.

Using the tools of biotechnology, researchers are working to reduce the bitterness in citrus fruits, reduce saturated fats in cooking oils, produce more flavorful tomatoes, and even lessen the gassiness caused by beans. Grains, fruits and vegetables that contain more nutrients and potatoes that absorb less oil when made into chips and french fries are also in the development pipeline.

As the tools and techniques used in biotechnology become more complex and a broader range of plants are researched for a wider variety of uses, the FDA must prepare for the safety and regulatory challenges that novel genetically engineered foods may present.

One of these challenges is evaluating food for its potential to cause allergic reactions. People who have food allergies are usually allergic to specific proteins in foods.

FDA biochemical engineer Tong-Jen Fu, Ph.D., is analyzing methods currently used by scientists to determine the allergenic potential of new proteins that may be introduced in food. "The only way people can avoid allergic reactions to food is to avoid eating those offending foods," says Fu. "But we know that there is some possibility that a new protein in food may be an allergen for some individuals. So it is important to have sound scientific methods for assessing whether a new protein will be an allergen."

Fu is analyzing a current test that assumes a correlation between digestive stability and allergenic potential. Using simulated gastric and intestinal fluids, she has found that this correlation isn't always present. Fu's work is improving the FDA's knowledge about proteins and their likelihood of being allergens, which ultimately will help agency regulators determine if a food is safe.

To further assure that the FDA has the best scientific knowledge available to assess the safety of genetically engineered foods, the agency has increased the number of staff experts in plant genetics, molecular biology, immunology, and agricultural biotechnology.

In addition to its own scientists who evaluate safety data, the FDA looks to outside experts, such as the NAS, for advice on food safety assessments. In response to public concerns about the unknown long-term effects of consuming genetically engineered foods, the FDA, USDA and EPA requested assistance from the NAS. The NAS is currently conducting a study to assess the potential for unintended health effects resulting from genetically engineered foods.

"We have no reason to believe there are any adverse effects from the long-term use of these foods," says Maryanski, "but we've asked the NAS to look into it as part of our continuing effort to make sure that our decisions are based on the best science available today."

The FDA has added members with agricultural biotech expertise to its advisory committees that address scientific questions related to bioengineered foods and animal feeds. These committees also include consumer representatives.

"The FDA will continue to reach out to the public to help consumers understand the scientific issues and the agency's policies regarding genetically engineered food," says McClellan. "FDA, in cooperation with USDA and EPA, will continue its oversight of new and emerging food biotechnology products and will be vigilant in ensuring the safety and integrity of the food supply."

From *FDA Consumer*, November/December 2003, pp. 29–34.

What Does Science Say You Should Eat?

Most diets aren't realistic or advisable, including the U.S. agriculture department's famous food pyramid. Instead, a Harvard scientist recommends a new way of eating based on the world's largest and longest food study.

BRAD LEMLEY

America clearly needs dietary guidance.—More than 44 million people are clinically obese compared with 30 million a decade ago, putting them at increased risk for heart disease, stroke, type 2 diabetes, and breast, prostate, and colon cancers. In the meantime, the noun *diet* seems to attract a different adjective every week, including Atkins, Ornish, Cooper, grapefruit, rice, protein, Scarsdale, South Beach, Beverly Hills, Best Chance, Eat Smart, and Miracle, not to mention Help, I'm Southern and I Can't Stop Eating. While some of these plans overlap, others seem to specifically contradict each other, notably the meat-intensive regime of the late Robert Atkins versus the near-vegetarian program of Dean Ornish.—No wonder Americans are tempted to follow Mark Twain's admonition to "eat what you like and let the food fight it out inside." But still, we wonder: Is there really an optimum way to eat?—Although debate rages, academic nutrition researchers have begun to form a consensus around a plan with an important advantage—it is based on a preponderance of sound science. The regime does not as yet have a name, but it might well be called the Willett diet, after its leading proponent, Walter Willett, chairman of the department of nutrition at the Harvard School of Public Health.—Featuring abundant fruits, vegetables, whole grains, and vegetable oils, as well as optional portions of fish and chicken, Willett's plan resembles the much-touted Mediterranean diet shown in several studies to reduce the risk of heart disease. Nonetheless, Willett resists the comparison. "The Mediterranean diet is specific to a certain climate and culture," he says, adding that by focusing on healthy ingredients rather than specific dishes, "anyone can adapt this plan to his own tastes." The results: stable blood-sugar levels, easier weight control, clearer arteries, and overall better health.

In this case it's hard science, not just opinion. Willett's plan is based on the largest long-term dietary survey ever undertaken: the 121,700-participant Nurses' Health Study, begun in 1976 by Harvard Medical School professor Frank Speizer, with dietary assessments supervised by Willett since 1980. The study isn't just big: Willett carefully crafted it so that he and others could extract specific recommendations about food intake. Participants even surrender blood and toenail samples so that Willett can track absorption of trace elements and other nutrients. If a participant reports a major illness, such as heart attack or cancer, "we write for permission to obtain medical records for further details," says Willett. To ensure that the data include both sexes and two generations, Willett and several colleagues also launched the Health Professionals Follow-Up Study, which includes 52,000 men, and the Nurses' Health Study II, a survey of 116,000 younger women.

In the past, nutritional scientists have largely relied on studies of animals, small groups of people, and/or petri-dish biochemistry that may not reflect the vagaries of human metabolism, although Willett uses such studies when he deems it appropriate. His access to a unique quarter-million-person pool of humans who carefully track both their diets and their health lends added credibility to his research. "When you put animal, metabolic, and epidemiological studies together and they all point in the same direction, you can be pretty confident about your conclusions," Willett says.

'Nutrition used to be like religion. Everyone said, I have the truth, everyone else is wrong'

While soft-spoken and self-effacing in person, Willett isn't shy about using this formidable database to take on the federal establishment. His Healthy Eating Pyramid differs radically from the Food Guide Pyramid pushed by the U.S. Department of Agriculture. "At best, the USDA pyramid offers wishy-washy, scientifically unfounded advice," Willett argues in his book, *Eat, Drink, and Be Healthy: The Harvard Medical School Guide to Healthy Eating.* At worst, he adds, "the misinformation contributes to overweight, poor health, and unnecessary early deaths."

The numbers back him up. Men and women in Willett's studies whose diets most closely paralleled the Healthy Eating Pyramid's guidelines lowered their risk of major chronic disease by 20 percent and 11 percent respectively, according to an

WILLETT VS. ORNISH VS. ATKINS

Walter Willett's dietary recommendations are similar in many ways to those advanced by another doctor-nutritionist, Dean Ornish, who pioneered an ultralow-fat, near-vegetarian regime that has been shown to halt or reduce coronary blockage in most heart patients. Both Willett and Ornish emphasize whole grains, fruits, and vegetables, and both minimize animal proteins. But they part ways on fats: Willett recommends replacing saturated fats in the American diet with unsaturated ones, while Ornish suggests sharply cutting fat intake altogether, especially for those at risk for heart disease. "No one has shown that the kind of diet that Walter Willett recommends can reverse heart disease," says Ornish.

For his part, Willett insists that "replacing saturated fats with unsaturated fats is a safe, proven, and delicious way to cut the rates of heart disease." He says the Lyon Diet Heart study, a French trial that tracked heart-attack survivors on an oil-rich Mediterranean diet versus those on the low-fat American Heart Association diet, showed a significant drop in second attacks for the Lyon group. Ornish responds that the drop in deaths in that study was most likely due to increasing heart-healthy omega-3 fats and decreasing intake of omega-6 fats, saturated fats, animal protein, and cholesterol, not to high overall consumption of fat. Ornish recommends that everyone consume three grams of omega-3 fats daily, either through eating fish or taking supplements.

In contrast with both Willett and Ornish, the late Robert Atkins recommended a meat-intensive, protein-rich regime. "Studies at Duke University, the University of Cincinnati, and the University of Pennsylvania all show that people can lose significant weight, lower their triglycerides, and improve their HDL [high-density lipoprotein] cholesterol levels by consuming protein and limiting carbohydrates," says Stuart Trager, an orthopedic surgeon who assumed the spokesman's mantle for the diet after Atkins's death in April 2003. Trager believes the real strength of the Atkins diet is that "it is something people are willing and able to do."

Willett concedes that Atkins "was really onto something. He believed, correctly, that most people can better control their weight by reducing the glycemic load of the diet than by other means. But there is evidence that the traditional Atkins diet, which is high in animal fat, is not optimal. There are benefits to having cereal in one's diet. There is relief from constipation, and we do see [in the Nurses' Health Study] some benefit for heart disease and diabetes. This is probably partially from the fiber in whole grains, and also partly from the other minerals and vitamins that come along with whole grains that are in short supply in many people's diets."

While at first blush the three approaches seem sharply divergent, Trager sounds a conciliatory note. "No one has ever bothered to point out that we are compatriots on many points," he says. All three nutritionists share an emphasis on reducing blood-sugar spikes by reducing the glycemic load. Moreover, all three condemn trans fats, white flour, and sugar. "There really is universal agreement that you should cut those things out of your diet," Trager says. —*Brad Lemley*

---

article published in the December 2002 issue of *The American Journal of Clinical Nutrition*. That compares with reduced risks of 11 percent and 3 percent for those whose diets most closely mirrored the USDA pyramid's guidelines.

"Nutrition used to be like religion. Everyone said, 'I have the truth, everyone else is wrong,' and there wasn't much data to refute that," says Willett. "Now we're starting to have a real scientific basis for understanding what you should eat."

JUST INSIDE THE DOOR OF WILLETT'S OFFICE AT the Harvard School of Public Health in Boston sits his bicycle, mud-spattered from his daily commute over the Charles River from his home in Cambridge. Past that, on top of a pile of medical journals, perches a plastic bag full of plump, homegrown cherry tomatoes, a late-season-harvest gift from his administrative assistant. Willett knows good tomatoes. As a member of a fifth-generation Michigan farming family, he paid his undergraduate tuition at Michigan State by raising vegetables, and today he grows "as much as possible" in his tiny urban backyard.

Behind the cluttered desk sits Willett himself, trim, toned, and turned out in a sharp gray suit. "All you have to do is take a look at Walter to see the value of his research. The proof is in the pudding," says David Jenkins, a nutrition researcher at the University of Toronto. Willett vigorously follows his own plan and at age 58 reports that his weight, cholesterol, and triglycerides are all where they should be. He is, in short, the picture of where applied nutritional science might deliver us all, if we had the proper information.

That's the problem. In recent years, Willett says, the American public has been victimized by dodgy advice. Not only has obesity skyrocketed but "the incidence of heart disease is also not going down anymore. It has really stalled."

What happened? In Willett's view, things began to go awry in the mid-1980s, when a National Institutes of Health conference decreed that to prevent heart disease, all Americans except children under 2 years old should reduce their fat intake from 40 percent to 30 percent of their total daily calories. The press touted the recommendation as revealed truth, and the USDA's Food Guide Pyramid, released in 1992, reflects this view, calling for 6 to 11 servings of bread, cereal, rice, and pasta daily, while fats and oils are to be used "sparingly."

Too bad, says Willett. "The low-fat mantra has contributed to obesity. The nutrition community told people they had to worry only about counting fat grams. That encouraged the creation of thousands of low-fat products. I call it 'the SnackWell revolution.'" Blithely consuming low-fat foods full of carbohydrates is a prescription for portliness, says Willett, adding that any farmer knows this. "If you pen up an animal and feed it grain, it will get fat. People are no different."

The problem with overeating refined carbohydrates such as white flour and sucrose (table sugar) is that amylase, an enzyme, quickly converts them into the simple sugar called glucose. That goads the pancreas to overproduce insulin, the substance that conducts glucose into the cells. But excessive sugar is toxic to cells, so after years of glucose and insulin overload, the cells can become insulin resistant and may no longer allow insulin to easily push glucose inside them. That keeps blood glucose levels high, forcing the pancreas to make even more insulin in a desperate attempt to jam the stuff through cell membranes. Willett likens the effect to an overworked, undermaintained pump that eventually wears out. Type 2 diabetes can be one result, but Willett contends that insulin-resistant people who don't develop full-blown diabetes still face significant health risks.

Other researchers agree. Stanford endocrinologist Gerald Reaven coined the term Syndrome X to describe the constellation of health problems that spring from insulin resistance. Until the late 1980s, Reaven says, "the common scientific view was that insulin resistance only mattered if it led all the way to type 2 diabetes. Looking at the data, it's clear that most people who are insulin resistant don't get diabetes but are greatly at risk for coronary heart disease, hypertension, non-alcoholic-type liver disease, polycystic ovary syndrome, and several kinds of cancer."

In the case of heart disease, Reaven says that high blood concentrations of insulin and glucose can damage the endothelium that lines coronary arteries and set the stage for the formation of plaques. "A big problem is the lack of drugs to treat this problem," he adds. "A lot of doctors' education comes from drug companies. They know about cholesterol because everyone is pushing their statin. They know about hypertension because there are multiple hypertensive drugs. But they know a lot less about insulin resistance and its consequences, and that's unfortunate."

Syndrome X, also known as metabolic syndrome or insulin-resistance syndrome, is largely unknown to the public as well. While many people avoid cholesterol and fat-laden foods, few understand the threat posed by carbohydrate excess. That needs to change, says Willett. "Cholesterol is relevant, but the danger is overblown," he says. "Syndrome X is the global public-health problem of the 21st century. Almost certainly the vast majority of Americans have a higher degree of insulin resistance than is optimal."

The Willett plan aims to even out the glucose roller coaster through an emphasis on foods with low glycemic loads—foods that convert to glucose slowly—like whole grains, plant oils, and vegetables. This keeps blood glucose levels relatively constant, sparing the pancreas overwork. Steady blood glucose also helps keep the appetite in check, which makes maintaining a healthy weight easier, says Willett. So instead of high carb, low fat, one might summarize the Willett plan's directive as good carb, good fat.

"People are being told to reduce fat and eat more carbohydrates. For many people, particularly overweight people with a high degree of insulin resistance, that produces exactly the opposite of what they need," says Willett. Randomized trials, he says, show that people on low-fat diets generally lose two to four pounds after several weeks but then gain back the weight even while continuing the diet. "Most of them would be better off reducing carbs, switching to better carbs, and increasing their intake of healthy fats."

'Instead of high carb, low fat, one might summarize the Willett plan's directive as good carb, good fat'

Willett, like virtually every other nutrition researcher, advises eating vegetables in abundance, consuming alcohol in moderation, and taking a daily multivitamin to cover nutritional gaps. He also touts fish as a source of protein and heart-protective n-3 fatty acids, which are also known as omega-3 acids. (Those who worry about mercury contamination in fish got some good news recently: In one study conducted in the Seychelles, a group of islands in the Indian Ocean, scientists from the University of Rochester Medical Center tracked pregnant women who ate an average of 12 fish meals a week, about 10 times the quantity of fish eaten by the average American. "We've found no evidence that the low levels of mercury in seafood are harmful," said lead author Gary Myers. Moreover, various tests indicated that the women's children suffered no adverse cognitive, behavioral, or neurological effects.)

High on the list of food ingredients Willett counsels avoiding are hydrogenated fats, often referred to as trans fats, which are found in shortening, margarine, deep-fried foods, and packaged baked goods. That advice was controversial when Willett published a groundbreaking paper on the subject in 1991, but it has since become close to dogma. "Both controlled-feeding studies that have examined the effects of trans fat on blood cholesterol and epidemiological studies of trans-fat intake in relation to the risk of heart disease and diabetes indicate they are considerably worse than saturated fats," he says.

Daily exercise is essential, Willett adds, and he confirms the often-cited advice that walking is the best choice for many people. The Nurses' Health Study revealed a "very strong link" between walking and protection against heart disease: Women who walked an average of three hours a week were 35 percent less likely to have a heart attack over an eight-year period than those who walked less. It may seem odd that Willett includes exercise in his Healthy Eating Pyramid, but he is adamant that exercise and diet cannot be teased apart. "It doesn't have to be extreme. I run along the Charles for 25 minutes most mornings." A half hour daily of moderate activity offers "impressive health benefits," he says, but there is "added benefit for greater intensity for longer times."

GOOD CARBS/BAD CARBS

The glycemic index (GI) is a way of measuring how quickly the carbohydrate in a given food raises the level of blood sugar. So eating a low-GI food causes a slow, mild rise, while the same quantity of carbohydrate in a high-GI food will trigger a faster, bigger rise. A GI of 55 or less is considered low, 56 to 69 is medium, and 70 or more is high.

But the GI is of limited use in the real world of pears, pork, and pudding because it ignores how much of that food a person eats. A few years ago, Walter Willett pioneered the concept of the glycemic load (GL), a measurement that factors in the quantity of carbohydrates eaten in a single serving of a particular food. The carbohydrates in parsnips, for example, are quickly converted to glucose, so parsnips have a rather high index of 97, plus or minus 19 (the numbers are sometimes imprecise because they are based on feeding foods to test subjects and monitoring their blood-sugar response, which can vary for many reasons). But parsnips have a GL of just 12, because a single 80-gram serving contains a relatively small amount of carbohydrate. A GL of 10 or less is considered low, 11 to 19 is medium, and, 20

or more is high. Consistently eating low-GL foods evens out blood-sugar peaks and valleys, which Willett says helps keep appetite and weight under control. Eating low-GL foods also reduces the risk of developing type 2 diabetes. When Willett says "good carbs," he is essentially referring to fiber-rich, low-GL foods.

Generally, whole grains have lower glycemic loads than refined grains. For example, a 150-gram serving of brown rice has a GL of 18, while the same serving of quick-cooking white rice has a GL of 29. Although the photographs in this story tally the "sugar equivalence" of the carbohydrates in various American foods, the glycemic index and glycemic load of each of these foods needs to be considered as well. The glycemic numbers accompanying the photographs in this article are from Janette Brand-Miller of the University of Sydney, based on a table published in the July 2002 issue of *The American Journal of Clinical Nutrition*. An adaptation of that table can be seen at **diabetes.about.com/library/mendosagi/ngilists.htm.**

—*B. L.*

Willett's more iconoclastic conclusions include the heretical notion that soy—touted as a miracle food that fights cancer, obesity, and virtually every other human ill—may have "a dark side." He points to a British study in which 48 women with suspicious breast lumps were randomly assigned to receive either no supplement or one containing soy isoflavones (a compound in soybeans molecularly similar to estrogen) for 14 days. Those taking the supplement showed substantially more cell growth in the tissue removed than the women who were not taking the soy. Another troubling study showed memory loss and other cognitive declines in elderly Japanese men in Hawaii who stuck to their traditional soy-based diet, as opposed to those who switched to a more of a Western diet. "In moderation, soy is fine," says Willett. "Stuffed into everything, you could get into trouble." And soy isoflavone supplements, he counsels, should be regarded as "totally untested new drugs."

Willett also counsels that dairy products—which supply concentrated calories and saturated fat—are not the best way to get calcium and that the recommended daily intake of 1,200 milligrams daily for adults over 50 appears to be more than what's needed. His advice: Eat calcium-bearing vegetables, including leafy greens, take calcium supplements if you're a woman, and exercise. "The evidence for physical activity being protective against fractures is huge," he says.

'No research has ever shown that people who eat more eggs have more heart attacks than people who eat fewer eggs'

And he defends eggs. Although cholesterol fears have caused American per capita egg consumption to drop from 400 to 250 per year, "no research has ever shown that people who eat more eggs have more heart attacks than people who eat fewer eggs," Willett says. A 2001 Kansas State University study identified a type of lecithin called phosphatidylcholine in eggs that interferes with cholesterol absorption, which may explain why many studies have found no association between egg intake and blood cholesterol level. If the breakfast menu option is a white-flour bagel or an egg fried in vegetable oil, says Willett, "the egg is the better choice."

Perhaps the most comprehensive studies Willett has assembled compare the health consequences of eating saturated versus unsaturated fat. The term *saturated* means that every available site along each fat molecule's carbon chain is filled with a hydrogen atom; such fats—including butter and animal fat—are solids at room temperature. There are two types of unsaturated fats: monounsaturated fats such as olive oil, which are missing one pair of hydrogen atoms, and polyunsaturated fats such as soy, corn, and canola oils, which lack more than one pair. Both sorts are liquid at room temperature.

Some researchers have questioned whether saturated fat is dangerous. In his book, *The Cholesterol Myths: Exposing the Fallacy That Saturated Fat and Cholesterol Cause Heart Disease*, Swedish physician Uffe Ravnskov asserts that as of 1998, 27 studies on diet and heart disease had been published regarding 34 groups of patients; in 30 of those groups investigators found no difference in animal fat consumption between those who had heart disease and those who did not. "Anyone who reads the literature in this field with an open mind soon discovers that the emperor has no clothes," Ravnskov writes.

Willett turns to his Nurses' Health mega-study for the definitive word. "The amounts of specific fats did make a difference," he says. "Women who ate more unsaturated fat instead of saturated fat had fewer heart problems." Willett calculated that replacing 5 percent of saturated fat calories with unsaturated would cut the risk of heart attack or death from heart disease by 40 percent. Other studies—notably the French Lyon Diet Heart study, begun in 1988—show a similar correlation.

A healthy diet plan is worthless if people won't stick to it, and Susan Roberts, director of the energy metabolism laboratory at Tufts University, contends that Willett's regimen is too severe. "Most people would say his recommendations are healthy but that other, less difficult diets are healthy too," she says.

Difficult is in the palate of the eater. The last half of Willett's book aims to dispel any taint of Calvinism with recipes that verge on the sybaritic, including pork tenderloin with pistachio-gremolata crust, chicken enchilada casserole, and grilled salmon steaks with papaya-mint salsa. On the other hand, some resolve might be required to soldier through a few of the other dishes listed there, including hearty oat-wheat berry bread or the onion-crusted tofu-steak sandwich. But most people, Willett believes, can summon the willpower to substitute whole-wheat flour for white and plant oils for shortening or lard, and eat less sugar overall. "I think what I suggest is not severely restrictive, because it can be achieved mainly by substitution," rather than slavishly following recipes, Willett says. In any case, "it does not mean you cannot eat any of those foods but rather that they should be de-emphasized."

So take heart. Even Willett has a little chocolate now and then.

Food News Blues

FAT IS BAD, BUT GOOD FAT IS GOOD. WHAT ABOUT FISH? WINE? NUTS? A NEW APPETITE FOR ANSWERS HAS PUT SCIENCE ON A COLLISION COURSE WITH THE MEDIA.

BARBARA KANTROWITZ AND CLAUDIA KALB

YOU COULDN'T MISS THE HEADLINES. The New York Times: LOW-FAT DIET DOES NOT CUT HEALTH RISKS, STUDY FINDS. The Atlanta Journal-Constitution: REDUCING FAT MAY NOT CURB DISEASE. The Boston Globe: STUDY FINDS NO MAJOR BENEFIT OF A LOW-FAT DIET. The Los Angeles Times: EATING LEAN DOESN'T CUT RISK. When the results of a massive, federally funded study were released last month, TV, newspapers and, yes, magazines around the country trumpeted what seemed to confound conventional wisdom and standard medical advice. Fat, these articles seemed to say, wasn't so bad for you after all. In fact, the results of the study, the Women's Health Initiative (WHI), were actually more complex—as all these articles explained to readers who got beyond the headlines.

> **'America, step away from the french fries ... Despite new reports, less is still best.'**
> —USA TODAY, Feb. 28, 2006

It wasn't (as many of us might have hoped) a signal to rush out and gorge on cheeseburgers—especially if you're a man of any age or a woman under 50. That's because the study involved only older women—from 50 to 79. And the primary goal was far narrower than those headlines implied: to test whether cutting fat would reduce the risk, specifically, of breast cancer. After an average of eight years, researchers found no statistically significant difference in breast-cancer risk between women on a low-fat diet and women who had made no changes in what they ate. But that is not the bottom line. The results showed what researchers call a "trend" toward a low-fat diet reducing breast-cancer risk; this effect was actually significant in those who started with the highest levels of fat. Scientists will observe the women until 2010, when we could hear a whole new message. "I wouldn't worry about the headlines of today as far as low fat and breast cancer are concerned," says Dr. Jacques Rossouw, the WHI project officer. "They may be wrong."

To those of us without an M.D., it sometimes seems as if scientists are deliberately trying to mess with our heads—especially when it comes to nutrition research. The WHI study is the latest in what appears to be a series of dietary flip-flops. All fat was bad; now some fat is good. Eggs were bad; now they're OK in moderation. Nuts were *verboten*; now their fats are beneficial. Coffee has been up and down more often than hemlines. We've even been reading that chocolate could be a health food. (We've got some bad news on that. Read on.) Meanwhile, Americans are getting fatter and fatter. Two thirds are overweight or obese, and we're shelling out millions annually in a futile effort to shed those excess pounds.

Why all the mixed messages? Three words: too much information. Not so long ago patients got all their medical knowledge from their doctors. But now a media explosion has transformed that intimate relationship into an orgy of Web sites, cable- and network-TV medical reports, and magazine and newspaper stories heralding one breakthrough after another. Americans are more likely to hear first reports of the latest cancer treatment from CNN's Sanjay Gupta or ABC's Tim Johnson (both doctors) than from their own oncologist. From 1977 to 2004, the number of newspaper front-page stories on science tripled, from 1 to 3 percent, while foreign-affairs coverage plummeted from 27 to 14 percent, according to the Project for Excellence in Journalism, a group that monitors media coverage. In news magazines, the number of pages devoted to health and medical science has quadrupled since 1980. Last year, 10 out of 50 NEWSWEEK cover stories were on such health issues as lung cancer, autism and heart disease. The WHI fat story led TIP SHEET section in our Feb. 20 edition.

The pharmaceutical industry, wise to this proliferation of outlets and heightened consumer interest, spent $1.3 billion in magazine advertising last year, according to TNS Media Intelligence, a media-tracking service. An additional $2.4 billion went to network and cable TV.

Scientists themselves have become part of the media machine. In the old days, researchers who went public with their petri dishes were scorned by colleagues. Some still are. But the pressure to talk to reporters is enormous. Hospitals and universities send out press releases and publish glossy magazines about scientific advances within their ranks to generate buzz and maybe even research dollars. Drug companies hire physicians as consultants, then tout them as experts, setting up interviews with reporters about developments in a disease when the real motive is to promote a drug. And then there are the truly aggressive doctors—many of them in fields like dermatology and plastic surgery, where they are vying for patients—who hire their own public-relations reps who then mail press kits to reporters, complete with 8-by-10 photos. Even the most guarded scientists know that it's hard to hide, especially if their research is being paid for by the taxpaying public. They may seem like geeks in lab coats, but scientific research is hugely competitive—for attention, recognition and funding. The most egregious example: the South Korean stem-cell debacle. A supposed milestone in the controversial science—cloning human embryos to create stem cells—turned out to be a fraud. "Science is a contact sport," says Dr. Jeffrey Drazen, editor of the prestigious New England Journal of Medicine. "People think about it being genteel, but it's a tough game."

'Hold on to your olive oil. This study … did not differentiate between "good" and "bad" fats.'
—KNIGHT RIDDER, Feb. 28, 2006

All this coverage would be fine, perhaps even beneficial, if medical progress were as straightforward as it's often reported. Unfortunately, it's not. Headlines and sound bites can't capture the complexity of research. Science works in small steps, and failure and mistakes are an integral part of the process. Experiments flame out; hypotheses crash and burn. "Most science isn't a breakthrough," says Dr. Judah Folkman, the famed cancer researcher at Children's Hospital Boston who was involuntarily thrust into the spotlight by a 1998 New York Times story about his research. "It's incremental, brick by brick." But the public has big expectations. "Science and medicine have promised a lot," says Dr. Jerome Groopman of Harvard Medical School and a writer for The New Yorker. "We have all this technology, this information and resources, and we're making promises to people. In many cases, we still don't have the answers."

Published studies on the same topic can vary enormously in terms of sample size (small, medium, big), demographics (age, gender), data (self-reported versus objectively measured information) and length (weeks, months, years). Then there's the design of the study, a critical factor. The gold standard, a randomized, double-blind, placebo-controlled trial, is considered the most reliable because neither researchers nor participants know who is taking the medication being tested and who is taking the placebo (essentially a sugar pill).

Some studies, like the WHI, are prospective, which means a group of patients is watched from the beginning of a treatment, procedure or intervention. Others are retrospective: they look back at patient records to uncover hints about disease onset or

patterns. Still others are "meta-analyses," overviews of existing studies on a similar theme. Even bad studies can get published in journals with less rigorous standards. "The media reports all studies as if they have the same degree of certainty," says Dr. Elias Zerhouni, director of the National Institutes of Health. "There's no real label of quality."

To really understand what's going on, you also have to follow the money. The government pays for much of basic science, but industries with a stake in the outcome often fund food and drug studies. An industry connection doesn't necessarily mean a study is wrong. Scientists have to rely on different sources of support in the increasingly ferocious battle for dollars. But, says Dr. Richard Deyo, professor of medicine at the University of Washington in Seattle, "when corporate sponsors fund research, it's more likely to show beneficial effects." For example, industry-funded studies have consistently concluded that soda can be part of a healthy diet. But non-industry studies find that sugary beverages contribute to obesity. The National Dairy Council pays for research on the link between dairy food and weight loss. The California Raisin Marketing Board underwrote a study showing that raisins fight oral bacteria. If raisins hadn't done the job, the public might never have known. Industry-funded studies with negative results are often not published.

The stars in this vast medical-research universe were perfectly aligned in the early 1990s, when the WHI began. Women's health advocates had been pushing for more research. The NIH had its first female director, Dr. Bernadine Healy. And there were serious questions about older women's health that needed answers. Observational studies, which follow people over time without intervening in their behavior, had suggested that estrogen might prevent heart disease; millions of women were urged to take it. Scientists also decided to study the role of a low-fat diet and the use of calcium and vitamin D supplements to protect against fractures from osteoporosis. Together, heart disease, breast cancer and osteoporosis represent major causes of death and disability in older women. Preventing these diseases could affect millions.

The WHI was a massive undertaking—the largest federally funded study of women's health, ultimately costing $725 million over 15 years. In the early to mid-1990s, WHI researchers recruited 161,808 women age 50 to 79 from all over the country. This in itself was a major achievement because joining the study was a serious commitment. The women had to agree to be tested regularly, fill in lots of forms, take medication without knowing whether it would help them or hurt them, and, in the case of the dietary study, learn to cook and eat in a completely different way.

From the beginning, the WHI was controversial. Scientists especially questioned the diet trial, which enrolled 48,835 women. Psychologist Kelly Brownell, director of Yale's Rudd Center for Food Policy and Obesity, was on a committee convened at the request of Congress in 1993 to review the WHI. He says committee members were concerned about the design. Cancer and heart disease can take decades to develop. Would an eight-year trial be long enough? Would the women in the test group fully report their eating habits? Self-reports of dietary intake are notoriously inaccurate. On average, the participants weighed 170 pounds at the outset and reported that they ate 1,700 calories a day. By the end, they reported eating 1,400 to 1,500 calories daily. "They should have lost loads of weight," says Brownell. "Yet the women in the test group only lost three or four pounds. The control group actually gained about a pound. A scale is a scale. It won't lie. That screams out to me that the dietary records were inaccurate." It could mean that the difference in fat intake between the test and control groups wasn't large enough to show a distinct effect.

Docs may seem like geeks in lab coats, but scientific research is hugely competitive—for attention, recognition and funding.

The calcium and vitamin D study also had its critics. When it was designed, calcium was considered so important that researchers thought it would be unethical to tell women in the control group to stop taking supplements. In the end, the test subjects and the placebo group were both taking in roughly the same amount of calcium. So when the final results showed little difference in the fracture rate between the two groups, some scientists blamed the study design. And there was a second problem. The amount of vitamin D they were given is considered inadequate today. Most doctors still recommend calcium supplements if women can't get enough in their diets. "It was a disappointment that it was not better designed," says Joan Lappe, professor of medicine at the Osteoporosis Research Center at Creighton University. She and her colleagues are worried that the public is getting the message that calcium and vitamin D don't matter.

WHI investigators fired off their first bombshell in 2002, when they stopped the hormone study early after a safety-monitoring board concluded that the risks outweighed the benefits. Gynecologists' phones rang off the hook as millions of patients demanded to know if they'd been duped. That study continues to be a source of fierce debate. Although the results showed an increased risk of breast cancer, stroke, blood clots and heart disease in women who took estrogen and progestin, some scientists say the reaction was too strong. Many doctors believe younger women who take hormones for a short time to relieve menopausal symptoms like hot flashes are generally at low risk. There's also some evidence that estrogen might protect younger women against heart disease. Researchers are only beginning to study that issue.

Years ago this debate would have been confined to scientific circles. Medical journals would have filtered new research and doctors would have read the journals, discussed studies with colleagues and then figured out how to translate data into clinical practice. All this was hidden to patients. Now even the most respected journals have had to adapt to the growing demand for health information. When The Journal of the American Medical Association (JAMA) and The New England Journal of Medicine were launched in the 19th century, they would have had no conception of a "publicity" department. But today, JAMA, which has published several WHI studies, spends $1 million annually on its

media and communications program, says Dr. Catherine DeAngelis, the editor. Half goes to packaging video interviews, which TV reporters use in their stories. DeAngelis says the JAMA footage hits an average of 20 million viewers a week through local, national and international outlets. The other half of the money is used to run the communications office, hold press conferences and prepare press releases about upcoming studies, which reporters receive before the studies are published—if they tacitly agree not to print anything before the journal's publication date. If they agree to these "embargo" terms, they can question the scientists involved in the study and others who might have a more objective view of the research.

'Didn't the study find there's no value in taking calcium supplements?'
—THE WASHINGTON POST, Feb. 28, 2006

All that was in place last month when the WHI released its diet study. The headline in the main JAMA article, published on Feb. 8, gave no hint that some readers might be tempted to head for Krispy Kreme: LOW-FAT DIETARY PATTERN AND RISK OF INVASIVE BREAST CANCER. Two other articles in the same issue discussed the impact of the diet on heart disease and colorectal cancer. Like any journal report, all three were laden with details, including the number of women in the trial (48,835) and the goals (to reduce fat to 20 percent of calories and to increase consumption of vegetables, fruit and grains). The conclusion of the breast-cancer study—that a low-fat diet did not lower risk—was fairly nuanced. It suggested that if the women were observed for a longer time, there might be more of an effect. At a conference last week at the National Institutes of Health, which sponsors the WHI, researchers were even more direct, saying that they hoped women would not start eating fat because of this study, but that message got lost in the headlines.

The diet study was a victim of its time. Fifteen years later, we know a lot more and understand that some fatty foods, like olive oil and avocados, may actually be beneficial. And some food labeled fat-free is full of calories, which might have accounted for some of the participants' weight issues. "These studies are more complicated than a simple headline or sound bite can convey, and that's an important lesson for all of us," says Dr. Elizabeth Nabel, director of the National Heart, Lung, and Blood Institute, which administers the WHI.

But to the average American, the WHI study just seemed like one more example of scientists unable to make up their minds. Dr. Mary Altz-Smith, a rheumatologist in Birmingham, Ala., is worried about the message it sent to her patients, many of whom are already overweight. "This information is all too likely to encourage patients to slide," she says. And who could blame them? Every day, the "truth" about diet seems ever more elusive even while scientists insist the picture is becoming clearer. A classic case is margarine. Early on, it was touted to be better than butter, which contains saturated fat. But that was before scientists realized that margarine had an even more noxious ingredient: trans fat. Margarine became poison. Now the pendu-

Coffee

- Experts used to believe that coffee could cause hypertension and heart disease.
- But in the 1990s studies refuted the link with heart attacks; a 2002 Johns Hopkins study found that, while male drinkers had higher blood pressure than nondrinkers, coffee was not a major factor.
- Although recent studies suggest that java may help ward off Parkinson's and diabetes, pregnant women may want to limit their intake.

Red Wine

- In the early '90s, red wine, which contains compounds like resveratrol, was thought to be especially good for heart health.
- But a 1996 Harvard study of beer, wine and spirits showed that drinking any alcoholic beverage in moderation—not just red wine— can be linked to lower rates of heart disease.
- Now experts say that 1–2 glasses a day may lower the risk of heartattack—but caution against starting to drink for health benefits alone.

Milk

- Nutritionists have long hyped calcium-rich milk for its strengthening effect on bones and teeth
- But recently some leading experts have questioned the need to drink milk in the government-recommended quantities. A 1997 Harvard study found that older women who drank more milk didn't suffer fewer fractures.
- The USDA still recommends 3 cups a day of low- or non-fat dairy, but also suggests leafy green veggies for calcium.

Nuts

- Thanks to the "carbs are good, fat is bad" trend of the '80s and '90s, dieters avoided nuts, which are high in fat.
- But most fat in nuts is "good," unsaturated fat that—when combined with nuts' fiber and antioxidants—could lower risk of heart disease. Recent studies—including 1998 Harvard research on women eating 5 oz. of nuts a week—have solidified the connection.
- Cut bad fats; sub in several ounces of nuts each week.

Eggs

- For decades, doctors believed that cholesterol-laden eggs were a major contributor to heart disease; in the '80s, Americans started to limit their intake.
- A '99 analysis by Harvard scientists found that eating up to one egg a day didn't increase the risk of heart disease or stroke in healthy people. Other studies have suggested that eggs don't raise cholesterol levels appreciably.
- Experts say eggs are fine in moderation.

Tuna

- Fish, including tuna, has traditionally been lauded as a good source of protein and other nutrients (most recently omega-3 fatty acids).
- But in 2001, growing concerns over mercury levels led the FDA to issue warnings directing children and pregnant women to limit consumption of certain fish. Tuna was added to the list in 2004.
- Those at risk should cut fish intake to 12 oz. a week; choose canned light tuna over albacore.

Olive Oil

- The USDA's 1992 food pyramid placed fats and oils at the very tip, telling Americans to consume these foods "sparingly."
- In 1999, a major clinical trial by French researchers showed that a diet high in olive and canola oils helped prevent heart attacks; other scientists have since singled out olive oil as a source of heart-healthy mono-unsaturated fat.
- Experts now recommend olive oil as an alternative to butter or margarine.

lum has shifted back a bit as manufacturers removed the bad fat and put in non-hydrogenated oils. "Those are better," says Dr. Walter Willett, chair of nutrition at the Harvard School of Public Health. "But it's still better to use liquid vegetable oils, like olive oil." And as for butter, the fact that margarine was worse doesn't make butter good. "It's not health food," Willett says.

'Diet fads and their alleged benefits have us eating in circles.'
—SAN FRANCISCO CHRONICLE editorial, Feb. 20, 2006

More recently, chocolate appeared to be heading for that coveted health-food status, and the public was more than ready to gobble it up. It began when a 2001 study (funded by the American Cocoa Research Institute) found that cocoa powder and dark chocolate boosted good cholesterol by 4 percent. What most people didn't realize is that there were only 23 participants in this study, hardly enough to produce any serious conclusion. Nonetheless, it made headlines and was followed by additional chocolate studies that seemed to find even more benefits. But most of that research focused on a group of compounds in chocolate called flavanols—which unfortunately tend to get processed out of the chocolate you buy at the grocery store. And chocolate still has lots of fat, sugar and calories.

Just last week a study from the Netherlands published in the Archives of Internal Medicine found that participants who ate the most food containing chocolate (candy bars, spreads, pudding) had slightly lower blood pressure and were half as likely to have died from heart disease at the end of the 15-year follow-up. However, it's not clear that the results were strictly from chocolate. The biggest challenge in dietary research is that nobody eats only one thing. In this case, the chocolate lovers also ate less meat and more nuts. "This study is another piece of the puzzle," says Harold Schmitz, chief science officer of Mars Inc., the candy manufacturer. "As much as I'd love to say it puts the capstone on the research, it doesn't." And it could be years before there's a definitive answer.

Everyone's looking for an immediate solution, but science takes time. It took Judah Folkman decades to confirm his pioneering theory that cancerous tumors rely on a blood supply to grow. When The New York Times heralded his research on the front page with a headline that proclaimed HOPE IN THE LAB, TV, newspapers and magazines (including NEWSWEEK) picked up the story. Desperate patients flooded Folkman's lab with phone calls seeking help. But at the time, his research was only in mice, not men—a detail that many readers overlooked. It was years before Folkman's theory—called angiogenesis—translated into drugs that can actually help people. More than anybody, Folkman understands how difficult it is to balance enthusiasm for scientific progress with the danger of hyping new developments. "That's the fundamental problem," he says. "We scientists don't always know how to share our excitement with the public without making our research sound overdone."

It's even more complicated with a study like the WHI, which is paid for by taxpayers and is of enormous interest to a wide range of people. What may have seemed like flip-flopping is actually an evolutionary process, says Stanford's Marcia Stefanick, chair of the WHI steering committee. "As we acquire new scientific information, we need to modify public-health recommendations." If the diet results were misinterpreted, there's probably blame all around. Journalists wanted juicy headlines and the public wanted a quick fix for fat. Scientists were trying to report their findings in the most digestible form while acknowledging that reality was more complex. It would be nice to think that everybody is a little bit wiser. For all their differences, scientists and journalists are on the same path. They should keep asking questions, not be discouraged by dead ends and be open-minded to surprising truths.

UNIT 4

Exercise and Weight Management

Unit Selections

Key Points to Consider

- How can exercise affect mental health and mental abilities?

- How important is exercise to achieving optimal health? Explain.

- Why should exercise be included in any weight control program?

- How do the three components to the Female Athlete Triad affect health status?

- How do you feel about people who are overweight? Has your weight ever been a problem for you? If so, what have you done about it?

- Do you exercise on a regular basis? If not, why not? What would it take to get you exercising on a regular basis?

- Is there such a thing as too much exercise?

- Should obesity be classified as a disease rather than a lack of willpower?

- What role does volumetrics play in weight management?

Student Website
www.mhcls.com/online

Internet References
Further information regarding these websites may be found in this book's preface or online.

American Society of Exercise Physiologists (ASEP)
http://www.asep.org

Eating Disorders Awareness and Prevention, Inc.
http://www.edap.org

Cyberdiet
http://www.cyberdiet.com/reg/index.html

Shape Up America!
http://www.shapeup.org

Recently, a new set of guidelines, dubbed "Exercise Lite," has been issued by the U.S. Centers for Disease Control and Prevention in conjunction with the American College of Sports Medicine. These guidelines call for 30 minutes of exercise, 5 days a week, which can be spread over the course of a day. The primary focus of this approach to exercise is improving health, not athletic performance. Examples of activities that qualify under the new guidelines are walking your dog, playing tag with your kids, scrubbing floors, washing your car, mowing the lawn, weeding your garden, and having sex. From a practical standpoint, this approach to fitness will likely motivate many more people to become active and stay active. Remember, since the benefits of exercise can take weeks or even months before they become apparent, it is very important to choose an exercise program that you enjoy so that you will stick with it. While a good diet cannot overcome lack of exercise, exercise can overcome a less than optimal diet. Exercise not only makes people physically healthier, it may also keep their brains healthy. While the connection hasn't been proven, there is evidence that regular workouts may cause the brain to better process and store information which results in a smarter brain.

While exercise and a nutritious diet can keep people fit and healthy, many Americans are not heeding this advice. For the first time in our history, the average American is now overweight when judged according to standard height/weight tables. In addition, more than 25 percent of Americans are clinically obese, and the numbers appear to be growing. Why is this happening, given the prevailing attitude that Americans have toward fat? One theory that is currently gaining support suggests that while Americans have cut back on their consumption of fatty snacks and deserts, they have actually increased their total caloric intake by failing to limit their consumption of carbohydrates. The underlying philosophy goes something like this: fat calories make you fat, but you can eat as many carbohydrates as you want and not gain weight. The truth is that all calories count when it comes to weight gain, and if cutting back on fat calories prevents you from feeling satiated you will naturally eat more to achieve that feeling. While this position seems reasonable enough, some groups, most notably supporters of the Atkins diet, have suggested that eating a high-fat diet will actually help people lose weight because of fat's high satiety value in conjunction with the formation of ketones (which suppress appetite).

Whether people limit fat or carbohydrates, they will not lose weight unless their total caloric intake is less than their energy expenditure.

America's preoccupation with body weight has given rise to a billion-dollar industry. When asked why people go on diets, the predominant answer is for social reasons such as appearance and group acceptance, rather than concerns regarding health. Why do diets and diet aids fail? One of the major reasons lies in the mind-set of the dieter. Many dieters do not fully understand the biological and behavioral aspects of weight loss, and consequently they have unrealistic expectations regarding the process.

Being overweight not only causes health problems; it also carries with it a social stigma. Overweight people are often thought of as weak-willed individuals with little or no self-respect. The notion that weight control problems are the result of personality defects is being challenged by new research findings. Evidence is mounting that suggests that physiological and hereditary factors may play as great a role in obesity as do behavioral and environmental factors. Researchers now believe that genetics dictate the base number of fat cells an individual will have, as well as the location and distribution of these cells within the body. The study of fat metabolism has provided additional clues as to why weight control is so difficult. These metabolic studies have found that the body seems to have a "setpoint," or desired weight, and it will defend this weight through alterations in basal metabolic rate and fat-cell activity. While this process is thought to be an adaptive throwback to primitive times when food supplies were uncertain, today, with our abundant food supply, this mechanism only contributes to the problem of weight control.

It should be apparent by now that weight control is both an attitudinal and a lifestyle issue. Fortunately, a new, more rational approach to the problem of weight control is emerging. This approach is based on the premise that you can be perfectly healthy and look good without being pencil-thin. The primary focus of this approach to weight management is the attainment of your body's "natural ideal weight" and not some idealized, fanciful notion of what you would like to weigh. Unfortunately, for many female athletes, the desire to have a perfect body has led some to develop eating disorders that can lead to osteoporosis. In "The Female Triad," authors Lola Ramos and Gregory L. Welch discuss a condition that affects female athletes who eat too little and exercise too much. The concept of achieving your natural ideal body weight suggests that we need to take a more realistic approach to both fitness and weight control and serves to remind us that a healthy lifestyle is based on the concepts of balance and moderation. That sentiment is echoed in "Exercise Abuse: Too Much of a Good Thing." Author Kate Jackson addresses individuals who abuse exercise by overdoing it to the point of physical injury, and other negative side effects.

Exercise Abuse

Too Much of a Good Thing

Know when your client has tipped the scales from healthy fitness to obsession.

KATE JACKSON

Imagine a client who's diligent about exercise and walks every day for one hour. Sounds healthy, right? What if she never misses a day and exercises rain or shine, even after spraining an ankle or when she has the flu? As the picture becomes more complex, the client's behavior begins to sound less healthy and more obsessive and compulsive.

Excessive exercise—sometimes called *exercise abuse* or *addiction*—is defined as activity that has a deleterious effect on physical and psychological well-being, says Kelly Pedrotty, MA, exercise coordinator and program coordinator at the Renfrew Center of Philadelphia, a residential treatment center for individuals with eating disorders. "People who have a healthy view of exercise," she explains, "exercise because they enjoy it."

Those who exercise excessively have negative feelings about their workouts and may consider it painful. It's often difficult to discern, say experts, but the key difference between moderate and pathological exercise is that the latter is compulsive. The individuals have to do it all the time—every day—or they become anxious. "This need to engage in a behavior, such as exercise every day or repeatedly, is a sign of compulsion," says Elizabeth Carll, PhD, a psychologist and eating disorders specialist in private practice in Long Island, N.Y.

Rigorous activity by all means isn't always pathological. "Goals such as training for an athletic event or weight loss that is medically necessary are appropriate, and once those goals are reached, people cut back on the level of exercise intensity," explains Carll. "Exercise is compulsive and considered a disorder, however, when it is in response to free-floating anxiety, an obsessive need to improve the way one looks, or chronic dissatisfaction with one's appearance. The key difference is that those who have an addiction or compulsion can't stop."

Although men, women, and children can abuse exercise, it appears to be more common in women and is often linked with other psychological disorders such as depression or obsessive compulsive disorder. Compulsive patterns of exercise often go hand in hand with eating disorders, particularly anorexia nervosa.

"Many girls with anorexia also exercise compulsively in addition to restricting their intake of food in order to lose weight,"

Don't Go Gung-Ho

Juliet Zuercher, RD, director of nutrition at Remuda Ranch, cautions dietitians that gung-ho attitudes about healthful eating and regular exercise can be misinterpreted by individuals with exercise addiction or eating disorders. "Dietitians tend to be health-conscious and knowledgeable about exercise," she says, "and sometimes those who are not as adept or really experienced with eating disordered clients can almost feed into what might be a brewing exercise addiction."

All in the name of health, she says, dietitians not experienced in eating disorders may affirm, support, and unknowingly encourage what may sound like a healthy exercise pattern, not recognizing the extreme nature of the client's thinking. A dietitian, she warns, can unwittingly feed into distorted thought patterns by emphasizing low-fat foods, fewer calories, or extremely healthy foods—all good ideas for normal clients, but easily misconstrued by those with compulsive tendencies.— KJ

---

says Carll. For these individuals, she explains, exercise and eating are linked, so that every time they eat, they feel they must exercise. They engage in activity, says Pedrotty, solely to compensate for eating.

Excessive exercise is also frequently associated with bulimia nervosa, says Christian Lemmon, PhD, department of psychiatry and health behavior, MCG Health Systems in Atlanta, a psychologist who specializes in treating people with eating disorders. In patients with bulimia, excessive exercise is another form of compensation for eating, such as inducing vomiting or taking laxatives or diuretics. It exists independently of eating disorders as well, most commonly in men, but appears to be more common in individuals who struggle with food-related issues.

Typically viewed as merely exercising too much, exercise abuse can be manifested in other behaviors, explains Pedrotty, especially when eating disorders are involved. Bulimic women in particular may exhibit what she calls all-or-nothing patterns of exercise: "They'll engage in a period of intense exercise, and then they'll avoid it. Perhaps they'll train hard for a month and then back off for three months because they feel burned out. Or their approach may vary from day to day. They may wake up one day and feel like they ate too much the day before and therefore they exercise like crazy and then take a week off." Another associated behavior is obsessing about exercise but never actually working out, says Pedrotty.

At the Root

Exercise abuse may have a gradual or quick onset and typically begins as a healthy pattern that goes wrong, often in people with propensity for compulsivity. Molly Kimball, sports and lifestyle nutritionist at Ochsner Clinic's Elmwood Fitness Center in New Orleans, notes that it can arise easily among perfectionists. "Usually it occurs in very driven people—those who are over-achievers and people who get great grades in school, excel at work, are well liked, and tend to do things for the approval of others."

Individuals who have eating disorders and who abuse exercise often do so out of a lack of self-esteem and in an effort to punish themselves. "A lot of our patients use it as a form of self-harm, believing that they can't stop until they've experienced pain, until their heart rate reaches the maximum, until they're dripping with sweat, or until their bodies burn," says Pedrotty. They may feel they're not worthy of eating and that they must abuse their body. Many people derive a lot of self-esteem from their ability to maintain a certain kind of exercise regimen, agrees Lemmon, and it's difficult for them to see other reasons to feel good about themselves.

It's also highly likely to arise in people who by nature or circumstance have a need to control. Observes Kimball, "When other things feel out of control, exercise may become a control issue because it's one thing they can master. No one makes them do it and they don't let anyone or anything interfere." A person might have been a recreational exerciser for years, she says, but something happens to trigger the obsession, such as a divorce or death of a parent. It might even be a less drastic milestone—a move, a new job, or the start of college—that erodes control and causes exercise to become an excessive focus.

Carll suggests that the root of overzealous exercise is an obsession—along the lines of an anxiety disorder—with one's appearance, used as a way of reducing weight and changing shape. "Frequently, individuals are both anxious and depressed and display behaviors similar to those seen in people with obsessive compulsive disorder, which is an anxiety disorder." Exercise, she explains, is a way of coping with the anxious feelings and taking control of one's body, much like anorexia. Most clients she sees with anorexia started out by dieting, but the diets got out of control. These girls and women kept losing weight, thinking that eventually they'd reach their ideal weights and goals. "They never do," she says. "It's always 5 pounds more. The same thing happens with exercise addiction."

Telltale Signs: Spying the Hidden Problem

Since exercise abusers, like those with eating disorders, are typically skillful dissemblers, simple and straightforward questions may not always cut through their disguises. Nutrition and exercise professionals offer the following telltale signs of excessive exercise:

- using exercise merely as a way to lose weight, especially by an individual with an eating disorder;
- a strong emotional commitment to exercise;
- a sense of duty or obligation about exercise manifested by an inability to take a day off or anxiety when exercise is not possible;
- a strong relationship between intake and output—having to exercise after eating;
- talking about exercise in a regimented way, not having a relaxed attitude about exercise, and not expressing enjoyment about activity;
- exercising through illness or injury, in inclement weather, or in severe times of stress;
- using exercise as the only means of stress control or mental health;
- exercising at the expense of one's social life or responsibilities;
- expressing guilt about not exercising;
- spot training—picking a particular part of the body and focusing excessively on it (eg, doing 1,500 crunches per day);
- being inflexible about exercise schedules or having rigid patterns (eg, having to use the same equipment at the same time in the same amount);
- always talking about exercise;
- exercising secretively—hiding or lying about exercise;
- visiting the gym more than once per day;
- having all-or-nothing exercise patterns—going from extremes of no exercise to constant exercise; and
- having a preoccupation with health food, weight loss, or performance supplements and products. — KJ

Exercise abuse may also develop out of a habit that's widely promoted and generally considered healthy: working out to ward off stress. But once again, in vulnerable individuals, there's a tendency to turn a plus into a minus. According to Juliet Zuercher, RD, director of nutrition at Remuda Ranch, a treatment center for women and girls with eating disorders and related issues such as exercise addiction, "A client may dabble with exercise as a means of stress release, and it feels good, so they think more will be better." Then they get into higher intensity exercise, she explains, and are essentially self-medicating with endorphins. "If they were depressed or stressed, they exercise and they feel better. That's positive reinforcement that goes to the extreme and until the activity becomes compulsive and the person thinks he or she will be depressed if they don't run 10 miles every day."

Physicians and psychotherapists often recommend exercise as a means to keep depression and stress at bay, but it must be both moderate and balanced by proper nutrition. "I feel great when I exercise," says Lemmon, "but too much of anything isn't good for you." Exercise abusers, he says, also use negative reinforcement for their behaviors. "They engage in excessive exercise to avoid a noxious set of stimuli—the anxiety that comes from not exercising," he explains.

Lemmon observes that many teens' parents worry that their kids may sneak out of the house at night and engage in sexual or drug-related behaviors. Young people with exercise disorders, however, may tiptoe out to engage in exercise surreptitiously. He recalls one patient who waited until her parents were asleep to go out and run five miles each night and another who got up every day at 5 am to ride on a stationary bike for 25 minutes, run on a treadmill for 45 minutes, and then do hundreds of crunches.

In all these cases, a good thing has gone too far. "It's an extremist way of thinking. If a certain amount is good, then a lot more is better," explains Carll. "These individuals think that if it's great to exercise three or four times a week, imagine how much better shape they could be in and how much healthier they'd be if they exercised all the time."

"Healthy" Symptoms

Regular exercise is healthy, but compulsive exercise becomes pathological. It's more often than not a hidden problem, and the line that divides healthy from obsessive activity is seldom clear. One of the reasons the problem goes unnoticed and and that many eating disorders programs don't have exercise abuse components, says Pedrotty, is that exercise is the only symptom of an eating disorder that's actually healthy. "It's never healthy to binge-purge or use laxatives, but exercise is healthy when used in moderation and when there's a healthy mind-set motivating it, so it's challenging to find the balance."

It's important that healthcare professionals know how to assess for excessive exercise, says Lemmon, who acknowledges that it's a hard set of behaviors to define. "If someone says he or she exercises seven days a week, that's almost culturally sanctioned. We would all envy a person who can work out seven days a week, not only because they'd be in good health but because we'd wish we had the time to do the same. So problems such as exercise addiction are actually reinforced by our society."

For these reasons, professionals in the field suggest that dietitians ask all clients—men or women, young or mature, thin or obese—about exercise. By asking about it routinely, RDs can begin to see beyond the camouflage exercise abusers wear. Even in the ordinary course of practice with all clients, dietitians need to know about daily input and output of energy since they can't determine recommended dietary allowances without knowing how much energy a person is burning, says Lemmon. It's an opportunity to expand the conversation, he suggests, and dig a bit deeper.

Zuercher says that since excessive exercise is a problem that can easily be missed, it makes sense for RDs to question all clients about their feelings about exercise in the initial intake or interview. It's not necessary to go into great depth with all clients,

The Toll of Exercise Abuse

In addition to the psychological toll of excessive exercise, a host of physical complaints may arise, including the following:
- bone and muscle injuries
- inflamed joints, tendons, and ligaments
- decreased bone density
- disruption of the menstrual cycle
- infertility
- overuse injuries
- stress fracture
- plantar fasciatis

— KJ

but when responses to simple questions about activity levels and exercise patterns suggest a problem, further probing is warranted.

"Clients who exercise a lot may appear to have a healthy attitude. It's only after you ask specific questions to assess the degree of exercise that it may become apparent that it's no longer healthy," explains Carll. In our very health-oriented culture, exercise is seen as positive, so most people might not pursue an avenue of questions about it. Dietitians, she adds, should ask specific questions to determine what kind of exercise their clients engage in and how much time they spend exercising.

It's especially important, adds Pedrotty, to probe clients with eating disorders about their activity. "Their exercise patterns may seem to be healthy and normal, but you really have to get in there and figure out their mind-sets." The crux of the program she codesigned with Rachel Calogero, MA, at the Renfrew Center, she says, is geared toward getting at the thoughts and feelings clients have about exercise.

Lemmon says he'd begin simply by asking clients to tell him about their physical activity. "If she tells me that she does aerobics six days a week, would I worry about that? Not necessarily, but I'll begin to ask more questions. I'll want to know if she has a tendency to exercise more on or after days when she feels as if she's eaten too much, or if she eats less on a day when she didn't get a chance to work out. If she says yes to those kinds of questions, warning signals go off in my head and I'm going to ask more questions." He'll then want to explore whether clients' exercise regimens get in the way of their ability to function otherwise—if the behaviors disrupt their ability to function occupationally, academically, interpersonally, or socially. Many exercises abusers, especially those with eating disorders, he notes, make exercise their top priority. "They start limiting themselves socially because their social obligations can't fit into the structure to which their eating disorder symptoms bind them."

How to Help

Dietitians can help by discussing with clients the basics of energy balance, says Lemmon, explaining the need for a proper diet to compensate for exercise rather than the need for exercise to compensate for diet. They can also make a difference by educating clients to recognize unhealthy patterns and attitudes and understand the limits of healthy exercise.

For people in healthy body weight range, says Zuercher, "we suggest exercising for an hour at a time, three to five times a week—an amount based upon recommendations to the American College of Sports Medicine." She stresses the importance of taking one or two days off per week and advises people with weight issues to increase the cardio segment of each day's hour of exercise or increase exercise to six days per week rather than attempting to do more exercise each day. Anywhere from 30 to 60 minutes per day from three to six times per week—mostly cardiovascular exercise—is in the range of normal, suggests Kimball.

Ultimately, the healthy amount is different from person to person, says Pedrotty. Olympic athletes may exercise six days per week for eight hours per day, but that's not necessarily unhealthy because they fuel themselves appropriately, they enjoy what they're doing, and they take care of their bodies. "It's not the amount of exercise, it's the mind-set."

The simplest way dietitians can transform their clients' unhealthy attitudes about exercise is by being good role models, says Pedrotty. "They should have healthy views about exercise, know how much is enough and how much is too much, and understand and communicate that the sole purpose of exercise is not weight loss but rather that there are many purposes: to rejuvenate the body, to create a connection between the mind and body, to have fun, and to relieve stress." In the end, she says, make sure to promote the idea that we eat to exercise. We don't exercise to eat." Then follow up by providing healthy eating and exercising strategies.

Referring Clients

That said, more often than not, clients with exercise issues will need more help than you alone can provide. It's important to keep in mind that an eating or exercise disorder is a psychological illness, says Carll, so it's necessary to refer patients to mental health professionals who specialize in treating people with compulsive behaviors. These types of issues, she adds, have typically existed for some time and are not likely to change without therapeutic intervention. And the consequences of continuing these behaviors can be extremely serious. "Exercise by anorexic individuals with low body weight and low blood pressure can result in cardiac problems, including heart failure," says Carll.

In most cases, she says, people who exercise compulsively may not recognize that they have a problem because their behaviors give them a false sense of control. Your clients may not be receptive to the recommendation that they seek the care of a mental health professional, says Carll, who advises that it's still helpful to make the suggestion.

"If you see someone who has a very low body fat percentage and you discover that their intake isn't appropriate or their amount of exercise seems far in excess of what it needs to be, ask questions," says Lemmon, who stresses above all the need to be sensitive. "Communicate concern but also understanding, and recognize that if your clients are truly addicted to exercise, they're probably going to be a little bit skittish about seeking treatment and may even get downright angry or upset with you."

In a very loving, kind, empathic way, he urges, tell them your concerns and offer to help them find someone with whom they can talk about their issues. Then, ideally, he says, dietitians would continue to be part of an interdisciplinary team that includes physicians and psychotherapists working together to help clients with exercise addiction.

— Kate Jackson is a staff writer
for *Today's Dietitian*.

The Female Triad

LOLA RAMOS AND GREGORY L. WELCH, M.S.

In the past 30 years the opportunities for adolescent girls and young adult women to participate in all levels of sports competition have increased tremendously. This is certainly a positive direction for women because with increased physical activity comes associated wellness benefits. Chronic physiological adaptation to exercise training is well documented in regard to improved cardiovascular efficiency, muscular strength, self-esteem and overall body image (Wilmore and Costill 1999).

In addition to women who train at a competitive level, many non-competitive women exercise vigorously as well. It is not just that they train at high intensities but that their ambition to train surpasses that of individuals who are more moderate in their exercise programs. This mindset is such that training becomes a lifestyle philosophy as well as a passion. While this is generally an admirable trait, it is not without significant risk. For example, "over training" injuries in the form of muscular strain, tendonitis and stress fractures will likely occur to many individuals who overprioritize their workouts at the expense of sufficient recovery and nutrition. Specifically for young women, there is an even greater health concern that far outweighs typical "overuse syndrome"—the female triad. If not dealt with appropriately, the female triad can damage women's wellness throughout their lives.

Defining the Female Triad

The female triad is a combination of three coexistent conditions associated with exercise training: disordered eating, amenorrhea and osteoporosis (Hobart and Smucker 2000). Originally termed "female athlete triad," the name was derived at a meeting led by members of the American College of Sports Medicine in the early 1990s (Yeager et al. 1993). Papanek (2003) reports that the meeting was called in response to the alarming increase in stress fracture rates, documented decreases in bone mineral density and menstrual dysfunction in otherwise healthy female athletes. Furthermore, the depiction of the triad as a triangle was developed to demonstrate the interrelationship between the three disorders normally considered independent medical conditions.

Over the last decade, the triad's definition has evolved to be more precise about the involvement of related clinical conditions. Anorexia nervosa (AN) and bulimia nervosa (BN) are the most common clinical disorders. A third category for eating disorders not otherwise specified (EDNOS) was created in an effort to expand treatment access for patients at high risk for an eating disorder (Papanek 2003). In other words, an athlete who falls short in meeting the criteria for AN or BN could still be recognized as needing treatment by being placed in the EDNOS category. *See Table 1.*

However, not all restrictive eating behaviors necessarily reach the clinical level (Beals and Manore 2000). Even with the addition of the EDNOS category, female athletes with the triad display a wide range of food-related pathologies. Therefore, the term "eating disorder" was found to be too restrictive and replaced by "disordered eating" to include the various forms of aberrant eating behaviors that disrupt caloric balance (Papanek 2003). Common disordered eating patterns exhibited by female athletes include food restriction, prolonged fasting as well as abuse of diet pills, diuretics and laxatives (Donaldson 2003).

Eumenorrheic or regular menstrual cycles are defined as regular flow occurring every 21 to 45 days, with 10 to 13 cycles per year, and oligomenorrhea refers to three to six cycles occurring per year (Rome 2003). Marshal (1994) classifies amenorrhea as primary or secondary and defines them as follows: primary amenorrhea or delayed menarche is defined as not having experienced a single menstrual cycle by the age of 16 and secondary amenorrhea is the absence of menses for six months or a length of time equivalent to at least three of the woman's previous menstrual cycle lengths. The main difference is that in secondary amenorrhea, at least one menstrual period has occurred. Physiologically, this means all parts of the reproductive axis (i.e., hypothalamus, pituitary, ovaries and uterus) worked together once, but for some reason, this integrative function has changed (Papanek 2003).

Osteoporosis is a systemic, skeletal disease characterized by low bone density and microarchitectural deterioration of bone tissue, with a consequent increase in bone fragility and fracture susceptibility (O'brien 2001). To clarify, the term osteoporosis, as referred to in this writing, is actually secondary osteoporosis because it is caused or exacerbated by other disorders (Stein and Shane 2003). Additionally, osteopenia, which is abnormally low bone density and believed to be an osteoporosis precursor (Nelson 2000), has also been included when identifying the female triad syndrome. Amenorrheic adolescent athletes do not acquire proper bone mass and, thus, will be osteopenic in their early adult years (Elford and Spence 2002).

Table 1 Diagnostic criteria and warning signs for eating disorders

	DIAGNOSTIC CRITERIA	WARNING SIGNS AND SYMPTOMS
Anorexia Nervosa (AN)	1. Refusal to maintain body weight at or above 85 percent of normal weight for age and height 2. Intense fear of gaining weight or becoming fat, even though underweight 3. Disturbance in the way in which one's body weight or shape is experienced, undue influence of body weight or shape on self-evaluation or denial of the seriousness of current low body weight 4. Amenorrhea	1. Fat and muscle atrophy 2. Dry hair and skin 3. Cold, discolored hands and feet 4. Decreased body temperature 5. Lightheadedness 6. Decreased ability to concentrate 7. Bradycardia (i.e., slowness of the heartbeat, so that the pulse rate is less than 60 per minute) 8. Past history of physical or sexual abuse
	DIAGNOSTIC CRITERIA	**WARNING SIGNS AND SYMPTOMS**
Bulimia Nervosa (BN)	1. Recurrent episodes of binge eating 2. Sense of lack of control over eating during the episode (e.g., feeling that one cannot stop eating or control what or how much one is eating) 3. Recurrent inappropriate compensatory behavior to prevent weight gain (e.g., diuretics, enemas, self-induced vomiting, misuse of laxatives or other medications, fasting or excessive exercise) 4. The binge eating and inappropriate compensatory behaviors occur, on average, at least twice a week for three months 5. Self-evaluation is unduly influenced by body shape and weight 6. The disturbance does not occur exclusively during episodes of anorexia nervosa	1. Swollen parotid glands 2. Chest pain, sore throat 3. Fatigue, abdominal pain 4. Diarrhea or constipation 5. Menstrual irregularities 6. Callous formation or scars on knuckles
	DIAGNOSTIC CRITERIA	
Eating Disorder Not Otherwise Specified (EDNOS)	1. For females, all of the criteria for AN are met except the individual has regular menses 2. All criteria for AN are met except that, despite significant weight loss, the person's current weight is in the normal range 3. All the criteria for BN are met except that the binge eating and inappropriate compensatory mechanisms occur at a frequency of less than two per week for a duration of less than three months	4. Regular use of inappropriate compensatory behavior by an individual of normal body weight after eating small amounts of food (e.g., self-induced vomiting after consumption of two cookies) 5. Repeatedly chewing, but not swallowing, and spitting out large amounts of food 6. Binge-eating disorder: recurrent episodes of binge eating in the absence of the regular use of inappropriate compensatory behaviors characteristic of BN

Disordered Eating

Society has done a great disservice to adolescent females by perpetuating the "ideal" body image. For young women, this can intensify the pursuit of a thin physique at a time when nutrition plays a key role in proper growth and development. According to a 1997 Youth Risk Behavior Surveillance Survey, 34 percent of adolescent females were likely to consider themselves "too fat" and, therefore, limited their dietary intake (Kann et al. 1998). Hobart and Smucker (2000) add that many factors may create poor self-image and pathogenic weight-control behaviors in female athletes. Likewise, frequent weigh-ins,

punitive consequences for weight gain, pressure to "win at all costs," an overly controlling parent or coach and social isolation caused by intensive sports involvement may increase a female athlete's risk of disordered eating behavior.

Disordered eating occurs in 5 percent of the general population (Donaldson 2003), but affects as many as two thirds of young female athletes (Nativ et al. 1994). According to Gidwani and Rome (1997), 32 percent of female athletes, at all levels of competition, practice pathogenic behavior for weight control. Rosen and Hough (1988) reported disordered eating behavior in 15 to 62 percent of female college athletes. Even before the triad was officially recognized as a distinct syndrome, Calabrese (1985) performed a study with collegiate gymnasts and discovered 62 percent displayed some type of disordered eating—26 percent vomited on a daily basis, 24 percent used diet pills, 12 percent fasted and 75 percent had been told by their coaches that they weighed too much. Disordered eating behavior is believed to contribute to a disruption in the hypothalamic-gonadal axis, resulting in amenorrhea (Donaldson 2003).

The Interrelationship of the Triad

The three components of the female triad—disordered eating, amenorrhea and osteoporosis—pose serious health concerns for young athletic women. Shafer and Irwin (1991) state that the adolescent growth spurt accounts for approximately 25 percent of adult height and 50 percent of adult weight. Additionally, girls develop reproductive capacity during this time and dieting behaviors and nutrition can have an enormous impact on their gynecologic health (Seidenfeld and Rickert 2001).

While they can all occur independently, the interrelationship between the three parts of the triad is such that one component will affect another. In order to understand the physiological beginning of this syndrome, one must first realize that, in addition to the calories required for basal metabolic rate and physical activity, calories are required for menstruation, building and repairing muscle, healing and, in younger athletes, growth (Papanek 2003). The pathophysiology of the triad can be explained by a caloric deficit which disrupts the release of gonadotropin-releasing hormone, resulting in low levels of gonadotropins and secondarily reduced levels of estrogen and progesterone, leading to amenorrhea and osteopenia (Elford and Spence 2002).

Disordered eating behavior affects the number of calories available for normal life function. Manore (1999) states that any athlete, regardless of size, who consumes less than 1,800 calories per day is unable to meet caloric and nutrient requirements. Furthermore, a female athlete exercising 10 to 20 hours per week requires at least 2,200 to 2,500 calories per day to maintain body weight.

Negative Caloric Balance and Amenorrhea

Dueck, et al., (1996) reported that the average difference between amenorrheic and eumenorrheic athletes was only a caloric balance deficit of 250 calories per day. Many athletes do not realize the nutritional demands of their sports and, thus, it is this disordered eating that causes a negative caloric balance leading to amenorrhea (Papanek 2003). Even as early as 1981, Frisch, et al., found that amenorrheic competitive runners had an average intake of 1,700 calories per day, whereas eumenorrheic runners consumed 2,200 calories per day.

In addition to a caloric deficit due to disordered eating, physical training intensity plays an important role in the triad syndrome. Even if caloric deprivation does not occur through

disordered eating, negative caloric imbalance can result from failing to support the training regimen with adequate recovery. Primary and secondary amenorrhea can occur in the context of eating disorders or intense athletics (Rome 2003). DiPietro and Stachenfeld support this by adding that a chronic negative energy balance, being underweight and exercise stress are important elements in the pathway to amenorrhea (1997). Cobb, et al., (2003) write that female athletes with disordered eating may limit their calorie and/or fat intakes but maintain high training levels, often resulting in a state of chronic energy deficit. Athletic amenorrhea occurs more frequently in activities such as running, ballet and gymnastics, in which intense physical training is combined with the desire to maintain a lean build (Warren 1980).

Osteoporosis and Negative Caloric Balance

Bones require a normal level of systemic hormones, adequate caloric intake (including protein, calcium and vitamin D, in particular) and regular, weight-bearing exercise throughout life (O'brien 2001). Exercise's effects on the growing skeleton are complex and influenced by many factors, including the nature and intensity of the activity, skeleton area primarily involved, body weight and dietary calcium intake (Stein and Shane 2003). Although moderate exercise protects against osteoporosis, too little or excessive exercise may actually cause it (O'brien 2001).

> **"In general, women struggle with the perception of the 'perfect body image' society has unfairly placed upon them. Regardless of the circumstances, we as health care providers, coaches and parents are ultimately responsible for protecting the wellness of the young women in our care. Therefore, we must provide a proper wellness environment by nurturing sound physical training and nutritional habits."**

The minimum daily calcium requirement is 1,300 milligrams for people ages 11 to 23. Unfortunately, 85 percent of adolescent females do not consume this amount (National Institutes of Health and Child Development Publication 2001). Attitudes about their bodies during puberty can contribute to the dietary changes adolescent females make. This can lead to possible chronic dieting disorders, resulting in low bone mass and a risk for osteoporotic fractures later in life (Ali and Siktberg 1996).

Osteoporosis is a prevalent AN complication. In fact, the duration of AN is a predictor of low bone mineral density because the longer the illness lasts, the greater bone mineral density is reduced (Mehler 2003). For example, more than 50 percent of female patients with AN develop osteoporosis (Treasure and Surpell 2001). Miller and Klibanski (1999) add that the lack of nutrition is so severe in anorexics that an increased osteoporosis risk may exist due to associated endocrine abnormalities, including estrogen deficiency.

Amenorrhea and Osteoporosis

Continuing the triad syndrome's assault on the female athlete's wellness is the relationship between the absence of menses and bone deterioration. Some athletes see amenorrhea as a sign of appropriate training levels, while others regard it as a great solution to a monthly inconvenience (National Institutes of Health 2003). There is a prevailing myth in women's athletics that equates a disrupted menstrual cycle with the appropriate level of elite training (Papanek 2003). Mickelsfield, et al., (1995) state that amenorrheic/oligomenorrheic athletes on average have lower bone mineral density than eumenorrheic controls. Stein and Shane (2003) agree that low bone mineral density is a consequence of exercise-induced amenorrhea. Osteopenia or significantly reduced bone mass occurring with prolonged loss of menses has been associated with an increased risk of stress fractures (Mansfield and Emans 1993).

Summary

The female triad is a unique phenomenon that does not occur overnight but rather appears to gradually infiltrate female adolescents' lifestyle. Under intense pressure from parents, coaches teammates and often themselves, many young women begin to fall into patterns of disordered eating and/or overintense caloric expenditure without the support of adequate rest and nutrition. The triad is especially troubling due to the fact that, while each affliction can occur independently, they often are interrelated by a chain reaction. Amenorrhea/oligomenorrhea is likely to follow the caloric imbalance, which leads to osteopenia and ultimately osteoporosis. This downward spiral can result in termination of an athletic career as well as a chronically unhealthy adult life.

Identification of the triad can be difficult. When confronted by family, friends, coaches and physicians about their eating behavior, athletes can be anywhere from elusive in their explanation to perfectly convincing that nothing is wrong. Although it is more common to find this syndrome affecting athletic women, it is certainly not exclusive to this population. In general, women struggle with the perception of the "perfect body image" society has unfairly placed upon them. Regardless of the circumstances, we as health care providers, coaches and parents are ultimately responsible for protecting the wellness of the young women in our care. Therefore, we must provide a proper wellness environment by nurturing sound physical training and nutritional habits.

References

Ali, N. and Siktberg, L. "Osteoporosis prevention in female adolescents: Calcium intake and exercise participation," *Pediatr. Nurs.* 1996, 27 (2), 132-9.

Beals, K.A. and Manore, M.M. "Behavioral, psychological and physical characteristics of female athletes with subclinical eating disorders." *Int. J. Sports Nutr. Exerc. Metab.,* 2000, 10, 128-43.

Calabrese, L.H. "Nutritional and medical aspects of gymnastics." *Clin. Sports Med.,* 1985, 4, 23-37.

Cobb, K.L., et al. "Disordered eating, menstrual irregularity, and bone mineral density in female runners." *Med. Sci. Sports Exerc.,* 2003, 35 (5), 711-9.

DiPietro, L. and Stachenfeld, N.S. "The female athletic triad: American College of Sports Medicine position." *Med. Sci. Sports Exerc.,* 1997, 29, I-IX.

Donaldson, M.C. "The female athlete triad: A growing health concern." *Orthop. Nurs.,* 2003, 22 (5), 322-3.

Dueck, C.A., Manore, M.M. and Matt, K.S. "Role of energy balance in athletic menstrual dysfunction." *Int. J. Sports Nutr.,* 1996, 6, 165-190.

Elford, K.J. and Spence, J.E.H. "The forgotten female: Pediatric and adolescent gynecological concerns and their reproductive consequences." *J. Pediatr. Adolesc. Gynecol.,* 2002, 15 (2), 83-105.

Frisch, R.E., Gotz-Welbergen, A.V. and McArthur, J.W. "Delayed menarche and amenorrhea of college athletes in relation to age of onset of training." *JAMA,* 1981, 246, 1559.

Gidwani, G. and Rome, E. "Eating Disorders." *Clin. Obstet. Gynaecol.,* 1997, 40 (3), 601.

Hobart, J. and Smucker, D. "The female triad." *Am. Fam. Physician,* 2000, 61, 3357-64, 3367.

Kann, L., et al. "Youth risk behavior surveillance-United States, 1997." *MMWR,* 1998, 47 (SS-3), 1-89.

Manore, M.M. "Nutritional needs of the female athlete." *Clin. Sports Med.,* 1999, 18, 549-63.

Mansfield, M.J. and Emans, S.J. "Growth in female gymnasts: Should training decrease puberty?" *J. Pediatr.,* 1993, 122, 237-40.

Marshal, L.A. "Clinical evaluation of amenorrhea in active and athletic women." *Clin. Sports Med.,* 1994, 13, 371-87.

Mehler, P.S. "Osteoporosis in anorexia nervosa: Prevention and treatment." *Int. J. Eat. Disord.,* 2003, 33 (2), 113-26.

Mickelsfield, L.K., et al. "Bone mineral density in mature, premenopausal ultramarathon runners." *Med. Sci. Sports Exerc.,* 1995, 27, 688-96.

Miller, K.K. and Klibanski, A. "Amenorrheic bone loss." *J. Clin. Endocrinol. Metab.,* 1999, 84, 1775-83.

National Institutes of Health. "Fitness and Bone Health: The skeletal risk of overtraining." *National Resource Center,* 2003, Bethesda, Maryland.

National Institutes of Health and Child Development Publication. "Why milk matters now for children and teens under childhood adolescent nutrition." January 2001, no. 00-4864.

Nativ, A., et al. "The female athlete triad." *Clin. Sports Med.,* 1994, 13, 405-18.

Nelson, M. *Strong Women, Strong Bones.* New York: G.P Putnam's and Sons, 2000.

O'brien, M. "Exercise and osteoporosis." *Ir. J. Med. Sci.,* 2001, 170 (1), 58-62.

Papanek, P.E. "The female athlete triad: An emerging role for physical therapy." *J. Orthop. Sports Phys. Ther.,* 2003, 33 (10), 594-614.

Rome, E.S. "Eating disorders." *Obs. Gyn. Clin.,* 2003, 30 (2), 353-77.

Rosen, L.W. and Hough, D.O. "Pathogenic weight-control behaviors of female college gymnasts." *Phys. Sports Med.,* 1988, 16, 140-3.

Seidenfeld, M.D. and Rickert, V.I. "Impact of anorexia, bulimia and obesity on the gynecologic health of adolescents." *Am. Fam. Physician,* 2001, 64 (3), 445-50.

Shafer, M.B. and Irwin, C.E. "The adolescent patient." In Rudolf A. M., ed. *Rudolf's Pediatrics.* 19th ed. Norwalk: Appleton & Lange, 1991: 39.

Stein, E. and Shane, E. "Secondary osteoporosis." *Endocrinol.* Metab. Clin., 2003, 32 (1) 889-92.

Treasure, J. and Serpell, L. "Osteoporosis in young people. Research and treatment in eating disorders." *Psychiatr. Clin. North Am.,* 2001, 24 (2), 359-70.

Warren, M.P. "The effects of exercise on pubertal progression and reproductive function in girls." *J. Clin. Endocrinol.* Metab., 1980, 51, 1150.

Wilmore, J.H. and Costill, D.L. *Physiology of Sport and Exercise.* Champaign: Human Kinetics, 1999.

Yeager, K.K., et al. "The female athlete triad: disordered eating, amenorrhea, osteoporosis." *Med. Sci. Sports and Exerc.,* 1999, 25: 775-7.

LOLA RAMOS is pursuing her bachelor's degree in kinesiology and health promotion at California State University, Fullerton. She has recently completed an academic internship through the SpeciFit Foundation.

GREGORY L. WELCH, M.S., is an exercise physiologist and president of SpeciFit, An Agency of Wellness and Competitive Performance Enhancement, located in Seal Beach, California. He is also founder and CEO of the SpeciFit Foundation, a non-profit entity providing wellness concepts for adolescent women. Welch has published several articles regarding wellness of older adults and through his foundation has added adolescent women to the category of special populations. He can be reached at (562) 431-5206 and www.specifit.com.

How Sleep Affects Your Weight

DAVID SCHARDT

Are the sleepless counting doughnuts and pies instead of sheep? "Americans sleep less than they used to, and this could be part of the reason why more of us are now overweight," says David Dinges, Chief of the Division of Sleep and Chronobiology at the University of Pennsylvania School of Medicine.

Over the past 40 years, Americans have cut their snooze time by one to two hours a night. We now sleep less than people in any other industrialized country. And researchers are discovering that sleep affects hormones that regulate satiety, hunger, and how efficiently you burn calories.

Too little sleep may make you hungry, especially for calorie-dense foods, and may prime your body to try to hold on to the calories you eat. It may also boost your insulin levels, which increases the risk of heart disease and diabetes.

The Sleep-Weight Link

"Obesity is obviously a very complex issue, and no one is suggesting that lack of sleep is the cause of the obesity epidemic," says Carl Hunt, director of the National Center on Sleep Disorders Research at the National Institutes of Health in Bethesda, Maryland.

"But new research certainly supports the idea that sleeping less may be a previously unknown but important contributor to the obesity epidemic in the U.S."

The link between sleep and weight was first noticed in the 1990s, when European researchers were puzzling over why so many children were getting heavier.

"They were surprised to discover that it wasn't how much TV a child watched, but how much sleep the child got, that best predicted whether he or she was overweight," says Dinges. "The less children slept, the heavier they were."

Researchers in the U.S. are finding the same link in adults.

In the Wisconsin Sleep Cohort Study, which tracks the sleep habits of nearly 3,000 middle-aged state government employees, those who reported that they typically slept less than eight hours a night were more likely to be overweight.[1]

And researchers at Columbia University in New York City found that people who slept six hours a night were 23 percent more likely to be obese than people who slept between seven and nine hours. Those who slept five hours were 50 percent

more likely—while those who slept four hours or less were 73 percent more likely—to be obese.

The connection between hours slept and weight wasn't significant for people 60 and older, says James Gangwisch, a psychiatric epidemiologist at Columbia, "probably because the sleep problems that are so common in older people obscure the link." (The analysis hasn't yet been published.)

Leapin' Leptin

Why would people who sleep less weigh more?

"The results are somewhat counterintuitive," says Gangwisch, since people burn more calories when they're awake. "We think it has more to do with what happens to your body when you deprive it of sleep, as opposed to the amount of physical activity you get."

What happens involves two hormones: Leptin, which is released by fat cells, signals the brain to *stop* eating. Ghrelin (pronounced GRELL-lin), which is made in the stomach, is a signal to *keep* eating. The two influence whether you go for a second helping or push yourself away from the table.

"Studies have shown that leptin levels are lower and ghrelin levels are higher in people who sleep fewer hours," says Gangwisch.

In the Wisconsin Sleep Cohort Study, those who slept for five hours had 15 percent lower leptin levels and 15 percent higher ghrelin levels than those who slept for eight hours.[1]

While the study wasn't designed to prove whether sleep deprivation causes changes in leptin and ghrelin levels, new research at the University of Chicago suggests that it does.

When Eve Van Cauter and co-workers limited 12 healthy young men to just four hours of sleep for two consecutive nights, their leptin levels were 18 percent lower and their ghrelin levels were 28 percent higher than after two nights of sleeping for ten hours.[2]

"The combination of low leptin and high ghrelin is likely to increase appetite," says Wisconsin Sleep Cohort Study researcher Emmanuel Mignot of Stanford University (though "short sleepers may also have more time to overeat," he points out).

In fact, the men in Van Cauter's study said that they were more hungry—and that they'd be more likely to eat salty foods like chips and nuts; sweets like cake, candy, and ice cream; and starchy foods like bread, cereal, and potatoes—after four hours of sleep than after ten hours.

Compounding the problem: the brain interprets a drop in leptin as a sign of starvation. So it responds not only by boosting hunger, but by burning fewer calories. That means you put on more weight even if you don't eat any more food.

Sweet Dreams

Sleep deprivation may stimulate more than your appetite.

"It also affects insulin resistance and blood glucose levels, which are two important components of the metabolic syndrome," says Carl Hunt of the National Center on Sleep Disorders Research.

The metabolic syndrome, also called insulin resistance syndrome, is a cluster of symptoms that increases the risk of heart attack, stroke, and diabetes. Signs of the syndrome are abdominal obesity, low HDL ("good") cholesterol, and elevated (though not necessarily high) triglycerides, blood pressure, and blood sugar.

When the University of Chicago's Eve Van Cauter and her colleagues limited 11 healthy men in their 20s to four hours of sleep for six straight nights, "it brought them to a nearly prediabetic state."

Their bodies were 40 percent less able to clear glucose from their blood and 30 percent slower in releasing insulin than when they were allowed to sleep for twelve hours.[3] In fact, four hours of sleep for six consecutive nights gave the young men the insulin sensitivity of 70- or 80-year-olds.

"We didn't expect to see a change of that magnitude," says Van Cauter.

(Insulin is a hormone that lets glucose, or blood sugar, enter the body's cells, where the sugar is burned for energy. When people are insulin insensitive, or insulin resistant, their insulin doesn't work efficiently.)

"The consensus that prevailed until recently was that sleep is for the brain, not for the rest of the body," says Van Cauter. "But sleep really affects everything. We are not wired biologically for sleep deprivation. We're the only animal that intentionally sleeps less than we need to."

Notes

1. *PLoS Med. 1:e62* 2004 (Epub.).
2. *Ann. Intern. Med. 141:* 846, 2004.
3. *Lancet 354*: 1435, 1999.

"Fat Chance"

Doesn't "everyone know" that serving supersize meals to a young couch potato with plus-size parents is a sure recipe for an obese child? So why is the current epidemic of childhood obesity such a mystery to science?

SUSAN OKIE

Rudolph L. Leibel's genes may have predisposed him to become a scientist, but his decision to spend his life trying to discover the causes of obesity was environmental happenstance, the result of a chance encounter. In the spring of 1977, Randall, a severely overweight child, and Randall's mother showed up at the pediatric clinic of Cambridge Hospital in Massachusetts, where Leibel was a specialist in hormone disorders. Leibel could find no evidence that hormone deficiency or, indeed, any other known medical condition, was the cause of Randall's obesity. But what struck the young doctor was the response of Randall's mother when Leibel told her there was little he or anyone else could do for her son: "Let's get out of here, Randall," she snapped. "This doctor doesn't know s--t."

Chastened by her words, Leibel soon traded his hospital post for the low-paying toil of a rookie laboratory scientist. At the Rockefeller University laboratory of Jules Hirsch, a leading figure in research on obesity, Leibel and Hirsch conducted extensive studies of weight homeostasis: how the body responds both to weight gain and weight loss by fighting to restore the status quo ante.

In one of the studies, volunteers were induced to overeat to gain weight—a task that proved remarkably difficult. Whether they were fat or lean at the outset, the volunteers' bodies responded by turning up the metabolic rate, boosting the levels of certain hormones, reducing hunger, and burning up more calories as heat—all in a coordinated effort by the autonomic nervous system to restore the body's original weight. By contrast, when volunteers' food intake was restricted in order to promote weight loss, their bodies fought back even more fiercely: metabolisms slowed; the volunteers moved around less often and, even when they were exercising, their muscles burned fewer calories; and everyone felt constantly and uncomfortably hungry. A host of physiological defense mechanisms had swung into play, all aimed at regaining the lost pounds.

Such tight physiological regulation of body weight persuaded Leibel that a chemical signal from the body's stores of fat was being sent to the brain. Leibel's hypothesis led to the discovery of a gene that coded for the hormone leptin, which is produced by fat cells. Animal studies soon proved that leptin does indeed pass through the circulatory system to the brain.

Could leptin be the key player in the signaling system Leibel had envisioned? If the brain detected enough leptin, would it decide that enough fat cells were storing energy, and so conclude that it was safe to stop eating? Sure enough, mice that could not produce leptin ate nonstop and grew enormously obese. Treating such mice with leptin normalized their body weight.

The gene for leptin was identified and sequenced as the result of an intensive collaborative effort between Leibel and his Rockefeller colleague Jeffrey M. Friedman. When the announcement was made in 1994, it was greeted with much fanfare. Many people (along with some drug companies) predicted that the newly identified gene would enable the hormone to become a miracle cure for obesity. It has not turned out that way.

Some evidence suggests body weight reaches a "set point" during puberty. So untreated childhood obesity can lead to the medical risks of adult obesity.

Today, instead, the United States and many other countries are faced with an epidemic. Most people tend to think of an epidemic as an outbreak of a contagious illness. But to public health officials, obesity rates since the mid 1980s have exploded dramatically and unexpectedly, just as if they reflected the outbreak of a new infectious disease. Noting that obesity and physical inactivity, along with tobacco smoking, are the major causes of "noncommunicable diseases," the World Health Organization estimated that 60 percent of the 56 million deaths worldwide in 2001 were caused by such obesity-related illnesses as heart disease and type 2 diabetes. Among children, obesity can have adverse effects that persist for life, just as surely as a virus can. For example, there is evidence suggesting that a person's general body weight reaches a "set point" sometime during puberty, and so extreme obesity in childhood, left untreated, carries with it all the health risks of obesity for the rest of one's life: substantial increases in the risks of diabetes, heart disease, and other adverse medical consequences. Some officials have even begun to respond with the kind of alarm that might greet the global resurgence of polio. As David L. Katz of the Yale School of Public Health puts it:

Children growing up in the United States today will suffer more chronic disease and premature death because of the way they eat and [because of] their lack of physical activity than [they will] from exposure to tobacco, drugs, and alcohol combined.

Even though the discovery of leptin has not led to a cure for childhood obesity, it has helped to show that the condition is largely biological, and not simply the result of faulty parenting or lack of willpower. And the years since the discovery have been hailed as a golden age for obesity research. In little more than a decade, investigators have sketched, in broad outlines, the biological system that regulates body weight. They have also learned a great deal about genetic vulnerability to obesity.

The control centers for tracking energy balance and regulating body weight are situated primarily in the hypothalamus, a small part of the brain that specializes in integrating messages from many parts of the body and orchestrating the organism's response to its environment [see illustration on opposite page]. The hypothalamus communicates via nerve pathways and chemical signals with many other areas of the brain, as well as with the organs of the cardiovascular, digestive, reproductive, and endocrine systems (the latter encompasses the glands that secrete the hormones circulating in the blood).

The output of the hypothalamus can fine-tune a number of unconscious processes that affect a person's weight, such as the rate at which the body burns calories in carrying out certain cellular processes or through spontaneous muscle activity, such as fidgeting. Conceptually, at least, understanding how the body controls such unconscious processes is fairly straightforward. What is surprising for some people is that signals from the hypothalamus also affect the cerebral cortex, the "thinking" part of the brain. The hypothalamus can modify such conscious, purposeful behaviors as food-seeking, simply by increasing or decreasing the appetite. As Leibel puts it, those unconscious signals contribute to such conscious actions as ordering a pizza or having a second piece of pie. Just because a behavior is conscious, he adds, doesn't mean that all aspects of it are voluntary.

To exert its control, the hypothalamus needs reliable, relevant information about the body's current need for food. But where does that information come from? Leptin and, to a lesser extent, insulin carry information about long-term energy depots. The level of leptin in the blood reflects how much fat is stored in the body. Its chief function seems to be to protect energy stores and prevent starvation. When a human or other mammal's food intake is severely restricted, leptin levels drop within twenty-four hours—well before fat stores have been materially depleted by being burned for energy. The fall in leptin immediately prompts the hypothalamus to lower the metabolic rate, increase the appetite, and, to some extent, suppress the reproductive and immune systems so as to focus the body's resources on gaining food.

Insulin, the hormone produced by the beta cells of the pancreas, is released into the bloodstream in response to glucose from food. It helps the body maintain a balance between storing glucose and fat and burning them. Insulin also serves as another signal to certain nerve cells in the brain, informing them about the body's overall nutritional status. The brain also receives messages from the digestive tract. Constant updates about food availability and the timing of meals are relayed to the hypothalamus by various messenger molecules released by cells in the stomach and intestinal tract.

What about the genetics? If Randall were Leibel's young patient today, the boy might undergo testing for a genetic cause of his obesity. A few unlucky people are born with a single genetic mutation that stacks the deck against them so overwhelmingly that they become severely overweight almost no matter what the environment. At least five distinct "obesity genes" have been identified so far. Each of them is so critical to the regulation of appetite and food intake that certain mutations in any of them can lead to extreme obesity.

The mutations that cause such "monogenic," or single-gene, obesity are quite rare. Moreover, even if a physician can diagnose such a condition, there is still no guarantee that it can be treated successfully. Nevertheless, monogenic cases of severe obesity have helped investigators understand how the body regulates food intake and fat stores in people without such debilitating mutations. And even though monogenic obesity is rare, Leibel notes, it does reinforce the idea that specific molecules are highly potent in determining energy balance and body weight in humans.

What about the vast majority of overweight children and adults, whose obesity is not the result of a single defective gene? The scientific consensus is that such people may have multiple genes whose net effect predisposes them to eat a few extra calories, burn up a bit less energy than they take in, or store the excess as fat. Like the members of a band, the genes in each person's personal collection play together, along with various factors in the environment, to determine the person's specific vulnerability to becoming overweight.

How many genes might be at play? Investigators don't yet know. At first, just after leptin was discovered, many people thought there must be a single obesity gene, and some believed it had been found. Now at least sixty genes are being investigated, and some workers fear that as many as a hundred genes could be contributing to the obesity risk.

Leibel's own suspicion, after examining patterns of obesity inheritance in families drawn from various populations and ethnic groups, is that the number of important players is much smaller. He suggests that each person may have as many as a dozen genes that combine to determine the individual risk of obesity. Some genes—perhaps six or seven of them—are probably major players that help determine the likelihood of obesity in people all over the planet. The rest of the dozen or so genes may have arisen from gene variants more common in one ethnic population than in another. That, says Leibel, is what makes the genetics so complicated. No one knows which genes are major players, and which genes are minor ones. And so the geneticists have no way of knowing how to apportion their efforts.

Most people, of course, do not become severely obese, even in today's calorie-rich environment. The average person consumes between 7.5 million and 10 million calories per decade, yet Americans and people in other developed countries typically gain only half a pound to a pound a year throughout their adult lives. To gain any weight at all, they must eat more calories than they burn—but the amount needed to account for the typical weight gain is only about ten to twenty calories a day. That's about the equivalent of one Ritz cracker, or less than 1 percent of the average adult's daily intake.

A calorie imbalance that small can't be reliably measured by studying people in their normal habitat. To study how weight gain and loss quantitatively affect people's appetite and metabolism, Leibel and his associates had to confine volunteers to hospital research wards and measure every mouthful. They found, surprisingly, that obese people do not eat more than lean people in proportion to their body size. Nor do obese people have slower metabolisms than lean ones, as long as they remain at what is their own "normal" weight. They still balance their calorie intake and output very precisely to maintain a constant weight, just as lean people do. It's just that the weight they maintain is higher.

To gain half a pound to a pound a year, an adult needs to eat just ten to twenty calories a day more than she burns. That's about the equivalent of one Ritz cracker.

Yet the laws of thermodynamics dictate that people who are overweight must, at some point, have taken in more energy than they spent in order to gain the extra pounds. "There's no way around it," Leibel says. "You cannot eat like a canary and become the size of a pterodactyl." But in most cases, once obese people have reached a personal set point determined by their own physiology, their weight stabilizes. Their food intake and their metabolic rates, when adjusted for their body size, are similar to those of lean people.

When a person loses weight, however, the circumstances shift dramatically. Whether people start out lean or obese, when they lose 10 to 20 percent of their body weight, their bodies respond by becoming more efficient and using less energy, in an effort to conserve calories and replenish lost reserves of fat. The reduction in energy expenditure is about 15 percent larger than would be expected for the amount of weight lost. That almost certainly accounts for some of the tremendous recidivism among dieters, Leibel says. Studies suggest that some 95 percent of people who lose weight by dieting gain it back within five years.

So though genes determine individual vulnerability to weight gain, environmental factors help dictate the outcome—the weight that a person reaches during childhood or adulthood. Imagine, Leibel says, that you can rank a hundred people, on the basis of their genetic endowment, from 1 to 100 according to their tendency to store excess calories as body fat. Then that same genetic ranking will tell you how they'll line up relative to one another in most environments. What it won't tell you, though, is what those hundred people will look like in any particular environment. For example, if a hundred people were ex-

posed to famine and had to subsist on a starvation diet, they would all become thin—but some would lose less weight than others, according to their genetic endowments.

In spite of the scientific progress made in disentangling the body's complex systems for regulating food intake, energy use, and energy storage, no one really knows how to treat most cases of obesity. Meanwhile, most of the developed world is facing an expanding public health crisis that clearly has not arisen because of newly mutated genes. Obesity is increasing at an unprecedented rate in the United States, and in many other countries as well. For example: in a study conducted in Europe between 1983 and 1986, more than half of the adults between the ages of thirty-five and sixty-five were either overweight or obese; and even in Japan and China, and throughout Southeast Asia, obesity rates have risen sharply during the past two decades. Recent shifts in the modern environment are undoubtedly at the root of the epidemic. People eat more and move around less. Most of us in the developed world enjoy an abundance of cheap, tasty, high-calorie foods, rely on cars, elevators, and other forms of motorized transportation, and lead sedentary lifestyles, in part because of the difficulty of incorporating walking and other kinds of activity into our daily routines.

Such a "toxic environment," in the words of Kelly D. Brownell, a health psychologist at Yale University, is playing on individual genetic vulnerability, thereby causing unhealthy weight gain in increasing numbers of people. And if environmental factors are at fault, then by changing the environment—or by learning ways whereby we can consciously change our responses to it—it may be possible to slow down or even reverse the trend. Nevertheless, one must sound a cautionary note on what may be too sanguine an assessment: obesity experts who are studying the epidemic think that a comprehensive solution to the rise in obesity will require broad environmental and social changes—a daunting task.

Leibel is proud that his genetic research has helped put a stop to "blaming the victim," shifting the blame for fatness away from the people who suffer from it. The continuing discovery of obesity genes is proof that biological variation in vulnerability to weight gain is the main reason some people are fat and others are lean. That's why Leibel views much of the current national debate about measures to prevent obesity with some concern. He points out that no one yet knows precisely what actions will be most effective. "On some level this is a disease that everybody thinks they understand, and yet in fact nobody understands," he says. "We really don't know what has happened, other than on a very macro, thermodynamic level. Food intake is greater than energy expenditure. Period."

This article was adapted from Susan Okie's forthcoming book, *Fed Up! Winning the War against Childhood Obesity*, which is being published by Joseph Henry Press (http://www.jhpress.org) in September 2006.

From *Natural History,* February 2005, pp. 34-37. Excerpted from FED UP! WINNING THE WAR AGAINST CHILDHOOD OBESITY by Susan Okie.

Why We're Losing the War Against Obesity

About two-thirds of all adult Americans are fat, but what's alarming is that more children and teenagers are overweight, and as they grow up, their health problems will have huge repercussions for our society.

LOUISE WITT

The first time Krista Pournaras, 16, remembers dieting was when she was 6 years old. She was gaining weight like "mad," packing on 30 pounds in one year alone. By second grade, it was obvious Pournaras was fat. That's when her mother Lynn Katekovich, a nurse, took her to a pediatrician, who put the young girl on a strict diet that didn't allow any between-meal snacks, not even an apple.

That diet didn't work. Neither did the others. Pournaras went on low-fat diets, she tried Weight Watchers, she even took diet pills. She'd bike around the neighborhood, go to the gym and swim at the local YMCA. Pournaras would lose a few pounds, but then she'd gain them back or gain even more. This year, when Pournaras, who stands slightly taller then 5'2", started her junior year at the local vo-tech in Conway, Pa., north of Pittsburgh, she weighed 245 pounds. She couldn't play with her dogs without becoming short of breath and feeling achy. This summer Pournaras discovered her weight had seriously affected her health: She had high blood pressure and elevated insulin levels, putting her at risk for Type 2 diabetes, and Polycystic Ovarian Syndrome, a condition in which a female has heightened levels of testosterone.

After Katekovich, who owns a medical staffing company, found out her daughter was likely to develop heart disease and diabetes, she cried. That's when she decided to talk to her about having bariatric surgery. Katekovich and her two sisters had had the drastic procedure in January 2003. Since then, the 44-year-old Katekovich, who had weighed 264, has lost 100 pounds. With bariatric surgery the stomach is reduced by 90 percent—to the size of the top joint of the thumb—and the large intestines are bypassed. On Nov. 12, Dr. Philip Schauer, director of Bariatric Surgery at Magee Women's Hospital in Pittsburgh, operated on Pournaras.

"I was against the surgery," Pournaras says. "But my mom and Dr. Schauer talked to me and said that if I didn't do something about my health, I'd die much younger, younger than usual. I want to be happier about myself and not have as many health problems."

Getting Worse Faster

Pournaras's extreme solution may be unusual, but her weight problem isn't. About 9 million children and adolescents in the U.S. are overweight or obese. That's roughly 15 percent of the children and adolescents between the ages of 6 and 19 who are overweight or obese, according to the latest data compiled during 1999 and 2000 by the Centers for Disease Control and Preventions National Center for Health Statistics. Health officials and physicians blame children's poor eating habits—having supersized portions of junk food and sweetened soft drinks—and physical inactivity, such as watching TV; playing video games or clicking away on PCs, instead of playing. Just take a look at the numbers from a little more than 30 years earlier to see how rapidly children's health has deteriorated: In a similar CDC survey taken from 1971 to 1974, 4 percent of children between the ages of 6 and 11 were overweight or obese, and 6 percent of adolescents between the ages of 12 and 19 were overweight or obese.

And, the nation's obesity problem will only worsen. As today's young people grow older, it's estimated that 3 in 4 overweight children will become fat adults and will suffer from obesity-related diseases at earlier ages than previous generations. Already, about two-thirds of all adults are overweight and about 31 percent of those are considered obese. Generally, if someone weighs more than 30 pounds above his ideal weight, then he's considered obese. The CDC considers someone overweight if his body mass index, or BMI, a calculation based on height and weight, is more than 25. If a person's BMI is over 30, then he is considered obese. Health officials have now deemed obesity in America a health epidemic.

Weighing in

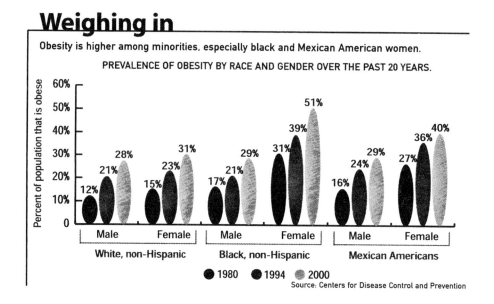

Obesity is higher among minorities, especially black and Mexican American women.

PREVALENCE OF OBESITY BY RACE AND GENDER OVER THE PAST 20 YEARS.

Percent of population that is obese

White, non-Hispanic — Male: 12%, 21%, 28% / Female: 15%, 23%, 31%
Black, non-Hispanic — Male: 17%, 21%, 29% / Female: 31%, 39%, 51%
Mexican Americans — Male: 16%, 24%, 29% / Female: 27%, 36%, 40%

● 1980 ● 1994 ● 2000

Source: Centers for Disease Control and Prevention

By 2010, only six years away, about 40 percent of all adult Americans, or 68 million, will be obese. If trends continue, almost every single American will be overweight, or obese, (except the few that are genetically prone to have higher metabolisms) by 2040, says John Foreyt, director of Behavioral Medicine Research Center at Baylor College of Medicine in Houston. "It may happen more quickly," he says. "Twenty years ago, it was unusual to see a 300-pound person in my clinic, now we see it all the time. And it used to be we'd see obesity only in adults, but now we see it in children. This may be the first generation of children who will die before their parents."

Foreyt based his projections on data collected from the CDC's Health and Nutritional Examination Surveys, which record actual weights and heights of Americans surveyed, showing that the U.S. population has become much heavier in the past 20 years. In 1980, 46 percent of the adult population was overweight or obese. In 1990, 56 percent was overweight or obese. In 2000, the percent jumped to 64.5 percent. That's 1 percentage point gain a year. Foreyt says part of the problem is that Americans eat 200 more calories a day than they did 10 years ago. Over a year, those extra calories add up to 20 pounds.

Efforts to Reverse Trend

In an effort to slow the rate of increase in obesity, and maybe even reverse the trend, the U.S. Surgeon General's office requested $125 million in the 2004 budget to expand the Healthier US Initiative, a campaign President George W. Bush announced in June 2002 to encourage Americans to eat healthier and exercise more. The 2003 budget was $25 million. In November, the Surgeon General teamed up with the American Academy of Pediatrics, Nike Inc. and McNeil Nutritionals, maker of Splenda artificial sweetner, to launch Shaping America's Youth. Initially, this program intends to find out the scope of children's weight problems and identify community resources available to help them.

"It's an extraordinary project because there are children out there who are sedentary and who eat indiscriminately," says Dr. Richard H. Carmona, the U.S. Surgeon General. "When [these children] are middle-aged and overweight, or obese, they will have Type 2 diabetes, hypertension and cardiovascular disease. We're making an unhealthy society for our children. We have to break that cycle; it affects all of us."

Costs Add Up

It's difficult to put a price tag on what it costs people who are overweight to live in a society that values thinness and fitness. What's the price of a chubby teenager who is so fearful of being mocked by classmates that he decides not to go college? Yet, for more tangible expenses, the CDC estimates that in 2000, the latest figures available, obesity cost $117 billion: $56 billion in lost productivity and $61 billion in medical treatments. About 300,000 deaths a year are attributed to obesity-related diseases. "That's approaching the costs for treating people with tobacco-related diseases," says Mary Kay Sones, a spokesperson with the CDC's National Center for Chronic Disease Prevention and Health Promotion in Atlanta.

That may be an underestimate, because obesity has so many ramifications. It contributes to higher incidences of cancer, specifically kidney cancer, and orthopedic complications, due to the excess stress on bones and cartilage. Diabetes alone costs about $130 billion a year. The disease can cause blindness, kidney failure, strokes and heart disease. It's estimated that diabetes shortens a person's life by 10 to 15 years. Dr. K.M. Venkat Narayan, chief of the CDC's diabetes epidemiology section, says the disease "has a high impact economically and in terms of suffering" for the patients.

The CDC estimates that 1 American in 3 born in 2000 will develop Type 2 diabetes, as they grow older; some while they're still young. In the past, people weren't usually diagnosed with the disease until they were in their 50s or 60s. If obesity trends con-

It's a Big Country

The maps compare obesity levels across the country in 1991 and today. It seems Colorado residents have been watching their weight, while Midwesterners and Southerners have been spreading out.

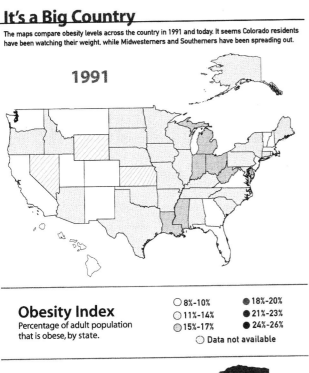

1991

Obesity Index
Percentage of adult population that is obese, by state.

○ 8%-10% ● 18%-20%
○ 11%-14% ● 21%-23%
◐ 15%-17% ● 24%-26%
○ Data not available

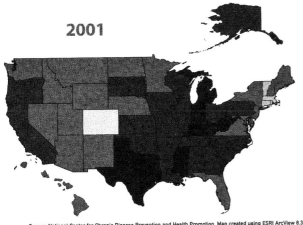

2001

Source: National Center for Chronic Disease Prevention and Health Promotion. Map created using ESRI ArcView 8.3

tinue, Narayan projects that in 50 years 28 million Americans will have diabetes, up from 17 million in 2003.

Ronald Sturm, an economist at Rand Corp., a think tank in Santa Monica, Calif., says the number of severely obese people is increasing at an even higher rate. To be considered severely obese a person has to have a BMI of 40 or higher. In 1986, 1 in 200 were considered severely obese. In 2000, that increased to 1 in 50. An average adult male would be roughly 100 pounds more than his ideal weight. For instance, a man who is 5'10" would weigh more than 300 pounds, and a woman who is 5'4" would be more than 250 pounds. Sturm, who studied people between the ages of 50 and 60, projects that by 2020, more than half of men will be obese and about a quarter of those will be severely obese.

Sturm estimates that in 2003 medical costs for an obese man who is 50 years old are $1,000 more a year than they are for a similarly aged man of normal weight. Costs for a severely obese

man would be $10,000 more. Sturm figures the costs would be slightly less for severely obese women: about $7,000 a year. That's not even taking into consideration more pricey measures. Bariatric surgery, for instance, costs about $25,000.

Ed Bernstein, executive director of the North American Association for the Study of Obesity in Silver Springs, Md., wants patients' who are under a doctor's care to be reimbursed for weight-loss costs. Currently, patients pay for their treatments, but then they can deduct those expenses from their federal income taxes. "We ridicule people for their health problem," Bernstein says. "We wouldn't do that for someone with diabetes, cancer or heart disease, but we do that with people who are obese....Your body fights you very hard when you try to lose weight. People do it; there are a few success stories. We're learning about what helps keep weight off, but it's not simple."

Who's Responsible Anyway?

Weight gain seems to be a simple calculation: more calories are consumed than are burned. But it's more complicated. Genes aren't solely responsible for the increase in obesity, but they do play a role. Forty percent of people's weight problems can be blamed on their genes, says Patrick O'Neil, a psychologist and director of the Weight Management Center at the Medical University of South Carolina in Charleston. That's because Homo sapiens evolved under conditions, requiring vigorous physical activity at a time when food supplies were uncertain.

"We're programmed to be able to store energy from our earlier days," O'Neil says. "As far as evolution goes, it's only yesterday that human beings have been on the planet." Today, Americans have ready access to tasty, cheap, high-caloric food. And in our modern society, we're less active. We drive instead of walking. We use a remote to change our TV channels instead of getting up to switch them. And we buy our food in supermarkets rather than hunt animals or raise crops. As he says, "Genes load the gun and the environment pulls the trigger."

Scientific studies suggest that many modern conveniences and luxuries lead to obesity, especially in children. One showed that school-age children who drank sweetened soft drinks had a total energy intake 10 percent higher than those who did not. Fast food is also thought to contribute to obesity because it tends to be high in saturated and trans fat—which increases LDL cholesterol, or bad cholesterol—high in sugar and served in large portions. Fast food also tends to be low in dietary fiber, nutrients and antioxidants.

Local Efforts in Schools

Faced with the burgeoning number of overweight students, state and local government have begun their own initiatives. Two of the nation's largest public school systems, New York City and Los Angeles, banned soda vending during school hours. (The L.A. ban becomes effective January 2004.) New York went a step further, prohibiting snack-food vending machines in schools and reducing the fat content in the school cafeteria food. In October, the L.A. school district followed, banning fried chips, candy and other junk foods from vending machines. The

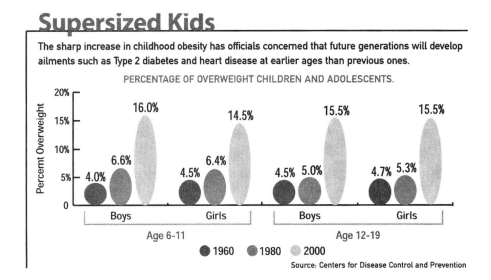

Supersized Kids

The sharp increase in childhood obesity has officials concerned that future generations will develop ailments such as Type 2 diabetes and heart disease at earlier ages than previous ones.

PERCENTAGE OF OVERWEIGHT CHILDREN AND ADOLESCENTS.

Source: Centers for Disease Control and Prevention

plan also calls on school administrators to end contracts with vendors who sell pizzas and burgers at some institutions.

Last summer, South Carolina started the South Carolina Nutrition Research Consortium, pooling the resources of Clemson University, the University of South Carolina and the Medical University in Charleston to tackle the state's growing overweight population. Almost 22 percent of the state's residents are obese, according to CDC data. "We were concerned about being a chubby state," says Peter Kent, a spokesman for Clemson University. "We're a state at risk."

Surgeon General Carmona says he would like food producers to assume a greater role in fighting obesity. He'd like them to make the nutritional contents of their products more available to consumers, make sure animals are raised under healthy conditions, promote healthy eating messages and offer healthier food options. Suing companies isn't the answer, he says. In 2002, two obese teenagers sued McDonald's, blaming the chain's poor labeling of the nutritional and caloric content in its fast food for their weight gain. The lawsuit was thrown out.

"Rather than make an enemy of corporate America, let's talk to them," Carmona says. "Let's make them part of the solution, rather than the problem."

Food Marketers Respond

Indeed, food companies have been taking steps to promote healthier eating habits. Kraft Foods Inc., maker of Oscar Mayer cold cuts, Velveeta and Oreo cookies, launched a global anti-obesity effort in July, which calls for smaller portion sizes and improving the nutritional content of some Kraft products. It also includes ending marketing in schools and setting up guidelines for marketing aimed at children. (A San Francisco man dropped a lawsuit last year against Kraft, after it agreed to reduce trans fat in Oreos.)

Recently, Pizza Hut added low-fat items and salads to its menu. Dubbed Fit 'N' Delicious, the pizzas have 25 percent less fat and 30 percent fewer calories. Ruby Tuesday, a restaurant chain, changed its cooking oil from soybean to canola and intro-

duced a low-carbohydrate menu. Burger King began offering salads and a new low-fat chicken sandwich, and KFC has a low-fat barbecue sandwich.

Liz Castells-Heard, president of Castells & Asociados Advertising in Los Angeles, says she used reports on the alarming number of overweight Hispanic youngsters to convince McDonald's to reach out to Hispanic customers with healthier menu items in its California and Texas markets. As a result, Castells-Heard says, the fast-food giant developed three new salads, a veggie burger, a chicken sandwich on whole wheat bread and yogurt parfaits.

Castells-Heard approached McDonald's after noticing that a higher number of Hispanics, especially youngsters, were overweight or obese than the overall U.S. population. According to the NCHS, 27.3 percent of Mexican American boys between the ages of 6 and 11 are overweight, compared with 12 percent of white non-Hispanic boys of the same age. For Mexican American males between 12 and 19 years old, 27.5 percent are overweight, compared with 12.8 percent of white non-Hispanics males in that age group. For Mexican American girls between the ages of 6 and 11, 19.6 percent are considered overweight. For Mexican American females between 12 and 19, about 19.4 percent are considered overweight, compared with 12.4 percent of their white non-Hispanic counterparts. "It's part of the Hispanic culture," says Castells-Heard. "They don't have that obsession that younger females have about getting so skinny, or being anorexic or bulimic—that's the good news. The bad news is that we have a higher rate of obesity."

Yet, Americans think that they are slimming down. In its latest survey, released in October, Port Washington, N.Y.-based NPD Group found that Americans said they weren't gaining weight. Of the 5,000 people in the study, 55 percent said they were overweight, compared with 56 percent the year before. "I've never seen that," said Harry Balzer, NPD's vice president, in a statement. "Looks like we're focusing on health again, a return to the '80s. People are interested in a balanced diet; they ate more fruits and vegetables last year than the year before and snacked less in the evening."

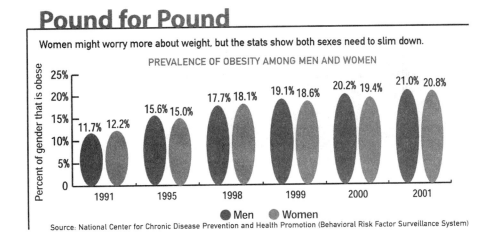

Pound for Pound

Women might worry more about weight, but the stats show both sexes need to slim down.

PREVALENCE OF OBESITY AMONG MEN AND WOMEN

Percent of gender that is obese

1991	1995	1998	1999	2000	2001
11.7% 12.2%	15.6% 15.0%	17.7% 18.1%	19.1% 18.6%	20.2% 19.4%	21.0% 20.8%

● Men ● Women

Source: National Center for Chronic Disease Prevention and Health Promotion (Behavioral Risk Factor Surveillance System)

NPD survey's respondents were more concerned with fat, cholesterol, sugar and food additives. Thirty-five percent said they plan nutritious meals, up from 32 percent in 2001. And 66 percent said they were strenuously exercising at least once a week, up from 63 percent in 2002. Fifty-three percent said they check food labels to avoid harmful substances, that's up from 51 percent in 2002. But Belzer added: "The question is which trends are the beginning of a new direction and which are short-term disruptions."

Tougher Measures Needed

The nation's anti-smoking campaign may be an indication of how hard it is to change people's lifestyles. The Surgeon General warned about the dangers of cigarette smoking in 1964. "Forty years down the line and we're still seeing 440,000 smoking-related deaths a year," says Dr. Carmona. "Obesity kills over 300,000. So, it's rapidly catching up and becoming the fastest growing killer of Americans. It will eclipse smoking in the near future. People are used to eating a certain way from their family and friends. We're talking about changing American culture. It's not cool to be the Marlboro man, but look how long it took us to get to that point."

Kelly D. Brownell, director of the Yale Center for Eating and Weight Disorders, doesn't think the Surgeon General's new anti-obesity program goes far enough. Americans have been bombarded with public service messages to eat healthier and exercise more for years with disappointing results. Brownell, coauthor of *Food Fight* (Contemporary Books, 2003) about America's food industry and the growing prevalence of obesity, thinks banning soft drinks and fast food in schools is a step in the right direction. But he says food advertising geared toward children must change. The average child is inundated with ads for fast food, candy, sugared cereals and soft drinks. "If parents ate every meal with their children and persuaded them to eat healthier, then that would be 1,000 messages for the parents and 10,000 for them," he says. "The advertisers have Britney Spears, Shaquille O'Neal and Beyonce Knowles. It's not a fair contest."

Brownell thinks food and drink ads marketed toward children will eventually change, just as cigarette ads did. "Our nation is quick to respond when it feels children are being victimized and American children are suffering in record numbers with poor diets and physical inactivity," he says.

For some children, these changes can't come soon enough. After her bariatric surgery in November, Krista Pournaras hopes her life will improve. She thinks that she will be a better student when she is thinner, because she won't be afraid to participate in class discussions. Pournaras thinks other obese teens could benefit from this surgery. "I figure if this can help me, and make me happier, why not help other adolescents?

Reprinted by permission of *American Demographics,* December 2003/January 2004, pp. 27-31. Copyright © 2004 by Crain Communications Inc.

UNIT 5

Drugs and Health

Unit Selections

Key Points to Consider

- What are the risks associated with college students' drinking?

- Do you think America has a drug problem? Defend your answer.

- Why do teenagers use drugs despite the messages they've heard from DARE and "Just Say No"?

- What are the risks of taking over the counter pain medications?

Student Website

www.mhcls.com/online

Internet References

Further information regarding these websites may be found in this book's preface or online.

Food and Drug Administration (FDA)
http://www.fda.gov/

National Institute on Drug Abuse (NIDA)
http://www.nida.nih.gov/

Prescription Drugs: The Issue
http://www.opensecrets.org/news/drug/

As a culture, Americans have come to rely on drugs not only as a treatment for disease but also as an aid for living normal, productive lives. This view of drugs has fostered both a casual attitude regarding their use and a tremendous drug abuse problem. Drug use and abuse has become so widespread that there is no way to describe the typical drug abuser.

There is no simple explanation for why America has become a drug-taking culture, but there is certainly evidence to suggest some of the factors that have contributed to this development. From the time that we are children, we are constantly bombarded by advertisements about how certain drugs can make us feel and look better. While most of these ads deal with proprietary drugs, the belief is created that drugs are a legitimate and effective way to help us cope with everyday problems. Certainly drugs can have a profound effect on how we feel and act, but research has also demonstrated that our mind plays a major role in the healing process.

Growing up, most of us probably had a medicine cabinet full of over-the-counter (OTC) drugs, freely dispensed to family members to treat a variety of ailments. This familiarity with OTC drugs, coupled with rising health care costs, has prompted many people to diagnose and medicate themselves with OTC medications without sufficient knowledge of their possible side effects. While most of these preparations have little potential for abuse, that does not mean that they are innocuous. Generally speaking, OTC drugs are relatively safe if taken at the recommended dosage by healthy people, but the risk of dangerous side effects rises sharply when people exceed the recommended dosage. Another potential danger associated with the use of OTC drugs is the drug interactions that can occur when they are taken in conjunction with prescription medications. The gravest danger associated with the use of OTC drugs is that an individual may use them to control symptoms of an underlying disease and thus prevent its early diagnosis and treatment.

Another category of over the counter medications, herbal preparations, has become extremely popular. They include approximately 750 substances such as herbal teas and other products of botanical origin that are believed to have medicinal properties. Many have been used for centuries with no ill effects, but others have questionable safety records. One drug with a

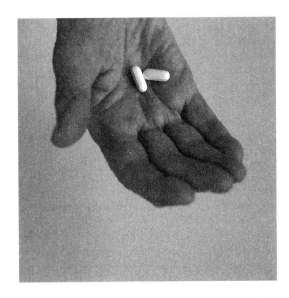

checkered history is the herb ephedra, used in over the counter weight control products sold in pharmacies, mall kiosks, and via the Internet. The death of 23-year-old Baltimore Orioles pitcher Steve Bechler in February 2003, attributed to the use of ephedra, brought attention to the risks of the herb. Soon after Bechler's death, minor league baseball banned the herb, joining other sports organization that had already banned its use. Health officials caution consumers against the use of the drug, especially if it's combined with other stimulants such as caffeine, or if strenuous exercise is involved.

As a culture, we have grown up believing that there is, or should be, a drug to treat any malady or discomfort that befalls us. Would we have a drug problem if there were no demand for drugs? One drug which is used widely in the U.S. and especially on college campuses is alcohol. Every year over 1,000 students die from alcohol-related causes, mostly drinking and driving. In "Drinking Too Much: Too Young, author Garry Boulard discusses other risks associated with student drinking including missed classes, falling behind in school work, damage to property, and injuries which occur while under the influence of alcohol.

Rx for Fraud

The government is about to spend $720 billion over the next decade on medicines for old people. How much of this is going to be wasted or stolen?

NATHAN VARDI

I t won't be long before bad guys start helping themselves to the giant honeypot created by the new Medicare drug benefit, beginning next January. How do we know? Because they're already busy going after the much smaller drug program—a warm-up to the big act—in place today.

The 2003 Medicare law included, for the first time in the 40-year-old program's history, broad prescription coverage. To start, people over 65 could apply for discount cards good for 25% off and for some other subsidies. This was a warm-up to the deeper coverage that kicks in next year.

No sooner was the ink dry on the 25% benefit than complaints started coming in about hucksters and providers violating the rules. The first calls came from Atlanta, where door-to-door salesmen were pitching phony $30 cards. (Even legitimate issuers of the cards were not permitted to hustle them door-to-door.) Then callers weighed in from other states, reporting cases of insurers and pharmacy benefit managers (PBMs) enrolling Medicare beneficiaries without their consent and billing them the $30 enrollment fee—or trying to lure them into other services and products, like medical devices, that Medicare reimbursed. One operator tried to pay pharmacies a fee for directing patients to its card, also verboten. Then there was the alleged scheme by Eileen and Leonardo de Oliveira, involving Canadian and U.S. telemarketers, who bilked 103 people in Illinois of $90,000 by offering them bogus cards, then forwarded their checking account numbers to the De Oliveiras' Florida company, which debited the accounts, according to Illinois Attorney General Lisa Madigan. She charged them civilly with consumer fraud; the De Oliveiras deny any wrongdoing.

Peanuts, compared with what's coming. In November an expected 29 million people 65 and older will start enrolling in Medicare's fully launched prescription drug insurance plan, costing an estimated $720 billion over the first decade. "This is the largest new social benefit program in the history of the country, and it is going to take effect not in pieces but all at once," says James Sheehan, the associate U.S. Attorney in Philadelphia, who has overseen 500 health care fraud cases, including the $330 million settlement by the former SmithKline Beecham for fraudulent billings, and the government's current case against Medco Health Solutions, alleging kickbacks and false claims. "There are vulnerabilities, and there is going to be fraud in the first year or two."

Or, more likely, starting on Jan. 2. Why? Because the work of guarding the henhouse has been subcontracted, in large measure, to foxes. This vast and complex plan will be run by private middlemen—chiefly HMOs and PBMs, with assists from pharmaceutical companies—some of whom have been offenders in the past. Uncle Sam is relying on their honest accounting to determine how to dispense massive subsidies to them. To make matters worse, the three-phase benefit—each with its own set of rules—creates powerful incentives for old people, with the connivance or even the active participation of doctors and druggists, to pad their pill expenses.

Medicare has long been easy prey. The program has lured such small-time crooks as Mark Little, an Orange County, Calif. podiatrist sentenced to 51 months in April for billing Medicare $800,000 for phantom procedures, and big players like Tenet Healthcare, which, while it denied any wrongdoing, paid $51 million to settle charges that one of its hospitals tried to collect on unnecessary cardiac surgeries. Kickbacks are rife. Dialysis provider Gambro Healthcare agreed to pay $350 million in criminal and civil fines last December to settle charges it paid for doctor referrals; psychiatrist Lewis Gottlieb was convicted last year of taking $200 from wheelchair sellers for each of the hundreds of fraudulent certificates of medical necessity he signed for Medicare beneficiaries (*see box*).

HHS has repeatedly "missed opportunities to use claims data to target areas vulnerable to fraud."

How widespread is the abuse? In the Sept. 30 fiscal year, ending just before the big drug benefit starts up, Medicare will disburse $295 billion. The division of the Health & Human Services Department that runs the program estimates that last year $20 billion in improper claims were paid out in fee-for-service care, the bulk of Medicare payments. How much of that was deliberate? Don't look to the feds for answers. HHS, says the Government Accountability Office, has repeatedly "missed opportunities to use claims data to target areas vulnerable to fraud."

Safeguarding the new benefit, which applies only to pills, may be even tougher. As Daniel Levinson, acting HHS inspector general, put it to the Senate in February: "Prescription drugs are especially vulnerable to fraud, waste and abuse."

Start with how complicated the three-part plan is. In part one most enrollees will pay $450 or so in annual premiums and a $250 deductible for coverage of 75% of their prescription drug costs up to $2,250—from Lipitor to Viagra. Then comes the controversial "doughnut hole" (*see box*), which leaves participants in financial limbo, paying all drug costs out of their own pockets until they've spent $3,600. (Couples are treated as individuals for insurance purposes.) At that point, phase three, catastrophic coverage kicks in, with Medicare paying 95% of expenses.

For its part the government is trying to identify and anticipate certain types of cheating. In March law enforcement officials and bureaucrats gathered in Omaha to discuss scenarios in which bad guys piggybacked on the new benefit to commit identity theft, or signed up without being qualified. The cops worried about how to prevent legitimate beneficiaries from being used to funnel lucrative and potentially dangerous drugs like OxyContin to black markets. They contemplated how easy it would be for older people qualifying for 95% coverage to buy more drugs than they intend to take, passing along the pills to relatives who aren't covered. Or simply giving, say, their Tamiflu to a sick neighbor or their Enbrel to a 59-year-old friend with arthritis. For that matter, what's to stop physicians from bulking up their prescription pads? After several decades of private insurance, doctors have come to rationalize a little fudging of diagnoses if that helps the patient with his insurance. No reason to expect the ethical dilemma to come out any differently when the victim is Uncle Sam rather than UnitedHealthcare.

In April HHS identified 33 different areas of potential flimflammery. Among them:

Shifty Discounting

A bone of contention for the medicaid program, which shells out some $37 billion a year for poor patients' drugs, is whether the government is paying a fair price. The drug companies are forbidden to charge any more than they charge private-sector insurers. But sometimes they do. They give secret rebates to the private sector but bill Medicaid for the list price. "Inadequate oversight" and "limited checks" by the government mean complete rebates often do not get reported, leading to overpaying by the federal government, said the Government Accountability Office in February.

Schering-Plough settled a Medicaid case for $345 million last year that shows how tough it can be to track rebates. The feds claimed the maker of Claritin, in a price war with the producer of the competing drug Allegra, gave concealed discounts to Cigna and PacifiCare Health Systems in the form of "data processing fees," interest-free loans and "risk share" rebates tied to growth in an insurer's outlays for antihistamine-like drugs.

The temptations will be all the larger in Medicare's new drug program. Suppose a manufacturer has a high-priced, branded

The Black Hole

There are those on Capitol Hill who still remember what happened 16 years ago to Dan Rostenkowski, the former Democratic head of the House Ways & Means Committee. After he backed an $800 per capita surtax to pay for Medicare's catastrophic illness insurance, Medicarees in Chicago jumped on the hood of his car and chased him down the street. The surtax was repealed within months.

Nearly 7 million people will end up in the doughnut hole next year, says the Kaiser Family Foundation. This is the bracket (from $2,250 to $3,600 in drug outlays) in which Medicare recipients are supposed to cover 100% of their costs. Moreover, 7.4 million people will spend more on drugs than they currently do. Of those, according to the foundation, 2.4 million are retirees who will see a significant surge in their costs because they will be shifted from more generous employer plans to the new Medicare benefit.

They are prey for the unscrupulous—from those peddling nonexistent coverage to pharmaceutical firms that offer cash or in-kind drug assistance specifically to lure old people to a particular plan or help push them out of the doughnut hole and into catastrophic coverage, so that Medicare picks up almost the whole tab. The government offers no guidance to patients or corporations about how to fill the gap.

Political pressures will be hard to resist. Especially since the number of doughnut-hole denizens will peak right around election time next year. Plugging the hole could be "astronomically expensive," says Edmund F. Haislmaier, a research fellow at the Heritage Foundation, probably costing the government hundreds of billions of extra dollars.   —N.V.

drug for asthma, used mostly by younger patients, and a high-priced drug for arthritis, used mostly by the old. Both drugs face competition from equivalent remedies sold by other pharma companies. To win slots on the drug formulary of a middleman (PBM or HMO), the pharma outfit has to offer some discounts. Would it be 10% across the board? There's little to stop the negotiators from coming up with a package deal in which the asthma medication gets a 20% discount but the arthritis medication gets no discount. In other words, a disproportionate share of the nation's pharmacy bill gets shifted onto the taxpayer. "We're going to have a whole new creative urge, and such bundling is plausible," says Keith Korenchuk, a Washington, D.C. lawyer who advises drugmakers.

Drug Switching

HHS is already on record that this is a potential trouble spot. In this scenario a doctor prescribes Lipitor ($2.30 a pill), but the pharmacy benefit manager pushes the physician to use a more expensive drug, say, Zocor ($4). What the doctor and patient don't know, in an improper switch, is that the PBM gets some benefit from the manufacturer of the more expensive pill.

Associate U.S. Attorney Sheehan sued Medco in 2003, accusing the nation's largest PBM of, among other things, improper drug switching "to enhance its revenue regardless of health plan costs, or of any potential adverse or life-threatening clinical outcomes to patients." The government claimed Medco received "substantial sums" from Merck and other pillmakers to advocate switches to their drugs even when the disfavored drugs were cheaper or more effective. It also alleged the switches "resulted in increased costs to health plans and patients, primarily in follow-up doctor visits and tests." Medco got $440 million in 2001 from Merck, its then-parent, that was not disclosed to its clients, to favor Merck's products, the suit said. Reaping a financial benefit in return for health care referrals can qualify as an illegal kickback under federal law. Medco settled the drug-switching allegations last year without admitting wrongdoing, agreeing to pay $29 million to 20 states. It also agreed to disclose financial incentives for drug switches and not substitute more expensive drugs for cheaper ones.

Prescription Shorting

It's the oldest trick in the medicine cabinet and still has authorities worried. A pharmacy distributes high doses of AstraZeneca's Nexium, for example, billing the Medicare drug plan and the beneficiary for $380 for 90 tablets, but dispensing only 88.

In a recent case the Eckerd pharmacy chain paid $9 million in 2002 to the feds and 18 states to settle claims that it dispensed partial prescriptions but billed Medicaid and other programs for full quantities. Its Eckerd ECK MD affiliate also paid a $1.7 million fine to deal with a related criminal investigation in 2001. In both these cases inventories at drugstores were low, and customers did not return to stores to pick up the outstanding pills owed to them. Eckerd blamed the problem on processing limitations, adding that new systems were installed to deal with what was an "industrywide issue." Indeed, Walgreen Co., the nation's biggest pharmacy chain, settled governmental short-filling claims for $7.6 million in 1999.

Palm Greasing

Why would a doctor prescribe a $6 antibiotic instead of one that costs 12 cents? The pill industry is rife with incentives. "You can bet pharmaceutical companies do what they can to seduce doctors," says Jerome Kassirer, a kidney specialist and former editor-in-chief of the *New England Journal of Medicine*. "They entertain them at expensive restaurants, engage them as consultants and put them on their speakers' bureaus."

Pfizer paid $430 million last year to settle government charges that its Warner-Lambert unit dangled money and trips to persuade doctors to use its epilepsy drug, Neurontin, to treat other conditions for which it was not approved, like migraines, attention deficit disorder and alcohol withdrawal. The feds claimed Warner paid physicians consulting fees to attend dinners and trips to Florida, Hawaii and the Olympics, even though "there was little or no significant consulting provided by the physicians."

Scam on Wheels

Government spending on power wheelchairs climbed 450% between 1999 and 2003, to $1.2 billion. A report released last year by Health & Human Services' inspector general found that only 13% of those it surveyed who got the most popular wheelchair met the Medicare coverage requirements. This is what happens when someone is spending other people's money.

The four contractors that process Medicare's wheelchair claims—Palmetto GBA, Cigna HealthCare, AdminaStar Federal and HealthNow New York—saw a spurt in spending as early as 1997, but the office that runs Medicare and Medicaid did not lead a coordinated response until 2003, says the Government Accountability Office.

In one egregious case last year the U.S. Attorney in Houston charged two physicians, Charles Skripka Jr. and Jayshree Patel, for conspiring to defraud Medicare of $40 million between February 2002 and June 2003. The duo allegedly approved wheelchairs for up to 50 Medicare beneficiaries per day, in return for kickbacks from the suppliers. The doctors have pleaded not guilty; the owner of their clinic, Lewis Gottlieb, has put in a guilty plea and is helping the government.

The feds in April sued the Scooter Store of New Braunfels, Tex., which billed Medicare for $400 million or so since 1997. In ads, the Scooter Store suggested to old folks that the government would pay for scooters. But, the government alleges, when customers called the company to inquire about reimbursement, the Scooter Store pushed motorized wheelchairs on them, with the result that Medicare ended up paying for expensive and unnecessary equipment. The government is supposed to pay for a motor-driven chair only if the patient would be confined to bed without one. The Scooter Store says it has done nothing wrong and that the government is trying to get out of repaying legitimate claims. —N.V.

HHS is thinking about all manner of other kinds of skullduggery that haven't yet surfaced but surely will. Among them: A pharmacy submits bills for pills not provided and alters prescriptions to secure fatter payments, or bills for branded drugs but dispenses generics; an insurer gooses enrollment counts in order to increase subsidies.

Perhaps the biggest invitation to shenanigans is the doughnut hole—where old people pay for their own drugs. The incentive to produce fake receipts to inflate a patient's out-of-pocket spending and push him into 95% coverage is all too obvious. "If pharmacies or pharmaceutical companies are working to milk the system, they will all have an interest in getting them through the coverage gap by producing paperwork to show inflated volumes," says Malcolm Sparrow, a professor of public management at Harvard.

PBMs and HMOs that operate plans also have a financial interest in steering discounts they get from pill companies to the early part of the plan. That's because they receive a fixed, direct subsidy from Medicare unaffected by discounts from drugmakers during the first phase of 75% coverage. In the 95% bracket, by contrast, HMOs receive subsidies that vary, based on pill costs, and are reduced by discounts they receive from pharmas.

Watchdogging all this will be hellish. "We have some new electronic systems in place to help us stay on top of it," says Mark McClellan, M.D., Medicare's chief. Yet the HHS division that will do the work has lost one quarter of its executives in the last three years, and 46% of its workforce will be eligible for retirement in the next four years. Most oversight—auditing claims and reviewing Medicare payments—will be farmed out to private contractors.

The biggest invitation to abuse is the doughnut hole—where the elderly pay for their own drugs.

Palmetto GBA of Columbia, S.C., a BlueCross BlueShield unit of the state, was supposed to be minding the Medicare store in Florida. But according to a government suit against a Miami supplier, Palmetto okayed $144 million worth of claims for artificial limbs, many of which were not required by the recipients. A federal judge in Miami was recently quoted in the *Miami Herald* as saying, "It is unclear why Palmetto GBA is not a subject of the ... investigation into criminal wrongdoing." Palmetto blames the overpayments on, among other things, a lack of government funding for its oversight, and notes that it denied $149 million of Medicare artificial-limb claims in the last two years.

The HHS Office of Inspector General is receiving a one-time $25 million boost to fight fraud associated with the prescription drug benefit. The FBI unit overseeing health care lost 121 agents between 2000 and 2003. As for the $114 million the FBI receives each year to fight health care fraud, the GAO says some of the funds may have been improperly used to fight other crimes, like terrorism. The government probably won't invest heavily in protecting its $720 billion investment until a fair amount of money has been lost.

Drinking Too Much, Too Young

Trying to find an answer to the persistent habit of binge drinking among young people vexes the nation's policymakers.

GARRY BOULARD

The stories have been shocking, abruptly reminding a nation of a problem that remains unsolved: in the last half of 2004, six college-age students in Colorado died as a result of binge drinking.

Although each fatality was different in its circumstance—Samantha Spady, 19, a sophomore at Colorado State University, died after drinking vanilla vodka and more than two dozen beers, while Benett Bertoli, 20, also a CSU student, was found dead on a couch at an off-campus party from a combination of alcohol, methadone and benzodiazepene—the events leading up to the deaths were maddeningly familiar.

In almost every case, the fatalities were the unexpected ending to a boisterous party almost always involving large gatherings of young people on weekend nights consuming prodigious amounts of alcohol, sometimes for two days straight.

The number of Colorado deaths from binge drinking in late 2004 was exceptionally large, but the state is not alone. It killed Thomas Ryan Hauser, 23, a student at Virginia Tech in September. Blake Hammontree, 19, died at his fraternity house at the University of Oklahoma, also in September. Bradley Kemp, 20, died in October at his home near the University of Arkansas, where he was a student. Steven Judd died celebrating his 21st birthday with fraternity friends at New Mexico State University in November.

Those deaths did not occur in a vacuum. According to statistics from the National Institute for Alcohol Abuse and Alcoholism, more than 1,400 college students die from alcohol-related deaths each year including motor vehicle crashes. Unfortunately, that number has remained constant even though both high school and college-age drinking has decreased.

"The numbers have been going in the right direction," says Peter Cressy, the president of the Distilled Spirits Council of the United States. "There is today less regular use of alcohol on college campuses than there was 20 years ago. There has been a drop in the number of college students both of age and not of age who drink at all during any given month. And the data for eighth, 10th, and 12th graders who consume alcohol has also shown a downward trend."

Bucking the Trend

But what hasn't changed, industry, health and alcohol experts all agree, is the stubborn number of young people who continue to engage in destructive behavior.

"The issue is not the 30,000 kids on the campus of the University of Colorado, or any other school, who drink legally or illegally, but somehow manage to do it without any great peril," says Ralph Blackman, the president of the Century Council, a not-for-profit organization dedicated to fighting drunk driving and underage drinking.

"The issue is binge drinking and the continuing large numbers of kids who insist on over consumption to a level that has a very decided risk for a dangerous result," continues Blackman. "That is a phenomenon that very much remains with us."

Trying to find a specific reason for the persistence of binge drinking among the young is a subject that both vexes and causes great debate among the nation's policymakers. Do younger people just naturally like to get drunk, or in some cases, very drunk? Is it a matter of upbringing or income? Is it a reflection of a troubled and anxious society?

"You could ask questions like that all day, and not really get any solid answers," says Paul Hanson, a professor emeritus of sociology at the State University of New York, Potsdam.

"The only thing you could be sure of is that no matter how many different ways we approach it with different solutions, binge drinking continues among the very young, generation after generation."

But some experts believe one thing that is different with those who are a part of what demographers call the Millennials—those born in 1980 or after—and their predecessors, is that binge drinking today is out of the closet and celebrated on almost a worldwide basis due to the Internet.

"There is a huge difference from when many of us went to school in the 1960s and '70s and today," says Stephen Bentley, a coordinator of substance abuse services at the Wardenberg Health Center at the University of Colorado.

"Back in our day we really did not want any attention of any kind, we did not want adults or the world to know that we were drinking and partying excessively," continues Bentley.

"But today young people who engage in this kind of behavior are actually very proud of what they are doing, they post their own Web sites about their parties so that everyone else can see what they did."

One of the Web sites, called shamings.com, features pictures of drunken young men, updated on a regular basis, sometimes sleeping in their own vomit, often half naked, and many times covered with magic marker salutations alluding to their drinking prowess or lack thereof.

One of the Web site creators, Ricky Van Veen, explained to the Washington Post the guidelines used by the Web site in determining whether or not to post a binge drinker's picture: "The standard rule is, if you fall asleep with your shoes on, you're fair game," he said.

Youth Targets

For Julia Sherman, field director with the Center on Alcohol Marketing and Youth, binge drinking self-promotion is almost a natural outgrowth of what she says is the alcohol industry's "preoccupation with the young."

"The ads that are being put out there today are not your Mom and Pop, 'Mabel, Black Label,' ads of another era, but ads that are very much geared toward an exceedingly young demographic," she says.

"The whole ad focus of the alcohol industry has changed both in tenor and in numbers," says Sherman. "Their Web site ads now feature computer games and premiums for downloading music. They run ads in what are called the 'laddie magazines,' that are edgier than anything adults are seeing in their magazines. It is all part of a non-stop, never-ending pitch for the youth market."

According to a study released by the Center on Alcohol Marketing and Youth last October, the number of alcohol ads on TV jumped by nearly 90,000 between 2001 and 2003, with some 23 percent of the ads "more likely to be seen by the average underage person for every four seen by the average adult."

Cressey of the Distilled Spirits Council, among other industry leaders, disputes that there has been any concerted targeting of young people, and notes that his group will not permit any member to advertise where the media is not at least a 70/30, adult to minor, demographic.

"We also require through our code that all models in our ads be at least 25 years old," adds Cressey, a requirement that is also generally followed by members of the Beer Institute.

But even working within those parameters, the impact of drinking ads, usually showing young people at a beach party, rap concert, or skate boarding, remains a matter of contention.

"The problem is that how we view television has changed greatly in the last generation," says Sherman. "It used to be that there was one TV and the entire family was watching it, which meant that there would probably be some sort of adult filtering or response to whatever the ad message was. But that is much harder today when over 30 percent of kids aged two to eight, and two-thirds over the age of eight, have their own TVs in their own rooms."

BINGE DRINKING— THE FACTS

- In 2001, 44% of U.S. college students engaged in binge drinking; this rate has not changed since 1993.
- 51% of the men drank five or more drinks in a row.
- 40% of the women drank four or more drinks in a row.
- Students more likely to binge drink are white, age 23 or younger, and are residents of a fraternity or sorority.
- 75.1% of fraternity residents and 62.4% of sorority residents report binge drinking.
- Binge drinkers in high school are three times more likely to binge in college.
- From 1993 to 2001, more students abstained from alcohol (16% to 19%), but more also frequently drank heavily (19.7% to 22.8%).
- Just as many freshman (those under 21) as seniors binge drink.
- Frequent binge drinkers are eight times more likely than others to miss a class, fall behind in schoolwork, get hurt or injured, and damage property.
- 91% of women and 78% of the men who are frequent binge drinkers consider themselves to be moderate or light drinkers.
- 1,400 college students every year die from alcohol-related causes; 1,100 of these deaths involve drinking and driving.

Sources: Harvard University's School of Public Health; Robert Wood Johnson Foundation

The end result may not only be a message received early on that drinking alcohol is attractive, but an actual inability at an age leading all the way up to college to discern alcohol's potential danger. "There is a lot of research out there showing that even up to the age of 21 and beyond a young body is not fully developed and it does not absorb alcohol as well as it might in an older person," says Blackman of the Century Council. "Just as important is the evidence that your brain is not fully developed at that point either, so that issues of risk-taking and behavior are assessed in a different way."

To make matters worse, State University of New York's Hanson says, zero tolerance alcohol programs or efforts to make campuses virtually alcohol-free have a funny way of backfiring. "Prohibition is a classic example of how the laws in these matters can end up being counterproductive by actually making the thing that is being prohibited more attractive. That remains especially true for young people who don't like to be told what not to do."

And when that happens," says Hanson, "young people very often find themselves involved in these dangerous events centered around heavy episodic drinking, which is the very last thing we want to see happen."

Teaching Moderation

Hanson has also noticed in his own research that the percentage of students who drink tends to decrease as they go from being freshmen to seniors. He says policymakers would be wiser to focus on what he calls "harm reduction policies" that acknowledge young people are going to drink no matter what, but emphasize responsible drinking through education—even to minors.

Similarly Colorado University's Bentley has noticed the effectiveness of the restorative justice approach on many college campuses that require students who have engaged in binge drinking to face the people who suffered the consequences of their behavior when they were drunk.

"That means the neighbors who were trying to study when the party was blaring," says Bentley, "or friends who had to take care of them when they were throwing up all over themselves or were otherwise dead drunk."

Legislatively, some lawmakers are looking at keg-registration laws in order to keep better track of who buys what for whom, particularly when such kegs end up at parties heavily populated with minors. So far, 24 states and the District of Columbia have adopted keg registration laws of varying severity.

"It is only a tool that might possibly reduce binge drinking and underage drinking," says Arizona Representative Ted Downing, who has introduced legislation requiring the state to put tracking numbers on every keg of beer sold.

"The way my legislation reads is that if you want to buy a keg, you have to show identification, fill out a form, leave a deposit, and detail where the keg is going to go and for what purpose" says Downing.

Other lawmakers believe that by making underage consumption and distribution more legally challenging, they can, at the very least, chip away at the roughly 33 percent of the nation's college students who are below the age of 21.

"It's worth a try," says Colorado Representative Angie Paccione, who has introduced legislation making it a class one misdemeanor to distribute alcohol to someone under the age of 21, with jail time of up to 18 months and fines topping out at $5,000.

"We want to give the DAs a tool that they can use for prosecuting and that the police can use in order to effect behavior changes," Paccione says, adding that problem college drinking is very often proceeded by problem high school drinking.

"I was a dean in a high school and have seen more than my share of kids who have had liquid lunches," she says. "So I know that this is a problem that begins very early."

Education Works

And although a new look at both underage and binge drinking from the legislative perspective may be in order, Jeff Becker, president of the Beer Institute, says lawmakers should not lose sight of the progress that has already been made in reducing both high school and college drinking.

"The education and awareness programs have really worked, whether it is at the college or high school level; and I think lawmakers should take credit for any support they have given to those efforts and continue those programs," says Becker.

"Maybe these most recent deaths will serve as a wake-up call and get all of us to look once more at what works and what doesn't work," he adds. "But from the community, family and school level it is very clear that making kids aware of the dangers has also made them smarter. And I don't think we should stop doing that."

In Connecticut, Senator Biagio "Billy" Ciotto, a long-time advocate of programs that educate high school students on the harmful effects of both drinking and driving and binge drinking, says he remains convinced that lawmakers should concentrate on what he calls the "realistic goal of reduction" vs. the "impossible idea," of elimination.

"You are never going to get rid of this kind of drinking completely," Ciotto says. "But I have no doubt in my mind that you can reduce the abuse simply by staying with it, never giving up, always trying to let kids know, without lecturing them, about the harmful effects of alcohol abuse."

Ciotto's efforts have even won the support of the Connecticut Coalition to Stop Underage Drinking, which named him "Outstanding Legislator in Reducing Underage Drinking" in 2004.

"I think they and just about everyone else recognize that we have to work on the big majority of kids who will not abuse alcohol if they know the dangers, and just figure that there is always going to be a minority that will do what they want to do no matter what, he says."

Arizona's Downing agrees: "It would be very foolish for any state representative or senator to feel that you can propose a bill that will somehow magically get rid of the problems of binge drinking or underage drinking."

"You can't," says Downing. "And we have to admit that. All you can really do is nudge things in a certain direction, which is what so many of our laws do anyway. If people are going to behave in the wrong way no matter what, there is only so much we can do. But we can help those who want to do the right thing, or don't want to break any laws just to have a little fun. That is the group we need to appeal to."

Free-lancer Garry Boulard is a frequent contributor to State Legislatures.

Just Say No Again

The old failures of new and improved anti-drug education

RENEE MOILANEN

I'm at the February 2001 Teens at the Table conference, a feel-good event sponsored by a coalition of Los Angeles youth organizations and high schools. It's designed to boost self-esteem and teach teenagers how to make smart decisions. In one of the sessions, a group of students is about to learn how easy it is to stay off drugs. It doesn't require anything as lame as red ribbons or "Just Say No" chants. It just takes knowing what constitutes a healthy decision—one that is all your own—coupled with a little real-life practice.

The kids test their skills with a role-playing skit. The scenario: Two girls are walking home from a party late at night when a car full of boys pulls up to offer them a ride. "The boys have been drinking and smoking," the script reads. "Trouble is imminent."

Here is where the teenagers are supposed to call on their newfound decision making skills in choosing whether to get into the car. They're asked to think about their options, weigh the consequences, and decide what to do based on what would be best for them—no judgments, no right or wrong, none of that thoughtless Just Say No stuff from the 1980s and early '90s. Today's drug prevention lessons, scientifically crafted and tested, are supposed to be all about teaching teenagers how to make choices, not telling them what to do; respecting their autonomy, not treating them like ventriloquist's dummies.

So the teenagers choose. If they don't get into the car, they walk home and everything is fine. But if they do ...

Boys: Hop in girls!
(Eventually the boys get out of hand and come on to the girls.)
Girls: Stop it!
Boys: Come on, it will be fun!
Girls: No!
(Car accident.)

The teachers say there's a choice here, but these kids aren't stupid. They can stay out of the car and live, or get in the car and die. So ... just say no.

Dare to Keep Your Kids off DARE

That three-word mantra "Just Say No" became a national punch line for a reason: It didn't keep kids away from drugs. Drug use among teenagers dropped steadily from the early 1980s until 1992, mirroring a decline in drug use among adults. But this downward trend began before the anti-drug curricula developed in the 1980s, exemplified by Drug Abuse Resistance Education (DARE), could have had any impact. The drop was detected in surveys of students who had never heard of DARE or Just Say No. And by the early 1990s, when students who were exposed to DARE and similar programs in grade school and middle school reached their late teens, drug use among teenagers was going up again. In the 2002 Monitoring the Future Study, 53 percent of high school seniors said they had used illegal drugs, compared to 41 percent in 1992. Past-month use rose from 14 percent to 25 percent during the same period.

Meanwhile, the leading model for drug education in the United States has been DARE, which brings police officers into elementary and middle school classrooms to warn kids away from drugs. DARE claims to teach kids how to resist peer pressure and say no to drugs through skits, cartoons, and hypothetical situations. Founded by Los Angeles Police Chief Daryl Gates in 1983 and organized as a nonprofit corporation (DARE America) in 1987, DARE is still used in around three-quarters of the nation's school districts. At the annual DARE Officers Association Dinner a few years ago, Bill Clinton's drug czar, Barry McCaffrey, declared that "DARE knows what needs to be done to reduce drug use among children, and you are doing it—successfully." But as McCaffrey should have known, the effectiveness of DARE has never been demonstrated, a fact DARE America itself implicitly conceded when it announced, half a year after the drug czar's praise, that it was revamping its program.

During the last decade DARE has been widely criticized as unproven and unsophisticated. In one of the most damning studies, published in 1999, a team of researchers at the University of Kentucky found that 10 years after receiving the anti-drug lessons, former DARE students were no different from non-DARE students in terms of drug use, drug attitudes, or self-esteem. "This report adds to the accumulating literature on DARE's lack of efficacy in preventing or reducing substance use," the researchers noted. In a 2003 report, the General Accounting Office reviewed six long-term evaluations of DARE and concluded that there were "no significant differences in illicit drug use between students who received DARE ... and students who did not." The surgeon general, the National Academy of Sciences, and the U.S. Department of Education also have declared DARE ineffective.

Determined not to repeat past mistakes and prodded by a federal government that lately has been demanding accountability in education, teachers today are turning to prevention programs backed by "scientifically based" claims of effectiveness. In 1998 the Department of Education, concerned that money was being wasted on a mishmash of ineffective programs, decided to fund only those proven by "scientifically based research" to reduce or prevent drug use. Testimonials and we-think-it's-working assurances like those cited by DARE would no longer pass muster. Every prevention program now needed hard numbers, objective experiments, and independently reviewed conclusions based on long-term follow-ups to prove they worked.

In 2000 the Department of Education convened an expert panel that judged nine prevention programs "exemplary" for their proven effectiveness and 33 others "promising." Comprised mostly of educators and health professionals, the panel gave the "exemplary" or "promising" nod only to programs backed by at least one scientific evaluation of effectiveness (DARE did not make the cut). Schools using programs that were not on the list would risk losing their slice of the Department of Education's $635 million drug prevention budget. In 2001 President George W. Bush included the "scientifically based research" criterion for drug education in his No Child Left Behind Act, signing into law what had previously been only administrative practice.

But the officially endorsed alternatives to DARE aren't necessarily better. Once you remove the shiny packaging and discard the "new and improved" labels, you'll find a product that's disappointingly familiar. The main thing that has changed is the rhetoric. Instead of "Just Say No," you'll hear, "Use your refusal skills." The new programs encourage teachers to go beyond telling kids that drug use is bad. Instead, they tell teenagers to "use your decision making skills" to make "healthy life choices." Since drugs aren't healthy, the choice is obvious: Just say no.

The persistence of this theme is no accident. Prevention programs can get the federal government's stamp of approval only if they deliver "a clear and consistent message that the illegal use of drugs" is "wrong and harmful." But this abstinence-only message leaves teenagers ill-equipped to avoid drug-related hazards if they do decide to experiment.

After examining some of the new anti-drug curricula and watching a sampling of them in action, I strongly doubt these programs are winning many hearts and minds.

The Class Struggle Against Drugs

In September 2001, I join a class of middle schoolers in the upscale Los Angeles suburb of Palos Verdes Estates as they run through a series of hypothetical scenarios ostensibly designed to put their decision making skills to work. The program, called Skills for Adolescence, is used in about 10 percent of the nation's 92,000 K–12 schools. The curriculum, which the Department of Education deems "promising," "teaches the social competency skills young adolescents need for positive development," according to program literature.

Clustered into small groups, each student fingers a wallet-size blue card. The card—titled "Will it lead to trouble?"—lists the five questions adolescents should ask themselves when confronted with a difficult choice. It's laminated, presumably so teenagers can keep it in their back pockets and whip it out whenever they're faced with a tough decision and need a quick reminder about how to make one.

If the answer to any of these questions is yes, the students are supposed to say no: "Is it against the law, rules, or the teachings of my religion? Is it harmful to me or to others? Would it disappoint my family or other important adults? Is it wrong to do? Would I be hurt or upset if someone did this to me?"

The questions clearly are designed to elicit a complete rejection of drug use. Is it against the law? Yes, drugs are against the law. Therefore, you must reject them. Is it harmful? Yes, they can be harmful. Reject them. Would it disappoint my family or other adults? Yes, reject. There's no way to make any other decision. "If the only decision that's the right decision is the decision to say no, you've effectively cut off the discussion again," observes Marsha Rosenbaum, director of the West Coast office of the Drug Policy Alliance and author of *Safety First: A Reality-Based Approach to Teens, Drugs, and Drug Education.*

Another program praised by the Department of Education is Project ALERT, which it calls "exemplary." A series of anti-drug and anti-tobacco lessons used in about a fifth of the nation's 15,000 school districts, Project ALERT boasts that it "helps students build skills that will last a lifetime," including "how to identify the sources of pressure to use substances," "how to match specific resistance techniques with social pressures," "how to counter pro-drug arguments," and "how to say 'no' several different ways."

Eliminate the psychobabble, and Project ALERT's message is almost indistinguishable from that of the 1980s anti-drug programs that teachers now roundly scorn: Peer pressure is bad. Drugs are bad. Just say no.

In a room plastered with posters titled "Pressures" and "Ways to Say No," I join a class of Los Angeles middle schoolers in November 2002 as it breaks into small groups to plod through an anti-drug lesson from Project ALERT. The adolescents have just finished watching a video about smoking cigarettes featuring former teenaged smokers who say things like, "Life is too short. I'm not eager to die."

Each of the four groups is assigned a different question to answer: How can you help people quit? What's good about quitting? How do people quit? What gets people to quit?

There is little discussion. The kids know what the teacher expects. How can you help people quit? Tell them smoking is dumb. Don't hang out with them anymore.

When asked if she knows anyone who smokes, one girl nods.

Do you think any of this helps?

"No," she says without hesitation.

Why not?

The girl barely lifts her eyes from the paper, where she is decorating the "Smoking is dumb" and "Don't hang out with them anymore" list with bright red hearts. She shrugs. "Some people just don't care," she says.

The students are asked why they think kids use drugs.

They respond in unison, "Peer pressure"—the answer they know is expected. When asked to explain what this means, the students conjure up images of older kids hassling younger ones. "Sometimes they're your friends, but sometimes they're crazy people that come up and ask if you want some," one boy says, drawing on concepts that prevailed during the Just Say No era but have little basis in real life.

One boy defines peer pressure as other students "trying to force you, trying to convince you to do it." When asked if he's ever experienced peer pressure, he shakes his head. He's waiting for a group of sinister strangers to thrust drugs in his face. Drug education apparently has not helped him realize that peer pressure is far subtler, like wearing the same clothes as your friends or sharing inside jokes. And the teachers, by continuing to portray peer pressure as a palpable evil, fail to protect their students from anything.

Everything Old Is New Again

Today's anti-drug programs claim to have replaced all the scare tactics of years past with good, solid information about the physiological effects of drug use. But these programs, which are based on the same flawed "scientific" information that adults have been using for years to keep kids off drugs, are a lot like anti-alcohol propaganda from the late 19th and early 20th centuries.

Back in the late 1800s, health lessons endorsed by the Woman's Christian Temperance Union (WCTU) and its Department of Scientific Instruction portrayed alcohol as a wicked poison that created an uncontrollable appetite for more: "Many persons who at first take only a little beer, cider, or wine, form a great desire for them....The appetite for alcoholic liquors usually grows rapidly, and men who use but little at first often become drunkards in a short time." This selection comes from *The House I Live In,* a schoolbook written in 1887 and heartily endorsed by the WCTU.

A century later, another popular textbook offers a similar perspective on drug use. This passage comes from *Making Life Choices* (1999), lauded by teachers for its scientific content: "Attachment to the drug becomes almost like a great love relationship with another person. The only sure way to escape drug addiction is never to experiment with taking the drugs that produce it."

In the popular classroom video *Marijuana Updates,* produced in 1997, teenagers and Leo Hayden, a former college football player turned drug counselor, describe how pot ruined their lives. They say the drug made them feel invincible, tired, hungry, and numb. Soon they were slacking off in school, shirking responsibilities, and turning to harder drugs for a better high. Their testimonials, which suggest that pot turns people into useless zombies eager to snort cocaine and shoot heroin, draw on two major themes in anti-marijuana propaganda: "amotivational syndrome" and the "gateway effect."

> **"[Drug eduators] make you feel as bad as they can if you do it," says one Los Angeles teenager. Still, he says, "almost every person I know has tried marijuana. Even good people."**

A century ago, kids heard the same warnings about tobacco, another target of the so-called temperance movement. *Our Bodies and How We Live* (1904) warned that "the mind of the habitual user of tobacco is apt to lose its capacity for study or successful effort." According to the 1924 *Primer of Hygiene,* a smoker "forgets the importance of the work he has to do, and idles away his time instead of going earnestly to work to finish his task." *The Essentials of Health* (1892) worried that cigarettes would lead to harder stuff: "It is to be feared that if our young men continue the use of cigarettes we shall soon see, as a legitimate result, a large number of adults addicted to the opium habit."

The scientific studies allegedly proving the effectiveness of the new drug education programs aren't much more impressive than the tired rhetoric. Consider Life Skills Training, a fast-growing program that reaches about 2 percent of the nation's 47 million schoolchildren and tops the list of "exemplary" programs. Generally touted as the future of drug education, Life Skills Training purports to cut tobacco, alcohol, and marijuana use by up to 75 percent; to reduce the use of multiple drugs by two-thirds; and to decrease the use of inhalants, narcotics, and hallucinogens. These claims aren't based on testimonials or case studies about 12-year-old Johnny turning his life around after a few Life Skills Training lessons. The program's supporters cite actual scientific studies, reported in journals published by the American Medical Association and American Psychological Association.

But the lead scientist on those evaluations, Cornell University epidemiologist Gilbert Botvin, is the creator of Life Skills Training and the one profiting from its success. Botvin also sits on the expert panel that deemed his prevention program "exemplary." He is not the only program developer sitting on the expert panel; two other panelists have participated in rating prevention programs they helped develop. All of their programs have received "exemplary" marks.

Such conflicts of interest aren't proof that the conclusions are flawed. But independent researchers such as Joel Brown at the Center for Educational Research and Development in Berkeley have found problems with the Life Skills Training studies. Brown charges that the evaluations often focused only on positive outcomes and omitted results indicating that teenagers who went through the prevention program were *more* likely to use drugs or alcohol than their peers.

You Gotta Believe

In a 2001 analysis published by the *Journal of Drug Education,* Brown noted that a six-year evaluation of Life Skills Training reported data only from students who had completed 60 percent or more of the curriculum, just two-thirds of the original 2,455-student sample. The students left out were the ones who missed many of the anti-drug lessons—probably students who skipped class a lot or were less motivated. Such students, other research suggests, would be especially prone to drug use. Carving them out of the picture inflated the program's apparent effectiveness, Brown's study shows.

Brown also found that when students completed anything less than 60 percent of the Life Skills Training curriculum, even 59 percent, their drug use was no lower, and in many cases higher, than that of students who did not participate in any lessons at all. Since the researchers don't give a good reason for using 60 percent as the cutoff point (only saying it was "a reasonably complete version of the intervention"), it seems they simply chose the point at which the outcomes turned positive.

Furthermore, Brown says, real students in real classrooms are unlikely ever to see 60 percent of the curriculum, because most teachers simply pick out lessons and squeeze them in whenever possible. The Life Skills Training research reinforces this caveat: Even under pristine conditions, with teachers getting constant training and monitoring, one-third of the students failed to reach the 60 percent mark. And those kids, Brown's research shows, were more likely to use drugs than the students who did not participate at all.

What all of these programs continue to ignore is the most crucial piece in the drug prevention puzzle—the kids, and their stubbornly independent reactions to propaganda. They aren't fooled by "decision making" skills or "healthy choices."

The National Academy of Sciences found similar gaps in drug education research in its 2001 report *Informing America's Policy on Illegal Drugs: What We Don't Know Keeps Hurting Us.* Too many studies omit negative results, exclude students from the original sample, and inflate statistical evidence, the report concluded. But because the federal government only requires a prevention study to demonstrate a single positive outcome, programs backed by weak evidence stay in business.

Another problem with many of the new "science-based" prevention programs is that they continue to rely on statistics measuring student attitudes toward drugs. Project ALERT celebrates outcomes such as these: "Anti-drug beliefs were significantly enhanced," among them "intentions not to use within the next six months," "beliefs that one can successfully resist pro-drug pressures," and "beliefs that drug use is harmful and has negative consequences." But whether a student *intends* to

abstain or *believes* he can resist drugs does not tell us whether he actually will do so.

DARE officials likewise tried to counter bad publicity by falling back on beliefs, trumpeting that 97 percent of teachers rated DARE as good to excellent, 93 percent of parents believed DARE teaches children to avoid drugs, and 86 percent of school principals believed students would be less likely to use drugs after DARE. With only beliefs to cite, DARE was left off the federal government's list of "exemplary" and "promising" prevention curricula in 2000. Many schools have dropped it from their anti-drug lineups or scaled it back to the point of irrelevance, a fact that DARE officials concede while refusing to release numbers on the decline.

Desperate to retain its dominance in the prevention market, DARE has embarked on a dramatic retooling of its lessons to keep up with the current emphasis on scientific research, decision-making skills, and resistance techniques. The Robert Wood Johnson Foundation has given DARE a $13.7 million grant to create a new middle school curriculum, which teachers began testing last fall. DARE officials said the new curriculum was drastically different.

"It's not just say no, it's not Nancy Reagan," says Charlie Parsons, executive director of DARE America. "We're teaching kids *how* to say no."

It remains to be seen how this revamped DARE curriculum is going to be any different from the old one—or, for that matter, how any of the new prevention programs are different from the old DARE. Many of the DARE tactics now scorned by educators are quite similar to those used in the new, supposedly revised programs. Project ALERT and Life Skills Training have "Ways to Say No" almost identical to the ones taught in DARE.

Drug Education as if Reality Matters

What all of these programs continue to ignore is the most crucial piece in the drug prevention puzzle—the kids, and their stubbornly independent reactions to propaganda. They aren't fooled by "decision making" skills or "healthy choices." They know what the teachers expect: Just say no.

"They make you feel as bad as they can if you do it," says one Los Angeles teenager. Still, he says, "almost every person I know has tried marijuana. Even good people."

At Mira Costa High School in Manhattan Beach, California, a 10th-grade summer health teacher, Guy Gardner, recognizes his difficult position. About one in four Manhattan Beach students are "current" (past-month) marijuana users, according to the district's own studies, which puts them near the national average. "A lot of them know more than I do," Gardner confesses. Yet he plays the game, rattling off a list of warnings—cocaine will rot out your nose, marijuana could kill you, there's no such thing as recreational drug use—even as most of his students know how unlikely or just plain wrong it all is.

In one lesson, Gardner asks students to name the first thing that comes to their minds when they hear the word *drugs.*

"Don't give me answers I want to hear, give me your answers," he urges.

A couple of kids call out: Crime. Death. Stupid. Something that alters your mind and screws up your body.

But a few offer another point of view.

"I think it's bad, but people have the choice to do it, and if they do it, it's their problem," says one boy.

"If you really want to do it, you're going to do it," says another, even going so far as to advocate legalizing drugs. "We'd be so much more chill in the nation."

That may be, but saying so is untenable in the abstinence-only world of drug education. Gardner pulls back the debate. You can't legalize drugs, he tells the students, because they're harmful. "The ultimate message" of legalization, he says, "is it's OK to do drugs." And that, he implies, just isn't true.

In the end, meaningful drug education reform probably won't come from educators. It will have to come from those who have far more at stake when it comes to drug use by teenagers: their parents. They are the ones who see their kids stumble home with bloodshot eyes, who can't fall asleep when their kids are partying the night away, who know their kids are experimenting with drugs and want, above all, for them to be safe.

That's why drug experts such as *Safety First* author Marsha Rosenbaum are calling for a truly new approach to drug education, one that abandons the abstinence-only message and gives kids the unbiased, factual information they need to stay safe, even if they choose to experiment. Such information could include now-forbidden advice on real but avoidable hazards such as driving under the influence, having sex when you're high, mixing alcohol with other depressants, and overheating while using Ecstasy.

One possible model is Mothers Against Drunk Driving (MADD), which recognized that if it couldn't stop young people from drinking, it could at least stop them from getting behind the wheel while intoxicated. MADD's efforts, which made *designated driver* a household term, seem to have worked: Since 1982, according to the National Highway Traffic Safety Administration, the number of teenagers killed in drunk driving accidents has plunged 57 percent. MADD thus helped prove that we can make drug use safer without eliminating it entirely.

"There are kids who are not going to use drugs for religious reasons, because they're athletes, because they're focused on school, because they don't like the way they feel," Rosenbaum notes. "These kids don't need a program to tell them no. They're already not using. But for the kids who are amenable to the experience, it doesn't matter how many DARE programs they sit through; they're going to do it anyway … If we can't prevent drug use, what we can prevent is drug abuse and drug problems. But we have to get real."

RENEE MOILANEN (rmoilanen@adelphia.net) is a freelance journalist studying drug policy at UCLA.

Strategies To Reduce Medication Errors

How the FDA is working to improve medication safety and what you can do to help

MICHELLE MEADOWS

When Jacquelyn Ley shattered her elbow on the soccer field two years ago, her parents set out to find her the best care in Minneapolis. "We drove past five other hospitals to get to the one we wanted," says Carol Ley, M.D., an occupational health physician. Her husband, an orthopedic surgeon, made sure Jacquelyn got the right surgeon. After a successful three-hour surgery to repair the broken bones, Jacquelyn, who was 9 at the time, received the pain medicine morphine through a pump and was hooked up to a heart monitor, breathing monitor, and blood oxygen monitor. Her recovery was going so well that doctors decided to turn off the morphine pump and to forgo regular checks of her vital signs.

Carol Ley, M.D., chairwoman of the board of the National Patient Safety Foundation, says her daughter's medication error strengthened her involvement in patient safety.

Carol Ley slept in her daughter's hospital room that night. When she woke up in the middle of the night and checked on her, Jacquelyn was barely breathing. "I called her name, but she wouldn't respond," she says. "I shook her and called for help." The morphine pump hadn't been shut down, but had accidentally been turned up high. The narcotic flooded Jacquelyn's body. She survived the overdose, but it was a close call. "If three more hours had gone by, I don't think Jacquelyn would have survived," Ley says. "Fortunately, I woke up."

Ley was pleased with the way the hospital handled the error. "They came right out and said the morphine pump was incorrectly programmed, they told me the steps they were going to take to make sure Jacquelyn was OK, and they also told me what they were going to do to make sure this kind of mistake won't happen again. And that's very important to me." The hospital began using pumps that are easier to use and revamped nurse's training. Ley believes there were many contributors to the error, including the fact that it was Labor Day weekend and there were staff shortages. "It goes to show that this can happen to anyone, anywhere," says Ley, who now chairs the board of the National Patient Safety Foundation.

Multiple Factors

Since 1992, the Food and Drug Administration has received about 20,000 reports of medication errors. These are voluntary reports, so the number of medication errors that actually occur is thought to be much higher. There is no "typical" medication error, and health professionals, patients, and their families are all involved. Some examples:

A physician ordered a 260-milligram preparation of Taxol for a patient, but the pharmacist prepared 260 milligrams of Taxotere instead. Both are chemotherapy drugs used for different types of cancer and with different recommended doses. The patient died several days later, though the death couldn't be linked to the error because the patient was already severely ill.

The IOM reported that more than 7,000 deaths each year are related to medication errors.

An elderly patient with rheumatoid arthritis died after receiving an overdose of methotrexate—a 10-milligram daily dose of the drug rather than the intended 10-milligram weekly dose. Some dosing mix-ups have occurred because daily dosing of methotrexate is typically used to treat people with cancer, while low weekly doses of the drug have been prescribed for other conditions, such as arthritis, asthma, and inflammatory bowel disease.

One patient died because 20 units of insulin was abbreviated as "20 U," but the "U" was mistaken for a "zero." As a result, a dose of 200 units of insulin was accidentally injected.

A man died after his wife mistakenly applied six transdermal patches to his skin at one time. The multiple patches delivered an overdose of the narcotic pain medicine fentanyl through his skin.

A patient developed a fatal hemorrhage when given another patient's prescription for the blood thinner warfarin.

These and other medication errors reported to the FDA may stem from poor communication, misinterpreted handwriting, drug name confusion, lack of employee knowledge, and lack of patient understanding about a drug's directions. "But it's important to recognize that such errors are due to multiple factors in a complex medical system," says Paul Seligman, M.D., director of the FDA's Office of Pharmacoepidemiology and Statistical Science. "In most cases, medication errors can't be blamed on a single person."

A medication error is "any preventable event that may cause or lead to inappropriate medication use or patient harm while the medication is in the control of the health care professional, patient, or consumer,' according to the National Coordinating Council for Medication Error Reporting and Prevention. The council, a group of more than 20 national organizations, including the FDA, examines and evaluates medication errors and recommends strategies for error prevention.

A Regulatory Approach

The public took notice in 1999 when the Institute of Medicine (IOM) released a report, "To Err is Human: Building a Safer Health System." According to the report, between 44,000 and 98,000 deaths may result each year from medical errors in hospitals alone. And more than 7,000 deaths each year are related to medications. In response to the IOM's report, all parts of the U.S. health system put error reduction strategies into high gear by re-evaluating and strengthening checks and balances to prevent errors.

In addition, the U.S. Department of Health and Human Services (HHS) and other federal agencies formed the Quality Interagency Coordination Task Force in 2000 and issued an action plan for reducing medical errors. In 2001, HHS Secretary Tommy G. Thompson announced a Patient Safety Task Force to coordinate a joint effort to improve data collection on patient safety. The lead agencies are the FDA, the Centers for Disease Control and Prevention, the Centers for Medicare and Medicaid Services, and the Agency for Healthcare Research and Quality.

Bar coding is a promising way to automate aspects of medication administration.

The FDA enhanced its efforts to reduce medication errors by dedicating more resources to drug safety, which included forming a new division on medication errors at the agency last year. "We work to prevent medication errors before a drug reaches the market and to also monitor any errors that may occur after that," says Jerry Phillips, R.Ph., director of the FDA's new Division of Medication Errors and Technical Support.

Here's a look at key areas in which the FDA is working to reduce medication errors.

Bar code label rule: After a public meeting in July 2002, the FDA decided to propose a new rule requiring bar codes on certain drug and biological product labels. Health care professionals would use bar code scanning equipment, similar to that used in supermarkets, to make sure that the right drug in the right dose and route of administration is given to the right patient at the right time.

"It's a promising way to automate aspects of medication administration," says Robert Krawisz, executive director of the National Patient Safety Foundation. "The technology's impact at VA hospitals so far has been amazing." The Department of Veterans Affairs (VA) already uses bar codes nationwide in its hospitals, and the result has been a drastic reduction in medication errors. For example, the VA medical center in Topeka, Kan., has reported that bar coding reduced its medication error rate by 86 percent over a nine-year period.

Here's how it works: When patients enter the hospital, they get a bar-coded identification wristband that can transmit information to the hospital's computer, says Lottie Lockett, R.N., a nursing administrator at the Houston VA Medical Center. Nurses have laptop computers and scanners on top of medication carts that they bring to patients' rooms. Nurses use the scanners to scan the patient's wristband and the medications to be given. The bar codes provide unique, identifying information about drugs given at the patient's bedside. "Before giving medications, nurses use the scanner to pull up a patient's full name and social security number on the laptops, along with the medications," Lockett says. "If there is not a match between the patient and the medication or some other problem, a warning box pops up on the screen."

The FDA's proposed rule on bar code labeling was published on March 14, 2003. The rule, which would take effect in 2006, applies to prescription drugs, biological products such as vaccines, blood and blood components, and over-the-counter (OTC) drugs that are commonly used in hospitals. Manufacturers, repackers, relabelers, and private label distributors of prescription and OTC drugs would be subject to the bar code requirements. The agency continues to study whether it also should develop a rule requiring bar code labeling on medical devices.

Drug name confusion: To minimize confusion between drug names that look or sound alike, the FDA reviews about 300 drug names a year before they are marketed. "We reject about one-third of the names that drug companies propose," says Phillips. The agency tests drug names with the help of about 120 FDA health professionals who volunteer to simulate real-life drug order situations. "We're also creating a computerized program that will assist in detecting similar names and that will help us take a more scientific approach to comparing names," Phillips says.

After drugs are approved, the FDA tracks reports of errors due to drug name confusion and spreads the word to health professionals, along with recommendations for avoiding future problems. For example, the FDA has reported errors involving the inadvertent administration of methadone, a drug used to treat opiate dependence, rather than the intended Metadate ER (methylphenidate) for the treatment of attention-deficit/hyperactivity disorder (ADHD). One report involved the death of an 8-year-old boy after a possible medication error at the dispensing pharmacy. The child, who was being treated for ADHD, was found dead at home. Methadone substitution was the suspected cause of death. Some FDA recommendations regarding drug name confusion have encouraged pharmacists to separate similar drug products on pharmacy shelves and have encouraged physicians to indicate

GlaxoWellcome

**IMMEDIATE ATTENTION REQUIRED
DISPENSING ERRORS ALERT**

June 6 ??

Dear Pharmacist:

Glaxo Wellcome Inc. has received reports of prescription dispen~~~ ·
LAMICTAL® (lamotrigine) Tablets and LA~~~~ ·
~~us adver~~ ··

Letters alert health care professionals about drug mix-ups, such as dispensing errors between the antiepileptic drug Lamictal and the antifungal drug Lamisil.

both brand and generic drug names on prescription orders, as well as what the drug is intended to treat.

The last time the FDA changed a drug name after it was approved was in 1994 when the thyroid medicine Levoxine was being confused with the heart medicine Lanoxin (digoxin), and some people were hospitalized as a result. Now the thyroid medicine is called Levoxyl, and the agency hasn't received reports of errors since the name change. Other examples of drug name confusion reported to the FDA include:

- Serzone (nefazodone) for depression and Seroquel (quetiapine) for schizophrenia
- Lamictal (lamotrigine) for epilepsy, Lamisil (terbinafine) for nail infections, Ludiomil (maprotiline) for depression, and Lomotil (diphenoxylate) for diarrhea
- Taxotere (docetaxel) and Taxol (paclitaxel), both for chemotherapy
- Zantac (ranitidine) for heartburn, Zyrtec (cetirizine) for allergies, and Zyprexa (olanzapine) for mental conditions
- Celebrex (celecoxib) for arthritis and Celexa (citalopram) for depression.

Drug labeling: Consumers tend to overlook important label information on OTC drugs, according to a Harris Interactive Market Research Poll conducted for the National Council on Patient Information and Education and released in January 2002. In May 2002, an FDA regulation went into effect that aims to help consumers use OTC drugs more wisely.

The regulation requires a standardized "Drug Facts" label on more than 100,000 OTC drug products. Modeled after the Nutrition Facts label on foods, the label helps consumers compare and select OTC medicines and follow instructions. The label clearly lists active ingredients, uses, warnings, dosage, directions, other information, such as how to store the medicine, and inactive ingredients.

As for health professionals, the FDA proposed a new format in 2000 to improve prescription drug labeling for physicians, also known as the package insert. One FDA study showed that practitioners found the labeling to be lengthy, complex, and hard to use. The proposed redesign would feature a user-friendly format and would highlight critical information more clearly. The FDA is still reviewing public comments on this proposed rule. The agency has also been working on a project called DailyMed, a computer system that will be available without cost from the National Library of Medicine next year. DailyMed will have new information added daily, and will allow health professionals to pull up drug warnings and label changes electronically.

The FDA educates the public on an ongoing basis to prevent repeat errors.

Error tracking and public education: On March 13, 2003, the FDA announced a proposed rule that would revamp safety reporting requirements. For example, the proposal would require that reports on actual and potential medication errors be submitted to the agency within 15 calendar days. FDA's Seligman says, "This rule is part of FDA's overall effort to understand the sources of medication errors and prevent them."

The FDA reviews medication error reports that come from drug manufacturers and through MedWatch, the agency's safety information and adverse event reporting program. The agency also receives reports from the Institute for Safe Medication Practices (ISMP) and the U.S. Pharmacopeia, or USP (see "Who Tracks Medication Errors?").

A recent ISMP survey on medication error reporting practices showed that health professionals submit reports more often to internal reporting programs such as hospitals than to

Who Tracks Medication Errors?

The Food and Drug Administration

Accepts reports from consumers and health professionals about products regulated by the FDA, including drugs and medical devices, through MedWatch, the FDA's safety information and adverse event reporting program. For information on how to report, call 1-800-332-1088 or go to **www.fda.gov/medwatch/how.htm.**

Institute for Safe Medication Practices

Accepts reports from consumers and health professionals related to medication. Publishes *Safe Medicine*, a consumer newsletter on medication errors. 1800 Byberry Rd., Suite 810, Huntingdon Valley, PA 19006-3520 215-947-7797 **www.ismp.org/ Pages/Consumer.html**

U.S. Pharmacopeia

MedMARX is an anonymous medication error reporting program used by hospitals. **www.medmarx.com** 12601 Twinbrook Parkway, Rockville, MD 20852 1-800-822-8772 **www.usp.org**

---

external programs such as the FDA. According to ISMP, one reason may be health professionals' limited knowledge about external reporting programs.

The FDA receives and reviews about 250 medication error reports each month, and classifies them to determine the cause and type of error. Depending on the findings, the FDA can change the way it labels, names, or packages a drug product. In addition, once a problem is discovered, the FDA educates the public on an ongoing basis to prevent repeat errors.

If you see different doctors, it's important that they all know what you are taking.

In 2001, the agency released a public health advisory to hospitals, nursing homes, and other health care facilities about the hazards of mix-ups between medical gases, which are prescription drugs. In one case, a nursing home in Ohio reported four deaths after an employee mistakenly connected nitrogen to the oxygen system.

ISMP reports medication errors through various newsletters that target health professionals in acute care, nursing, and community/ambulatory care. Recently, ISMP launched a newsletter for consumers called *Safe Medicine*.

In December 2002, LISP released an analysis of medication errors captured in 2001 by its anonymous national reporting database, MedMARX. Of 105,603 errors, 3,361 errors (3.2 percent) involved children. Most of the errors were corrected before causing harm, but 190 caused patient injury and of those, two resulted in death. As a result of this analysis, USP released recommendations for preventing drug errors in children in January 2003.

Patient Safety Proposals

In March 2003, Health and Human Services Secretary Tommy G. Thompson announced two proposed roles from the FDA that will use state-of-the-art technology to improve patient safety. Here is a snapshot of each rule:

- **Bar codes:** Just as the technology is used in retail and other industries, required bar codes would contain unique identifying information about drugs. When used with bar code scanners and computerized patient information systems, bar code technology can prevent many medication errors, including administering the wrong drug or dose, or administering a drug to a patient with a known allergy.
- **Safety Reporting:** The proposed revamping of safety reporting requirements aims to enhance the FDA's ability to monitor and improve the safe use of drugs and biologics. The rule would improve the quality and consistency of safety reports, require the submission of all suspected serious reactions for blood and blood products, and require reports on important potential medication errors.

What Consumers Can Do

In one case reported to ISMP, a doctor called in a prescription for the antibiotic Noroxin (norfloxacin) for a patient with a bladder infection. But the pharmacist thought the order was for Neurontin (gabapentin), a medication used to treat seizures. The good news is that the patient read the medication leaflet stapled to his medication bag, noticed the drug he received is used to treat seizures, and then asked about it. ISMP president Michael Cohen, R. Ph., Sc.D., says, "You should expect to count on the

Hospital Strategies

Hospitals and other health care organizations work to reduce medication errors by using technology, improving processes, zeroing in on errors that cause harm, and building a culture of safety, Here are a couple of examples.

Pharmacy intervention: It was a challenge for health care providers, especially surgeons, at Fairview Southdale Hospital in Edina, Minn., to ensure that patients continued taking their regularly prescribed medicines when they entered the hospital, says Steven Meisel, Pharm. D., director of medication safety at Fairview Health Services. "Surgeons are not typically the original prescribers," he says. The solution was to have pharmacy technicians record complete medication histories on a form. In a pilot program, the technicians called most patients on the phone a couple of days before surgery. A pharmacist reviewed the information and then the surgeon decided which medications should be continued. After three months, the number of order errors per patient dropped by 84 percent, and the pilot program became permanent.

Computerized Physician Order Entry (CPOE): Studies have shown that CPOE is effective in reducing medication errors. It involves entering medication orders directly into a computer system rather than on paper or verbally. The Institute for Safe Medication Practices conducted a survey of 1,500 hospitals in 2001 and found that about 3 percent of hospitals were using CPOE, and the number is rising. Eugene Wiener, M.D., medical director at the Children's Hospital of Pittsburgh, says, "There is no misinterpretation of handwriting, decimal points, or abbreviations. This puts everything in a digital world."

The Pittsburgh hospital unveiled its CPOE system in October 2002. Developed by the hospital and the Cerner Corporation in Kansas City, Mo., Children'sNet has replaced most paper forms and prescription pads. Wiener says that, unlike with adults, most drug orders for children are generally based on weight. "The computer won't let you put an order in if the child's weight isn't in the system," he says, "and if the weight changes, the computer notices." The system also provides all kinds of information about potential drug complications that the doctor might not have thought about. "Doctors always have a choice in dealing with the alerts," Wiener says. "They can choose to move past an alert, but the alert makes them stop and think based on the specific patient indications."

—M.M.

health system to keep you safe, but there are also steps you can take to look out for yourself and your family."

• Know what kind of errors occur. The FDA evaluated reports of fatal medication errors that it received from 1993 to 1998 and found that the most common types of errors involved administering an improper dose (41 percent), giving the wrong drug (16 percent), and using the wrong route of administration (16 percent). The most common causes of the medication errors were performance and knowledge deficits (44 percent) and communication errors (16 percent). Almost half of the fatal medication errors occurred in people over 60. Older people are especially at risk for errors because they often take multiple medications. Children are also a vulnerable population because drugs are often dosed based on their weight, and accurate calculations are critical.

• Find out what drug you're taking and what it's for.

Rather than simply letting the doctor write you a prescription and send you on your way, be sure to ask the name of the drug. Cohen says, "I would also ask the doctor to put the purpose of the prescription on the order." This serves as a check in case there is some confusion about the drug name. If you're in the hospital, ask (or have a friend or family member ask) what drugs you are being given and why.

There are steps you can take to look out for yourself and your family.

• Find out how to take the drug and make sure you understand the directions. If you are told to take a medicine three times a day, does that mean eight hours apart exactly or at mealtimes? Should the medicine be stored at room temperature or in the refrigerator? Are there any medications, beverages, or foods you should avoid? Also, ask about what medication side effects you might expect and what you should do about them. And read the bottle's label every time you take a drug to avoid mistakes. In the middle of the night, you could mistake ear drops for eye drops, or accidentally give your older child's medication to the baby if you're not careful. Else the measuring device that comes with the medicine, not spoons from the kitchen drawer. If you take multiple medications and have trouble keeping them straight, ask your doctor or pharmacist about compliance aids, such as containers with sections for daily doses. Family members can help by reminding you to take your medicine.

• Keep a list of all medications, including OTC drugs, as well as dietary supplements, medicinal herbs, and other substances you take for health reasons, and report it to your health care providers. The often-forgotten things that you should tell your doctor about include vitamins, laxatives, sleeping aids, and birth control pills. One National Institutes of Health study showed a significant drug interaction between the herbal product St. John's wort and indinavir, a protease inhibitor used to treat HIV infection. Some antibiotics can lower the effectiveness of birth control pills. If you see different doctors, it's important that they all know what you are taking. If possible, get all your prescriptions filled at the same pharmacy so that all of your records are in one place. Also, make sure your doctors and pharmacy know about your medication allergies or other unpleasant drug reactions you may have experienced.

• **If in doubt, ask, ask, ask.** Be on the lookout for clues of a problem, such as if your pills look different than normal or if you notice a different drug name or different directions than what you thought. Robert Krawisz of the National Patient Safety Foundation says it's best to be cautious and ask questions if you're unsure about anything. "If you forget, don't hesitate to call your doctor or pharmacist when you get home,' he says. "It can't hurt to ask."

For More Information

Agency for Healthcare Research and Quality Brochures: "20 Tips. to Help Prevent Medical Errors" and "20 Tips to Help Prevent Medical Errors in Children" 1-800-358-9295 Food and Drug Administration

"Think it Through: A Guide to Managing the Benefits and Risks of Medicines" (www.fda.gov/cder/consumerinfo/ think.htm) 1-888-878-3256

From *FDA Consumer,* May/June 2003, pp. 21-27.

The Price of Pain

You get relief. You also get some health risk. This is the deal you cut

AMANDA SPAKE AND JILL KONIECZKO

In the past few months, David Borenstein's life and his Washington, D.C., rheumatology practice have become something of a nightmare. Most of his patients suffer chronic pain and inflammation from arthritis, back pain, or muscular-skeletal diseases. "I see over 100 patients a week," says Borenstein. "My life is about trying to keep these people functional."

And that mission is becoming an increasingly difficult challenge every day. In the past few weeks, both Celebrex and Bextra—which belong to a popular class of pain relievers known as Cox-2 inhibitors—and the widely used over-the-counter pain reliever naproxen, sold as Aleve, have been linked to an increase in heart attacks and strokes. Two large government-funded trials of these drugs to prevent colon cancer and Alzheimer's disease have been stopped, though officials admit that the heart risk revealed in these studies is preliminary and conflicts with data from other studies. The drugmaker Pfizer agreed to stop direct-to-consumer advertising of Celebrex after patients taking the drug had a 2.5-fold increased risk of major cardiovascular events. The Food and Drug Administration issued an advisory recommending that doctors limit use of the Cox-2 inhibitors and that consumers adhere to the label directions for nonprescription pain pills, taking them no longer than 10 days without physician supervision.

Nation in pain. As a result, many doctors have been deluged with calls from frightened patients. "Everybody takes these drugs," says Elizabeth Tindall, president of the American College of Rheumatology and in private practice in Portland, Ore. Indeed, pain reliever sales are estimated by Kalorama Information at more than $18.8 billion in 2004, not surprising when over 30 million Americans take a nonsteroidal anti-inflammatory drug, or NSAID, every day.

Until recently, the NSAID naproxen was thought to be mildly protective of the heart. Available over the counter for the past decade, naproxen is recommended to treat everything from the muscle soreness suffered by weekend jocks to severe joint pain among rheumatoid arthritis sufferers. Yet, a $26 million, five-year Alzheimer's trial was suspended by the National Institutes of Health last month after naproxen was linked to a 50 percent increase in cardiovascular events.

"They stopped the trial for an unclear reason," says Eric Topol of the Cleveland Clinic. "This would be the only study of its kind to show harm with naproxen. A 50 percent increase in heart attacks and strokes? Fifty percent of what?" But no additional data have been forthcoming, and NIH refused to provide any scientist to answer questions about why the trial was stopped or what it might reveal.

Topol is one of many scientists skeptical of the unconfirmed results and critical of this type of medicine by press release. "It had already been a terrible situation for patients on Vioxx," says Topol, who believes the FDA should have insisted on warnings about the drug sooner, so patients could evaluate their heart risk with their doctors. Now, he says, stopping the Aleve study has "added to the fear and panic that already exists about pain relievers."

Danger for the heart. The panic over pain relievers has raged since Vioxx was withdrawn from the market in September. Patients taking the drug in a cancer prevention trial experienced a more than twofold increase in heart attacks and strokes. Like Vioxx, Celebrex and Bextra also block the Cox-2 enzymes, which trigger the body's pain and inflammatory responses.

Studies show that the pain relief from older NSAIDs like aspirin and ibuprofen is comparable to that from the Cox-2s. But researchers have also learned that blocking only the Cox-2 enzyme may protect the stomach but also endanger the heart. The Cox-2 inhibitors reduce production of a natural body fat that prevents blood platelets from clumping together. Reducing this lipid "is like removing a natural break to clotting," explains Garret FitzGerald, chairman of pharmacology at the University of Pennsylvania. FitzGerald was the first to identify the mechanism by which the Cox-2s enhance clotting and may hasten hardening of the arteries.

"The phase we're moving into now," says FitzGerald, "is that these drugs have value, and we need to conserve their value while managing the risk. The main question to answer is what exactly is the cardiovascular risk in people with conditions the drugs were designed to treat, namely arthritis." The problem, says Cleveland's Topol, is that we don't have the data to make that calculation: "We know from some surveys that about half of arthritis patients have heart disease. But we have never looked at this enormous population of patients."

Janet Woodcock, acting deputy commissioner for operations at the FDA, agrees that the lack of studies is a problem in evaluating all pain relievers. "Look at naproxen. It's always looked better against other NSAIDs, more like aspirin. But we don't know if that's because it is better, or the other NSAIDs are worse, in that they increase the risk of heart attack more than naproxen." And none of this uncertainty will be resolved until an FDA advisory committee meets next month on the safety of arthritis drugs.

So what are patients to do? "It's a good time to review family history of strokes, heart attacks and try to make the best possible decision with limited information," says Oregon's Tindall. Internist A. Mark Fendrick, at the University of Michigan Hospital, agrees. "If you are taking any chronic nonsteroidal anti-inflammatory drug—over the counter, prescription, Cox-2, or not—it's very important to talk to your doctor and evaluate whether you need an NSAID in light of these real gastrointestinal and possible cardiovascular risks." Fendrick worries about the large number of people taking Cox-2s plus aspirin for heart protection, because aspirin eliminates the gastrointestinal benefit of Cox-2s."My preference is not to use an NSAID at all."

David Borenstein thinks that's unrealistic for many of his patients. Diseases like arthritis have enormous impact on cardiovascular health, he says. "If you can't move, your heart gets flabby and it doesn't work well. So whether to take these drugs, or what drugs to take, has to be a balance."

UNIT 6

Sexuality and Relationships

Unit Selections

Key Points to Consider

- Do you feel at risk of contracting AIDS or other STDs? If not, why not? If you do, what are you doing to reduce your risk?

- What is meant by a "love culture"?

- Should very young children be taught about sex?

- Is the viewing of pornography by couples a harmless or harmful activity?

Student Website

www.mhcls.com/online

Internet References

Further information regarding these websites may be found in this book's preface or online.

Planned Parenthood
   http://www.plannedparenthood.org/
Sexuality Information and Education Council of the United States (SIECUS)
   http://www.siecus.org/

Sexuality is an important part of both self awareness and intimate relationships.

How important is physical attraction in establishing and maintaining intimate relationships? Researchers in the area of evolutionary psychology have proposed numerous theories that attempt to explain the mutual attraction that occurs between the sexes. The most controversial of these theories postulates that our perception of beauty or physical attractiveness is not subjective but rather a biological component hardwired into our brains. It is generally assumed that perceptions of beauty vary from era to era and culture to culture, but evidence is mounting that suggests people everywhere share a common sense of beauty that is based on physical symmetry.

While physical attraction is clearly an important issue when it comes to dating, how important is it in long-term loving relationships? For many Americans the answer may be very important, because we tend to be a "Love Culture," a culture that places a premium on passion in the selection of our mates. Is passion an essential ingredient in love, and can passion serve to sustain a long-term meaningful relationship? Since most people can't imagine marrying someone that they don't love, we must assume that most marriages are based on this feeling we call love. That being the case, why is it that so few marriages survive the

rigors of day-to-day living? Perhaps the answer has more to do with our limited definition of love than love itself. "Promiscuous Plague" examines the state of America's sexual health through a presentation that includes current statistical data and interviews with individuals personally involved with unintended pregnancies, STDs, HIV/AIDS, homosexuality, and abortion. A related topic is that sex is good for health. Studies are showing that an active sex life may lead to a longer life, better ability to withstand pain, a healthy immune system, less heart disease and cancer, and lower rates of depression.

An important topic of interest and controversy in the area of human sexuality is sex education. While most states mandate some type of school-based sex education, many parents believe they should be the source of their children's sexuality education, not the schools. There is a growing number of parents who also believe that sex education should begin much earlier than school age and that it's never too early to teach children about sex. In "Sex Ed For the Stroller Set," Jodi Kantor reports on parents who are teaching sex education to children as young as two and three.

Perhaps no topic in the area of human sexuality has garnered more publicity and public concern than the dangers associated with unprotected sex. Although the concept of "safe sex" is nothing new, the degree of open and public discussion regarding sexual behaviors is. With the emergence of AIDS as a disease of epidemic proportions and the rapid spreading of other sexually transmitted diseases (STDs), the surgeon general of the United States initiated an aggressive educational campaign based on the assumption that knowledge would change behavior. If STD rates among teens are any indication as to the effectiveness of this approach, then we must conclude that our educational efforts are failing. Conservatives believe that while education may play a role in curbing the spread of STDs, the root of the problem is promiscuity, and promiscuity rises when a society is undergoing a moral decline. The solution, according to conservatives, is a joint effort between parents and educators in which students are taught the importance of values such as respect, responsibility, and integrity. Liberals, on the other hand, think that preventing promiscuity is unrealistic, and instead the focus should be on establishing open and frank discussions between the sexes. Their premise is that we are all sexual beings, and the best way to combat STDs is to establish discussions between sexual partners so that condoms will be used correctly when couples engage in intercourse.

While education undoubtedly has had a positive impact on slowing the spread of STDs, perhaps it was unrealistic to think that education alone was the solution, given the magnitude and the nature of the problem. Most experts agree that for education to succeed in changing personal behaviors the following conditions must be met: (1) The recipients of the information must first perceive themselves as vulnerable and, thus, be motivated to explore replacement behaviors, and (2) the replacement behaviors must satisfy the needs that were the basis of the problem behaviors. To date most education programs have failed to meet these criteria. Given all the information that we now have on the dangers associated with AIDS and STDs, why is it that people do not perceive themselves at risk? It is not so much the denial of risks as it is the notion that when it comes to choosing sex partners most people think that they use good judgment. Unfortunately, most decisions regarding sexual behavior are based on subjective criteria that bear little or no relationship to one's actual risk. Even when individuals do view themselves as vulnerable to AIDS and STDs, there are currently only two viable options for reducing the risk of contracting these diseases. The first is the use of a condom and the second is sexual abstinence, neither of which is an ideal solution to the problem.

You, Me, and Porn Make Three

Pornography can be a harmless pleasure—or a source of bitter resentment. How do you prevent the XXX explosion from undermining your relationship?

LIZA FEATHERSTONE

When her new boyfriend confessed that he looked at porn, Donna, 37, made her views clear to him. "I'm very anti-pornography," she says. "I think it's very degrading to women. I told him: This is something I can't have in a relationship." He assured her that he'd only been interested in porn because he was single and lonely. Then, last year, after the two had been married nine months, she found out he'd never stopped, at times spending as much as $120 a month on Internet raunch.

Donna, who lives in a small town in Connecticut, was stunned. "I blamed myself—I wasn't attractive enough. I have a weight problem—I blamed it on that." She also worried that she was overreacting: "Was I too strict? Too moral? Missing something?" Beyond her doubts about herself, she had a larger problem to deal with: "It broke my trust in the marriage."

Porn-gazing—whether chronic or casual—can become an explosive issue for a couple, corroding intimacy and demolishing the sexual connection. But reactions to pornography can be as varied as human desire itself, and fault is often in the eye of the beholder. For couples who already have sexual conflicts or difficulty trusting each other, porn can play a particularly destructive role. Yet in some situations, erotic material can be a healthy outlet for sexual fantasy, possibly bringing a couple closer together. Even a conflict over pornography, handled constructively, can improve a relationship.

Erotic images are more available—and more mainstream—than ever. According to comScore, which measures Internet traffic, 66 percent of Internet—using men between the ages of 18 and 34 look at online porn at least once a month. In the past, guys hid their liking for smut; now, they can openly embrace it, thanks to Jenna Jameson, *Stuff* magazine and a porn-friendly culture. As a result, pornography-related conflicts among couples are becoming more common, marriage counselors say. The argument often has a similar refrain: He looks at it, she hates it and each resents the other. In a 2003 study published in the *Journal of Sex and Marital Therapy*, Ana Bridges and her co-authors found that while most women weren't bothered by their partner's X-rated interest, a significant minority were extremely distressed by it. But are they right to be worried? Is the anguish misdirected—or is there something to fear about porn?

The Facts of Life

Many women feel betrayed by porn, even though their mates don't necessarily perceive it as a transgression. "It was infidelity," says Suzanne Vail, 43, of Nashua, New Hampshire, describing her ex-boyfriend's habit. "I felt cheated on." More than a quarter of the women in Bridges's study agreed. The feelings may arise from an unrealistic understanding of fantasy in adult sexuality, suggests marital therapist Michele Weiner-Davis, author of *The Sex-Starved Marriage* and founder of Divorce-Busting, a therapy and coaching service aimed at saving marriages. Partners, even long-term ones, may have never discussed fantasies. "On the conservative end of the spectrum, some wives are upset that the husband would think about any other images or other women," she says. "I'm just amazed at that—some of these couples have been together a long time!"

Weiner-Davis will often try to "do a little sexual education," explaining that fantasy is normal and that a lot of people enjoy sexually explicit images—especially men, who tend to be more visually oriented. If that "doesn't make a dent, if the wife is truly beside herself, it is a betrayal and I treat it as such." Weiner-Davis doesn't necessarily agree that a husband in this situation is cheating, but the emotional dynamics are much the same: The porn user needs to understand his partner's hurt feelings, and she needs to find a way to forgive him.

Looking at porn in terms of right or wrong isn't helpful. The question is: What can couples do about it?

Many women feel that the guy who looks at porn must harbor some hostility toward women. Yet research hasn't established a link between pornography consumption and misogyny. One 2004 study found that porn users actually had slightly more positive and egalitarian views of women than other men did, though porn users were also more likely to hold stereotypical beliefs—for example, that women are more moral.

It's a counterintuitive finding, likely to annoy both conservatives and antiporn feminists. But simultaneously liking porn and respecting women is consistent with a liberal outlook, which typically combines tolerance with an egalitarian perspective. If your boyfriend has an abortion-rights bumper sticker and a stash of hardcore smut on his computer, he may be Jerry Falwell's worst nightmare, but he's not all that unusual. Or perhaps the connection between porn watching and pro-female attitudes is more fundamental, suggests James Beggan, a University of Louisville sociologist who co-authored the study with psychologist colleagues at Texas Tech University. "If you spend your time looking at pictures of naked women," he observes, "that's not really consistent with not liking women. It's consistent with liking them."

Living Up to the Fantasy

Phil, a 46-year-old writer in New York City, doesn't enjoy porn that much. But when it first became readily available online, the novelty sucked him in. "In the early days of the Internet, I would sometimes surf through reams of online flesh," he recalls wryly, "but I found it numbingly repetitive, and the opposite of arousing." Partly out of boredom, Phil (not his real name) used some of the images to teach himself graphic design. When his wife found the files on his computer, "she freaked," he recalls. "I was just pasting women's heads on different naked bodies—you know, perfectly normal behavior," he jokes, "but it did not sit at all well with the real-life woman I was living with."

Phil's wife was the kind of gorgeous blonde that most men only fantasize about, yet he suspects that his looking at porn made her feel inadequate. He was bewildered. Any notion that he was looking at cheesy Internet images because she wasn't good enough, he says, "would have been wildly misguided." (The couple has since divorced for other reasons.)

That fear is very real for many women, who worry they can't compete with the airbrushed perfection of the porn star. And they are "absolutely right," says Barry McCarthy, author of *Rekindling Desire*, and a therapist in Washington—they can't. But not measuring up to an illusion shouldn't be cause for worry, he adds. What makes the woman in porn so erotic is not her red lips and her fake breasts, but the fact that she's "crazy," says McCarthy: she's ever ready, always willing to do anything to please a man. No real woman could or would want to be that way.

Psychologically healthy men don't have much trouble distinguishing between reality and the weird world of commercial raunch. The trouble emerges, McCarthy says, when a person "can't differentiate between fantasy and reality: 'Why isn't my girlfriend like that? Why isn't she into sex with animals? Why won't she let me ejaculate on her face?'" Suzanne Vail, who operates an online group for women who believe their partners are sex addicts, says women in her group have attempted to please porn-obsessed men through liposuction, breast surgery and crash dieting. If a man has a driving need to make his real-life partner into a porn star, he's got a problem. A woman who acquiesces in such an impossible pursuit may quickly find that she's got one, too.

When Porn Is Good for You

Porn can actually help foster emotional and sexual intimacy, says Colorado psychologist David Schnarch, author of *Resurrecting Sex*, who runs a couples therapy practice with his wife. He explains: "A significant portion of our work in helping couples develop a deeper sexual connection is through erotic images. Erotica, as well as couples' own masturbatory fantasies, can be useful tools for helping them develop as adults." How couples intensify their sexual relationship differs radically depending on the individuals and on the dynamic between them. But fantasy is certainly a part of a healthy sex life, and porn does contribute significantly to the archive of sexy scenarios in our heads. It can also inspire couples to experiment more.

Interestingly, in Ana Bridges's study, the women with the most positive views of porn's role in their relationship were engaged in a more creative activity: The couples were taking sexy pictures of one another, removing entirely the problem of competition with the busty and lascivious commercial sex bomb. "It's very validating," says Bridges. "It's me turning you on. Even in my absence, you want to look at me."

She's Looking, Too

While men do look at porn more than women do, the ease and privacy of the Internet allow many women who would never have dared in the past to explore this realm. Fully half of the women in Bridges's study said they looked at pornography themselves.

And women can become just as obsessed as men. Jennifer Schneider, an M.D. who has studied sex addicts, interviewed several women who became hooked on smut. One 35-year-old married woman said the pictures (especially those depicting S&M scenarios) "would haunt me day and night." The habit began to erode her marriage. "My husband could no longer satisfy me," she told Schneider. "I wanted what I saw in the videos and pictures and was too embarrassed to ask him for it." The woman said she was freed from her obsessions by God, but a good marital therapist might have viewed this as an opportunity for the couple to learn to talk to each other about their desires—and perhaps try something new.

There is little solid research on how men feel about their female partner's porn use—or, for that matter, on how porn figures into gay relationships, which could help illuminate how much a straight couple's porn conflict is really a matter of gender differences. Some men clearly find it sexy, perhaps seeing her porn interest as a sign of a woman's experimental nature or aggressive libido. But writer Pamela Paul argues in her new book, *Pornified: How Pornography Is Transforming Our Lives, Our Relationships and Our Families*, that while many men hope their partner approves of (or at least tolerates) their own porn interest, they may be critical of a girlfriend or wife who uses pornography herself. A 2004 *Elle*MSNBC.com poll found that six in ten men were concerned about their partner's interest in Internet smut.

Drawing the Line

Dose matters. According to research by the late Alvin Cooper of the Silicon Valley Psychotherapy Center, people engaged in any kind of online sexual activity for less than an hour a week said it had little impact on their lives; people using it for 11 or more hours a week said it affected both their self-image and their feelings about their partners. Anywhere between one and ten hours a week is ambiguous terrain. It may just be a way to release stress, but as Cooper has pointed out, "the Internet is...a very powerful force that people can quickly develop a problem with, like crack cocaine."

Because it's sexual, porn is a more loaded distancing strategy than golf or too much time at the office.

Donna's husband, Steve, was just such a person. "Before, the pain and embarrassment of buying a magazine or going into a sex shop would stop him," she says. "Once he got the computer, that was it." Some individuals are vulnerable to compulsive porn use because of their own psychological makeup. Steve is a diagnosed obsessive-compulsive, and in his case, the availability and anonymity of Internet porn lent itself to ritualistic, uncontrollable behavior. But online pornography can become an obsession even for people without psychological disorders, simply because it is so easily available and taps into such a powerful appetite.

Sometimes a Dirty Picture Isn't Just a Dirty Picture

Not everyone is going to embrace porn as a positive force. But it is usually possible to work through the conflicts posed by pornography use. Michele Weiner-Davis encourages couples to explore what it means in the dynamic of the relationship: Why does it bother her so much? Is there something he gets from it that he could be getting from the relationship? "Sometimes it is relational," she says. "For example, the wife may not understand the importance of a good sex life. Sometimes she's not experimental or passionate. If, in a long-term marriage, couples don't have a common goal of keeping marriage passionate," she says, an X-rated habit can be a symptom of restlessness.

A heavy reliance on porn may be an outgrowth of other sexual discontents. Many men complain that their wives have gained weight and are no longer very attractive, says Weiner-Davis. Others prefer smut to real sex because while they're viewing porn, they're in control, McCarthy and Weiner-Davis agree. Says McCarthy, "Couple sex is much more complicated." Says Bridges, "People think it's just a way to masturbate, but in a relationship it can be a punishment: 'I don't want to be with you right now.'"

In the case of one couple Bridges saw, the husband had pulled away from his wife's constant criticism and retreated into fantasy. She had to learn not to be so mean, says Bridges. While there are countless ways to withdraw from a spouse, porn is both satisfying and readily available. And because it's sexual, it's a far more loaded distancing strategy than playing golf or spending too much time at the office.

One solution to the porn dilemma that clearly doesn't work: surveillance. It undermines trust and can foster its own obsessions. Suzanne Vail says partners may get compulsive about monitoring, just as those married to drug addicts or alcoholics can become overly involved in policing addictions.

Researchers and therapists concur that couples are better off treating the conflict as a practical matter rather than a moral issue. Faith may not be such an important consideration: Bridges found that nonreligious women were just as likely as religious women to be upset over a partner's porn use. "Looking at this in terms of right or wrong isn't helpful," says Weiner-Davis. "There's a great deal of variation in what turns people on, and the question is: What can we as a couple do about it?" As she points out, couples work hard to reach agreement on many issues—how they will spend money, where they will live, whether they will have children—but often neglect to achieve any sort of consensus on their sex life: how often, what sort of activities, how much extracurricular interest is acceptable.

A couple may never see eye-to-eye on porn; even if he's not compulsive, she may always feel that it's disgusting (or immoral). As David Schnarch has often pointed out, tolerating discomfort—and recognizing that a partner's desires may be different from yours—is critical to a fully adult, intimate sexual relationship. Then again, if porn is repellent to someone you love, it may be worthwhile to call it quits, like smoking or other cherished habits we give up for the sake of a relationship. As Weiner-Davis says of porn, "You won't get a disease, but it could cost you your marriage."

LIZA FEATHERSTONE is a Manhattan-based freelance writer.

Sex Ed for the Stroller Set

JODI KANTOR

This September 3-year-old Halley Vollmar of Bellmore, N.Y., was having her annual checkup when her pediatrician paused. "I'm going to check your peepee now," he warned, and tugged down her underwear. But Halley protested. "Mommy, why he call my vagina a peepee?" she scolded, telling the startled physician he was a "silly doctor" before allowing him to proceed.

Last week Kristin Hansen, Halley's mother, recounted the story to several other women with a satisfied laugh. The gathering in Wantagh, N.Y., was something of a reunion. Over the summer the mothers had convened weekly for lessons in how to educate their toddlers about sex, a program they found so necessary they are already planning to reconvene next year.

Halley may be surprisingly articulate about her private parts, but she is in excellent company. Like many other parents and educators, the mothers chatting over lemonade and coffee cake in Susan Vartoukian's toy-strewn home maintain that sex education—once and mostly still an awkward fixture of the pubescent years—should begin early. And when they say early, they mean it: preferably from birth, or if not that, from toilet training age. "Parents don't have the luxury of silence anymore," said Nanette Ecker, a sex educator at the Nassau County chapter of Planned Parenthood, who led the group.

For most adults, knowledge of intercourse came as a distinct moment of revelation: an "aha" moment in the schoolyard or the living room when the mysterious connection between body parts and babies was made suddenly and shockingly clear. But now children who are practically babies themselves are learning how babies are made.

For most parents and educators, it's never too early for the facts.

According to this approach, toddlers should learn words like "vulva" at the same time they learn "ears" and "toes," benign-sounding myths about storks and seeds constitute harmful misinformation, and any child who can ask about how he or she was created is old enough for a truthful answer.

"People have been told by experts that there's a right age" to learn about intercourse, said Dr. Justin Richardson, a assistant professor of psychiatry at Cornell and Columbia medical

schools and an author of "Everything You Never Wanted Your Kids to Know About Sex (But Were Afraid They'd Ask)," one of a number of recently published guides that advocates early tutelage.

"If you're talking about how babies are made, there's no age at which it is harmful to learn that the penis goes into the vagina," he said. "Yes, it's true that exposing a child to sexual stimulation is harmful. But telling a kid how babies are made is very different."

The general cultural environment has become so vulgar, the early-approach advocates say, that sex education has become a race: parents must reach children before other forces—from misinformed playground confidantes to pubescent-looking models posed in their skivvies—do. "We need to get there first," said Deborah M. Roffman, a sex educator and the author of "But How'd I Get in There in the First Place? Talking to Your Young Child About Sex."

If not, these advocates warn, children will gather their impressions anywhere and everywhere: from prime-time television jokes about threesomes, Internet pop-up ads for penis enlargement pills or even more explicit Web sites. When the Rev. Debra Haffner's son typed "Katrina images" into Google's search box for a school project, he ended up staring at photographs that had nothing to do with the hurricane, said Ms. Haffner, a Unitarian Universalist minister and the author of "From Diapers to Dating."

"When parents say to me, 'But my child is too young, I want to keep them safe and innocent for as long as I can,' I say, 'Do you take them grocery shopping?'" Ms. Haffner said, referring to the naughty poses and headlines featured on magazines at the checkout counter.

Early sex education is a small and hard-to-measure movement, but it's a growing one, with advocates like Ms. Roffman, Ms. Haffner and Dr. Richardson writing books and conducting seminars for parents, preschool teachers and day care providers. Many chapters of Planned Parenthood offer workshops on the topic and so do some evangelical Christian churches.

"The classic approach in religious circles has been, shield their innocence for as long as you can, until they're 13, then give them The Talk," said Stanton L. Jones, a professor of psychology and the provost of Wheaton College in Illinois. Dr. Stanton and his wife, Brenna Jones, wrote "The Story of Me," a sex education book for 3-to-5-year-olds. (The book emphasizes

God's contribution and traditional gender roles, and says less about intercourse than many of its secular equivalents).

Lately the Joneses "have found a lot of acceptance" for starting sex education early, Mr. Jones said; pastors teach their approach at conferences on family life, and the book is sold by the conservative evangelical group Focus on the Family.

Teaching babies how babies are made.

Robie H. Harris, a leading author of sex education books for children, started on the topic in 1994 with "It's Perfectly Normal" for preteenagers. (There are now 400,000 copies in print in the United States and more than a million worldwide.) Since then she has found herself addressing progressively younger audiences: first with "It's So Amazing," geared to 7-year-olds and up, and now "It's Not the Stork," due this summer, and intended for children as young as 4. In 2008 she is to publish a volume aimed at 2½-year-olds. Her steady downward demographic shift, she said, is purely in response to parental demand. "Everyplace I would speak, I would hear, 'I don't know how to talk about this,'" Ms. Harris said.

On the whole, early sex education has attracted little organized resistance. While Ms. Harris's "It's Perfectly Normal" often appears on the American Library Association's annual list of most frequently challenged books—critics object to its references to homosexuality, contraception and masturbation—her work for younger children has drawn less attention. Perhaps this is because early sex education is a matter of parental choice or because the materials tend to concentrate on basic biology and safety.

Rather, the resistance comes from parents who cannot imagine initiating a conversation about sex with children who cannot read a book or ride a bicycle, and haven't yet displayed any curiosity about the matter. Rachel Wolman of Chevy Chase, Md., said she "would definitely not" sit her 3-year-old daughter down "for a birds-and-bees discussion."

"I'm guessing that kids wise up pretty quick by the time they get to 5," she added, "but even at that point, I'm not prepared to have a sit-down to run through how things work."

Jaymi Offir, a mother in Caldwell, N.J., said that introducing the topic to her daughter, Zoe, nearly 4, "would only confuse her."

"Being proactive at sex ed would be more appropriate for 9- or 10-year-olds," she said.

But even if parents of kindergarten-age children aren't prepared to discuss intercourse, early-childhood sex educators urge parents to abandon the usual litany of babyish names for private parts: the rather insulting "weenie" for boys, the murky "down there" for girls and so on. (A 1997 study in the journal Gender and Psychoanalysis showed that fewer girls are taught names for their genitals than boys, and that while girls learn the names of male genitals, the reverse is often not the case.)

When showing children their eyes and noses, "we don't say 'blink blink' or 'blow blow,'" said Ms. Ecker of Planned Parenthood.

Instead some toddlers are learning startlingly specific, biologically correct terms that even adults tend to confuse. "It's Not the Stork" includes a drawing of the vas deferens (the tubes that carry sperm); many educators emphasize the difference between the vagina (the tract that connects the uterus to the outside of the body) and the vulva (a collective term for all of the external female genital organs).

Early childhood sex educators also caution parents about never—no matter how mortifying the question—lying to children. Or feeding them benign-sounding half truths. Or even distracting them. "Kids have a right to have this information," Ms. Harris said. "If we ignore it, then the myths and fears start coming in."

The solution, they agree, is to give correct but simple answers. Parents have a tendency to blurt out more than what's needed: answering a question about nipples, say, with a flustered, halting lecture on sexual pleasure.

"If a child holds up a tampon and says, 'What's this?'" said Bill Taverner, the director of education for Planned Parenthood of Greater Northern New Jersey, "the best answer may just be, 'that's a tampon.' Having a name for something is sometimes enough."

The early education approach has exaggerated the already wide disparities in what various kids know, and some arrive at school so fluent that they fluster their teachers. (Though some public elementary schools do teach sex education, especially HIV awareness, it's a scattered affair, varying enormously not only by state but by district and even classroom.)

Take Mr. Taverner's son Rob, whose first-grade teacher refused to hang on the bulletin board a drawing on which the child had scrawled, "Sex is when two married people join the egg and the sperm."

Even parents who have embraced this kind of frankness seem somewhat taken aback by it. Back in Wantagh, Diana Lee shook her head over the difference between the rich sexual education her daughter, Alexandra, already had, and the skimpy one she received as a child.

"I was surprised I had to tell her so much at 3 years old," she said. "I'm still waiting for The Talk," she added of her own parents' silence on the matter.

"It's a fun time at dinner now," Ms. Vartoukian, the host of the Wantagh gathering, said, gesturing at her two small boys. "We have The Talk every single night."

It's Just Mechanics

Viagra is just the start: we'll soon have pills that make you feel deep love and video games that give vibrations. Ziauddin Sardar on the masturbatory society

ZIAUDDIN SARDAR

Is your sex life normal? The question was raised recently on the *Oprah Winfrey Show*. Tell us, the show asked its 20 million viewers, what turns you on, what turns you off, and what makes good sex.

The problem with such questions is that there are no "normal" answers. The normal is problematic because our ideas about sex have changed fundamentally. What constitutes normal is constantly refurbished. Its boundaries shift rapidly, and continue to shift. So what was abnormal yesterday—say, pornography—becomes normal today. And what is shunned today (say paedophilia) may just as easily become normal tomorrow.

One huge jump was provided by Viagra. In less than six years since the impotence pill came on the market, Viagra and its competitors, Levitra and Cialis, have transformed sexual norms and practices. As Meika Loe argues in *The Rise of Viagra* (New York University Press), it has redefined the concept of normal and changed the language of sex.

From the beginning, this was a treatment branded and marketed as normal. Impotence was called "erectile dysfunction", or simply ED—a common condition, as the football legend Pele assured us in TV ads, but not normal. Moreover, it did not arise from psychological causes or physical damage; rather, it was a simple medical condition rectified by a pill. Suddenly, drug company surveys discovered that more than half the US adult male population suffered from ED; figures for Europe were not far behind.

So if you can't get it up because you're pissed, stressed out, simply not in the mood or no longer find your partner attractive, you are actually suffering from a disease. And like all diseases, it must be cured. The cure is to swallow a pill and have sex no matter what, any where, any time, whenever. This has now become the norm.

Viagra is another step in stripping sex of all its complexity. Sex has been reduced to a simple question: for men, "how big?"; for women, "how long?". Combine these conundrums with other features of a market economy, such as availability on demand, choice, flexibility to mix'n'match, and we have new definitions not just of sex and love but of what it means to be human.

Today, to be normal, humans have sex right up to their last breath. It's the way to go. Sex is no longer the indulgence of the young. Nowadays, it is people over 50 who are having the most sex. With demographic shifts, high divorce rates and early retirement, the erstwhile golden generation of Sixties swingers who let it all hang out are now the "silver singles" (as they are called in America). The preoccupations of their youth have been sustained through their later years by medical enhancements. The wet dreams of 60-year-olds, who turned on to chemical enhancement in the Sixties, are a manifest example of future normality for us all.

What Viagra actually treats is loss of male power. In a confusing, depersonalising world busy reassigning status, regendering the social order, manipulating the ever-increasing demands of a commodified existence, sexual potency is the last bastion. Men, who have lost status and power almost everywhere, from workplace to home, must repair to the bedroom. Only there can they find the redemption of their true nature.

However, in an age of sexual equality, men cannot be left alone with their predicament. The other half of humanity, too, finds it is not exempt from malfunction. Just a few months ago, the disease "female sexual dysfunction" hit the headlines. But female sexuality being what it is, women probably need something more than a pill. Simple enhanced blood flow, as laboratory tests have shown, is not good enough. So a female Viagra won't do the job as well as a vibrator or a dildo—soon to be widely and cheaply available from a Boots near you. A vibrator outperforms even a man on Viagra.

More serious aids to female performance are in the pipeline. In the next few years, patches and drugs to enhance vaginal lubrication and sensitivity will become available. A US surgeon has already patented a pacemaker-sized device which, implanted under the skin, triggers an orgasm. Last month, clinical trials for the device were approved by the US Food and Drug Administration. Within a decade, it will be normal for every woman to have a perpetual orgasm whenever she wants it, wherever she needs it.

Love, too, will be available on demand. Recent research on love suggests that it consists of three basic biochemical elements. First, testosterone—which produces lust. Second, a group of amphetamine-like chemicals (dopamine, noradrenaline and phenylethylamine) produces feelings of euphoria that lead to infatuation. Third, if a relationship survives the first two rushes, a new biochemical response emerges, based on oxytocin, vasopressin and endorphins. This produces feelings of intimacy, trust and affection. Pharmaceutical companies are currently working on this third phase. So a "love pill" that modulates your subtler emotions and takes you straight to deep feelings of intimacy, trust and affection is just over the horizon. Science will fulfil the fairy tale. It will come up with a genuine love potion.

Science will fulfill the fairy tale. It will come up with a genuine love potion, modulating your subtler emotions

The sexual liberation of every woman and man approaches its apotheosis: availability on demand with peak performance, assured gratification and enduring emotion. But much more has been let out of the bottle. The physical and psychological barriers to sex, identified as the ultimate metaphor for all the ills of humanity, had to be overcome. The consequence is that most sexual taboos have evaporated. No matter how dark your thoughts, how unethical your desires, how absurd your fetish, everything is normal. Your desire to dress up as a stuffed toy, your dreams of having sex with obese or dead people, your obsession with plastic or rubber, your fixation with asphyxiation—all that is sexually driven is OK.

Pornography's status as a taboo is rapidly disappearing. It has become part of the mainstream of western culture. Ancient Egyptians, Greeks and Romans had their erotica as esoterica on scrolls, pottery and frescos. Hindus have their erotic sculptures on temples. But in western culture pornography in unparalleled quantities and forms is communicated in every mass medium. Never before in history has there been so much pornography to be had by so many in such numerous ways.

Everyone is now just a click away from explicit, hard-core material. It is impossible to miss pornography on the internet because it seeks you out persistently, unannounced, at every opportunity. It is there on Channels 4 and 5, Sky and innumerable digital channels every night.

On MTV's reality show *The Real World*, you can witness bisexual group sex. Explicit sex, including shots of erect penises, can be viewed on Sky's revisionist western drama *Deadwood*. Michael Winterbottom's *9 Songs*, which will go on general release shortly, offers a stream of close-ups of intercourse, fellatio, ejaculation and cunnilingus. The French art-house director Catherine Breillat has pioneered the transfer of porn stars into mainstream cinema. Her new film, *Anatomy of Hell*, is as graphic as it is bizarre. And if that doesn't satisfy you, you can go to a new breed of "pornaoke bars", just opened in Edinburgh, where you can groan and grind karaoke-style to porno tapes.

When pornography becomes normal, where will we go next?

There are only two taboos left: sex with children, and incest. Attempts to "normalise" paedophilia have begun. A thesis by Richard Yuill, awarded a PhD by Glasgow University in December 2004, suggests that sex between adults and minors is a good and positive thing. Yuill's research, based on interviews with paedophiles and their victims, "challenges the assumption" that paedophiles are inherently abusive. It is only a matter of time before other academics start arguing that incest, too, is decent and wholesome. Graphic art films and television documentaries will follow. The organisations campaigning for the rights of paedophiles will have their case for "normality" made for them.

They may then be able to take their place among the bewildering array of sexual orientations already being normalised. Once upon a time, there were heterosexuals and the love that dared not speak its name. Gay men and lesbians have long since lost their reticence. Then bisexuals, transsexuals and the "kinky" found their identity. Now we have intersexuals and the polyamorous. A few months ago, *New Scientist* announced the discovery, in breathless prose, of asexuals. These folk don't like to have sex—horror of horrors—with *anybody*. There are even orientations within orientations. So we have such self-definition as non-op transsexual, TG butch, femme queen, gender-queer, cross-dresser, third gender, drag king or queen and transboy. In one recent episode of Channel 5's *CSI: crime scene investigation,* a murder victim was said to be part of a community of "plushies", people who enjoy sex while dressed up as stuffed animals.

It is now normal to have your breasts removed or added to, have new genitals constructed, or sprinkle a dash of hormones for the appropriate, desired effect. Things are about to become even more complex. Within a decade or so, you will be able to modify your body almost totally, as you wish. You will be able to turn off all physical signs of gender, switch off the hormones and get rid of all secondary sexual characteristics. Then you can add on the bits you wish and "sculpt" your body in any shape you like. When gene therapy becomes common, things will be even easier. Already, there are people who are experimenting with this; and a "body-mod" subculture is thriving on the internet.

The shifting of the boundaries of what is normal and our obsession with sex have not improved our sex lives

What you can't do in reality will soon be available in simulation. The emerging technology of haptics, or the telecommunication of sensation using a computer interface, will enable you to live your most horrific dreams in virtual reality. Haptic technologies simulate physical sensation of real objects and feed them to the user. The first generation of haptic technology can be experienced in certain video games for the Sony PlayStation where the joystick is used to simulate vibrations. The next generation, on its way from Rutgers University, will simulate pressure, texture and heat. Combine this with state-of-the-art graphics and some innovative software and you have a complete pornographic universe. As Eric Garland points out in the December 2004 issue of the American magazine *The Futurist*, among its first uses could be "pornography involving children and featuring violence". But what's the harm, as it is only a digitised child?

Am I the only person to wonder if the constant shifting of the boundaries of the normal, while increasing our obsession with sex, has really improved our sex lives? On the contrary, I would argue, it has led to a decline in real sex. Genuine intimacy cannot be generated through a pill. Neither can sincere, uncondi-tional love be simulated. When sex is reduced to mechanics and endurance, there is little to differentiate it from plumbing and maintenance. When gender becomes meaningless, sex becomes empty. When sexual choice becomes an end in itself, then the end is destined to be tragic.

Sex used to be intercourse because it was part of a context, a loving relationship. When sex is just sex, without any context, what good does it do you? That is the crux of the problem. It becomes the ultimate narcissism, the sole gratification of self-love.

Welcome to the masturbatory society.

ZIAUDDIN SARDAR is editor of *Futures*, the monthly journal of policy, planning and futures studies.

Promiscuous Plague

Sexually transmitted diseases (STDs) are the single greatest health threat affecting our youth. A girl is four times more likely to contract an STD than she is to become pregnant, and a young mother has had an average of 2.3 STDs.

KAREN TESTERMAN

We are facing a plague of massive proportions, a plague made more sinister because it attacks not only adults but our youth. What is this crisis? It is a pandemic of sexually transmitted diseases (STDs) that is encouraged by a message of "safe sex" and an adult population that acts as if self-control and traditional morality are outdated and without value.

Society focuses on out-of-wedlock and teen births. Meanwhile STDs tear through our youth and adult population at alarming and deadly rates. They are "not your father's" STDs, which were few and easily cured with penicillin (see sidebar).

In the 1960s, syphilis and gonorrhea were the two most prevalent STDs; today, there are more than 20 and some have as many as 80-100 strains. Despite the fitting publicity that the deadly epidemic of human immunodeficiency virus/acquired immune disorder syndrome (HIV/AIDS) commands, according to research at the University of New Mexico, human papilloma virus (HPV), not HIV, is the most common STD transmitted today.

What is the magnitude of the problem? According to recent testimony before the House Committee on Energy and Commerce, "Three to four million STDs are contracted yearly by 15- to 19-year-olds, and another five to six million STDs are contracted annually by 20- to 24-year-olds."

Perhaps the most tragic aspect of this plague is the role adults play in it. Failures by grown-ups are the primary cause of the pandemic among our youth. Adults are failing our children by promoting a fatal message about sex: both in education and in actions. Youth are allowed to believe that there is such a thing as safe sex outside of marriage and that any sexual practice is acceptable as long as the participants are smiling.

Marketing Sex

Billboards, TV, magazines, movies, and catalogs promote the message that sex is the way to be cool, to fit in, to solve life's challenges. Today, the initial onset of sexual activity is occurring at younger ages, while couples delay the decision to marry or prefer cohabitation. Dr. Meg Meeker, a pediatrician and au-

Not So Free Sex

(!) There are physical and emotional consequences of engaging in sexual activity outside of marriage.

(!) Unwed childbearing costs American taxpayers $29 billion a year in social services, lost tax revenue, and the consequences of delinquency and poverty among the teenage parents.

(!) In 1960, 15 percent of teen births in the United States were out-of-wedlock.

(!) More recently, despite the reduction in teen pregnancy, the out-of-wedlock birthrate was 78 percent.

(!) Adolescents raised by single parents or stepfamilies are more likely to engage in sexual intercourse and to be sexually active at an earlier age.

(!) Most sexually active, infected youth do not know they have a disease.

thor of *Epidemic: How Teen Sex Is Killing Our Kids*, reports that half of all students in the ninth through twelfth grades have had sexual intercourse. Additionally, the average age for the onset of puberty in girls has dropped from 12 to 10.

There are physical and emotional consequences of engaging in sexual activity outside of marriage. Unwed childbearing costs American taxpayers $29 billion a year in social services and lost tax revenue, and results in delinquency and poverty among teenage parents. These teens will enter adulthood disadvantaged and will convey this disadvantage to their children.

In 1960, 15 percent of teen births in the United States were out-of-wedlock. More recently, despite the reduction in teen pregnancy, the out-of-wedlock birthrate was 78 percent among teens, according to the National Center for Health Statistics (2000).

Meanwhile, a primary indicator of poverty in our nation is single-parent households among 15- to 19-year-olds. Ninety percent of these young people will never attend college. Eighty percent of women who choose to parent while they are teens will live at the poverty level for 10 years or more.

STDs: Yesterday and Today

The basic types of organisms responsible for STDs are bacteria, parasites, and viruses. Bacterial diseases are treatable with antibiotics such as penicillin, but the organism often develops a resistance to the antibiotic, complicating treatment. Most parasitic diseases are treatable, but viruses often remain in the host for life. Many produce symptoms with a secondary impact to the host—a reduced immune system, stress, or another infection. There are no known cures for viruses, and many hosts infected with them exhibit no symptoms.

In 1960 there were 5 primary STDs: gonorrhea, syphilis, granuloma inguinale, chancroid, and lymphogranuloma venereum. Today there are over 20. Unless otherwise noted, the following figures refer to the United States.

Herpes simplex virus (HSV) Types I and II—Genital herpes results from viral infection transmitted through intimate contact with the moist mucous lining of the genitals. Once in the body it remains, and there is no cure. A rash or ulcerations may be exhibited. Genital herpes can be transmitted without the host experiencing symptoms. Only 80 percent of those infected will test positive for the virus.

Human papilloma virus (HPV)—HPV is the most commonly transmitted STD. There are between 80 and 100 strains of the virus. Some cause genital warts, but the strains that cause cervical cancer and were recently linked to anal cancer do not produce symptoms in the host. HPV is spread through skin-to-skin contact.

Gonorrhea—A bacterial infection, gonorrhea is one of the oldest STDs. Estimates are that over 1 million women are infected with gonorrhea-causing bacteria, which infect the vagina, cervix, urethra, throat, and rectum. The disease is treatable.

Syphilis—A chronic disease, syphilis is caused by a bacterial spirochete that bores into the mucous membranes of the mouth or genitals. It is treatable but in the secondary stage is highly contagious, with a rash on the hands that can be transmitted through casual contact.

Chlamydia—A bacterial infection, first reported in 1984, chlamydia affects an estimated 3-5 million women annually. It infects the cervix, urethra, throat, and rectum. While treatable, it is highly destructive to the fallopian tubes and can cause infertility or ectopic pregnancies.

Human herpes virus 8 (HHV8)—HHV8 is a virus associated with Kaposi's sarcoma, an unusual skin tumor usually found in HIV-infected men. While the virus has been found in the semen of HIV-infected men, its impact is yet to be determined.

Trichomoniasis—Caused by *Trichomonas vaginalis*, a sexually transmitted parasite, trichomoniasis affects approximately 5 million people annually.

HIV/AIDS—Acquired immune deficiency syndrome is caused by the human immunodeficiency virus. An HIV infection weakens the body's immune system and increases the body's vulnerability to many infections as well as the development of certain cancers. AIDS is one of the most frightening of the STDs because it is the most uniformly fatal of the group.

Hepatitis A, B, C*, D*—These viruses cause inflammation of the liver and can lead to cirrhosis, liver failure, and liver cancer. The B virus form is transmitted through sexual intimacy in about 30 percent of the cases. The C form is spread mainly through blood contact, although it has been spread through semen.

Chancroid—One of the older bacterial STDs, chancroid is usually diagnosed through a culture of the ulcer. It must be distinguished from syphilis or herpes. All partners should be treated whether or not the ulcer was present at the time of exposure.

Lymphogranuloma venereum—Caused by a type of chlamydia, this disease affects the genitals, anus, or rectum. Another strain of the bacteria affects the urethra and can coexist with the former. Both are treatable with an oral antibiotic.

Donovanosis (granuloma inguinale)—A chronic bacterial infection of the genitals that is found in tropical areas, donovanosis can cause severe complications if left untreated.

Molluscum contagiosum—A common noncancerous skin growth, molluscum is caused by a viral infection in the top layers of the skin. The growths are similar to warts but are caused by a different virus. The virus and growths are easily spread by skin contact.

Ureaplasma urealyticum—A bacterial infection, generally asymptomatic in nature, ureaplasma is sexually transmitted between partners. The bacteria can survive undetected in the reproductive tract for many years, until a patient is specifically tested for the infection. Although generally asymptomatic, ureaplasma can lead to fertility problems including tubal disease, recurrent miscarriages, decreased sperm motility and count.

Shigellosis* and salmonellosis*—These bacterial infections cause diarrhea and are spread through contamination from the stool or soiled fingers of one person to the mouth of another. These are STDs common among men having sex with men.

Cytomegalovirus*—An asymptomatic disease, cytomegalovirus is caused by a virus that usually remains dormant in the body for life. Severe impairment of the immune system by medication or disease reactivates it. Infectious CMV may be shed in the bodily fluids of any infected person and thus may be found in urine, saliva, blood, tears, semen, and breast milk.

Giardiasis*—A diarrheal illness, giardiasis is caused by a one-celled, microscopic parasite that lives in the intestines of people and animals and is passed in the stool. The parasite is protected by an outer shell that allows it to survive outside the body for long periods. Giardiasis is more common at present among homosexuals, as it may be spread through oral-anal sexual contact.

Amoebiasis*—Caused by a one-celled parasite, amoebiasis is most commonly found in Mexico, South America, India, and South and West Africa. The parasite is harbored in the human intestinal tract and is passed along by contamination of food and water or by anal or anal/oral sex.

Bacterial vaginosis*—The condition is caused by excessive bacteria that may normally be present in the vagina. It is not clear whether it is sexually transmitted, but it is associated with other sexually transmitted diseases. Bacterial vaginosis is more common in women with multiple sexual partners, and it often develops soon after intercourse with a new partner. The disorder is relatively common among women with female partners, where the condition may be triggered by shared objects used in sexual acts.

*Sexual transmission occurs but is not the primary mode of transmission.

Linda Waite, professor of urban sociology at the University of Chicago, and Maggie Gallagher, affiliate scholar at the Institute for American Values, have found that children born to unmarried mothers are more likely to die in infancy. Boys raised in single-parent homes are twice as likely to commit a crime that leads to incarceration by their early thirties.

Adolescents raised by single parents or stepfamilies are more likely to engage in sexual intercourse and to be sexually active at an earlier age, according to Dawn M. Upchurch, professor at the UCLA School of Public Health. None of this takes into account the impact of post-abortive trauma or the emotional trauma of making tough decisions to allow adoption so that the child will have better opportunities.

A girl is four times more likely to contract an STD than she is to become pregnant. Today, a young mother has had on average 2.3 STDs. Syphilis, gonorrhea, herpes, chlamydia, hepatitis A and B, HIV, and HPV are the most common. Many of the viral STDs have multiple strains.

Sexual Russian Roulette

A leading risk factor is the number of sexual partners. Vital health statistics directly link this factor to the early onset of sexual activity. Consider the infected teen who has sex with 6 people, each of whom has 6 partners. According to Dr. Meeker, this means that 36 people have been exposed to disease.

Marcel T. Saghir, coauthor of *Male and Female Homosexuality: A Comprehensive Investigation*, cites the magnification of this problem in the homosexual community, even among those who define themselves as monogamous. The average such relationship among homosexual males lasts less than three years. Despite attempts to portray their choice for living as normal and healthy, homosexuals are in the highest risk group for several of the most serious STDs.

Evidence from the National Cancer Institute that smoking shortens a person's life by 7-10 years led to a multibillion-dollar lawsuit by state governments. However, despite numerous studies that reveal homosexual relationships can reduce male or female lives by 10-30 years, tolerance and political correctness reign.

As even homosexual supporters and the media admit, the increasing pressure to accept homosexual practices as mainstream is dramatically affecting our society. According to the *New York Blade News Reports,* gay men are in the highest-risk group for several of the most serious diseases, including STDs.

Instability and promiscuity are characteristic of homosexual relationships. Even the Gay Lesbian Medical Association agrees with mainstream reports that, despite decades of intensive efforts to educate, HIV/AIDS continues to increase among the homosexual community.

According to another homosexual newspaper, the *Washington Blade*, HPV is "almost universal" among homosexuals. HPV, often asymptomatic, is believed to be the causative vector of cervical cancer in women. It can also lead to anal cancer in men.

Add to this the confusion about what constitutes sexual activity. Is it just penile penetration of the vagina? Does oral sex count? Is heavy petting to be included? What about practices of homosexuals? Conventional wisdom seems to promote the idea that these questions are irrelevant, as a condom can prevent the passing of bodily fluids, and thus STDs.

Beyond Bodily Fluids

Sadly, this misconception leads to even more danger, as the passing of body fluids is not the only way to contract these diseases. Even a properly used and defect-free latex condom will not completely protect against all STDs. Any genital contact can cause an infection. Genital warts are the common name for HPV. The most common and contagious of STDs, HPV is passed by skin-to-skin contact. It is the leading cause of cervical cancer and in its cancerous form does not exhibit any symptoms.

Alas, most of our sexually active, infected youth do not know they have a disease. Some viruses can lie dormant in the body for up to 30 years before symptoms develop. Ninety percent of those infected with chlamydia exhibit no symptoms and receive no treatment.

According to abstinence speaker Pam Stenzel, the statistics of this disaster are staggering, especially among our youth. Every day in America, 12,000 teenagers contract a sexually transmitted disease.

The American Medical Association recommends that sexually active girls be tested for chlamydia every six months. Why just girls? Aren't boys infected as well? Yes, men carry the infection, but as is often the case, girls endure most of the consequences. Stenzel points out that the female reproductive system is open; scar tissue builds up on the cervix, fallopian tubes, and ovaries as a result of pelvic inflammatory disease (PID) from the chlamydia infection.

With a single chlamydia infection, there is a 25 percent chance of sterility. With a second infection there is a 50 percent chance of sterility. If there is a third infection, it is almost certain that the girl will be sterile—all due to PID.

This is why, some people reason, we should promote a dual message and sell teens on abstinence with "safe sex" as a backup. The dual message approach says that abstinence is best, but if you choose to engage in genital contact, use some form of contraception, usually condoms. This comprehensive message indicates that our youth are no more than bundles of uncontrollable hormones—that they are no more than mere animals. Many public school sexuality education programs instruct youth in the proper use of condoms and contraception. The information given is that condoms significantly reduce the chance of STD infection.

In reality, even if a condom is used 100 percent of the time, a sexually active young person is at risk to contract STDs including gonorrhea, chlamydia, and trichomoniasis. Even when used, a condom fails to prevent pregnancy 12 percent of the time, according to the Maryland Center for Mental and Child Health. Despite faithful use of the condom, the person who engages in genital contact is not immune from contracting an STD that spreads through skin-to-skin contact.

It is time that adults clean up their act and encourage youth to aspire to achieve the goal of being responsible, thinking people. Young people need adults who will trust them enough to give them the information they need to make good choices.

Knowledge is Power

Young people need to know that sex without boundaries is deadly. There are consequences when engaging in genital contact outside the bonds of marriage. Young people need to know that both parties should wait until they make a lifelong commitment to one another in marriage to have sex. Within marriage,

Homosexuality and Health

Little is heard today about the devastating health effects of homosexual promiscuity. A panoply of diseases—not only the well-publicized AIDS but lesser-known scourges such as hepatitis A, B, and C; herpes; cytomegalovirus; gay bowel syndrome; amoebiasis; anal warts and anal cancer; shigellosis; chlamydia; gonorrhea; and syphilis-serve to truncate the average gays life expectancy to roughly 50 years. And these pestilences not only shorten lives but sharply erode quality of life.

Behavioral disorders and mental illnesses also are far more prevalent among homosexuals than their heterosexual counterparts. High rates of alcoholism, drug addiction, "spousal" abuse, depression, and suicide all militate against living to old age.

Gay sex is of particular concern because among homosexuals, promiscuity is more the rule than the exception. For example, the December 1989 *Archives of Internal Medicine* refers to a Los Angeles report's finding that gay males averaged over 20 sex partners annually Some studies show that those in supposedly "steady" relationships are even more promiscuous, engaging in dozens of trysts a year outside the relationship.

A 1998 study that appeared in *Psychological Reports* used four databases to investigate the life spans of gays versus heterosexuals. It concluded that the homosexual lifestyle sliced 20 to 30 years from practitioners' life expectancy. Supporting this was a 1994 obituary investigation, which determined that the median age of death for gay males was 42 and for lesbians 49. It ran in the *Omega Journal of Death and Dying*.

Medical statistics show the gay community to be virtually awash in pathogens:

- Over 50 percent of all homosexual men are carriers of the human papilloma virus, which produces anal warts and can often lead to anal cancer, according to Stephen Goldstone, assistant clinical professor of surgery at Mount Sinai Medical Center, speaking at a 1999 Gay Men's Health Summit in Boulder, Colorado.
- Male homosexuals are about 1,000 times more likely to acquire AIDS than the general population (National Center for Infectious Diseases, 1992).
- A survey of more than 2,300 gays in New York and three other cities found that 37 percent of the men and 14 percent of the women reported having a non-HIV sexually transmitted infection (**Washington Blade**, October 9, 1998). Ten years earlier, male homosexuals (less than 1 percent of the population) accounted for 50 percent of U.S. syphilis cases (*Atlantic Monthly*, January 1988).
- Hepatitis B is about five times more prevalent among homosexuals than among heterosexual men, according to the National Health and Nutrition Examination Surveys, 1976-1994 (*American Journal of Public Health*).
- A young gay man has about a 50 percent chance of acquiring the AIDS virus by middle age, and the incidence of gonorrhea rose 74 percent among homosexuals from 1993-1996 (*New York Times*, November 23, 1997).
- Behavioral and mental disorders are likewise widespread in the gay community. Among the evidence is the following:
- A 1992 Boston study found that of 262 gay male subjects, 49 percent used drugs with sex, 9 percent weekly; 57 percent used alcohol with sex, 9 percent weekly (*AIDS*).
- Forty-six percent of homosexual and bisexual youths in a 1997 study of Massachusetts high-school students had attempted suicide in the preceding year (*Newsweek*).
- Forty percent of male homosexual subjects had a history of major depressive disorder (*Archives of General Psychiatry*, February 1991; *Comprehensive Psychiatry*, May/June 1993).

—The Editor

they have a better chance to be healthier, to attain a higher level of education, to be financially secure, to be happier and enjoy sex more, but only if that sex is with their marital partner.

The only way to protect against STDs that can have lifelong, physically and emotionally painful consequences is to abstain from genital contact outside of marriage. According to the University of Chicago research in *Sex in America*, researchers report that when a marriage is intact, the couple almost never have sex outside their marital relationship.

Promiscuous sexual practices, whether heterosexual or homosexual, are highly costly to Americans. The health of present and future generations is in jeopardy. Simply avoiding pregnancy or homosexual behavior is not enough. This attitude completely ignores the possibility and consequences of exposure to STDs. Add to this the disease of substance abuse and emotional trauma due to abortion, depression, anxiety, and subsequent problems, and it is clear that one should avoid promiscuity at all costs.

Despite the rhetoric, everyone is not doing it. Over 50 percent of our youth are not engaging in genital contact with one another. Given the information, our young people are capable of making informed decisions. Once we realize this, we can give them (and society) a future without this plague.

The promiscuous plague has many facets. Messages in the media, peer pressure, alcohol, and drugs all influence teen sexual behavior. The biggest influences, of course, are parents. The actions of young people reflect what adults transmit. This is done through how adults behave and what is communicated as acceptable. By allowing the media to undermine morality, the plague is fostered. By engaging in dangerous sexual practices, the plague is encouraged.

More important, by abdicating parental responsibility, the plague is promoted. A recent survey of teens conducted by L.B. Whitbeck, professor of sociology at the University of Nebraska, found that parents have the strongest effect on a teen's decision whether to have sex. Parents influence the attitude of their teens by their own marital status, their attitudes, the amount of supervision they provide, and how involved they are with their children.

Ultimately, the most effective inoculation against this plague is effective parenting. Certainly parenting would be made easier if the entertainment media reduced their hard sell of "anything goes" sex and schools truly taught nonmarital abstinence and credited our youth with the ability to use good sense. If given the opportunity, teens can and will make good choices. Our next generation needs to know it is okay to say no!

Young people need to know that sex without boundaries is deadly.

KAREN TESTERMAN is executive director of Cornerstone Policy Research, a family policy think tank located in Concord, New Hampshire. She has taught anatomy and physiology at the secondary-school level and sits on the New Hampshire Abstinence Task Force.

UNIT 7
Preventing and Fighting Disease

Unit Selections

Key Points to Consider

- What role might inflammation play in the risk of cardiovascular disease?

- What is the relationship between obesity and diabetes (Type 2)?

- What lifestyle changes could you make that would reduce your risk of developing cardiovascular disease, cancer, diabetes, and AIDS?

- Assuming that you live long enough, which chronic disease do you think you are most likely to contract, based on your family history and lifestyle?

- What are some steps individuals can take to reduce their risk of contracting cancer? What life changes could you make to reduce your risk of cancer?

- Why do fewer Americans consider AIDS a national health priority in 2006 as opposed to 20 years ago?

Student Website
www.mhcls.com/online

Internet References
Further information regarding these websites may be found in this book's preface or online.

American Cancer Society
http://www.cancer.org

American Heart Association
http://www.amhrt.org

National Institute of Allergy and Infectious Diseases (NIAID)
http://www3.niaid.nih.gov/

American Diabetes Association Home Page
http://www.diabetes.org

Cardiovascular disease and cancer are the leading killers in this country. This is not altogether surprising given that the American population is growing increasingly older and one's risk of developing both of these diseases is directly proportional to one's age. Another major risk factor, which has received considerable attention over the past 30 years, is one's genetic predisposition or family history. Historically the significance of this risk factor has been emphasized as a basis for encouraging at-risk individuals to make prudent lifestyle choices, but this may be about to change as recent advances in genetic research, including mapping the human genome, may significantly improve the efficacy of both diagnostic and therapeutic procedures.

Just as cutting-edge genetic research is transforming the practice of medicine, startling new research findings in the health profession are transforming our views concerning adult health. This new research suggests that the primary determinants of our health as adults are the environmental conditions we experienced during life in the womb. According to Dr. Peter Nathanielsz of Cornell University, conditions during gestation, ranging from hormones that flow from the mother to how well the placenta delivers nutrients to the tiny limbs and organs, program how our liver, heart, kidneys, and especially our brains function as adults. While it is too early to draw any firm conclusions regarding the significance of the "life in the womb factor," it appears that this avenue of research may yield important clues as to how we may best prevent or forestall chronic illness.

Of all the diseases in America, coronary heart disease is this nation's number one killer. Frequently, the first and only symptom of this disease is a sudden heart attack. Epidemiological studies have revealed a number of risk factors that increase one's likelihood of developing the disease. These include hypertension, a high serum cholesterol level, diabetes, cigarette smoking, obesity, a sedentary lifestyle, a family history of heart disease, age, sex, race, and stress. In addition to these well-established risk factors, scientists think they may have discovered several additional risk factors. These include the following: low birth weight, cytomegalovirus, *Chlamydia pneumoniae,* porphyromonasgingivalis, and c-reactive protein (CRP). CRP is a measure of inflammation somewhere in the body. In theory, a high CRP reading may be a good indicator of an impending heart attack. The article, "The Battle Within," addresses research related to yet another possible link to heart disease.

One of the most startling and ominous health stories was the recent announcement by the Centers for Disease Control and Prevention (CDC) that the incidence of Type 2 adult onset diabetes increased significantly over the past 15 years. This sudden rise appears to cross all races and age groups, with the sharpest increase occurring among people aged 30 to 39 (about 70 percent). Health experts at the CDC believe that this startling rise in diabetes among 30- to 39-year-olds is linked to the rise in obesity observed among young adults (obesity rates rose from 12 to 20 percent nationally during this same time period). Experts at the CDC believe that there is a time lag of about 10–15 years between the deposition of body fat and the manifestation of Type 2 diabetes. This time lag could explain why individuals in their 30s are experiencing the greatest increase in developing Type 2 diabetes today. Current estimates suggest that 16 million Americans have diabetes; it kills approximately 180,000 Americans each year. Many experts now believe that our couch-potato culture is fueling the rising rates of both obesity and diabetes. Given what we know about the relationship between obesity and Type 2 diabetes, the only practical solution is for Americans to watch their total calories and exercise regularly. 'Diabesity', a Crisis in an Expanding Country" examines the rapid rise in the incidence of Type 2 diabetes among our youth and young adults and suggests that the term "adult onset diabetes" may be a misnomer given the growing number of young adults and teens with this form of diabetes.

Cardiovascular disease is America's number one killer, but cancer takes top billing in terms of the "fear factor." This fear of cancer stems from an awareness of the degenerative and disfiguring nature of the disease. Today, cancer specialists are employing a variety of complex agents and technologies, such as monoclonal antibodies, interferon, and immunotherapy, in their attempt to fight the disease. Progress has been slow, however, and the results, while promising, suggest that a cure may be several years away. A very disturbing aspect of this country's battle against cancer is the fact that millions of dollars are spent each year trying to advance the treatment of cancer, while funding for the technologies used to detect cancer in its early stages is quite limited. A reallocation of funds would seem appropriate, given the medical community's position that early detection and treatment are the key elements in the successful management of cancer. Until such time that we have more effective methods for detecting cancer in the early stages, our best hope for managing cancer is to prevent it through our lifestyle choices. "Why We Are Still Losing the Winnable Cancer War" takes an extensive look at the major forms of cancer in the United States and provides useful suggestions on the steps one can take to lower one's risk. While many questions remain unanswered regarding both cardiovascular disease and cancer, scientists are closing in on important clues.

It has now been over 20 years since the CDC first became aware of HIV/AIDS, and over that period of time more than 58 million people worldwide have been infected with the HIV virus and 22 million have died of AIDS. Despite medical advances in the war against AIDS there is no cure in sight and a vaccination may be several years away. The complications associated with AIDS are not only medical, but include complex financial, political and social issues. With medical advances in the treatment of AIDS, complacency grew, and many people abandoned the philosophy of safe sex. Today many medical experts are worried that unless we remain vigilant in our fight against this disease we will find ourselves back where we were in the early days in terms of infection rates. "How AIDS Changed America" examines the disease, its origins, and its impact on America.

'Diabesity,' a Crisis in an Expanding Country

JANE E. BRODY

I can't understand why we still don't have a national initiative to control what is fast emerging as the most serious and costly health problem in America: excess weight. Are our schools, our parents, our national leaders blind to what is happening—a health crisis that looms even larger than our former and current smoking habits?

Just look at the numbers, so graphically described in an eye-opening new book, "Diabesity: The Obesity-Diabetes Epidemic That Threatens America—and What We Must Do to Stop It" (Bantam), by Dr. Francine R. Kaufman, a pediatric endocrinologist, the director of the diabetes clinic at Children's Hospital Los Angeles and a past president of the American Diabetes Association.

In just over a decade, she noted, the prevalence of diabetes nearly doubled in the American adult population: to 8.7 percent in 2002, from 4.9 percent in 1990. Furthermore, an estimated one-third of Americans with Type 2 diabetes don't even know they have it because the disease is hard to spot until it causes a medical crisis.

An estimated 18.2 million Americans now have diabetes, 90 percent of them the environmentally influenced type that used to be called adult-onset diabetes. But adults are no longer the only victims—a trend that prompted an official change in name in 1997 to Type 2 diabetes.

More and more children are developing this health-robbing disease or its precursor, prediabetes. Counting children and adults together, some 41 million Americans have a higher-than-normal blood sugar level that typically precedes the development of full-blown diabetes.

'Then Everything Changed'

And what is the reason for this runaway epidemic? Being overweight or obese, especially with the accumulation of large amounts of body fat around the abdomen. In Dr. Kaufman's first 15 years as a pediatric endocrinologist, 1978 to 1993, she wrote, "I never saw a young patient with Type 2 diabetes. But then everything changed."

Teenagers now come into her clinic weighing 200, 300, even nearly 400 pounds with blood sugar levels that are off the charts. But, she adds, we cannot simply blame this problem on gluttony and laziness and "assume that the sole solution is individual change."

The major causes, Dr. Kaufman says, are "an economic structure that makes it cheaper to eat fries than fruit" and a food industry and mass media that lure children to eat the wrong foods and too much of them. "We have defined progress in terms of the quantity rather than the quality of our food," she wrote.

Her views are supported by a 15-year study published in January in The Lancet. A team headed by Dr. Mark A. Pereira of the University of Minnesota analyzed the eating habits of 3,031 young adults and found that weight gain and the development of prediabetes were directly related to unhealthful fast food.

Taking other factors into consideration, consuming fast food two or more times a week resulted, on average, in an extra weight gain of 10 pounds and doubled the risk of prediabetes over the 15-year period.

Other important factors in the diabesity epidemic, Dr. Kaufman explained, are the failure of schools to set good examples by providing only healthful fare, a loss of required physical activity in schools and the inability of many children these days to walk or bike safely to school or to play outside later.

Genes play a role as well. Some people are more prone to developing Type 2 diabetes than others. The risk is 1.6 times as great for blacks as for whites of similar age. It is 1.5 times as great for Hispanic-Americans, and 2 times as great for Mexican-Americans and Native Americans.

Unless we change our eating and exercise habits and pay greater attention to this disease, more than one-third of whites, two-fifths of blacks and half of Hispanic people in this country will develop diabetes.

It is also obvious from the disastrous patient histories recounted in Dr. Kaufman's book that the nation's medical structure is a factor as well. Many people do not have readily accessible medical care, and still many others have no coverage for preventive medicine. As a result, millions fall between the cracks until they are felled by heart attacks or strokes.

A Devastating Disease

There is a tendency in some older people to think of diabetes as "just a little sugar," a common family problem. They fail to take it seriously and make the connection between it and the costly, crippling and often fatal diseases that can ensue.

Diabetes, with its consequences of heart attack, stroke, kidney failure, amputations and blindness, among others, already ranks No. 1 in direct health care costs, consuming $1 of every $7 spent on health care.

Nor is this epidemic confined to American borders. Internationally, "we are witnessing an epidemic that is the scourge of the 21st century," Dr. Kaufman wrote.

Unlike some other killer diseases, Type 2 diabetes issues an easily detected wake-up call: the accumulation of excess weight, especially around the abdomen. When the average fasting level of blood sugar (glucose) rises above 100 milligrams per deciliter, diabetes is looming.

Abdominal fat is highly active. The chemical output of its cells increases blood levels of hormones like estrogen, providing the link between obesity and breast cancer, and decreases androgens, which can cause a decline in libido. As the cells in abdominal fat expand, they also release chemicals that increase fat accumulation, ensuring their own existence.

The result is an increasing cellular resistance to the effects of the hormone insulin, which enables cells to burn blood sugar for energy. As blood sugar rises with increasing insulin resistance, the pancreas puts out more and more insulin (promoting further fat storage) until this gland is exhausted. Then when your fasting blood sugar level reaches 126 milligrams, you have diabetes.

Two recent clinical trials showed that Type 2 diabetes could be prevented by changes in diet and exercise. The Diabetes Prevention Program Research Group involving 3,234 overweight adults showed that "intensive lifestyle intervention" was more effective than a drug that increases insulin sensitivity in preventing diabetes over three years.

The intervention, lasting 24 weeks, trains people to choose low-calorie, low-fat diets; increase activity; and change their habits. Likewise, the randomized, controlled Finnish Diabetes Prevention Study of 522 obese patients showed that introducing a moderate exercise program of at least 150 minutes a week and weight loss of at least 5 percent reduced the incidence of diabetes by 58 percent.

Many changes are needed to combat this epidemic, starting with schools and parents. Perhaps the quickest changes can be made in the workplace, where people can be encouraged to use stairs instead of elevators; vending machines can be removed or dispense only healthful snacks; and cafeterias can offer attractive healthful fare. Lunchrooms equipped with refrigerators and microwaves will allow workers to bring healthful meals to work.

Dr. Kaufman tells of a challenge to get fit and lose weight by Caesars Entertainment in which 4,600 workers who completed the program lost a total of 45,000 pounds in 90 days. Others could follow this example.

The Battle Within

Our Anti-inflammation Diet

What do paper cuts, spicy foods, stubbed toes and intense workouts at the gym have to do with your odds of getting colon cancer, drifting into Alzheimer's or succumbing to a heart attack? A lot more than you might think.

The more scientists learn about these and other serious diseases, the more they are being linked with the long-term effects of inflammation on the body.

MICHAEL DOWNEY

The inflammation-disease connection has become a hot research topic. And it's about to explode.

Vital Nuisance

Inflammation is a vital immune response to infection, injury or irritation. It is the basis of humanity's earliest survival.

It's what causes the redness in that paper cut—the result of extra blood walling off the area and rushing macrophages, histamine and other bacteria-fighting immune factors to the wound.

The same inflammatory process is what makes your throat burn when you decide to impress your friends by chugging the extra-spicy suicide sauce—blood vessels leak fluid, proteins and cells to repair or remove damaged tissues. And fever is yet another form of that inflammatory burning.

Inflammation sparks the swelling in that stubbed toe—caused by fluid released into the banged-up cells to speed healing and cushion that toe against further injury.

It also causes that tenderness you feel after hours at the gym—because your immune system rushes fluids to the torn muscles to protect and repair them, compressing sensitive nerve endings in the process.

Inflammation isolates foreign invaders and rushes our strongest natural infection-fighters to the site deemed under attack. It cleans away debris from destroyed tissue; slows bleeding; starts clotting; and—if tissues cannot be restored—produces scar tissue. Without this sophisticated immune response, our species would have died out long ago.

But it's a double-edged sword. In addition to its telltale redness, heat, swelling or pain, inflammation can cause serious dysfunction.

Defensive Nutrition

- oily fish and fish oil supplements
- olive, walnut or flaxseed oil
- walnuts, flaxseeds and soy foods
- fruits and vegetables
- red wine
- antioxidant supplements
- garlic, ginger and turmeric (enreumin)
- sunflower seeds, eggs, herring, nuts or zinc tablets
- pineapple or bromelain supplements
- S-adenosyl-methionine (SAMe)

Problems begin when—for one reason or another—the inflammatory process becomes chronic, persisting long after it's needed.

Heart disease researchers were the first to notice that inflammation can play a role in cardiovascular disease.

Heart Mystery

Not long ago, doctors viewed heart disease as a plumbing problem. Cholesterol levels in the blood get too high, and, over the years, fatty deposits clog the pipes and cut off the blood supply.

There's just one problem with that explanation: Sometimes, it's dead wrong.

Half of all heart attacks occur in people with normal cholesterol levels and normal blood pressure. Something causes relatively minor deposits to burst, triggering massive clots that block the blood supply.

That something has turned out to be inflammation.

C-reactive protein (CRP)—a blood measure of inflammation—shoots up during an acute illness or infection. But CRP is also somewhat elevated among otherwise healthy people. And studies show that those with the highest CRP levels have three times the heart attack risk as those with the lowest levels. The inflammatory response, possibly reacting to cholesterol that has seeped into the lining of the artery, makes even normal fatty deposits unstable.

There are several causes of heart disease: smoking, high blood pressure and, yes, cholesterol. But we must now add inflammation to that list.

Runaway Reaction

Heart disease is just the tip of the inflammation iceberg. Studies over the past couple of years have suggested that higher CRP levels raise the risk of diabetes. It's too early to say whether lowering inflammation will keep diabetes from developing. But before insulin was isolated at the University of Toronto in the 1920s, doctors found that blood sugar levels could be decreased by using salicylates, a group of aspirin-like compounds known to reduce inflammation.

In the 1860s, German pathologist Rudolph Virchow speculated that cancerous tumors start at the site of chronic inflammation—basically, a wound that never heals. Then, in the middle of the 20th century, we came to understand the role of genetic mutations in cancerous tissue. Today, researchers are investigating the possibility that mutations and inflammation work together to turn normal cells into deadly tumors. Reducing chronic inflammation may yet become a prescription for keeping cancer at bay.

Researchers have found that people who take anti-inflammation medications—for arthritis, for example—succumb to Alzheimer's disease later in life than those who don't. Plaque and tangles accumulate in the brains of Alzheimer's patients. Perhaps the immune system mistakenly sees these abnormalities as damaged tissue that should be eliminated. Early information suggests that low-dose aspirin and fish oil capsules—both known to reduce inflammation—lower the risk of Alzheimer's.

The cause of asthma is still unknown, but some suspect the inflammatory attack. The treatments that help relieve asthma work by reducing the inflammation involved.

Sometimes, for reasons that are not clear, perfectly healthy cells trigger the body's immune system. The inflammatory response is launched against normal cells in the joints, nerves, connective tissue or any part of the body. These autoimmune disorders include rheumatoid arthritis, multiple sclerosis, lupus, vitiligo, psoriasis and other versions of a body at war with itself. Even Crohn's disease and cystic fibrosis are associated with inflammation.

Some level of inflammatory immune reaction is usually present in our bodies, whether we're aware of it or not. And if inflammation really is the biological engine that drives many of our most feared illnesses, it suggests a new and possibly much simpler way of warding off disease. Instead of different treatments for all of these disorders, simply turning down the degree of our inflammatory attack might be a partial prevention for all of them.

Dampening the Fires

Many attributes of a Western lifestyle—such as a diet high in sugars and saturated fats, accompanied by little or no exercise—make it much easier for the body to become inflamed.

Losing weight helps because fat cells produce cytokines, which crank up inflammation. Thirty minutes a day of moderate exercise dampens the fire as well. Flossing your teeth combats gum disease, another source of chronic inflammation. And, of course, you should avoid excess alcohol intake and smoking.

Despite the injury they can do to the stomach, anti-inflammatory drugs such as aspirin and ibuprofen are often prescribed for treatment of inflammatory diseases, but they're not appropriate for prevention. Fish oil capsules have been shown to produce the same reduction in inflammatory cytokines.

Inflammation-promoting prostaglandins are made from the trans fats found in partially hydrogenated oils. So avoid margarines and vegetable shortenings that are made with them.

Getting a good supply of omega-3 fatty acids—and a minimum of omega-6 fats—is key to an immune system that's not overreactive. Opt for oily fish such as salmon, sardines, herring and mackerel; and on days that you don't have fish, take a fish oil supplement, eat walnuts, freshly ground flaxseeds or flaxseed oil and soy foods. Steer away from safflower, sunflower, corn and sesame oils, as well as polyunsaturated vegetable oils. Use walnut, flaxseed or extra virgin olive oils instead.

Fruits and vegetables are full of antioxidants that disable free radicals and minimize inflammation. All are good, but you should focus your diet on those that produce the highest antioxidant activity: blueberries and kiwi. Consider antioxidant supplements such as resveratrol, grape seed extract, quercetin, pycnogenol or citrus bioflavonoids, as well as beta-carotene and vitamins, C and E. And drink red wine in small quantities.

Garlic, ginger and turmeric are natural anti-inflammatory agents. Include them in your diet.

Zinc controls inflammation while promoting healing. It is found in sunflower seeds, eggs, nuts, wheat germ, herring and zinc supplements.

S-adenosyl-methionine (SAMe), alpha lipoic acid and coenzyme Q1O act as inflammation fighters. Also, bromelain—found in pineapple and supplements—may reduce inflammation.

So if you want to stop inflammation, get off that couch and head out to pick up oily fish, fresh produce, garlic and supplements. And try not to stub your toe on the way.

Why We Are Still Losing the Winnable Cancer War

SAMUEL S. EPSTEIN, M.D.

For more than thirty years we in the United States have been losing the war on cancer because we've used the wrong "generals" and the wrong strategies. The war has been and continues to be waged using screening, diagnosis, treatment, and related research with the primary goal of "damage control." By contrast, cancer *prevention* through the reduction of avoidable exposures to carcinogens in the totality of the environment remains a minimal priority.

Ever since President Richard Nixon declared the "War on Cancer" in 1971 the country's primary generals—the federal National Cancer Institute (NCI) and the worlds wealthiest nonprofit organization, the American Cancer Society (ACS)—have misled the nation. At first they promised a cure in time for the United States' 1976 bicentennial. Then in 1984, and again in 1986, the NCI declared that cancer mortality would be halved by 2000. In 1998 the NCI and ACS trumpeted that the nation had "turned the corner" in the war on cancer. Most recently, in 2003, NCI Director Andrew C. von Eschenbach pledged unrealistically to "eliminate the suffering and death from cancer by 2015." This pledge was shortly followed by a joint NCI and ACS claim that "considerable progress has been made in reducing the burden of cancer."

On June 3, 2004, a joint NCI and ACS *Annual Report to the Nation on the Status of Cancer, 1975–2001* stated that "cancer incidence and death rates are on the decline from 1991–2001, due to progress in prevention, early detection, and treatment." This report prompted a flurry of positive headlines in national newspapers, such as "Cancer cases, death rates declining," supposedly by 7 to 8 percent from 1991 to 2001. But these decreases have largely resulted from the reduction of lung cancer cases and deaths due to decreased smoking by men and, to a lesser extent, women. Also, with few exceptions, the incidence rates of a wide range of nonsmoking related cancers continued to increase from 1991 to 2001. (These rates are based on statistics that are adjusted for the aging population.)

Confidence in the latest claim of the NCI and ACS of declining death rates was further shaken by the NCI's admission in a "Questions and Answers" release of "statistical uncertainties related to changes in data collection." These included discrepancies between the claim that death rates "are on the decline from 1991–2001" in contrast to their previous annual report that "death rates were stabilizing." Even more to the point is the alarming fact that death rates have remained virtually unchanged since 1975.

Today cancer strikes about 1.3 million people annually. Nearly one in two men and more than one in three women develop cancer in their lifetimes. This translates into approximately 56 percent more cancer in men and 22 percent more cancer in women over the course of just one generation. Cancer has become a "disease of mass destruction."

These trends have developed over the last three decades during which the NCI's annual budget has skyrocketed by about thirtyfold, now approaching $5 billion. By one recent estimate, total public and private spending on cancer will have amounted to $14 billion for 2004.

Paradoxically, it seems that the more money spent fighting cancer the more cancer is discovered in patients. Certainly, major funding is essential for early detection, treatment, and related research. But much less money would be needed if more cancers were prevented, resulting in less to treat. Representative John Conyers (Democrat, Michigan), the ranking minority member of the House judiciary Committee, recently warned that "so much carnage is preventable. Preventable that is, if the NCI gets off the dime and does its job."

The Cancer Establishment

The NCI is a federal agency funded by taxpayers while the ACS is a private, nonprofit "charity." However, despite their institutional independence, the NCI and ACS are joined at the hip. They are well dubbed the "cancer establishment."

The ACS powerfully and seemingly independently reinforces the NCIs strategies through well-orchestrated and aggressive public relations directed toward the public, the media, and Congress. This PR is underwritten by the multibillion dollar cancer drug industry ("Big Pharma"), other industries that are major ACS donors, and public donations. In spite of its smaller size and budget, the ACS is the dominant partner in the cancer establishment—"the tail that wags the NCI dog."

The institutional relationship between the NCI and the ACS is reinforced nationally at the rank-and file level. About half of ACS board members are surgeons, radiologists, oncologists, and basic scientists. Most are interlocked with the NCI, particularly with regard to finding for treatment and related research. And with the February 2002 appointment of ACS President elect von Eschenback as NCI director, the relationship between ACS and the NCI became further consolidated.

The Wrong Strategies

The cancer establishments strategies are overwhelmingly imbalanced. They are fixated on damage control—screening, diagnosis, and treatment—and related research to the virtual exclusion of prevention. These current strategies reflect professional mindsets within the establishment's leadership—predominantly oncologists, surgeons, radiotherapists, and research scientists. Such biases are exacerbated by strong and pervasive conflicts of interest.

At the April 2004 annual meeting of the American Association of Cancer Research, Leland Hartwell, president of the Fred Hutchinson Cancer Research Center and 2001 Nobel laureate, admitted the facts plainly when he said, "Congress and the public are not paying [NCI] $4.7 billion a year just to learn about cancer [through basic research]. They are paying to cure the disease." Hartwell further stressed that most resources for cancer research are spent on "promoting ineffective drugs" for terminal disease.

Hartwell wasn't the first establishment figure to admit these facts. As reported by the Associated Press on July 27, 2003, leading oncologists have questioned whether cancer "will ever be reliably and predictably cured." They also admitted that the biotech industry's new magic bullet, "targeted" drugs, have turned out to be "as powerless as old-line chemotherapy," increasing survival by a few months at best. In this connection, Memorial Sloan-Kettering's Leonard Saltz estimated that the price for new biotech drugs "has increased 500- fold in the last decade." Unchecked, these runaway costs could implode the entire health care system.

Hartwell also agreed with Clifton Leaf's March 22, 2004, *Fortune* article, "Why We're loosing the War on Cancer" which reports that cancer mortality rates have remained almost stable over the past five decades, during which time there have been major reductions in mortality from heart disease and stroke. Taken aback by Hartwell and Leaf's conclusions, von Eschenbach responded with an irrelevant stump speech; "You are transforming the world. You are saving lives. God bless you for it, and God continue to bless you in your work."

In this connection, it should be stressed that the standard criterion for the success of drug treatment is based on the shrinkage of tumor size by over 50 percent within six months, regardless of whether the patients life is prolonged. In fact, some "successful" treatments actually shorten survival due to drug toxicity while successes, particularly with the recent targeted drugs, are questionably based on brief increased survival in small trials.

When it comes to prevention, NCI and ACS strategies are fixated on faulty lifestyle, particularly smoking, to the virtual exclusion of a wide range of other avoidable causes of cancer. These include pervasive environmental contamination of air and water, hazardous waste sites, workplaces with carcinogenic industrial chemicals, contamination of food with carcinogenic

Incidence Rates of Non-Smoking Cancers

Cancer*	% Change, 1975–2001	% Change, 1991–2001
Melanoma	+137	+28
Liver	+100	+21
Kidney	+69	+13
Thyroid	+67	+48
Non-Hodgkin's Lymphoma (female)	+63	+8
Brain (childhood)	+61	+6
Testes	+46	+6
Breast (post-menopausal)	+37	+4
Acute Myeloid Leukemia	+15	+18
Multiple Myeloma	+8	−12
Colorectal	−13	−13

*Prostate cancer omitted because of diagnostic uncertainties relating to the PSA test

pesticides, carcinogenic prescription drugs and high-dose diagnostic radiation, and carcinogenic ingredients in cosmetics, toiletries, and household products.

Arthur Andersen's silence regarding Enron's misconduct pales in comparison to the cancer establishment's silence regarding reckless misconduct by the petrochemical and other industries. The former caused a financial meltdown while the latter has resulted in the cancer epidemic.

In sharp contrast to inflationary expenditures on treatment, the NCI's prevention budget has been and remains parsimonious. For instance, an unchallenged published analysis of its $2 billion 1992 budget revealed that less than 2.5 percent—not the 20 percent the NCI had claimed—was earmarked for research on avoidable causes of cancer, furthermore, no funds were allocated toward making any such information available to the public.

In 1998 U.S. Representative David Obey (Democrat, Wisconsin) asked then–NCI Director Richard Klausner to back up the claim that 20 percent of NCI's $2.5 billion budget was allocated toward research on environmental causes of cancer. Klausner simply increased his 20 percent figure to 40 percent without providing any supportive evidence. Another example of the NCI's frank misrepresentation of its prevention policies appears in the "Highlights" of its 2001 *Cancer Facts*. The opening sentence states, "Cancer prevention is a major component and current priority—to reduce suffering and death from cancer."

Sometimes NCI's false claims and indifference to avoidable causes of cancer extend to outright denial. For example, it holds that the causes of childhood cancer are largely unknown, in spite of substantial contrary evidence. The ACS takes a similar position. In the childhood cancer section of its 2003 *Cancer Facts & Figures,* no mention is made of any avoidable causes.

Indifference and denial can extend even to the outright suppression of information. At a 1996 San Francisco town hall meeting on

Avoidable Causes of Childhood Cancer

Environmental

- Proximity of residence to nuclear energy plants.
- Proximity of residence to petrochemical industries.
- Exposure to carcinogenic pesticides from agricultural and urban spraying and uses in schools, including wood playground sets treated with chromated copper arsenate.
- Maternal or paternal exposures (preconception, conception, and post-conception) to occupational carcinogens.

Domestic

- Drinking and cooking water contaminated with carcinogenic pesticides or other industrial pollutants.
- Exposure to carcinogenic pesticides from uses in the home and garden and pet flea collars.
- Contamination of infant and childhood food with carcinogenic pesticides.
- Nitrite preservatives in hot dogs (interacting with naturally occurring amines to form carcinogenic nitrosamines).
- Maternal or paternal carry home of occupational carcinogens.

Medical

- Maternal X-radiation during late pregnancy.
- Ionizing radiation for treatment of scalp ringworm or enlarged tonsils.
- High-dose diagnostic X radiation, particularly computerized tomography scans.
- Prescription drugs during pregnancy, such as DES and Dilantin.
- Pediatric prescription drugs, such as Lindane shampoos and Ritalin.

breast cancer, chaired by U.S. Representative Nancy Pelosi (a California Democrat, now the House minority leader), Klausner insisted that "low-level diagnostic radiation does not demonstrate an increased risk." Actually, the NCI's long-term studies on patients with scoliosis (spinal curvature) showed that such radiation was responsible for 70 percent excess breast cancer mortality.

Perhaps the most egregious violation of the public's right to know concerns the belated release in 1997 of decade-old data predicting up to 210,000 thyroid cancers from exposure to radioactive fallout following the hydrogen bomb tests in Nevada during the 1950s. Had the public been warned in time, these cancers, whose incidence almost doubled since 1973, could have been readily prevented with thyroid medication. In a 1999 hearing, the Senate Committee on Governmental Affairs charged that the NCI investigation was "plagued by lack of public participation and openness" and that failure to "release this information (to the public) was a travesty."

As long as the NCI shirks its job of providing Congress and regulatory agencies with scientific evidence on avoidable causes of cancer, corrective legislative and regulatory action remains discouraging. Meanwhile, this silence also encourages petrochemical and other industries to continue manufacturing carcinogenic products and corporate polluters to continue contaminating the environment unchallenged.

Responding to growing criticism of its policies, the NCI now claims to allocate 12 percent of its budget toward "prevention and control" and to require its nationwide Comprehensive Cancer Centers to have a "prevention component." However, prevention continues to be narrowly defined in exclusionary terms of faulty lifestyle and screening, with no reference to environmental causes due to exposure to a wide range of industrial carcinogens.

The NCI goes even further by defining environmental causes of cancer as those other than genetic in origin. Commenting on the NCI's June 17, 2004, news release, "The Majority of Cancers Are Linked to Environment," Dr. Aaron Blair, NCI's leading epidemiologist, explained that "environmental" causes include all causes of cancer other than genetic. Blair thus claimed that environmental causes are predominantly smoking, diet, alcohol, and obesity and that industrial pollutants of air, water, and the workplace account for 5 percent or less of all causes of cancer.

The ACS indifference to prevention extends to hostility, as reflected in a decades-long history of pro-industry bias and even collusion. Examples are legion. In 1978 the ACS in effect protected auto industry interests by refusing to support the Clean Air Act. In 1992 the ACS supported the Chlorine Institutes defense of the continued use of chlorinated pesticides, despite clear evidence of their carcinogenicity, persistence, and pervasive environmental contamination. In 1993, just before PBS aired a *Frontline* program warning of contamination of infant and children's food with carcinogenic pesticides, the ACS blanketed its forty-eight regional divisions and 3,000 local offices with false reassurances of safety crafted by the agribusiness industry. Then in its 2003 *Cancer Facts & Figures,* the ACS offered reassurance that carcinogenic exposures from dietary pesticides, "toxic wastes in dump sites," and radiation from "closely controlled" nuclear energy plants are all "at such low levels that risks are negligible."

The ACS pro-industry agenda is further exemplified by its lack of research on prevention. In spite of bloated contrary claims, less than 0.1 percent of its approximately $800 million budget has been assigned to address "environmental carcinogenesis."

Conflicts of Interest

The cancer establishment generals have longstanding conflicts of interest. A current case in point is the highly touted "anticancer" nutritional supplement, PC–SPES.

PC–SPES (*PC* for prostate cancer, and the Latin *spes* for hope) has been widely sold by International Medical Research (IMR) to prostate cancer patients, as well as to healthy men, to maintain "good prostate health without any adverse reaction." However, PC–SPES is laced with prescription drugs, including the potent carcinogen DES (diethylstilbestrol, a synthetic estrogen). Aside from the lack of any evidence of benefits, symptoms and prostate-specific antigen (PSA) levels in cancer patients are likely to have been dangerously masked by DBS in the supplement.

In February 2004 more than twenty personal injury suits filed in Los Angeles County Superior Court alleged that IMR directors Richard Klausner and Michael Milken (the latter a securities felon turned philanthropist and founder and chair of the Prostate Cancer Foundation) systematically promoted PC–SPES. Other IMR directors include leading oncologists and scientists in the NCI's twenty-plus nationwide Comprehensive Cancer Centers.

Conflicts of interest of the PC–SPES type aren't just matters of personal wrongdoing. The conflicts are deeply rooted in the NCI's institutional structure. Founded in 1937 and incorporated into the National Institutes of Health in 1941, the NCI was divorced from the NIH by the 1971 National Cancer Act. Far beyond a mere reshuffling of bureaucratic boxes, this action in effect politicized the NCI and effectively insulated it from the scientific and public health communities. The NCI director reports to the U.S. president through the Office of Management and Budget, bypassing the NIH and the Department of Health and Human Services.

Nixon created a three-member NCI executive President's Cancer Panel, naming as its first chair Benno C. Schmidt, an investment banker and senior drug company executive with close ties to the oil, steel, and chemical industries. Schmidt's successor in the 1980s was Armand Hammer, the late chair of Occidental Petroleum, one of the nation's largest manufacturers of industrial chemicals and infamous for its involvement in the Love Canal disaster. Not surprisingly, Schmidt and Hammer showed no interest in cancer prevention, Instead, they focused on the highly profitable development and marketing of cancer drugs.

The NCI's prototype Comprehensive Cancer Center, Memorial Sloan Kettering, jointly funded by the ACS, represents another example of entrenched conflicts of interest. An analysis of the center's board reveals the predominant representation of cancer drug industries and close affiliations with oil and petrochemical industries. Dr. Samuel Broder, NCI director from 1989 to 1995, admitted the obvious in a 1988 *Washington Post* interview: "The NCI has become what amounts to a government pharmaceutical company" Broder left the NCI to take executive posts at IVAX and Celera Genomics, two major manufacturers of cancer drugs.

This revolving door between the NCI and industry—particularly industries indifferent or hostile to cancer prevention—has been and remains commonplace. The late Dr. Frank Rauscher, appointed NCI director by Nixon to spearhead his cancer war, resigned in 1976 to become the ACS senior vice president for research. He then moved on to become executive director of the Thermal Insulation Manufacturers Association, which promoted the unregulated use of carcinogenic fiberglass. Dr. Richard Adamson, the NCI's former director of research and policy on cancer causation, left the NCI in 1994 to head the National Soft Drinks Association, which vigorously promoted the use of artificial sweeteners, particularly the carcinogenic saccharin.

In a June 30, 2003, CNBC program, "Titans of Cancer" hosted by Maria Bartiromo, four cancer "titans" enthused about alleged breakthroughs in treatment with targeted biotech drugs while at the same time they ignored cancer prevention. Included on the program was Dr. Harold Varmus, president of Memorial Sloan-Kettering Cancer Center and a past recipient of major NCI research grants. In 1995 Varmus, then NIH director, struck down the "reasonable pricing clause" that protected against gross industry profiteering from cancer and other drugs developed with taxpayer dollars. Varmus" action also gave senior NCI and NIH staff free rein to consult with the drug industry. Another titan on the program—Dr. John Mendelsohn, president of NCI's University of Texas M. D. Anderson Comprehensive Cancer Center has been embroiled in conflicts of interest over ImClone's targeted drug Erbitux.

Following the *Los Angeles Times* series of revelations on extensive private consulting by senior NCI scientists, some of whom have earned as much as $300,000 or more per year since 1995, the House Energy and Commerce Committee and the Senate Appropriations Subcommittee convened hearings in December 2003 and January 2004. An illustrative case was that of Dr. Jeffrey Schlom, head of NCI's Laboratory of Tumor Immunology and Biology since 1982. Schlom built himself another substantial career as consultant on Taxol to Cytoclonal Pharmaceuticals and on colorectal and prostate cancer vaccines to Jenner Biotherapie.

Meanwhile, further conflicts of interest hearings and a General Accounting Office investigation are pending. Klausner, now director of global health programs for the Bill and Melinda Gates Foundation, remains under congressional investigation for violating ethics rules. He allegedly accepted "lecture awards" from NCI's Comprehensive Cancer Centers while serving as NCI director more than two years ago. Congress is also investigating Klausners questionable travel arrangements and business connections.

For all that, the NCI's conflicts of interest are dwarfed by those of the American Cancer Society. The ACS openly trumpets its financial ties to Big Pharma and polluting industries. Designated as "Excalibur" donors for their annual contributions of $100,000 or more, these benefactors include such drug and biotech companies as Bristol-Myers Squibb, Pfizer, AstraZeneca, Eli Lilly, Amgen, Genentech, and Johnson and Johnson. Among polluting industries on the donor ledgers are more than ten major petrochemical and oil companies, including DuPont, Akzo Nobel, Pennzoil, British Petroleum, and Concho Oil.

A total of some 300 other industries and companies make similar contributions to the total annual ACS budget of about $800 million, not counting government grants or income from about $1 billion in reserves. The ACS honors these contributions with more than a wink and a nod. Such collusion between agency and industry is normally unthinkable. For example, one would never find the American Heart Association advocating low tar cigarettes. But the ACS continually crosses the line. Not surprisingly, a January 28, 1992, report in the *Chronicle of Philanthropy,* the nation's leading charity watchdog, has charged: "The ACS is more interested in accumulating wealth than saving lives."

Privatizing the War

The most disturbing development in the cancer war has been its privatization by ACS and NCI generals. In 1998 the ACS created and funded the National Dialogue on Cancer (NDC), co-chaired by former President George H. W. Bush and Barbara Bush. Members included cancer survivor groups, some 100 representatives of the cancer drug industry, and Shandwick International Public Relations. Dr. John Durant, executive president of the American Cancer Society for Clinical Oncology, charged that the hidden purpose of ACS was "protecting their own fund raising capacity...from competition from survivor groups. It has always seemed to me that this was an issue of control by the ACS over the cancer agenda."

Without informing the NDC, the ACS then spun off a small legislative committee, the explicit aim of which was to increase NCI's autonomy and budget and to shift major control of cancer policy to the ACS—in other words, from the public purse to private hands. Shandwick International played a key role in managing the NDC and drafting the proposed legislation.

When news surfaced that R. J. Reynolds Tobacco Holdings was one of Shandwicks major clients, the ACS claimed prior ignorance and fired Shandwick. Astoundingly, the ACS next hired Edelman Public Relations Worldwide, another well-known tobacco public relations firm, to conduct a voter cancer education campaign for the 2000 presidential election.

Ever since von Eschenbach was appointed NCI director, the National Cancer Program has been effectively privatized. Von Eschenbach obtained George W. Bush's agreement to continue as vice chair of NDC, of which he was a main founder. The NDC since has been spun off as a nonprofit organization and renamed C-Change. The group then again hired Edelman as its PR firm, following Edelmans signed pledge that it would sever its relations with the tobacco industry. Edelman represents the Brown and Williamson Tobacco Company and the Aitria Group, the parent company of Philip Morris, the largest cigarette maker in the United States. Edelman's clients also include Kraft and fast food and beverage companies now targeted by anti-obesity litigation.

In July 2003 it was discovered that Edelman, in violation of its pledge, was continuing to fight tobacco control programs from its Malaysian offices. Edelman executives apologized for this "oversight" and agreed once more to terminate its support of the tobacco industry. It further promised to donate this income to charity. Commenting on the ACS and NDC relationship with Edelman, Dr. Stanton Glantz, a prominent anti-smoking activist, commented, "It's like ... Bush hiring alQaeda to do PR, because they have good connections to al Jazeera."

Equally disturbing is the growing and secretive collaboration between the NCI and the C-Change organization. The latest example is the joint planning of a massive national tumor tissue bank for cancer drug and genetic research. According to the Washington insider *Cancer Letter,* this project would cost up to $1.2 billion to operate in addition to construction costs in the billions. This initiative would be privatized, ripe with conflicts of interest, and exempt from the public scrutiny required by the Federal Advisory Committee and Freedom of information acts.

Behind the scenes, strong support for privatization of the cancer war comes from Michael Milken. As noted in the *Cancer Letter,* "Milken is the single most influential player in cancer politics within the last decade."

How to Win the War

After all this time we don't need another thirty years of research on cellular mechanisms of cancer and treatment or more billions of dollars spent on illusory wonder drugs to start winning the war. The war must be fought with the right generals implementing the right strategies. This goal should be supported by an array of interlocking initiatives.

The National Cancer Institute: For over three decades, NCI generals have violated the mandates of the 1971 National Cancer Act and its amendments to "disseminate cancer information to the public" and to call for "an expanded and intensified research program for the prevention of cancer caused by occupational and environmental exposures to carcinogens." The highest priority should be directed toward drastically changing the NCI high command. Those responsible for prevention should be given at least the same authority as those responsible for damage control. Responsibility for prevention should also be extended to the twenty-member National Cancer Advisory Board, as the Cancer Act requires, and to presidents of NCI's Comprehensive Cancer Centers. NCI's generals, senior staff, and Cancer Center presidents involved in illegal activities or in flagrant conflicts of interest with the cancer drug industries should resign or face dismissal.

The American Cancer Society: The public and media should be fully informed of the ACS's hostile record on cancer prevention, beyond identifying the dangers of an unhealthy lifestyle. They should also be explicitly informed of flagrant conflicts of interest between the ACS and the cancer drug, petrochemical, and other industries as well as its close ties to the tobacco industry. Armed with this information, the public would then be in a position to decide whether to continue giving funds to this charity or to donate instead to individuals, groups, and organizations with strong scientific and public health policy concerns on cancer prevention.

Developing Grass-Roots National Support: Cancer affects virtually every family in the nation. Still, the epidemic is likely to be met with passivity or even denial unless citizens are provided with practical information on how to reduce their own risks. The most realistic strategy for developing broad public support for cancer prevention will stress self-interest rather than abstractions or ideology. Preventing smoking, particularly prior to addiction in adolescence, is obviously important. Much less recognized, though, is the critical need for user-friendly information on avoidable causes of a wide spectrum of nonsmoking cancers, incidence of which has escalated dramatically over recent decades.

The public's right to know about avoidable causes of cancer is the fundamental basis for building a national grass-roots coalition. The continuing failure of the NCI and the ACS to provide the public. Congress, and regulatory agencies with such information is a flagrant denial of this right. The right can be restored by empowering consumers, citizens, workers, and patients in a number of areas:

Instituting explicit label warnings on carcinogenic ingredients and contaminants in food, cosmetics and toiletries, and household products. Consumers then would be empowered to boycott mainstream companies selling unsafe products and reward smaller, "green" companies marketing safe alternatives. With increasing demand for the latter, economies of scale would reduce their higher prices.

Utilizing the "Environmental Defense Scorecard." Citizens have increasing opportunities for empowerment on an individual and community basis by plugging in their zip code on the scorecards website, **www.scorecard.org,** in order to obtain basic information on toxic and carcinogenic pollutants to which they are exposed locally by local chemical industries and power plants. They can then organize, alert the media, and join with environmental groups to express their concerns to local and state health authorities, including state governors. Regardless of their politics, governors are generally sensitive to citizen lobbies in their states.

Informing workers of potential high risks of cancers because of exposures to a wide range of occupational carcinogens can enable them to act to reduce such exposures both individually and through their unions and health and safety committees.

Advising patients to exercise their right to know by requesting full information on cancer and other risks of prescription drugs, as detailed in the "Precautions" section of the *Physicians Desk Reference,* empowers them to take charge of their own health. Thus, for the wide range of common prescription drugs carrying cancer risks, safe alternatives may be requested In accordance with legal as well as ethical requirements for informed consent. Made aware of the carcinogenic risks of high-dose X-ray procedures, particularly pediatric CT scans and fluoroscopy, patients can request dosage records for each examination, make informed decisions, and seek those (still few) informed radiologists and clinics practicing dose-reduction techniques.

Publicizing the Failure of the Cancer War: An aggressive critique of the cancer generals and their unwinnable strategies is well overdue. For decades the mainstream media have mostly ignored the failed cancer policies and conflicts of interest of the cancer establishment. Activist citizen groups could generate a mounting series of reports, initially in smaller independent newspapers and radio stations nationwide, focusing on hot button topics—local or regional exposures to environmental carcinogens, "cancer clusters" in the vicinity of petrochemical and nuclear power plants, and escalating rates of cancers in children and retirees, together with the known or suspect causes of such cancers.

Key to such media activities should be emphasis on the escalating rates of nonsmoking cancers, along with the cancer establishment's refusal to prioritize the overdue need to reduce exposures to environmental carcinogens and to recognize the public's right to know about these avoidable exposures. It might be argued that regulatory agencies, or industry itself, should be primary targets for media attention. However, considering the multibillion-dollar cancer establishment's responsibility for and control of basic information about cancer prevention, primary emphasis should be directed at exposing the establishments noninformation or, worse, willful misinformation.

Legislative Initiatives: In view of the NCI's exaggerated and inconsistent claims for its prevention budget, U.S. Representative Jan Schakowsky (Democrat, Illinois) recently asked the General Accounting Office to investigate the NCI's "fight against cancer." Specifically, she requested information on the dollar amounts spent on "funding for research on prevention" and "funding for outreach" to disseminate this information. Meanwhile, Congress is investigating conflicts of interest by NCI generals and scientists with particular reference to consulting with drug industries. This investigation should be extended by an order of magnitude to the NCI's institutional conflicts with the multi-billion dollar Big Pharma.

In response to congressional concerns about NCI policies, the National Academy of Sciences recently examined NCI's relationship with the NIH. In July 2003 the NAS reported that NCI's "special status" of independence from twenty-six other NIH bodies was problematic. It created "an unnecessary rift" between "the goals, mission and leadership of the NIH and those of NCI." In a startling statement that drew minimal media attention, the NAS emphasized, "Perhaps more important is the fact that the National Cancer Act has had little discernible effect on scientific and clinical progress for the diagnosis, treatment, or prevention of cancer."

The NAS report makes it clear that the NCI should be folded back into the NIH and integrated with the scientific community once again. But that is only the beginning of drastically needed reforms. Funding for cancer prevention should equal that of all other programs combined. Congress should direct the NCI to provide the public with all available information on avoidable and unknowing exposures to carcinogens in consumer products, prescription drugs, the workplace, and the environment.

Legislative initiatives should also be developed at the state and local levels. Since the 2002 midterm elections Congress has remained divided and grid-locked. Accordingly, leadership and innovative policies on domestic agendas is likely to shift further from the national to state, county, and city levels.

The Bottom Line: Citizens, the media, and Congress must belatedly recognize that, after spending thirty years and some $50 billion, we are now further from winning the war on cancer than when it was first declared. Furthermore, we all must recognize, albeit belatedly, that the cancer epidemic can still be arrested and reversed. But this goal will never be achieved until we recruit new generals and develop new strategies making prevention at least as urgent as damage control.

SAMUEL S. EPSTEIN, M.D., is professor emeritus of environmental and occupational medicine at the University of Illinois Chicago School of Public Health.

How AIDS Changed America

The plague years: It brought out the worst in us at first, but ultimately it brought out the best, and transformed the nation. The story of a disease that left an indelible mark on our history, our culture and our souls.

DAVID JEFFERSON

Jeanne White-Ginder sits at home, assembling a scrapbook about her son, Ryan. She pastes in newspaper stories about his fight to return to the Indiana middle school that barred him in 1985 for having AIDS. She sorts through photos of Ryan with Elton John, Greg Louganis and others who championed his cause. She organizes mementos from his PBS special, "I Have AIDS: A Teenager's Story." "I just got done with his funeral. Eight pages. That was very hard," says White-Ginder, who buried her 18-year-old son in 1991, seven years after he was diagnosed with the disease, which he contracted through a blood product used to treat hemophiliacs. The scrapbook, along with Ryan's bedroom, the way his mother left it when he died, will be part of an exhibit at the Children's Museum of Indianapolis on three children who changed history: Anne Frank. Ruby Bridges. And Ryan White. "He put a face to the epidemic, so people could care about people with AIDS," his mother says.

At a time when the mere threat of avian flu or SARS can set off a coast-to-coast panic—and prompt the federal government to draw up contingency plans and stockpile medicines—it's hard to imagine that the national response to the emergence of AIDS ranged from indifference to hostility. But that's exactly what happened when gay men in 1981 began dying of a strange array of opportunistic infections. President Ronald Reagan didn't discuss AIDS in a public forum until a press conference four years into the epidemic, by which time more than 12,000 Americans had already died. (He didn't publicly utter the term "AIDS" until 1987.) People with the disease were routinely evicted from their homes, fired from jobs and denied health insurance. Gays were demonized by the extreme right wing: Reagan adviser Pat Buchanan editorialized in 1983, "The poor homosexuals—they have declared war against nature, and now nature is exacting an awful retribution." In much of the rest of the culture, AIDS was simply treated as the punch line to a tasteless joke: "I just heard the Statue of Liberty has AIDS," Bob Hope quipped during the rededication ceremony of the statue in 1986. "Nobody knows if she got it from the mouth of the Hudson or the Staten Island Fairy." Across the

river in Manhattan, a generation of young adults was attending more funerals than weddings.

In 1995, Americans regarded HIV/AIDS as the nation's most urgent health problem. Today, only 17% rank it as the top concern.

All poll results are from the Kaiser family foundation's 2006 "Survey of Americans on HIV/AIDS," conducted among 2,517 Americans nationwide.

As AIDS made its death march across the nation, killing more Americans than every conflict from World War II through Iraq, it left an indelible mark on our history and culture. It changed so many things in so many ways, from how the media portray homosexuality to how cancer patients deal with their disease. At the same time, AIDS itself changed, from a disease that killed gay men and drug addicts to a global scourge that has decimated the African continent, cut a large swath through black America and infected almost as many women as men worldwide. The death toll to date: 25 million and counting. Through the crucible of AIDS, America was forced to face its fears and prejudices—fears that denied Ryan White a seat in school for a year and a half, prejudices that had customers boycotting restaurants with gay chefs. "At first, a ton of people said that whoever gets AIDS deserves to have AIDS, deserves to literally suffer all the physical pain that the virus carries with it," says Tom Hanks, who won an Oscar for playing a gay lawyer dying of the disease in 1993's "Philadelphia." "But that didn't hold." Watching a generation of gay men wither and die, the nation came to acknowledge the humanity of a community it had mostly ignored and reviled. "AIDS was the great unifier," says Craig Thompson, executive director of AIDS Project Los Angeles and HIV-positive for 25 years.

Without AIDS, and the activism and consciousness-raising that accompanied it, would gay marriage even be up for debate today? Would we be welcoming "Will & Grace" into our living rooms or weeping over "Brokeback Mountain"? Without red ribbons, first worn in 1991 to promote AIDS awareness, would we be donning rubber yellow bracelets to show our support for cancer research? And without the experience of battling AIDS, would scientists have the strategies and technologies to develop the antiviral drugs we'll need to battle microbial killers yet to emerge?

AIDS, of course, did happen. "Don't you dare tell me there's any good news in this," says Larry Kramer, who has been raging against the disease—and those who let it spread unchecked—since it was first identified in 1981. "We should be having a national day of mourning!" True. But as we try to comprehend the carnage, it's impossible not to acknowledge the displays of strength, compassion and, yes, love, that were a direct result of all that pain and loss. Without AIDS, we wouldn't have the degree of patient activism we see today among people with breast cancer, lymphoma, ALS and other life-threatening diseases. It was Kramer, after all, who organized 10,000 frustrated AIDS patients into ACT UP, a street army chanting "Silence equals death" that marched on the White House and shut down Wall Street, demanding more government funding for research and quicker access to drugs that might save lives. "The only thing that makes people fight is fear. That's what we discovered about AIDS activism," Kramer says.

Fear can mobilize, but it can also paralyze—which is what AIDS did when it first appeared. And no one—not the government, not the media, not the gay community itself—reacted fast enough to head off disaster. In the fiscally and socially conservative climate of Reagan's America, politicians were loath to fund research into a new pathogen that was killing mostly gay men and intravenous drug users. "In the first years of AIDS, I imagine we felt like the folks on the rooftops during Katrina, waiting for help," says Dr. Michael Gottlieb, the Los Angeles immunologist credited as the first doctor to recognize the looming epidemic. When epidemiologist Donald Francis of the federal Centers for Disease Control in Atlanta tried to get $30 million in funding for an AIDS-prevention campaign, "it went up to Washington and they said f--- off," says Francis, who quit the CDC soon after, defeated.

"Gay Cancer," as it was referred to at the time, wasn't a story the press wanted to cover—especially since it required a discussion of gay sex. While the media had a field day with Legionnaire's disease, toxic shock syndrome and the Tylenol scare, few outlets paid much attention to the new syndrome, even after scores of people had died. The New York Times ran fewer than a dozen stories about the new killer in 1981 and 1982, almost all of them buried inside the paper. (NEWSWEEK, for that matter, didn't run its first cover story on what "may be the public-health threat of the century" until April 1983.) The Wall Street Journal first reported on the disease only after it had spread to heterosexuals: NEW, OFTEN-FATAL ILLNESS IN HOMOSEXUALS TURNS UP IN WOMEN, HETEROSEXUAL MALES, read the February 1982 headline. Even the gay press missed the story at first: afraid of alarming the community and inflaming antigay forces, editors at the New York Native slapped the headline DISEASE RUMORS LARGELY UNFOUNDED

atop the very first press report about the syndrome, which ran May 18, 1981. There were a few notable exceptions, particularly the work of the late Randy Shilts, an openly gay journalist who convinced his editors at the San Francisco Chronicle to let him cover AIDS as a full-time beat: that reporting led to the landmark 1987 book "And the Band Played On," a detailed account of how the nation's failure to take AIDS seriously allowed the disease to spread exponentially in the early '80s.

Many gay men were slow to recognize the time bomb in their midst, even as people around them were being hospitalized with strange, purplish skin cancers and life-threatening pneumonia. Kramer and his friends tried to raise money for research during the 1981 Labor Day weekend in The Pines, a popular gay vacation spot on New York's Fire Island. "When we opened the collection boxes, we could not believe how truly awful the results were," says Kramer. The total? $769.55. "People thought we were a bunch of creeps with our GIVE TO GAY CANCER signs, raining on the parade of Pines' holiday festivities." The denial in some corners of the gay community would continue for years. Many were reluctant to give up the sexual liberation they believed they'd earned: as late as 1984, the community was bitterly debating whether to close San Francisco's gay bathhouses, where men were having unprotected sex with any number of partners in a single night.

With death a constant companion, the gay community sobered up from the party that was the '70s and rose to meet the unprecedented challenge of AIDS. There was no other choice, really: they had been abandoned by the nation, left to fend for themselves. "It's important to remember that there was a time when people did not want to use the same bathroom as a person with AIDS, when cabdrivers didn't want to pick up patients who had the disease, when hospitals put signs on patients' doors that said WARNING. DO NOT ENTER," recalls Marjorie Hill, executive director of Gay Men's Health Crisis in New York. Organizations like GMHC sprang up around the country to provide HIV patients with everything from medical care to counseling to food and housing. "Out of whole cloth, and without experience, we built a healthcare system that was affordable, effective and humane," says Darrel Cummings, chief of staff of the Los Angeles Gay & Lesbian Center. "I can't believe our community did what it did while so many people were dying." Patients took a hands-on approach to managing their disease, learning the intricacies of T-cell counts and grilling their doctors about treatment options. And they shared what they learned with one another. "There's something that a person with a disease can only get from another person with that disease. It's support and information and inspiration," says Sean Strub, who founded the magazine Poz for HIV-positive readers.

It took a movie star to get the rest of the nation's attention. In the summer of 1985, the world learned that Rock Hudson—the romantic leading man who'd been a symbol of American virility—was not only gay, but had full-blown AIDS. "It was a bombshell event," says Gottlieb, who remembers standing on the helipad at UCLA Medical Center, waiting for his celebrity patient to arrive, as news helicopters circled overhead. "For many Americans, it was their first awareness at all of AIDS. This prominent man had been diagnosed, and the image of him looking as sick as he did really stuck." Six years later, basketball legend Magic Johnson announced he was HIV-positive, and the shock waves were even bigger. A straight, healthy-looking superstar athlete had contracted the "gay" disease. "It can happen to anybody, even me, Magic Johnson," the 32-year-old announced to a stunned nation, as he urged Americans to practice safe sex.

Given the tremendous stigma, most well-known public figures with AIDS tried to keep their condition a secret. Actor Brad Davis, the star of "Midnight Express," kept his diagnosis hidden for six years, until he died in 1991. "He assumed, and I think rightly so, that he wouldn't be able to find work," says his widow, Susan Bluestein, a Hollywood casting director. After Davis died, rumors flew that he must have been secretly gay. "That part of the gossip mill was the most hurtful to me and my daughter," says Bluestein, who acknowledges in her book "After Midnight" that her husband was a drug addict and unfaithful—but not gay.

With the disease afflicting so many of their own, celebrities were quick to lend support and raise money. Elizabeth Taylor was among the first, taking her friend Rock Hudson's hand in public, before the TV cameras and the world, to dispel the notion that AIDS was something you could catch through casual contact. Her gesture seems quaint today, but in 1985—when the tabloids were awash with speculation that Hudson could have infected actress Linda Evans by simply kissing her during a love scene in "Dynasty"—Taylor's gesture was revolutionary. She became the celebrity face of the American Foundation for AIDS Research. "I've lost so many friends," Taylor says. "I have so many friends who are HIV-positive and you just wonder how long it's going to be. And it breaks your heart."

Behind the scenes, Hollywood wasn't nearly as progressive as it likes to appear. John Erman recalls the uphill battle getting the 1985 AIDS drama, "An Early Frost," on TV. "The meetings we had with NBC's Standards and Practices [the network's censors] were absolutely medieval," says Erman. One of the censors' demands: that the boyfriend of the main character be portrayed as "a bad guy" for infecting him: "They did not want to show a positive gay relationship," Erman recalls. Ultimately, with the support of the late NBC Entertainment president Brandon Tartikoff, Erman got to make the picture he wanted—though major advertisers refused to buy commercial time during the broadcast. Within a decade, AIDS had changed the face of television. In 1991, "thirtysomething" featured a gay character who'd contracted the disease. And in 1994, on MTV's "The Real World," 23-year-old Pedro Zamora, who died later that same year, taught a generation of young people what it meant to be HIV-positive.

If TV was slow to deal with AIDS, cinema was downright glacial. "Longtime Companion," the first feature film about the disease, didn't make it to the screen until 1990, nine years into the epidemic. "There was a lot of talk before the movie came out about how this was going to hurt my career, the same way there was talk about Heath Ledger in 'Brokeback Mountain',," says Bruce Davison, who received an Oscar nomination for his role. As for "Philadelphia," Hanks is the first to admit " it was late to the game."

Broadway was the major exception when it came to taking on AIDS as subject matter—in part because so many early casualties came from the world of theater. "I remember in 1982 sitting in a restaurant with seven friends of mine. All were gay men either working or looking to work in the theater, and we were talking about AIDS," recalls Tom Viola, executive director of Broadway Cares/Equity Fights AIDS. "Of those eight guys, four are dead, and two, including myself, are HIV-positive." By the time Tony Kushner's Pulitzer Prize-winning "Angels in America" made its Broadway debut in 1993, some 60 plays about the disease had opened in New York. Producer Jeffrey Seller remembers how he was told he "could never do a show on Broadway that's about, quote unquote, AIDS, homosexuality and drug addiction." He's talking about "Rent," which a decade later still draws capacity crowds.

The world of "Rent" is something of an artifact now. Just before it hit Broadway in 1996, scientists introduced the antiretroviral drug cocktails that have gone on to extend the lives of millions of patients with HIV. Since then, the urgency that once surrounded the AIDS fight in the United States has ebbed, as HIV has come to be seen as a chronic, rather than fatal, condition. But the drugs aren't a panacea—despite the fact that many people too young to remember the funerals of the '80s think the new medications have made it safe to be unsafe. "Everywhere I go, I'm meeting young people who've just found out they've been infected, many with drug-resistant strains of the virus," says Cleve Jones, who two decades ago decided to start stitching a quilt to honor a friend who had died of AIDS. That quilt grew to become an iconic patchwork of more than 40,000 panels, each one the size of a grave, handmade by loved ones to honor their dead. Ever-expanding, it was displayed several times in Washington, transforming the National Mall into what Jones had always intended: a colorful cemetery that would force the country to acknowledge the toll of AIDS. "If I'd have known 20 years ago that in 2006 I'd be watching a whole new generation facing this tragedy, I don't think I would have had the strength to continue," says Jones, whose own HIV infection has grown resistant to treatment.

Inner strength is what has allowed people living with HIV to persevere. "They think I'm gonna die. You know what, they better not hold their breath," Ryan White once told his mother. Though given six months to live when he was diagnosed with HIV, Ryan lived five and a half years, long enough to prod a nation into joining the fight against AIDS. When he died in 1990 at the age of 18, Congress named a new comprehensive AIDS funding act after him. But the real tribute to Ryan has been the ongoing efforts of his mother. "I think the hostility around the epidemic is still there. And because of religious and moral issues, it's been really hard to educate people about this disease and be explicit," says White-Ginder, who continues to give speeches about watching her son live and die of AIDS. "We should not still be facing this disease." Sadly, we are.

The Puzzling Origins of AIDS

Although no one explanation has been universally accepted, four rival theories provide some important lessons

JIM MOORE

Shortly after the 1983 discovery of the human immunodeficiency virus (HIV), the pathogen responsible for AIDS, investigators became aware of a strangely similar immune deficiency disease afflicting Asian monkeys (macaques) held in captivity in various U.S. research labs. Soon, virologists identified the culprit: a simian immunodeficiency virus (SIV) that is found naturally in a West African monkey species, the sooty mangabey (*Cercocebus atys*), but is harmless to that host. This virus, denoted SIVsm, is genetically similar to a weakly contagious form of the AIDS virus that is largely restricted to parts of West Africa, HIV-2, and thus is considered its likely precursor. More recent work has shown that the closest relative of the primary human immunodeficiency virus (HIV-1) is another simian immunodeficiency virus, one carried by chimpanzees (SIVcpz).

After comparing the SIVs in chimpanzees and sooty mangabeys with HIV-1 and HIV-2 strains, investigators concluded that there must have been multiple transmission "events" from simians to humans—at least seven for HIV-2 (some of which are known from only a single person who lives near mangabeys carrying a uniquely similar SIV) and three for HIV-1, the virus now infecting some 40 million people worldwide.

How did SIVcpz and SIVsm cross over into humans and become pathogenic? Given the lack of historical references to AIDS-like disease in Africa prior to the mid-20th century, as well as its absence previously in the New World (which imported some 10 million African slaves during the 16th through 19th centuries), that transfer appears to have happened relatively recently—exactly when is a point of considerable debate. And why did two distinct simian viruses with which humans have apparently coexisted for centuries, or even millennia, suddenly pass into humans multiple times within a few decades?

The answers to these questions have been slow in coming, despite the considerable efforts of molecular biologists to understand the nature and evolution of primate immunodeficiency viruses. I am not one of those molecular biologists; rather, I became a player in the field of AIDS-origin research through my interest in chimpanzee socioecology. Although I am partial to a theory I helped to fashion for why AIDS emerged when it did, with time it might become clear that a competing idea better ac-

counts for genesis of the epidemic. Or perhaps the answer will prove to lie with some complex combination of factors that no single explanation presently encompasses. Whatever the case, the solution almost certainly will come from one or more of four competing theories.

Theory 1: Tainted Polio Vaccine

The first theory is the most controversial. In a 1992 article in the magazine *Rolling Stone*, journalist Tom Curtis suggested that HIV could have resulted from the use in Africa of an experimental oral polio vaccine (OPV), one contaminated by a then-unknown SIV carried most probably (Curtis supposed) by African green monkeys. Green-monkey kidney cells were widely used as a substrate to grow viruses for research and vaccine production. And one of the first major trials of an experimental oral polio virus vaccine took place from 1957 to 1960 in what are now the Democratic Republic of the Congo, Burundi and Rwanda, seemingly the "hearth" of the global AIDS epidemic. When interviewed by Curtis, Hilary Koprowski, the polio-vaccine pioneer who mounted that massive campaign, could not recall or find documentary evidence as to whether his group had used kidney cells from green monkeys or Asian macaques (which do not naturally carry an SIV). If culture media contained SIV (a possibility, given that the techniques available during that era were unable to guard against unknown viruses that did not cause overt symptoms in their monkey hosts), more than 900,000 people might have received it with their medicine, laying the basis for the current epidemic.

Curtis credited this theory to Blaine Elswood, a Californian AIDS activist. Interestingly, the idea that the administration of a contaminated oral polio vaccine might have been involved in the genesis of AIDS was suggested independently by two others at about the same time. The first to do so was Louis Pascal, who like Elswood is not a scientist. After years of rejections, Pascal, a New Yorker, finally managed in 1991 to get the University of Wollongong in Australia to publish a paper describing his ideas. Not surprisingly, few noticed it. Attorney Walter Kyle also published a broadly similar theory in *The Lancet*, a British medical journal, in 1992. Since then, writer Edward Hooper, author of the controversial 1999 book *The River*, has become the contaminated-vaccine theory's most ardent supporter. Hooper, noting a passing mention by Curtis of a chimpanzee colony run by Koprowski's team, suggested that kidneys from these chimpanzees—not from green monkeys—may have been the original source of the virus.

Multiple localized strains of HIV have now been discovered, and mass vaccination appears unlikely to account for all of them. But the early distribution of the major pandemic strain, HIV-1 group M (for "main"), seems to fit reasonably well with the location of Koprowski's campaigns, and the OPV theory now is applied primarily to this strain.

Contamination of OPV is the only one of the four current theories that is readily falsifiable: Finding the HIV-1 group M virus in a tissue sample that predated the suspect vaccine would eliminate this possibility. So far that has not happened. Still, many investigators give the theory little weight for other reasons, which has led to the widespread belief that the theory has been definitively disproved. In 2001, for example, *Science* magazine published a piece titled "Disputed AIDS Theory Dies its Final Death," and *Nature* ran one under the heading "Polio Vaccines Exonerated." Earlier this year *Nature* also published "Origin of AIDS: Contaminated Polio Vaccine Theory Refuted"—a surprising title given that this theory ostensibly died three years ago.

The recent findings of various molecular biologists have indeed failed to provide support for the OPV theory. For example, in 2000 a few existing samples of the vaccine from Koprowski's home institution (the Wistar Institute in Philadelphia) were tested and found negative for both chimpanzee DNA and SIV. However, this result did not rule out the possibility, previously suggested by Hooper, that local amplification of the live-virus vaccine in Africa (to create more doses) could have introduced the SIV. The key issue is thus whether chimpanzee kidneys were used as a culture medium at any stage of Koprowski's vaccine program. There is eyewitness testimony on both sides of this question, and failure to find SIVcpz in a handful of samples of the live vaccine strain of the type used in Africa does not prove the virus was absent in (putative) locally produced batches.

A second reason to question the OPV theory also came to light in 2000, with a report in *Science* by Bette T. Korber (of Los Alamos National Laboratory) and colleagues. They used molecular differences among HIV-1 group M subtypes to estimate the date of their last common ancestor. The conclusion: 1931 (with 95 percent confidence limits giving the range 1915 to 1941), preceding OPV administration by decades. However, the calculation of such common ancestor dates can be thrown off by genetic recombination among subtypes ("viral sex"), which can make such dates come out too early, and there is increasing evidence that such recombination may be common with HIV. So maybe this date is not right. On the other hand, independent analyses using different methods have supported the date, and an analogous study of HIV-2 came up with an origin for the main group between 1940 and 1945.

Another objection to the OPV theory concerns the subspecies of chimpanzee kept near Kisangani (formerly Stanleyville) at a facility called Camp Lindi, which Koprowski and colleagues maintain was used for safety-testing their vaccine, but which Hooper suspects was the source of chimpanzee tissues used to produce vaccine locally. The SIVcpz strain that is most similar to HIV-1 has so far only been identified in a subspecies of chimpanzee native to west-central Africa, *Pan troglodytes troglodytes*. A second, less similar strain has been identified only in Pan troglodytes schweinfurthii, the subspecies found in east-central Africa—where Camp Lindi was located. The nearest known populations of P. *t. troglodytes* are more than 500 kilometers from Koprowski's chimp colony. So, this argument goes, the locally obtained captive chimps would not have been carrying the SIVcpz strain thought to have given rise to HIV-1.

One difficulty with this argument is that distance is not always measured in kilometers, particularly in Central Africa: Kisangani lies at the upstream end of the navigable portion of the Congo River, which borders the range of P. *t. troglodytes* for hundreds of kilometers, and river trade has been substantial since the colonial scramble for Africa in the late 19th century. If it became known that Americans were paying good money for young apes in Kisangani, it would be almost surprising if some hunters had not made the trip upriver. Another problem is the difficulty of proving the absence of something based on only a few samples, which requires some significant assumptions about the epidemiology of SIVcpz in the wild.

In short, although the majority of the biological evidence published in the last few years suggests that the OPV hypothesis is wrong, headlines reporting the death of this theory remain premature.

Theory 2: Cut Hunter

The main competing theory posits that SIV is occasionally transmitted to hunters via blood-to-blood contact with an infected primate. According to this view, the virus is usually cleared in its human host, but at least several times during the 20th century it survived and became established as HIV. It is not hard to imagine hunters suffering cuts or being injured by a wounded mangabey or chimpanzee, and some form of natural transfer between species presumably accounts for the widespread distribution of SIVs in African primates. Hence, one has the "cut hunter" or "natural transfer" theory, which is probably the most accepted idea today. According to that view, the timing of the widespread emergences of HIV-l and HIV-2 in the middle part of the 20th century is attributed to urbanization and regional commerce, which create conditions ideal for spreading a sexually transmitted disease.

Unlike the case with OPV, there is no easy way to disprove this theory—even a smoking gun linking oral polio vaccines to HIV-1 group M would leave multiple other HIV strains unaccounted for, and "modernization" is a diffuse enough explanation to cover any of them. Nor is the cut-hunter theory particularly limited in time. After all, many Africans began moving to colonial capitals and ports in the 19th century. A hypothesis that does not account for the timing of the AIDS epidemic and that is not falsifiable is of limited use. Still, the thinness of the theory does not make it wrong.

142

Theory 3: Contaminated Needles

The next proposal, a refinement of the cut-hunter theory, comes from Preston A. Marx, a virologist who holds positions at Tulane University and at the Aaron Diamond AIDS Research Center. In 1995 he noted (to Hooper) that a big change in medical practice took place in the 1950s with the worldwide introduction of disposable plastic syringes, making guaranteed sterile use possible and dropping the cost of syringe production by almost two orders of magnitude. The result was that the medical use of injections went up astronomically. Because doses can be measured and there is no possibility of patients losing or selling the medicine, injections became a popular way for doctors in the developing world to administer medicines, including vitamins, analgesics and other common drugs.

The problem is that trivial costs are still large to someone living outside the cash economy, and plastic syringes *cannot* be sterilized by boiling: they melt. According to this scenario, the widespread availability of disposable syringes increased the acceptance of injections to treat a variety of diseases, but the syringes were not so available (or cheap) as to permit users actually to dispose of them. The result was that unsterilized syringes were used again and again, spreading viruses, including those that eventually became HIV.

Marx suggests that people's immune systems would normally be able to overcome an SIV they acquired, say while butchering a monkey, within a week or two of infection. He further posits that the transition from SIV to HIV demands a series of mutations, with the probability of all the required mutations occurring being a function of viral population size. Thus, Marx contends, some way must be found to permit the SIV to remain at high levels in people for long enough that such spontaneous mutations might take place. He suggests that the required mechanism is "serial passaging" of virus through unsterile needles. That is, a cut hunter might get an injection while he is still harboring large numbers of viral particles in his bloodstream; that same needle would then be used to infect another person, who might soon receive a second injection, and so forth. High viral population levels can thus be maintained in a series of different people getting shots. With each transfer via contaminated needle, the virus finds itself in a fresh host, with an opportunity to proliferate before the infected person can mount an immune response. Chance mutations can thus accumulate, and eventually the SIV adapts, becoming HIV.

Theory 4: *Heart of Darkness*

Together with two undergraduate students, I am responsible for another variant to the cut-hunter theory, so perhaps I should explain how I became engaged in this field of inquiry. In late 1998 I became involved in an e-mail discussion about the conservation implications of the identification of central African chimpanzees as the source of HIV-1, a result that Beatrice H. Hahn of the University of Alabama at Birmingham and her colleagues had just published. At about the same time, a colleague urged me to read *King Leopold's Ghost,* Adam Hochschild's history of the Belgian Congo, and I was independently contacted by

two students, Amit Chitnis and Diana Rawls, who were interested in doing something involving the intersection of biological anthropology and medicine. Then came the catalyst: an article in *Discover* magazine that mentioned the idea that the origin of AIDS might have had something to do with the chaos that followed colonial withdrawal from central Africa. The notion was that the colonial authorities had kept things under control, but when they left, "there was a free-for-all" that provided the conditions for the establishment of a new disease.

King Leopold's Ghost had more impact on me than any other book I have read. I had vaguely heard that Belgian rule was harsh, but I had not realized that more Africans probably died as a result of colonial practices in French Equatorial Africa and neighboring Belgian Congo between 1880 and the onset of World War II than had been taken from Africa as slaves during the preceding 400 years. "Probably," because no record was kept of the dead. The first censuses, taken in the 1920s, estimated that the population of the two colonies was then about 15 million. Census-takers recorded that wherever they asked, local people (colonial and native) reported that about twice as many had lived there two or three decades before, indicating that some 15 million had died. Losing 50 percent of the population exceeds even the 35-percent fatality rate of the Black Death in Europe.

It seems Joseph Conrad's *Heart of Darkness* was as much fact as fiction, and the horror described in that famous novel reflected official policies in the Congo as much as individual insanity. What appeared to many as colonial "control" of the region in the late 19th and early 20th centuries brought chaos to the lives of the Africans who lived and died under it. Chitnis, Rawls and I set out to see what disease-promoting factors might have existed prior to the withdrawal of colonial powers around 1960.

Candidates were not difficult to find, at least during the years prior to World War I. Forced labor camps of thousands had poor sanitation, poor diet and exhausting labor demands. It is hard to imagine better conditions for the establishment of an immune-deficiency disease. Where imagination fails, let history serve. To care for the health of the laborers, well-meaning but under-supplied doctors routinely inoculated workers against smallpox and dysentery, and they treated sleeping sickness with serial injections. The problem is, the multiple injections given to arriving gangs of tens or hundreds were administered with only a handful of syringes. The importance of sterile technique was known but not regularly practiced: Transfer of pathogens would have been inevitable. And to appease the laborers, in some of the camps sex workers were officially encouraged.

And that was just the situation in the camps. Major efforts were made to eradicate smallpox and sleeping sickness elsewhere in the region (these diseases cut into productivity). The shortage of syringes was acute. One 1916 sleeping-sickness control expedition treated 89,000 people in Ubangi Shari (now Central African Republic) using just six syringes. And before the introduction of dried smallpox vaccine in about 1914, the only way to transport vaccine to the interior was by serially inoculating people, traveling during the eight-day interval required for the new carrier to develop pustules from which the next inoculation could be derived. There are records of at least 14,000 people receiving vaccine in this way. The method had been abandoned in Europe some 20 years before, because syphilis was all-too-often transmitted accidentally in the process.

Such circumstances easily could have promoted the evolution of HIV from SIVcpz. Imagine, for example, the following scenario:

> A fisherman flees his small village to escape a colonial patrol demanding its rubber quota; as he runs, he grabs one of the unfamiliar shotguns recently arrived in the area. While hiding for several days, he shoots a chimpanzee and, unfamiliar with the process of butchering it, is infected with SIVcpz. On return to the village he finds his family massacred and the village disbanded. He wanders for miles, dodging patrols, until arriving at a distant village. The next day he is seized by a railroad press gang and marched for days to the labor site, where he (along with several hundred others) receives several injections for reasons he does not understand. During his months working on the railroad, he has little to eat and is continually stressed, susceptible to any infection. He finds some solace in one of the camp prostitutes (themselves imported by those in charge), but eventually dies of an undiagnosed wasting—the fate of hundreds in that camp alone. Disease, starvation, abuse—no record is kept, none of the authorities knows, and those few doctors who care are overwhelmed.

We wrote up a short article laying out reasons to at least examine colonial-era practices seriously in regard to how they may have contributed to the origin and spread of HIV. It probably would have been ignored but for another coincidence: Our paper appeared in the journal *AIDS Research and Human Retroviruses* almost simultaneously with the report of Korber and her colleagues in *Science* placing the beginnings of HIV-1 Group M in the early decades of the 20th century. If this dating is correct, the colonial-policy theory offers an explanation. Note, however, that a version of the basic cut-hunter theory that does not rely on urbanization (or sets a much lower threshold for the critical level of city life) could also explain the genesis and initial spread of HIV during this period.

Neither of these scenarios neatly accounts for the decades between the postulated origin of HIV in the early part of the 20th century and the widespread emergence of AIDS in Africa, which did not take place until the early 1980s. But maybe that long delay is only an artifact of our perceptions: Starting with a single case and assuming a doubling in frequency every few years, one would need decades to pass for the prevalence to build appreciably; would colonial doctors have noticed an initially rare immune disease? Nor do these theories readily explain details of the spatial pattern in the early cases of HIV infection and AIDS, which indeed show a suggestive overlap with the sites of oral polio vaccination. But is that correspondence just a function of the distribution of population and doctors? As with all of the current ideas, one can suggest various explanations to account for intriguing observations or troubling discrepancies. For the moment, the fit between theory and observation remains loose enough that no one view has proved absolutely compelling.

Battling Theories

Arguments over rival theories of the origin of AIDS have raged viciously at times—far beyond the norms of most scientific debates. Indeed, both sides in the OPV controversy have in the recent scientific literature gone so far as to accuse their opponents of lying and manipulating evidence. I only became aware of the explosive nature of the debate after my students and I unwittingly wandered into this minefield.

Some of the participants in this controversy appear unwilling even to entertain the possibility of being wrong. Given the precarious status of each of the current theories, it seems more reasonable to try to keep an open mind until better evidence emerges and, in the meantime, to consider the literature on each of these origin stories as representing a highly refined simulation scenario. Insofar as there is any material benefit to come from understanding the origin of HIV in terms of cautionary tales, each model can and should be considered plausible—and worrisome. After all, unsterile needles *do* transmit diseases, contaminated polio vaccine *did* spread a simian virus (one called SV40) to millions of people, doctors *do* sometimes conduct risky research, colonial policies *did* have major health consequences, and contact with wild animals *can* introduce pathogens into humans.

An obvious general lesson can be drawn from all four theories: For some very puzzling reason, the origin of HIV was not fundamentally natural, given that humans apparently failed to acquire an immunodeficiency virus from simians during thousands of years of exposure. Instead, the emergence of HIV involved social change in one form or another: the abuses carried out at the hand of an invading foreign power; abrupt urbanization overwhelming the ability of medical and political authorities to manage the process; the undersupervised transfer of medical technology and half-measures in development programs; doctors taking liberties in distributing medicines without adequate precautions. It is worth noting that three of the four theories postulate an origin for AIDS that involves the inadvertent results of medical efforts, with what were then state-of-the-art health programs and technologies carrying with them unforeseen dangers.

Whether understanding the origin of HIV and AIDS is useful for evaluating risks associated with present-day concerns (say, the consumption of wildlife that might be the natural reservoir for emerging diseases like SARS, or evaluating the likelihood that the transplantation of animal organs into people will unleash a dangerous new virus) is a matter of opinion. My own view is that a firmer grasp of what happened in the past—and what might easily have happened had circumstances been slightly different—helps society to understand these dangers and to minimize the risk of sparking the next global scourge.

Bibliography

Apetrei, C., D. L. Robertson and P. A. Marx. 2004. The history of SIVs and AIDS: Epidemiology, phylogeny and biology of isolates from naturally SIV infected non-human primates (NHP) in Africa. *Frontiers in Bioscience* 9:225–254.

Chitnis, A., D. Rawls and J. Moore. 2000. Origin of HIV-1 in colonial French Equatorial Africa? *AIDS Research and Human Retroviruses* 16:5–8.

Cohen, J. 2001. Disputed AIDS theory dies its final death. *Science* 292:615.

Curtis, T. 1992. The Origin of AIDS. *Rolling Stone* issue 626 (19 March): 54–59+.

Dicko, M., A.-Q. O. Oni, S. Ganivet, S. Kone, L. Pierre and B. Jacquet. 2000. Safety of immunization injections in Africa: Not simply a problem of logistics. *Bulletin of the World Health Organization* 78:163–169.

Hochschild, A. 1998. *King Leopold's Ghost: A Story of Greed, Terror, and Heroism in Colonial Africa.* New York, Boston: Houghton Mifflin.

Hooper, E. 2000. *The River: A Journey to the Source of HIV and AIDS.* Boston: Back Bay Books.

Hooper, E. 2003. Dephlogistication, imperial display, apes, angels, and the return of Monsieur Émile Zola: New developments in the origins of AIDS controversy, including some observations about ways in which the scientific establishment may seek to limit open debate and flow of information on "difficult" issues. *Atti dei Convegni Lincei* 187:27–230.

Korber, B., M. Muldoon, J. Theiler, F. Gao, R. Gupta, A. Lapedes. B. H. Hahn, S. Wolinsky and T Bhattacharya. 2000. Timing the ancestor of the HIV-1 pandemic strains. *Science* 288:1789–1796.

Kyle, W. S. 1992. Simian retroviruses, polio vaccine, and origin of AIDS. *The Lancet* 339:600–601.

Lemey, P., O. G. Pybus, B. Wang, N. K. Saksena, M. Salemi and A.-.M. Vandamme. 2003. Tracing the origin and history of the HIV-2 epidemic. *Proceedings of the National Academy of Sciences of the U.S.A.* 100:6588–6592.

Peeters, M., V. Courgnaud, B. Abela, P. Auzel, X. Pourrut, F. Bibollet-Ruche, S. Loul, F. Liegeois, C. Butel, D. Koulagna, E. Mpoudi-Ngole, G. M. Shaw, B. H. Hahn and E. Delaporte. 2002. Risk to human health from a plethora of simian immunodeficiency viruses in primate bushmeat. *Emerging Infectious Diseases* 8:451–457.

Peterson, D. 2003. *Eating Apes.* Berkeley: University of California Press.

Reeler, A. V. 1990. Injections: A fatal attraction? *Social Science & Medicine* 31:1119–1125.

Salemi, M., K. Strimmer, W. W. Hall, M. Duffy, E. Delaporte, S. Mboup, M. Peeters and A.- M. Vandamme. 2001. Dating the common ancestor of SIVcpz and HIV-1 group M and the origin of HIV-1 subtypes using a new method to uncover clock-like molecular evolution. *The FASEB Journal* 15:276–278.

Weiss, R. A. 2001. Polio vaccines exonerated. *Nature* 410:1035-1036.

Worobey, M., M. L. Santiago, B. F. Keele, J.-B. N. Ndjango, J. B. Joy, B. L. Labama, B. D. Dhed'a, A. Rambaut, P. M. Sharp, G. M. Shaw, B. H. Hahn. 2004. Contaminated polio vaccine theory refuted. *Nature* 428:820.

JIM MOORE received his doctorate in biological anthropology from Harvard in 1985, where he studied demography and sociality in primates. Since then he has been on the faculty of the University of California, San Diego, where his research focuses on primate behavioral ecology. Address: Anthropology Department, University of California, San Diego, La Jolla, CA 92093. Internet: jjmoore@ucsd.edu

---

From *American Scientist,* November/December 2004, pp. 540, 542-547. Copyright © 2004 by American Scientist, magazine of Sigma Xi, The Scientific Research Society. Reprinted by permission.

UNIT 8

Health Care and the Health Care System

Unit Selections

Key Points to Consider

- Is health care just another commodity? Should it be treated differently from other consumer services?

- Is quality health care a right or a privilege? Defend your answer.

- What can you as an individual do to help reduce health care costs? Give specific actions that can be taken.

- What steps can you take to reduce your risk of injury during hospitalization?

- What can be done to reduce unnecessary medical treatment?

- Should pharmacists be permitted to refuse to fill certain prescriptions?

Student Website
www.mhcls.com/online

Internet References
Further information regarding these websites may be found in this book's preface or online.

American Medical Association (AMA)
http://www.ama-assn.org

MedScape: The Online Resource for Better Patient Care
http://www.medscape.com

Americans are healthier today than at any time in this nation's history. Americans suffer more illness today than at any time in this nation's history. Which statement is true? They both are, depending on the statistics you quote. According to longevity statistics, Americans are living longer today and, therefore, must be healthier. Still other statistics indicate that Americans today report twice as many acute illnesses as did our ancestors 60 years ago. They also report that their pain lasts longer. Unfortunately, this combination of living longer and feeling sicker places additional demands on a health care system that, according to experts, is already in a state of crisis.

Despite the clamor regarding the problems with our health care system, if you can afford health care, the American system is one of the best in the world. However, being the best does not mean that it is without its problems. Each year more than half a million Americans are injured or die due to preventable mistakes made by medical care professionals. In addition, countless unnecessary tests are preformed that not only add to the expense of health care but may actually place the patient at risk. Reports such as these fuel the fire of public skepticism regarding the quality of health care that Americans receive. While these aspects of our health care system indicate a system in need of repair, they represent just the tip of the iceberg. In "Medicine's Turf Wars," Christopher J. Gearon reports on the number of nonphysician specialists such as psychologists, chiropractors, and pharmacists who are moving into areas once managed solely by physicians. While some pharmacists are seeking greater medical autonomy, others are refusing to fill prescriptions for certain medications which violate their personal beliefs. These typically include oral contraceptives and morning after pills which some pharmacists believe cause abortions.

While choices in health care providers are increasing, paying for services continues to be a challenge as medical costs continue to rise. Why have health care costs risen so high? The answer to this question is multifaceted and includes such factors as physicians' fees, hospital costs, insurance costs, pharmaceutical costs, and health fraud. It could be argued that while these factors operate within any health care system, the lack of a meaningful form of outcomes assessment has permitted and encouraged waste and inefficiency within our system. Ironically, one of the major factors driving up the cost of health care is our rapidly expanding aging population—tangible evidence of an im-

proving health care delivery system. This is obviously one factor that we hope will continue to rise. Another significant factor that is often overlooked is the constantly expanding boundaries of health care. It is somewhat ironic that as our success in treating various disorders has expanded, so has the domain of health care, and often into areas where health care previously had little or no involvement.

Traditionally, Americans have felt that the state of their health was largely determined by the quality of the health care available to them. This attitude has fostered an unhealthy dependence upon the health care system and contributed to the skyrocketing costs. It should be obvious by now that while there is no simple solution to our health care problems, we would all be a lot better off if we accepted more personal responsibility for our health. While this shift would help ease the financial burden of health care, it might necessitate more responsible coverage of medical news to educate and enlighten the public on personal health issues.

Pharmacist Refusals: A Threat to Women's Health

MARCIA D. GREENBERGER AND RACHEL VOGELSTEIN

Pharmacist refusals to fill prescriptions for birth control based on personal beliefs have been increasingly reported around the world. In the United States, reports of pharmacist refusals have surfaced in over a dozen states. These refusals have occurred at major drugstore chains like CVS and Walgreens and have affected everyone from rape survivors in search of emergency contraception to married mothers needing birth control pills. Pharmacists who refuse to dispense also often have refused to transfer a woman's prescription to another pharmacist or to refer her to another pharmacy. Other pharmacists have confiscated prescriptions, misled women about availability of drugs, lectured women about morality, or delayed access to drugs until they are no longer effective.

Pharmacist refusal incidents have also been reported in other countries. For example, a pharmacist at a popular London pharmacy chain recently refused to fill a woman's prescription for emergency contraception (EC), or the "morning-after pill," due to religious beliefs; two pharmacists refused to fill contraceptive prescriptions for women at a pharmacy in Salleboeuf, France; and in the small country town of Merriwa, Australia, the local pharmacist refuses to stock EC altogether.[1-3] Pharmacists for Life International, a group refusing to fill prescriptions for contraception, currently claims to have over 1600 members worldwide and represents members in 23 countries.[4]

Pharmacist refusals can have devastating consequences for women's health. Access to contraception is critical to preventing unwanted pregnancies and to enabling women to control the timing and spacing of their pregnancies. Without contraception, the average woman would bear between 12 and 15 children in her lifetime. For some women, pregnancy can entail great health risks and even life-endangerment. Also, women rely on prescription contraceptives for a range of medical reasons in addition to birth control, such as amenorrhea, dysmenorrhea, and endometriosis. Refusals to fill prescriptions for EC (a form of contraception approved by the U.S. Food and Drug Administration and relied on worldwide) are particularly burdensome, as EC is an extremely time-sensitive drug. EC is most effective if used within the first 12 to 24 hours after contraceptive failure, unprotected sex, or sexual assault. If not secured in a timely manner, this drug is useless. Rural and low-income women, as well as survivors of sexual assault, are at particular risk of harm.

In the United States, most states have an implied duty to dispense. Personal beliefs are omitted from the enumerated instances where pharmacists are authorized to refuse; such as where the pharmacist has concerns about therapeutic duplications, drug-disease contraindications, drug interactions, incorrect dosage, or drug abuse. In New Hampshire, the pharmacy regulations' Code of Ethics states that a pharmacist shall "[h]old the health and safety of patients to be of first consideration and render to each patient the full measure of his/her ability as an essential health practitioner."[5] Pharmacists who refuse to fill valid prescriptions based on personal beliefs do not hold patient health and safety as their first consideration.

Illinois explicitly charges pharmacies with a duty to ensure that women's prescriptions for birth control are filled without delay or interference.[6] Massachusetts and North Carolina have interpreted their laws to ensure that women's access to medication is not impeded by pharmacists' personal beliefs.[7,8] However, Arkansas, Georgia, Mississippi, and South Dakota explicitly grant pharmacists the right to refuse to dispense prescriptions for birth control based on personal beliefs.[9]

In addition, a small number of administrative and judicial bodies have considered challenges to pharmacist refusals. In the United States, the Wisconsin pharmacy board found that a pharmacist's failure to transfer a birth control prescription fell below the expected standard of care and constituted a danger to the health and welfare of the patient. The board formally reprimanded the pharmacist for his actions, charged him with the $20,000 cost of adjudication, and conditioned his license on provision of proper notification to his employer about anticipated refusals and his assurances about steps he will take to protect patient access to medication.[10]

Outside of the United States, the European Court of Human Rights rejected an appeal of a conviction of pharmacists under the French consumer code for a refusal to sell contraceptive pills. The Court held that the right to freedom of religion does not allow pharmacists to impose their beliefs on others, so long as the sale of contraceptives is legal.[2]

Some have questioned how such rules comport with the treatment of other medical professionals. In general, medical professionals have a duty to treat patients, with only limited exceptions. The majority of refusal laws apply to doctors and nurses and are limited to abortion services. Allowing pharmacists to refuse to dispense prescriptions for contraception would dramatically expand the universe of permissible refusals. Moreover, unlike doctors and nurses, pharmacists do not select or administer treatments or perform procedures. Therefore, pharmacists' involvement is not as direct, nor would patients' safety be potentially compromised in the same way as would be the case if a doctor or nurse were forced to perform a procedure that they personally oppose.

Since 1997, 28 states have introduced legislation that would permit pharmacists to refuse to dispense, and sometimes to refer or transfer, drugs on the basis of moral or religious grounds. Fifteen states have introduced such bills in the 2005 legislative session alone; while some are specific to contraception, others apply to all medication. These bills have implications for future refusals to fill prescriptions, such as in HIV regimens or treatments derived from embryonic stem cell research. On the other hand, bills have been introduced in four state legislatures and the U.S. Congress that would require pharmacists or pharmacies either to fill prescriptions for contraception or ensure that women have timely access to prescription medication in their pharmacies.

Some professional and medical associations have issued guidelines that protect women against pharmacist refusals. Value VIII of the *Code of Ethics* of the College of Pharmacists of British Columbia requires pharmacists to ensure "continuity of care in the event of ... conflict with moral beliefs."[11] It permits pharmacists to refuse to dispense prescriptions based on moral beliefs, but only if there is another pharmacist "within a reasonable distance or available within a reasonable time willing to provide the service."

In the United States, several associations have issued similar, although not legally binding, policies. The American Public Health Association states that "[h]ealth systems are urged to establish protocols to ensure that a patient is not denied timely access to EC based on moral or religious objections of a health care provider."[12] The American Medical Women's Association has stated that "pharmacies should guarantee seamless delivery, without delay (within the standard practice for ordering), judgment, or other interference, of all contraceptive drugs and devices lawfully prescribed by a physician."[13]

The American Pharmacists Association (APhA) articulates a standard of professionalism in its *Code of Ethics* that is not legally binding. It mandates that pharmacists place "concern for the well-being of the patient at the center of professional practice"[14]. The code also emphasizes that pharmacists are "dedicated to protecting the dignity of the patient" and must "respect personal and cultural differences ..."[14] This language precludes refusals, lectures, and other barriers erected by pharmacists who disagree with a woman's decision, made in consultation with her health-care provider, to use birth control. Some state pharmacy associations have similar codes.

However, the APhA has another policy that conflicts with these principles. It allows for refusals based on personal beliefs, as long as pharmacists refer prescriptions to another pharmacist or pharmacy.[15] The APhA has not formally explained how to square this policy with its ethical principles of patient-protective care, let alone with state laws and regulations.

Recommendations

Women must be provided timely access to prescription medication. One solution is to require pharmacists to dispense all drugs despite their personal beliefs, in line with their professional duties and ethical obligations. Another solution is to shift the duty to fill from pharmacists onto pharmacies. Under this approach, pharmacies would be charged with ensuring that prescriptions for all drugs are filled without delay or other interference. Such a requirement would allow pharmacies to make arrangements to accommodate the personal beliefs of individual pharmacists. However, active obstruction by pharmacists of women's access to prescription medication—such as withholding or delaying prescriptions or providing misinformation—should be deemed unethical or unprofessional conduct subject to legal sanction.

References and Notes

1. "I Won't Sell Pill, It's Against My Religion," *Sunday Mirror* (27 February 2005).
2. Pichon and Sajous v. France, App. No. 49853/99, Eur. Court H.R. (2001).
3. "U.S. Firm Ships Free Contraceptives to Condom-Deprived Australian Town," *Financial Times,* 31 March 2005 [source: Agence France-Presse].
4. See www.pfli.org/main.php?pfli=locations.
5. N.H. Code Admin. R. Ph. 501.01(b)(1) (2005).
6. Illinois Pharmacy Practice Act, § 1330.91 (j)(1) (2005).
7. Massachusetts Board of Pharmacy, letter on file with the National Women's Law Center, 6 May 2004.
8. Conscience concerns in pharmacist decisions, *North Carolina Board Pharm. Newsl.* **26** (3), 1 (2005), 1; available as item 2061 at www.ncbop.org/Newsletters/NC012005.pdf.
9. Ark. Code. Ann. § 20-16-304 (1973); Ga. Comp. R. & Regs. r. 480-5-.03(n) (2001); Miss. Code. Ann. § 41-107-1 (2004); S.D. Codified Laws § 36-11-70 (1998).
10. See www.naralwi.org/assets/files/noesendecision &finalorder.pdf
11. See www.bcpharmacists.org/standards/ethicslong/
12. American Public Health Association (APHA), Policy statement 2003-15 (APHA, Washington, DC, 2003).

13. American Medical Women's Association (AMWA), Statement of AMWA supporting pharmacies' obligation to dispense birth control (Alexandria, VA, 2005) (on file with the National Women's Law Center).
14. See www.aphanet.org/AM/Template.cfm ?Section=Pharmacy_ Practice&CONTENTID=2903&TEMPLATE=/CM/HTMLDisplay.cfm.
15. S. C. Winckler, American Pharmacists Association (1 July 2004) (letter to the editor, unpublished); available at www.aphanet.org/AM/Template.cfm? Section=Public_Relations&Template=/CM/HTML Display.cfm&ContentID=2689.

The authors are with the National Women's Law Center, Washington, DC 20036, USA. For correspondence, e-mail: rlaser@nwlc.org.

A HIGH DOSE OF TECH

"Some grocery stores have better technology than our hospitals and clinics."

Tommy Thompson, secretary of health and human services

ROB TURNER

Eyebrows shot up at Thompson's uncharacteristically feisty zinger a couple of years ago. Technologically backward? Hospitals, where multimillion-dollar scanners painted finely detailed images of body parts? Where miniature restorative devices were threaded through tiny tubes into ailing vessels? Surely Thompson was engaging in a bit of hyperbole.

Not so—hospital administrators knew he was right on the money. Humble bar-code scanners, ancient technology at neighborhood supermarkets, had barely dented U.S. hospitals. Most patient records were still kept on paper and stuffed in bulging manila folders. Physicians in different parts of the same healthcare system couldn't send clinical data back and forth. Some doctors were technophobes and proud of it, boasting that real docs don't touch a keyboard.

And change was vital. Hospitals were inefficient—but worse, medical mistakes were killing tens of thousands of hospital patients a year. Available technology could slash the toll. Physicians' scrawled prescriptions could be entered directly into a computer, for example, eliminating errors that were causing complications and deaths. Thompson's message to hospitals: Make it happen.

And slowly but surely, hospitals are obeying—junking creaky old computer systems, cabling high-speed networks, and pumping up information-technology budgets that had bumped along hand to mouth for years.

But the few Seabiscuits are being trailed by thousands of also-rans, and last week, Thompson unveiled an ambitious 10-year initiative with a blunt bottom line: You're not wiring up fast enough, so we'll light a fire under you. The plan makes Medicare a vehicle for pilot programs ranging from handling prescriptions electronically to moving patient records online so that caregivers—and patients—can refer to them regardless of time or place. New standards, promised Thompson, will mesh the innovations into a seamless nationwide network.

"In most technology, America is the world leader," declared Thompson. "I can use my bank ATM card in Russia. Your pet has records that are likely kept electronically so you get an automatic E-mail reminder to bring in your dog for a checkup.

Don't you think we should do the same in medicine? Isn't it time to bring medicine into the 21st century?"

Percentage of most-wired hospitals that let patients preregister at home: 58.4%

Even minus a federal push, the number of plugged-in medical centers has climbed. Responses to annual "most-wired hospitals" surveys by *Hospitals & Health Networks*, an American Hospital Association trade publication, have risen steadily. The latest survey, released last week, represents nearly 1,300 hospitals, almost 20 percent above 2003.

Already, results are evident. Patients in intensive care, who usually are watched over by nurses during off-times, are being monitored by doctors miles away. Patients are being armed with more of their own medical information as medical records are converted from paper to digital bits. And the boom is spinning off amenities like bedside Web access and E-mail.

Hospital executives talk about saving lives, not saving money, as the reason to wire up. But the corporate community, pounded by rising healthcare costs, has also been pushing higher tech hard. Four years ago, a group of *Fortune* 500 companies and other major employers created the Leapfrog Group to reshape the delivery of hospital healthcare in ways that would save lives and reduce complications—and, not coincidentally, drive down costs. The sheer size of Leapfrog's members has given the group unusual muscle in dictating an agenda that includes a laundry list of 27 safety-related practices, computer entry of prescriptions, and improved ICU staffing.

But while hospitals are starting to embrace technology, many are doing so tentatively, having observed the bruises suffered by early adopters. It's not just high cost, or software that needs further tweaking. Old-fashioned stubbornness has been a source of frequent hiccups and occasional debacles. And notwithstanding Thompson's grand plan, a blueprint remains to be drawn up, so wiring up is being done piecemeal. A healthcare system with a number of small or rural hospitals might opt first to fund remote intensive-care monitoring. California hospitals, on the other hand, must submit detailed plans for reducing medication errors by next January, so they might focus on computerized drug orders.

Three features of wired hospitals are especially meaningful to patients: taking the guesswork out of ordering medications, preventing errors when medications are brought to the bedside, and giving patients access to their medical records through a website. For a closer look, read on.

Killer Prescription Pads

A small piece of paper doesn't look like a deadly weapon, but much of the concern over patient safety and hopes attached to technology have centered on the innocuous prescription pad. No one seriously argues that relying on handwritten drug orders is anything other than antiquated, inefficient, and dangerous. Many of the more than 1 million serious medication errors estimated by Leapfrog to occur in hospitals every year, killing 7,000 patients and driving up healthcare costs by an estimated $2 billion, start with a physician's sloppy scrawl.

The high-tech remedy is computerized physician order entry, or CPOE. Placing orders by computer for medications—and, as a side benefit, for lab tests, special diets, and other procedures—not only eliminates confusion caused by barely legible scrawls but moves medications to patients faster and minimizes the possibility of incorrect dosages and dangerous drug interactions.

In studies, CPOE has cut serious medical errors by 55 percent or more, and Mark Zielazinski, chief information officer for El Camino Hospital in Mountain View, Calif., thinks that may be too conservative. The hospital started using computerized order entry more than 30 years ago—the first in the country to do so, says Zielazinski—working in tandem with Lockheed Martin. Error rates weren't recorded until 1992, but since then, he says, the number of errors per 1,000 patient-days has dropped from approximately 12 to six last year and now stands at four, a decline of 67 percent in a 12-year span.

In a CPOE-equipped hospital, the physician logs in to a computer that might be a terminal in a corridor niche, a laptop on a wheeled cart, or even, as at El Camino, a wireless tablet PC. Depending on the system, the doctor might key in the name of the drug and the dose, or point and click from a list of medications she regularly prescribes. The order is automatically forwarded to the hospital pharmacy and to nurses responsible for administering the medication.

Even a relatively narrow application like CPOE, however, demands a substantial foundation. A database consisting of detailed medical records for each patient in electronic form must be created and scrupulously kept up to the minute. Custom hardware and software packages must be installed. The human beings who will make or break the new system must be trained. Their cooperation is vital, and winning it can be tough.

In 2002, Cedars-Sinai Medical Center in Los Angeles spent millions of dollars on CPOE but quickly scuttled the program because private physicians who sent patients to the hospital rebelled. "It was a noble attempt, but Cedars bit off more than they could chew," says Stephen Uman, an infectious disease

specialist who helped organize the movement to dismantle the program, which he believed demanded too much time and attention. Handwritten orders that could be dashed off in a few seconds were taking five to 10 minutes, adding up to hours daily. The system would not allow doctors to prescribe new drugs that hadn't been entered into the computer—and, says Uman, didn't tolerate the smallest misspellings. If a doctor keyed in penicillin with one "l," the computer would respond that no such drug existed. Cedars-Sinai executives did not return repeated requests for details.

"That's the nightmare everybody wants to avoid," says Steve Clark, chief information officer of the University of Colorado Hospital in Denver, which plans to switch to CPOE this fall. "Your success is dependent on the physicians' accepting the technology. It's far easier to just scribble something or tell a nurse what to do." Proper training is a must, says Clark, but it is just as important to demonstrate hospital commitment from the boardroom down.

Clark hopes for a reasonably smooth ride. At a university hospital, the majority of the physicians are on staff, so their choice is to go along or leave. But presumably, as employees they also are more loyal and committed to the hospital than outside physicians typically would be and, Clark agrees, should be easier to persuade. Hospital department heads and other managers also are emphasizing to caregivers the potential for improving patients' safety in ways that will show up in performance numbers.

At Children's Hospital & Regional Medical Center in Seattle, the conversion to CPOE last November was no cakewalk, especially for some older doctors. Tradition was the main obstacle, says Mark Del Beccaro, clinical director of information services—the idea that "I know how to use a pen to write an order—I don't want to spend hours learning a new way and then have to actually get used to doing it." Says Del Beccaro: "I told people,'This [is] going to be one of the hardest things you're ever going to do, because it really, fundamentally, changes the way we practice medicine, and there aren't too many times when you do that in your career.' "

Children's required private doctors to go through training if they wanted to retain their admitting privileges. "There was a little bit of grumbling," says Del Beccaro. "But now we have some people who didn't even open their own E-mail before; now they're doing their own orders. Once they get used to it, they find that it's actually quicker."

At Children's, the system has halved the time for medications to reach inpatients, meaning that critical drugs are reaching sick kids faster. Pharmacy errors due to hard-to-decipher prescriptions have dropped to zero. And orders for lab tests often move more rapidly, sometimes because of innovations made possible by new features that exploit clinical data. "Last night I was admitting a child with a new diagnosis of leukemia, and there's a bunch of labs we always have to get for those," says Del Beccaro. "Well, I can never remember what they are." The new software, however, displays a list of the required lab tests for new leukemia cases. "I pulled it up and bam, I sent it off. I can write those orders now in under two minutes. If I didit the old way, it would take me forever"—about 20 minutes longer, he says, which now seems like forever.

"AMERICA'S BEST" PLUGGED-IN HOSPITALS

Last week Hospitals & Health Networks, *a publication of the American Hospital Association, released its annual list of the "100 most-wired hospitals and health systems." Of the 100, the 38 below have additional appeal: They were also ranked in* U.S. News's *"America's Best Hospitals" this year.*

Advocate Lutheran General Hospital, Park Ridge, Ill*
Arthur G. James Cancer Hospital, Columbus, Ohio*
Baylor Institute For Rehabilitation, Dallas*
Baylor University Medical Center, Dallas*
Beth Israel Deaconess Medical Center, Boston*
Brigham And Women's Hospital, Boston*
Children's Hospital Of Philadelphia
Children's Hospital Of Pittsburgh*
Clarian Health Partners (Iu & Meth. Hosps.),
Indianapolis
Dartmouth-Hitchcock Medical Center, Lebanon, N.H.
Hackensack University Medical Center,
Hackensack, N.J.
Hamot Medical Center, Erie, Pa.
Hospital Of The University Of Pennsylvania,
Philadelphia*
Inova Fairfax Hospital, Falls Church, Va.*
Lehigh Valley Hospital, Allentown, Pa.*
Magee-Womens Hospital, Pittsburgh*
Massachusetts General Hospital, Boston*
Mclean Hospital, Belmont, Mass.*
Methodist Hospital, Houston

National Rehabilitation Hospital, Washington, D.C.*
New England Baptist Hospital, Boston*
North Carolina Baptist Hospital, Winston-Salem*
Northwestern Memorial Hospital, Chicago
Ochsner Clinic Foundation, New Orleans
Ohio State University Medical Center, Columbus*
Poudre Valley Hospital, Fort Collins, Colo.
Rush-Presbyterian-St. Luke's Medical Center, Chicago
Sentara Norfolk General Hospital, Norfolk, Va.*
Spaulding Rehabilitation Hospital, Boston*
Texas Heart Inst. at St. Luke's Episcopal Hosps.,
Houston
Union Memorial Hospital, Baltimore*
University Hospital Of Arkansas, Little Rock
University Of Alabama Hospital At Birmingham
University Of Pittsburgh Medical Center
University Of Utah Hospitals And Clinics, Salt Lake City
University Of Wisconsin Hospital And Clinics, Madison
Washington Hospital Center, Washington, D.C.*
Yale-New Haven Hospital, New Haven, Conn.
In a healthcare system named on the "100 most-wired" list

WHAT TO LIKE ABOUT WIRED HOSPITALS

A big reason hospitals wire up is to reduce prescription mistakes and other medical errors. But patients benefit in other ways, too, according to Hospitals & Health Networks' *yearly surveys.*

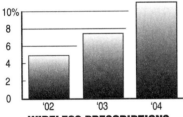

WIRELESS PRESCRIPTIONS
The percentage of hospitals where almost all doctors prescribe using wireless devices is rising, and nearly 22 percent of "most wired" hospitals prescribe that way.

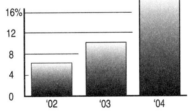

MATCHING DRUG TO PATIENT
Hospitals that use information technology to match most medications and doses with patients are increasing: Almost 35 percent of "most wired" hospitals do so.

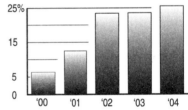

ONLINE SCHEDULING
At a growing number of hospitals, outpatients can book future appointments by logging on to a hospital website. Almost 54 percent of "most wired" hospitals allow it.

Percentage of most-wired hospitals that let patients query claims online: 30.7%

While adoption of CPOE has been steady, it has a long way to go. Fewer than 5 percent of hospitals in Leapfrog surveys had some form of CPOE in place as of last year. The two biggest barriers are large start-up costs—typically from $3 million to $10 million per hospital—and difficulty in showing bottom-line savings, according to an article last month in the journal *Health Affairs*. Fewer errors and higher productivity may more than offset the expense, but the savings are largely pocketed by health insurance carriers, not hospitals, because fewer complications and improved efficiency add up to shorter hospital stays.

Hospitals do benefit from increased patient safety, says internist Eric Poon, a coauthor of the article and a researcher at Brigham and Women's Hospital in Boston, but the high expense of CPOE still has to be justified. "Both the government and the insurance companies need to start thinking about providing financial incentives," he says. Part of the new federal program, says Mark McClellan, director of the federal Centers for Medicare and Medicaid Services, would do just that. A new Medicare pilot program will test the effect of higher payments to hospitals that meet various technology requirements.

Taking the long view, Leapfrog CEO Suzanne Delbanco is encouraged. About 16 percent of hospitals have told Leapfrog they plan to have some form of the system fully implemented by the end of 2005—which, she observes, "really is a sea change from where it was four years ago."

One Last Check

About one third of hospital medication errors happen at the front end, according to studies by Lucian Leape of the Harvard School of Public Health, when a doctor prescribes the wrong drug or the wrong dose. Another one third occur in the middle, because a hospital pharmacist misreads the doctor's handwriting or a transcriptionist writing up the doctor's dictated notes fumbles the name of the drug. That two thirds should shrink as hospitals adopt CPOE.

But then there is the back end: a medication administered to the wrong patient or to a patient who has a reaction because allergies, a health condition, potential drug interactions, or other medical information is missing from the record. To reduce those errors, more hospitals are bar-coding not only drugs but patients and nurses.

Before a medication is administered, the nurse scans in the bar codes on her badge, the patient's identification bracelet, and the medication. The computer alerts her to possible conflicts, such as a potentially dangerous interaction with another drug the patient is taking. It can also alert the nurse if the drug isn't being given at the proper time or at the proper dose.

At Eisenhower Medical Center in Rancho Mirage, Calif., 115 beds are wired for bar coding, and an additional 120 are in the works. "It's preventing medication errors daily," says Mary Ann McLaughlin, administrative director for medical-surgical services. Nurses there have come to rely on the system so much, along with pop-up screen alerts like "check blood pressure," says McLaughlin, that they don't "feel as protected" on floors still lacking the system.

All prescription drugs will have to come bar-coded by 2006 under Food and Drug Administration rules, and most likely before then, McClellan said last week, for Medicare patients. To Susan Bumatay, chief nurse at Sutter Delta Medical Center in Antioch, Calif., that's good news. Sutter currently spends millions of dollars to bar-code uncoded medications because keeping medications straight has become critical, says Bumatay. The number of drugs is burgeoning, and many have names that look or sound similar. More than 17,000 medications are currently marketed in Northern California, and processing 30 million prescriptions a year in Sutter Health's system offers plenty of opportunities for error. "We're human," she says. "That's why we need additional layers of safety." The hospital hasn't used the new system long enough to gauge overall results, says Bumatay, but her staff already can see the near misses that would have resulted without it. "We're dealing with lives here," she says emphatically. "We're not flipping hamburgers."

Digital Medical Records

Bruce Freedman was diagnosed with bladder cancer in 1992. Then, in 2001, he had triple coronary artery bypass surgery. He had a mild heart attack last October. And he has kidney problems on top of it all. As the years passed, Freedman, now 62, acquired new doctors with each new ailment. Each one would give him different drugs, and he couldn't keep track of all the instructions and advice.

Then Danny Sands, an internist at Beth Israel Deaconess Medical Center in Boston, became Freedman's primary-care physician. Sands had spent years developing electronic health records that patients could access at any time from home from a secure website.

It was a radical notion. Thanks to bureaucratic obstacles and physician resistance, patients rarely see their medical records. But Sands believed patients could help manage their own care if they felt more connected to information about their health. Besides, he says, studies show that patients forget 30 percent to 50 percent of what a doctor tells them during an office visit almost as soon as they walk out the door. If patients had their information available at a website, he reasoned, and could E-mail follow-up questions, they would be better informed and ultimately healthier.

So in 2000, Sands launched PatientSite on the Web, intended to contain everything that would go into the usual hospital medical record except for doctors' clinical notes (many doctors weren't comfortable including them and the patients weren't asking for them). Patients now could even see results of lab tests, usually as soon as their physicians got them. And patients could share the information with family members at home. As the site has evolved, Sands has added enhancements—such as the ability to schedule appointments and order refills online for maintenance medications. More than 20,000 patients at Beth Israel currently have access to their health records online, he says.

Freedman, a commercial real-estate broker, especially likes the E-mail feature. Before, he had trouble reaching Sands by phone, or they would play phone tag for days. Now he can fire off a message with a question and usually get an answer within a few hours to a day. "It saves me a lot of aggravation and time and effort," he says.

Not all doctors are as enthusiastic. About two thirds of doctors in national surveys would want to participate only if they were compensated, says Sands. The Beth Israel site doesn't charge for messaging capabilities, but that could change. (The Palo Alto Medical Foundation in California charges patients $60 a year for unlimited E-mailing.)

"Consumers have a right to know about their health," says Leapfrog's Delbanco. "That's why we are working so hard to promote a more transparent healthcare system, where we have as much information about our healthcare choices as we do about choosing a car or a dishwasher."

That's a theme heard repeatedly at hospitals that switch to electronic records and open them up to patients. At Palo Alto Medical, more than 25,000 patients now have 24-hour access. "In my mind, it levels the playing field," says Paul Tang, chief medical information officer, "so patients, not just their providers, are armed with information." He plans to launch a disease-management component on his site this fall to give diabetics specialized tools to help them monitor their own progress interactively—by, say, entering their cholesterol and glucose results. "It's one thing to be told your LDL cholesterol is 120," says Tang. "It's another to look at a graph and know what your target is."

Besides involving patients more directly, putting health records in electronic form makes patients safer. At Brigham and Women's Hospital in Boston and its many clinics scattered throughout the area, all patient records are electronic. A patient who comes to one hospital has her record available online at all of them. Perhaps an elderly woman from the suburbs breaks her hip and is taken to Brigham and Women's. The emergency physician calls up her records, says Robert Goldszer, vice chair of medicine, "and sees right away not to give her certain medications because she has a heart condition."

The University of Colorado Hospital in Denver experimented with the ultimate step in 2002, giving 54 regular outpatients at the hospital's heart center full access to their medical records, including clinical notes. Their behavior over the next year was compared with that of 53 other patients matched by age, sex, medical condition, and other qualities. Several physicians resisted, fearing they would have to censor themselves to keep from being E-mailed to death.

"Some of my colleagues may have felt a little threatened," says clinic cardiologist Gene Wolfel. "My philosophy is that these people should know what's going on. ... If they don't understand something, that's an opportunity for dialogue." Moreover, the feared hounding didn't happen. The 54 patients sent their seven doctors a total of 60 E-mails over the next year, barely more than one per patient. At the end of the study, the 53 other patients got total access, too.

Medicine's Turf Wars

Specialists without M.D.'s are pushing for more medical power. Are they ready—and are you?

CHRISTOPHER J. GEARON

You've probably noticed it at your own doctor's office, the subtle yet revolutionary changes in the way Americans receive their healthcare. The tipoff may have come when a physician assistant wrote your child a prescription instead of the pediatrician. If you've recently switched doctors, chances are you saw a nurse practitioner and not the primary-care physician listed on your health insurance card. Perhaps you live in a place where you can bypass the doctor and go directly to the pharmacist for immunizations. Or maybe you're one of the millions of patients directly spurring these changes, deliberately asking for these providers because you're fed up with your doctor, had to wait too long to see him, or simply couldn't afford it.

Nonphysician clinicians—nurse practitioners, nurse anesthetists, dentists, optometrists, chiropractors, and others—have become prominent health providers. Often working alongside doctors, well-trained, nonphysician clinicians provide frontline medical care to patients increasingly needing preventive care or monitoring for diabetes, congestive heart failure, and other chronic diseases. These new faces of American medicine are more willing to go to rural or inner-city areas and to work beyond the limited office hours typically kept by physicians. Minneapolis nurse practitioner May Hang, for instance, sees a wide variety of patients early mornings and nights at a Target store that houses her mini medical office, MinuteClinic. The clinic is designed to treat a limited set of common acute ailments, including ear, bladder, and sinus infections and strep throat. No appointments are necessary, and visits take only 15 minutes.

Yet as health professionals such as Hang have advanced into territory once held solely by doctors, a larger medical turf war has begun. The battles take place away from patients and are fought before state legislatures, the courts, and other venues as non-M.D. professions try to broaden their responsibilities even further. Oklahoma recently allowed optometrists to do limited surgery, podiatrists in California can perform partial foot amputations, and Idaho last year removed requirements of physician supervision over nurse practitioners and certified nurse midwives, giving them more freedom to practice. Nurse anesthetists in New Jersey have been lobbying for the same type of autonomy. And right now, psychologists in Tennessee are fighting for the right to write prescriptions—a battle the non-M.D.'s have already won in New Mexico and Louisiana.

Their primary weapons are the issues of access and patient safety. In Tennessee, for example, psychologists argue that patients must typically wait six weeks for an initial psychiatrist's appointment; low-income patients wait several months. The result is that many people don't get proper treatment, the psychologists contend. Roughly three quarters of the people in Tennessee who seek help for depression are treated by physicians with only limited training in mental disorders. Psychologists, who tout Ph.D.'s and many years of training, say they're better equipped than an internist or OB-GYN to prescribe drugs for emotional conditions.

Psychiatrists, not surprisingly, don't agree. "The cure to the access problem being proposed is worse than the disease," says Steven Sharfstein, president-elect of the American Psychiatric Association, adding that psychologists' proposed medical education equals a few weeks of what physicians get in medical school. "We need more psychiatrists, but I don't think the solution is to entitle or enable poorly trained physicians to provide a level of medical care that is potentially unsafe."

Behind the claims about safety for patients, however, lurks the specter of self-interest on both sides. "It's a political and economic issue," says physician Richard Cooper, professor of medicine and health policy at the Medical College of Wisconsin. Physicians want to maintain control of care and the financial rewards that come with it. They don't want to be undercut in the market by less costly providers.

Indeed, rising healthcare costs are a huge factor for consumers, health insurers, states, and employers all looking for less costly alternatives. "Nonphysician providers continue to achieve enhanced stature," notes Andrew McKinley, an analyst for Health Policy Tracking Service in Falls Church, Va. "There is growing support for the concept that the public health is best served by the broadest access to primary care, along with the safe use of pharmaceuticals." And for many, that concept is best supported by clinicians who don't have medical degrees.

Playing It Safe

The safety issue isn't just a "he said, she said" debate. Research has shown that many nonphysician providers perform safely, or at least as safely as physicians do, in their expanded roles. But that doesn't mean there's nothing to worry about. "In the main, it's been very safe," notes Cooper, "because roles have expanded commensurate with training and supervision." Cooper, who studies the enlarging roles of nonphysician clinicians and writes on quality and patient safety, adds that research, however, has not been done on leading-edge practices now being undertaken by some of these providers. "There are no outcomes on podiatrists doing amputations," and that's just one example, Cooper notes.

What research has established most notably is that an assortment of nurses with advanced training, including nurse practitioners and certified nurse midwives and other registered nurses with master's- or Ph.D.-level education, are safe. They relieve our pain during surgery, deliver our babies, treat our kids' asthma, care for our aging parents, and help alleviate the suffering of those with AIDS/HIV and other devastating conditions. More than 100 studies have examined, for example, the care delivered by nurse practitioners. "To my knowledge, there is not a single study showing negative impact of [nurse practitioner] practice on health," says Linda Aiken, director of the University of Pennsylvania's Center for Health Outcomes and Policy Research and a nursing professor. She adds that numerous studies of advanced practice nurses show the care they deliver is equal to or better than that delivered by physicians.

Robert Wise, vice president for standards and survey methods at the Joint Commission on Accreditation of Healthcare Organizations, the oversight group that inspects the nation's hospitals and healthcare facilities on quality and safety, says that "the critical issue here is not what they are allowed to do, but do they know what they can't do?" A wide scope of practice doesn't mean that a provider, physician or not, knows it all. They should refer patients to other clinicians when appropriate. "If they know what they can do and what they can't do, they are [most likely to be] a pretty safe practitioner."

Safety studies have played a major role in the mother of all turf battles, which has been waged between those two professions, anesthesiologists and nurse anesthetists, who ensure that, every year, more than 26 million Americans feel no pain when they go under the knife. In general, anesthesia is extremely safe (only one death occurs for every 250,000 times it's administered, a dramatic improvement since the early 1980s, when two deaths occurred per 10,000 anesthetics administered). And 65 percent of all anesthesia care is delivered by certified registered nurse anesthetists, critical-care nurses with a graduate degree in anesthesia, who train for several years in order to sit for certification. Medicare has long recognized their qualifications and reimbursed them for their services. The two professions are extremely courteous to one another when individuals meet in an operating room.

> **The federal government concluded that the psychologists were indeed trained to provide patients safe pharmacological care.**

But that courtesy masks a fierce dispute raging between the American Society of Anesthesiologists and the American Academy of Nurse Anesthetists. One part of this row involved nurse anesthetists' wanting to be paid for services rendered in hospitals and surgical centers without physician supervision. It has been left up to each state to allow—or disallow—that care without physician oversight.

To date, 12 mostly rural states have said there's no need for docs. The states have been swayed by safety data on anesthesia providers. "If there is a difference, the studies to date have not shown that," says Cooper.

Now the battle has shifted to doctors' offices. Florida has been the flashpoint. During the late 1990s, the number of office-based surgeries—largely lucrative cosmetic surgery operations—in the state skyrocketed. The practice wasn't well regulated, office facilities often lacked emergency care, and there were a number of highly publicized deaths.

"Office surgery is like the Wild West; it's the last frontier," says Rebecca Welch, president of the Florida Society of Anesthesiologists. While there are no data showing that CRNAs have trouble providing safe anesthesia in office settings, Welch says, "we feel like we are the experts" with a medical school background. Florida's state medical board apparently agreed and created standards for office-based surgeries that insisted anesthesiologists had to supervise CRNAs.

Nurse anesthetists felt the impact immediately. Victor Ortiz, a CRNA from Davie, Fla., says that right after the supervision rule took effect in 2002, "70 percent of my income got swept away." Why? Most surgeons concluded it wasn't economical or necessary to have both an anesthesiologist and a CRNA in their office. "[The medical board] was saying you're unsafe … but you read unbiased studies, and they show that you are safe. This was about control and turf," Ortiz says. So Ortiz sued the state medical board. Last summer, a Florida appellate court ruled the board overstepped its bounds with the anesthesiologist supervision rule, a decision affirmed last month by the Florida Supreme Court. "I'm elated," Ortiz says.

Now, another anesthesia battle is shaping up in New Jersey. The Garden State has passed an office-based-supervision rule similar to the one recently knocked down in Florida. It goes into effect in February. Local nurse anesthetists are gearing up for a court challenge, and they hope the outcome will be similar to Florida's as well.

Power of the Pad

The right to write prescriptions is the subject of another skirmish. The psychologists pushing for prescribing privileges in Tennessee and five other states will point to the gains they've made in New Mexico in 2002 and Louisiana last year, perhaps their best evidence and best way to assure doubters that they know what they are doing. In New Mexico, for example, psychologists have to take 450 hours of classes in psychopharmacology and other sciences, as well as log years of supervision and collaboration with physicians in order to prescribe. Advocates will also be holding up a Department of Defense experiment that followed the patients of 10 psychologists trained to prescribe medications, a demonstration that ran from 1991 to 1997 with program graduates going on to prescribe medications in conjunction with other kinds of therapy to active and retired members of the military and their families. The federal government and outside evaluators concluded the psychologists were indeed trained to provide safe pharmacological care. But psychiatrists argue about the results anyway. They say that the DOD training was more comprehensive than the training specified in legislation pushed in the states.

But Elaine LeVine, a Las Cruces psychologist, who helped persuade New Mexico's Legislature to give her colleagues prescribing privileges, says far from endangering her patients by writing them prescriptions, her patients will do better when she can choose their meds. She has no problems with psychiatrists—when enough of them are available for patients. It's physicians without mental health training but with a prescription pad who give her pause. While a patient may see his primary-care provider for only very short visits, she notes, psychologists' patients may spend an hour a week in therapy.

As the two professions debate the finer points, Carmen Catizone, who has seen a lot of prescription pads, chuckles. Catizone, executive director of the National Association of Boards of Pharmacy, has seen many professionals duke it out over non-physician prescribing privilege, including his own group. Pharmacists used to only make and hand out medications but today have authority to vaccinate patients in 37 states and can prescribe "morning after" emergency contraception in California, New Mexico, Alaska, and a handful of other places. Pharmacist prescribing generally is authorized under collaborative agreements with physicians but also allows pharmacists to monitor patients' ongoing conditions.

In the late 1960s and 1970s, the prescription battle was waged between M.D.'s and doctors of osteopathy. Today, like M.D.'s, D.O.'s have unlimited, independent prescribing authority in every state. In the early 1980s, optometrists battled ophthalmologists for the privilege. Now, optometrists can prescribe at least some eye-related medications in every state. Physician assistants, a profession devised by physicians to work under their supervision, had a much easier time in the early 1990s obtaining the ability to write prescriptions under the auspices of M.D.'s. Nurse practitioners have gotten some level of prescribing privileges in most states. Such battles cool as few significant problems are found and as more states grant a particular profession prescribing privileges. Instead, organized medicine focuses on preventing professions just starting to seek prescribing authority from getting it.

Knife Fights

Even mightier than the prescription pen, when it comes to medical practice, is the sword—actually, the scalpel. And fights are breaking out around the nation over whether non-physicians can wield one. Such fights, often fought in the absence of quality data, are among the feistiest around—and some of the most difficult for patients who need to choose which hand will do their surgery.

One such hand could belong to Richard Joseph. He finished his residency in 1977. He started out in trauma surgery, rebuilding faces mangled by car accidents and violence in Jacksonville, Fla. Eventually, he got permission from Jacksonville's Baptist Medical Center to perform face lifts as well. Now, his private practice includes face-lifts, eyelid surgery, Botox injections, and the occasional impacted wisdom tooth. Joseph is an oral surgeon, or, more properly, an oral and maxillofacial surgeon, a dental school graduate, and he's never been to medical school.

Oral surgeons are increasingly getting involved in doing cosmetic surgery. In a world of unhappy doctors and insurance hassles, cosmetic surgery looks like a good place to be. Oral surgeons are, technically, dentists. But they do at least four more years of training after dental school, when they learn to cut open, sew up, and improve the appearance of faces and necks, and they say they are just as qualified as plastic surgeons to do cosmetic surgery. Much of the facial trauma in the nation is handled by oral and maxillofacial surgeons; hospitals designated as Level I and Level II trauma centers are required to have one around to deal with facial injuries. And oral surgeons don't do the things you usually associate with dentists. Oral and maxillofacial surgeon Mark Steinberg, who teaches at Loyola University Medical Center in Chicago, says he hasn't filled a cavity in 25 years.

Plastic surgeons, for their part, go through medical school and several years of training in general surgery and plastic surgery. Oral surgeon training just doesn't match up, says Scott Spear, a plastic surgeon at Georgetown University Hospital and the president of the American Society of Plastic Surgeons. He and his colleagues insist that their concern is only for patient safety and good surgical results; predictably, oral surgeons shoot back that plastic surgeons just want to keep others off their lucrative turf.

State regulations that define dentistry have been the arena for the plastic surgeons' and oral surgeons' dust-ups. At issue is the American Dental Association's 1997 definition, which states that dentistry includes work on "the oral cavity, maxillofacial area and/or the adjacent and associated structures."

That is so ambiguous as to be useless, scoffs Bill Seward of the American Society of Plastic Surgeons. "The jaw is connected to the neck, which is connected to the torso. You can drive a Mack truck through that hole." He claims the "adjacent and associated structure" language gives oral surgeons the right to do breast augmentations, abdominal liposuction, or anything else they want, but oral surgeons point out that the definition also says they're only supposed to do work within the scope of their training.

Yet despite the plastic surgeons' objections, 16 states have adopted the ADA's definition, and several others also give permission for oral surgeons to do any procedures they have the training and credentials to do—which could include cosmetic surgery.

A patient who wants cosmetic surgery by a qualified surgeon—oral or any other—is bound to be a little confused. But there are some common-sense checks to make. Check to see if the surgeon is board certified, for example, and how many of the procedures the doctor does in a year. If the surgeon has hospital privileges to do your procedure, that's an indication that his or her peers think he or she is qualified.

These battles, without good information for patients to make good decisions, have made many people quite concerned.

In another cutting-edge battle, organized medicine has gone on the warpath in Oklahoma, the only state that allows optometrists to do laser and nonlaser eye surgeries. The state was apparently swayed by the access argument, specifically Oklahoma's greater supply of optometrists than ophthalmologists. Last year, ophthalmologists tried to overturn the law authorizing the scope of optometry practice, charging that it gave optometrists too much surgical authority. The challenge didn't quite work out. Instead, Oklahoma's Legislature and governor clarified optometrists' practice boundaries, allowing these nonphysicians to continue scalpel surgery around the eyelids and lashes and other eye-related surgeries. "It was politically motivated, and they picked a fight and it backfired on them," says Stillwater, Okla., optometrist David Cockrell, who is president of the Oklahoma Board of Examiners in Optometry.

These battles, without good information with which patients can make good choices, have many people concerned. "Unless we drastically change course, patients will see a much more fragmented system, and it will be more difficult to know whom to see and the quality of care they deliver," says Robert Phillips Jr., director of the Robert Graham Center, a policy center sponsored by family physicians looking at primary-care and quality issues. The course change that Phillips recommends is more collaboration and less conflict. He notes that the widening responsibilities allied health professionals are getting shouldn't leave them isolated from physicians. Most nurse practitioners, physician assistants, and others gaining more practice authority still work collaboratively and harmoniously with physicians. In fact, one thing physicians and allied health clinicians agree on is that a team approach to care is best for patients.

This spring, the Federation of State Medical Boards—a group that monitors physicians' licenses and practices—plans to release a document designed to help healthcare regulatory bodies and legislatures to make better-informed decisions on scope of practice changes. One would expect the FSMB document to boost the physician side in the turf battles, but FSMB President and CEO James Thompson, M.D., won't show his hand. Thompson does say that he believes calls from the Institute of Medicine to forge more collaborative relationships are getting the attention of physicians, and he expects to see that trend continue over the next five to 10 years.

Calls for collaboration are all very well, but many observers think that stronger intervention is needed. Market forces—in other words, money or the lack of it—are going to continue to draw primary-care physicians away from patients and draw allied health professionals in to take their places. "The system of medicine is pushing people to the edges of their competence," says the Medical College of Wisconsin's Cooper. "Is this a crisis? No, it's not a crisis. But is the system pushing nonphysicians to the limit of their capability? I think so."

Putting a Value on Health

The way to arrest spiraling costs is to admit that we already do what we say we never will—ration health care—and then figure out how to do that better

DON PECK

For all its flaws, medical care in the United States has improved enormously over the past several decades. Deaths from heart disease have fallen by 40 percent since 1970. In the mid-1980s HIV was an automatic death sentence; it's not anymore. Since 1990, thanks to better detection and treatment, cancer mortality rates have been falling. (Breast-cancer mortality is down by 20 percent since 1990.) Altogether, medical advances have helped to raise U.S. life expectancy from an average of sixty-eight years in 1950 to seventy-seven years today.

Not only have American lives grown longer, but their quality has improved. The proportion of people over sixty-five with one or more chronic disabilities—such as the inability to walk, or to get dressed, without aid—declined from greater than 25 percent in 1982 to less than 20 percent in 1999. And the development of Viagra and vision-correction surgery, among many other drugs and procedures, has allowed many Americans to prolong pleasures historically associated with youth.

Of course, not all the recent improvements in American health and longevity can be directly attributed to our health-care system; some are as much the result of adopting healthier habits (exercise, better diet) or of dropping unhealthy ones (smoking, excessive alcohol consumption). And even though life expectancy has been rising in America, it remains lower than in many other advanced nations—probably because those nations have lower rates of obesity, broader access to health care, and lesser degrees of wealth inequality. Still, better medical care is the principal cause of improvements in American health and life-span over the past fifty years.

The problem, of course, is that since 1960 health-care spending has grown significantly faster than the economy, meaning that we're spending an ever larger portion of our incomes on medical care. In 1960 health care constituted 5.1 percent of the U.S. economy; in 1980 it constituted 8.8 percent; today it constitutes 13.3 percent. The Centers for Medicare and Medicaid Services (CMMS) projects that healthcare spending will grow by an average of more than seven percent a year until 2012, even after adjusting for inflation. Meanwhile, private health-insurance premiums—which rose by 14 percent last year alone—are becoming unaffordable for ever more Americans.

It seems that cutting costs should be relatively easy. After all, health-care delivery in the United States is notoriously inefficient. Consumers lack sufficient information or expertise to make informed choices of physicians, hospitals, and treatments. Also, because most of their health care is paid for by insurance, they tend to overuse the system. Physicians, for their part, usually profit from the tests and procedures they order and perform—whether or not those tests and procedures are truly necessary. Shouldn't it be a simple matter to reduce waste and abuse?

Up to a point, yes. The frequency of a major surgical procedure such as coronary bypass surgery varies widely from physician to physician and region to region, with no discernible difference in health outcomes, on average, between patients who receive such treatments and those who don't. According to one study, 20 to 30 percent of health-care spending goes for tests, treatments, and visits that have no positive effect on either the quality or the length of our lives. If we could identify and prevent even half this spending, we would save some $25 billion to $35 billion each year on Medicare alone.

But this would do little to address the fundamental problem. That's because the largest driver of growth in health-care spending is not waste or price gouging or the slow aging of the population but, rather, the cost of technological innovation. Even when technological improvements make some treatments less expensive and more effective, overall spending often rises. Cataract surgery, for example, used to require up to a week in the hospital and offer only uncertain results. Now it's a quick, highly effective outpatient surgery. Per-procedure costs of this surgery have fallen, on average, by about one percent a year over the long term, after controlling for inflation. But because so many more people opt for cataract surgery today, real total spending on the procedure has risen by four percent a year over the same period. Given the overall growth in health-care spending currently projected by the CMMS, even an immediate drop, through waste reduction, of 20 percent in nationwide spending—which would be highly difficult to achieve—would be undone by new technology-fueled spending in just four years.

Most of the growth in health-care spending has produced real improvements in the scope of medical services and the

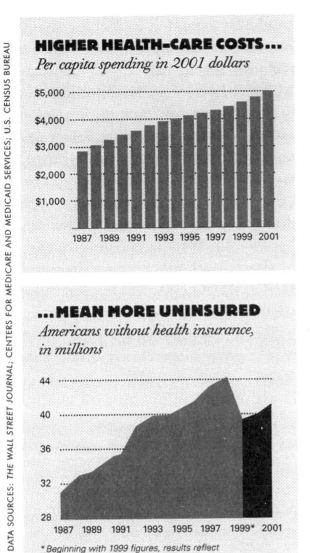

CHART DATA SOURCES: *THE WALL STREET JOURNAL;* CENTERS FOR MEDICARE AND MEDICAID SERVICES; U.S. CENSUS BUREAU

HIGHER HEALTH-CARE COSTS...

Per capita spending in 2001 dollars

...MEAN MORE UNINSURED

*Americans without health insurance,
in millions*

*Beginning with 1999 figures, results reflect
a change in Census Bureau question.*

technologies that barely improve the ability to detect or treat a disease are widely and rapidly adopted. Of course, not every health plan covers every test or treatment, but most health-insurance plans have been rapidly expanding what they cover. The result is a system in which patients with insurance can order up an expensive test that is one percent more effective than a test costing one third as much—indirectly pushing health-care premiums beyond the reach of many others.

- **THE NUMBER OF THINGS WE CAN DO TO PRESERVE HEALTH IS EXPANDING FASTER THAN THE ABILITY OF AMERICANS TO PAY FOR THEM.**
- **KEY FACTOR MISSING FROM REFORM EFFORTS IS RELIABLE INFORMATION ABOUT WHAT MEDICAL TREATMENTS WORK.**
- **THE SIMPLEST WAY TO ACHIEVE UNIVERSAL HEALTH INSURANCE IS TO REQUIRE AMERICANS TO BUY IT.**

Is there anything we can do about this? Unfortunately, the most obvious way to significandy reduce health-care costs without substantially decreasing the quality of care is rationing—that is, limiting the range of treatments and tests that insurance will cover in certain circumstances, a practice that runs counter to the prevailing any-care-at-any-cost ethos. Hardly a politician dares even to mouth the word "rationing," save as an expression of opprobrium.

Yet the fact is that the system already rations; we just don't acknowledge it openly. Every day on the front lines and in the back offices of the health-care profession ICU nurses, hospital executives, and Medicare and insurance-company administrators make difficult cost-versus-value decisions. How long should a man in a coma be allowed to linger in an expensive ICU bed while others who could benefit from the specialized care wait? Is it worth $7,000 to give Xigris—a drug to treat virulent infections that can develop in hospital settings—to an uninsured patient with less than three months to live? In a recent survey of 620 critical-care physicians, 68 percent said they had rationed medications or procedures in the preceding year. Such decisions are often morally complex, even agonizing—and often benefit patients with money: overall, people who have health insurance receive about twice as much medical care as those who lack it.

Without intervention this gap will most likely widen: a majority of Americans will continue to receive state-of-the-art care, whereas a growing minority will be shut out of the insurance system, finding themselves without access either to the cutting-edge treatments of 2004 or to proven forms of medical care that have been available for decades.

So the key question is not *whether* health care should be rationed in the United States; it already is. Rather, the question is *how* health care should be rationed. How should the potential benefits of reduced pain, improved quality of life, or extended life be weighed against the high costs of the medications or procedures involved? And who should weigh them? These are hard questions with high moral stakes. We do ourselves a disservice by dismissing them with a platitude like "You can't put a value

quality of care. But the number of things we can do to cure disease, eliminate discomfort and stave off aging is expanding faster than the ability of many Americans to pay for them. Indeed, it appears very likely that growth in medical spending will continue to outpace growth in personal income or GDP over the next few decades—even if we introduce temporary cost-saving measures.

That we spend enormous sums of money for even tiny improvements in health-care quality reflects a social ethos to which most Americans implicitly subscribe: anything that might improve health or extend life, however marginally, should be made available to everyone, at whatever cost. That may seem morally proper. But because of the way that health care is bought and financed in this country, we tend to be blind to the costs, both economic and moral, of taking this ethos too far. Because neither patients nor physicians pay for them directly, expensive tests, treatments, and procedures of only marginal value are routinely ordered, and expensive new

Insurance Required

If mandatory insurance is good enough for your car ...

Believe it or not, there is a politically appealing way to achieve universal health-care coverage: simply require all U.S. residents to buy insurance, with government help if necessary.

To understand why and how this might work, consider that the majority of those who lack health insurance are not unemployed. Nearly 60 percent of uninsured Americans work full time; another 16 percent work part time. These tend to be workers whose employers don't offer them health insurance (because they are low-wage or newly hired), or who cant afford to pay a share of the premiums.

In addition, about a third of the uninsured live in families with household incomes greater than $50,000 a year; many of these people could afford the costs of health insurance if they chose. Moreover, many of the uninsured are relatively young and healthy; about 40 percent are aged eighteen to thirty-four, and another 20 percent are under eighteen. This provides an opportunity. Requiring all these young, healthy Americans—who are currently gambling that they'll stay healthy—to enter the risk pool would drive down premiums for those Americans who currently have health insurance while lowering the cost of entry for those who don't.

Here's how it might work. States would establish insurance polls that would offer every American a choice among competing private insurance plans. Insurers offering coverage through these polls would be required to offer a core benefits package and could not discriminate on the basis of pre-existing conditions. Individuals could purchase more-comprehensive coverage if they wished.

Each year, according to a recent study published in the *Annals of Family Medicine*, 20 percent of people with insurance are forced to change health plans, resulting in higher costs and lower-quality care. A citizen-based (as opposed to employer-based) universal insurance program would eliminate this problem by enabling workers to keep their doctors and health plans when they changed jobs. And rather than being limited to the health plans chosen by their employers, workers could choose plans and levels of coverage from among competing private providers.

Under a universal citizen-based plan those employers who wished to continue administering health-care benefits could do so; but those who wanted to shed the administrative burden could choose instead to contribute a fixed amount (currently employers contribute more then $300 billion to employee health coverage each hear) to an insurance pool or to the plans of their employees' choosing.

This proposal would cost the federal government somewhere on the order of $80 billion a year, with most of that money going to provide subsidies to those who couldn't afford the minimum cost of coverage themselves. But the plan would also save the nation the cost of uncompensated care (currently some $35 billion, which is passed on to employers and insured employees in the form of rising premiums), and it would recoup some of the $65 billion to $130 billion of labor productivity that is lost to untreated health problems each year.

Won't Americans balk at a radical proposal that forces even those who don't want health insurance to buy it? Actually, it's hardly radical: Americans are already well accustomed to the idea of mandatory insurance. After all, almost anyone who wants to drive a car is required to buy car insurance, and anyone who wants to carry a mortgage must buy homeowner's insurance. The details are different, but the idea is the same. Applying this principle—universal coverage in exchange for universal responsibility—makes economic, moral, and practical sense.

—LAURIE RUBINER

Laurie Rubiner is the director of the Universal Health Insurance Program at the New America Foundation.

---

on health." That may be true in the abstract, but one *can* put a value on different treatments and practices. When we decline to do so, we are automatically putting a lower value on other areas, such as education and security, in which increased spending might in fact add more to life expectancy and quality of life. By refusing even to countenance sensible limits on the health care citizens have a right to demand, we make universal health-care coverage—a worthy goal that we are long overdue in attaining—nearly impossible. It would be un-American to suggest that those who can afford truly comprehensive insurance—call it "Cadillac insurance"—should be prevented from buying it. And no one is suggesting that. But if we will not consider that perhaps not everyone who pays premiums should be *guaranteed* Cadillac insurance, more Americans each year will be left unable to afford any coverage at all. At the very least we need to begin a national conversation about the meaning of "medical necessity"—for instance, does it include knee surgery for some-

one who is not in acute pain but wants to continue playing recreational tennis or touch football? what about bariatric surgery (stomach stapling) for those who are not morbidly obese?—and to launch an honest discussion about what kind of rationing would be fairest and most efficient.

To start the conversation, here's one scenario: Imagine a system in which everyone has insurance (including prescription-drug coverage) offering a basic standard of care almost equal to what the insured enjoy today, but people who want the very latest and most expensive treatments must eidier buy supplemental insurance or pay out of pocket. (For one vision of how coverage might be extended with little disruption, see Insurance Required.) As innovations prove to offer dramatically better care, or somewhat better care at roughly equal cost, basic coverage would be extended to include them; but the standard for what could be included would be set high (perhaps with the help of an institute like the one proposed by Shannon Brownlee on the facing page). With fewer patients opting for expensive new treatments that are only marginally more effective than older ones, research doctors, drug companies, and medical-hardware makers could devote more of their R&D resources to making existing treatments cheaper and more effective. Though health-care spending will never stop growing completely, it would grow more slowly under this scenario. Similarly, although the rate of improvement in health-care quality might slow marginally, improvement would continue. America would still have care equal to the best in the world—and the system would cover more people. Would that sort of rationing really be so bad?

DON PECK is the director of *The Atlantic's* editorial-research staff.

UNIT 9

Consumer Health

Unit Selections

Key Points to Consider

- What are some concrete examples of actions you can take to ensure that you get what you want from your doctor's visit?

- What should women know before they consider breast implants?

- What are the risks of daily use of tooth whiteners?

- Why are humans getting less and less sleep and what are the health implications?

Student Website

www.mhcls.com/online

Internet References

Further information regarding these websites may be found in this book's preface or online.

FDA Consumer Magazine
http://www.fda.gov/fdac

Global Vaccine Awareness League
http://www.gval.com

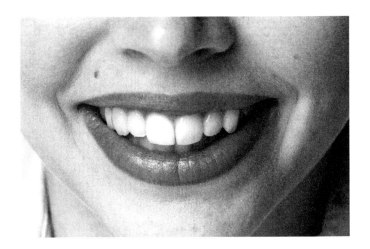

For many people the term "consumer health" conjures up images of selecting health care services and paying medical bills. While these two aspects of health care are indeed consumer health issues, the term consumer health encompasses all consumer products and services that influence the health and welfare of people. A definition this broad suggests that almost everything we see or do may be construed to be a consumer health issue whether it's related to products or recommendations such as getting enough sleep. In many ways consumer health is an outward expression of our health behavior and decision-making processes and as such is based on both our desire to make healthy choices, be assertive, and to be in possession of accurate information on which to base our decisions. These decisions are particularly important when it comes to pain management. Many people have fortunately turned to their doctors following the withdrawal of the pain medication Vioxx from the market. This, and other pain treatments, were found to increase the risk of cardiovascular disease. In "How to Ease Your Pain," consumers are offered advice on managing acute and chronic pain.

A health-related issue that is heavily promoted is the alleged safety of teeth whitening. In "Dentists Frown at Overuse of Whiteners," Natasha Singer discusses how many patients are overexposing themselves to bleach-base teeth whiteners. While dentists generally consider whiteners to be safe, they are concerned over the overuse of these products. There is also concern that continually whitening teeth will make them more sensitive and may permanently damage teeth and gums.

Breast implants are another known health risk that consumers demand. Many women want to increase their breast size via implants, while mastectomy patients seek implants to restore their breasts. For whatever reason, choosing implants is a decision that should be made only after a woman fully understands and acknowledges the potential harm and the importance of follow up medical care. While researchers have found that implants do not contribute to life-threatening systemic illnesses, there are many other concerns. Some of the risks of implants include pain, hardening of the scar tissue that forms around the implant, rupture of the saline-filled breast, nerve damage, and the potential inability to breast feed children. Most women with implants will also need at least one additional surgery over the course of their life for a variety of complications such as rupture or asymmetry.

The health-conscious consumer seeks to be as informed as possible when making dietary and medical decisions—but the best intentions come to no avail when consumers base their decisions on inaccurate information, old beliefs, or media hype that lacks a scientific basis. Knowledge (based on accurate information) and critical thinking skills are the key elements required to become proactive in managing your daily health concerns.

Dentists Frown at Overuse of Whiteners

NATASHA SINGER

Kevin Ross, a psychologist in Queens, is a serial tooth whitener. He started out seven years ago with custom-fitted bleaching trays, the kind dentists sell. When his teeth became sensitive, he switched to over-the-counter whitening strips, which use less bleach. These were gentler, but not as effective. So earlier this year Mr. Ross upgraded to professional-strength whitening strips dispensed by his dentist.

"I insist on having my teeth as white as possible," he said. "I guess it's like skinny people who always think they could be a little skinnier. I'd like to get another whitening treatment tomorrow."

But when Mr. Ross recently asked for a new set of whitening strips, his dentist said no. "I had to cut him off temporarily," said Dr. Marc M. Liechtung, who practices in New York City, "because his teeth are as white as they are going to get. It's our job not to indulge them when they want touch-ups they don't need."

Mr. Ross is not even the most avid whitener among Dr. Liechtung's patients. Some, Dr. Liechtung said, come back "like drug addicts pleading, 'Doc, sell me more just this once.'" "Meanwhile, on their own, they use every type of drugstore whitening product: not only the strips but also whitening toothpaste, floss, rinse and chewing gum."

More and more, dentists like Dr. Liechtung are putting their foot down for fear that these patients may be overexposing themselves to bleach. "In the long run," Dr. Liechtung said, "chronic whiteners could end up causing themselves tooth damage."

Dentists generally consider whitening to be a safe treatment when patients, following a proper dental exam, choose a bleaching product from a reputable brand, adhere to package instructions and don't overdo it. But tooth bleaching was never intended to become a daily grooming habit like shampooing or shaving. And some dentists suspect that uninterrupted whitening, using a hodgepodge of high-strength products, not only will make teeth more sensitive, but may also cause permanent damage to tooth enamel and gum tissue.

Until more studies have been done to assess the potential side effects of constant bleaching, these dentists say, consumers should take care to avoid going overboard.

"We see younger and younger patients wanting whiter and whiter teeth," said Dr. Bruce A. Matis, the director of the Clinical Research Section at Indiana School of Dentistry in Indianapolis. "We'll know in 10 years if they've damaged their teeth."

A fondness for pearly white teeth is ancient. In the Bible, Jacob hopes that his son Judah will have "teeth white with milk."

But never in history have paper-white teeth been as popular or easy to obtain as they are now. The market for dentist-dispensed tooth whitening products and in-office treatments is expected to reach more than $2 billion this year, up from $435 million in 2000, according to a report from Mintel International Group, a market research firm. Mintel expects sales of over-the-counter whitening kits to reach $351 million in 2005, up from $38 million five years ago.

All this bleaching has made teeth so white that manufacturers of dental materials used for bonding and filling have had to create ever-lighter shades to match them. The very whitest are an unnatural color that did not exist before bleaching, a shade dentists have nicknamed "Regis white."

Given that even short-term whitening can cause temporary tooth sensitivity and gum irritation, some dentists speculate that continuous bleaching could erode tooth enamel or cause gum inflammation. Some people's teeth have even taken on a translucent blue or gray color around the edges, dentists say.

Many clinical studies have indicated it is safe for teeth to be bleached—either professionally or with name-brand do-it-yourself kits—once or twice a year. Procter & Gamble, maker of Crest Whitestrips, has also done research on the safety of uninterrupted bleaching using the company's products; one of its clinical trials, conducted with researchers at Tufts University in Boston, found it was safe to use Whitestrips twice a day for six months.

Today's 'Regis white' may be tomorrow's gray, or worse.

Still, some dentist say that when people routinely use high-strength bleaches, or use whitening products in every step of their oral-care routine, it may add up to a level of exposure to bleaching agents that goes beyond what has been studied.

"We don't know how the body handles regular use of high concentrations of peroxide," said Dr. Van B. Haywood, a professor at the School of Dentistry at the Medical College of Georgia in Augusta, who in 1989 was an author of the first paper published on the effectiveness and safety of overnight bleaching trays.

The peroxides used in tooth bleach, hydrogen peroxide and carbamide peroxide (which contains hydrogen peroxide) produce free radicals that can damage cells of the gums or pulp inside teeth, said Dr. Yiming Li, the director of the Center for Dental Research at Loma Linda University School of Dentistry in California. "The lower your overall exposure," Dr. Li said, "the lower your risk."

Because of the unknown risks of high peroxide exposure, some dentists advise pregnant women as well as cancer patients and smokers (who are at risk of developing cancer) to avoid tooth whitening altogether.

Some dentists say certain over-the-counter bleaching products are riskier than professional whitening treatments because the bleach more easily strays from the teeth to the rest of the mouth. Ill-fitting one-size-fits-all trays easily leak bleaching material onto the gums and down the throat, Dr. Matis said.

Dentists say they prevent such leaks. "We protect the gums by painting on a semiplastic barrier, so no bleaching material touches the soft tissue," said Dr. Laurence R. Rifkin, a dentist in Beverly Hills, Calif. "We also make custom-fitted trays for home use that keep the whitening gel in close contact with your teeth."

In Europe only whitening products that are no more than one-tenth of a percent peroxide may be sold over the counter. Earlier this year, after examining the potential risks, the European Union's Scientific Committee on Consumer Products concluded that higher-strength bleaching is safe only when it is supervised by a dentist.

American products are much more powerful and getting stronger all the time, raising the risk of overexposure to bleach, dentists say. Fifteen years ago the first trays dispensed by dentists used gels that were 10 percent carbamide peroxide, equivalent to about 3 1/3 percent hydrogen peroxide. Today, Discus Dental Nite White ACP Deluxe Kit, dispensed by dentists, contains 22 percent carbamide peroxide gel (about 7 percent hydrogen peroxide). The Minute White Laser Speed Tooth Whitening System, sold on the QVC shopping channel, includes a 22 percent carbamide peroxide whitener. And the strongest bleaching strips sold by dentists now contain 14 percent hydrogen peroxide gels.

"Once you get above 15 percent carbamide, you are pushing the envelope," Dr. Haywood said.

Manufacturers counter that it is the amount of gel used, rather than the strength of its bleaching agent, that determines whether a product is safe. The gel in Crest Whitestrips Premium, for example, is 10 percent hydrogen peroxide, but the overall amount is small, the company said.

"The gel on each strip is as thin as two or three pieces of paper," said Dr. Robert W. Gerlach, a principal scientist at Procter & Gamble. "A tray-based system uses 4 to 10 times as much peroxide. And a whitening mouthwash could contain up to 20 times as much peroxide." Consumers often do not know how much bleach over-the-counter whiteners contain, however, because manufacturers are not required to quantify it on the label. Some dentists say that practice endangers consumers.

"The consumer cannot make an informed decision without concentrations listed on the labels," Dr. Matis said.

Dentists do not agree on how often their patients should use today's powerful whiteners. After his patients have completed their initial 10- to 14-day tray bleaching treatment, Dr. Rifkin permits them to wear the trays again once or twice a year for one- or two-day touch-ups. Dr. Matis advises patients to wait one to three years. And Dr. Haywood says that once a decade may be enough for some people.

Try telling that to Dale Michele Asti, a boutique owner in Beverly Hills who uses her 22 percent carbamide peroxide bleaching tray several times a week.

"I admit I'm obsessed," said Ms. Asti, a patient of Dr. Rifkin. "Whitening has become part of my routine when I'm getting ready for a date. I'll do it to make my smile sparkle while I'm shaving my legs or putting on makeup."

When told of Ms. Asti's habit, Dr. Rifkin said: "She shouldn't be doing that."

"It's not going to make her teeth any whiter," he added, "and it's potentially irritating. I may have to limit her number of whitening kits."

Making an Informed Decision about Breast Implants

Despite more than a decade of controversy over their safety, breast implants are more popular than ever among women who want to build upon what nature gave them or who want to restore what disease has taken away. Whatever the reason, opting for breast implants is a personal decision that should be made only after a woman fully understands and accepts the potential risks of the devices and the importance of follow-up evaluations with her physician.

CAROL RADOS

Some people see an enormous benefit to getting implants and are willing to accept associated risks. They say that using breast implants to rebuild the breast (reconstruction), or change its size and shape (augmentation), significantly improves the quality of life for many women. Advocates of breast implants also say that a woman's consent to the surgery should be considered valid as long as she weighs the risks and benefits of the procedure.

While every surgical procedure has potential risks, such as infection, bleeding, and scarring, there are risks that are specific to breast implants. Learning about them is key to being properly informed about the procedure.

A Primer on Breast Implants

According to the American Society of Plastic Surgeons (ASPS), there were nearly 255,000 breast enhancement implant surgeries in 2003, nearly twice the number done in 1998. Another 68,000 women received breast implants for reconstruction following mastectomy due to cancer or other disease.

But also in 2003, 45,000 augmentation patients and 17,000 reconstruction patients had their breast implants removed. The medical community and others, including the Food and Drug Administration, would like to better understand why.

Breast implants are designed for augmentation, a cosmetic procedure; reconstruction; and replacement of existing implants, called revision. There are two primary types: saline filled and silicone gel-filled. Depending on the type of implant, the shell is either pre-filled with a fixed volume of solution or filled through a valve during the surgery to the desired size.

Some allow for adjustments of the filler volume after surgery. Breast implants vary in shape, size, and shell texture.

While every surgical procedure has potential risks, such as infection, bleeding, and scarring, there are risks that are specific to breast implants.

At this time, there are two manufacturers with approved saline-filled breast implants. No manufacturer has yet received FDA approval to market a silicone gel-filled breast implant.

The Silicone Controversy

Breast implants were first marketed in the early 1960s, before the 1976 Medical Device Amendments to the Federal Food, Drug, and Cosmetic Act required a reasonable assurance of safety and effectiveness to be shown for certain medical devices. The 1976 law gave the FDA authority over such devices, but breast implants were "grandfathered" into the regulatory scheme, meaning that manufacturers were not required to provide the agency with scientific evidence of product safety unless questions arose about the safety and effectiveness of these already-marketed devices. Silicone was initially assumed by manufacturers to be biologically inactive and, therefore, to have no harmful effects.

But over the years, questions did arise about the effects of silicone on the body. In 1991, the FDA published a regulation that required manufacturers of silicone gel-filled breast implants to submit premarket approval applications (PMAs). This requirement meant that the FDA needed to agree that the manufacturer

Questions to Ask a Surgeon About Breast Augmentation

- What are the risks and complications associated with having breast implants?
- How many additional implant-related operations can I expect over my lifetime?
- How will my breasts look if I choose to have the implants removed without replacement?
- What shape, size, surface texturing, incision site, and placement site is recommended for me?
- How will my ability to breast-feed be affected?
- How can I expect my implanted breasts to look over time?
- How can I expect my implanted breasts to look after pregnancy? After breast-feeding?
- What are my options if I am dissatisfied with the cosmetic outcome of my implanted breasts?
- What alternate procedures or products are available if I choose not to have breast implants?
- Do you have before-and-after photos I can look at for each procedure and what results are reasonable for me?

Source: FDA

has presented data showing a reasonable assurance of safety and effectiveness in order for the devices to remain on the market.

In January 1992, the FDA called for a voluntary moratorium—a delay on the use of these implants—until new safety information could be thoroughly reviewed. The moratorium was not intended to "ban" the implants, but instead to allow time to review the new safety information.

In April 1992, the agency decided that no PMA yet submitted contained sufficient safety and effectiveness data to support approval. However, access to these silicone gel-filled breast implants would continue for women enrolled in certain clinical studies.

In the years that followed that decision, thousands of women filed lawsuits against the manufacturers of silicone gel-filled implants, claiming the devices had caused serious ailments, such as connective tissue diseases, neurological diseases, and cancer. Consumer groups repeatedly filed petitions urging more studies on the implants. But many women said they were pleased with their implants, including cancer patients who had pleaded for the opportunity to choose silicone gel-filled implants for reconstruction.

A Turn of Events

In October 2003, the FDA held a two-day advisory panel meeting to discuss a manufacturer's PMA for a silicone gel-filled breast implant. Some people complained that the meeting was premature in light of the fact that long-term studies had not been completed, but the FDA proceeded because the agency was required by law to consider the pending PMA within a specified time frame. The meeting also provided patients and others with timely access to information and expert analyses on

the issue. The issues before the panel reflected much of the decades-long debate over the implants. Moreover, the meeting provided a valuable public forum for discussing the issue from many diverse perspectives and for raising important additional questions.

As a panel member, Benjamin O. Anderson, M.D., voted with the majority to recommend that the FDA approve the new PMA, but only with specific conditions. Anderson says he wants to avoid getting into the business of determining how a woman defines the value of breast reconstruction or augmentation.

"The use of implants and augmentation conjures up some social judgments that may well be unfair," says Anderson, a professor of surgery and director of the University of Washington's Breast Health Center. Rather than deciding that no woman can have access to silicone gel-filled implants because a small number may be at risk for certain illnesses, he says, "I believe the better approach is to make the devices available and inform all women of the degree of risk involved."

That, according to Anderson, "is reasonable informed consent."

In January 2004—contrary to the recommendation of the agency's advisory panel—the FDA determined that the new silicone gel-filled breast implant PMA was "not approvable" at that time. This meant that the implants were not approved for marketing pending additional information, but that women would continue to have limited access to them by enrolling in clinical studies.

"The public scientific process that has been used to consider these devices is fully consistent with the FDA's mission —to use the best available science to protect and promote the public health interests of the American people," says Linda Kahan, deputy director of the FDA's Center for Devices and Radiological Health (CDRH).

Also in January 2004, the agency released a draft of its new guidelines for companies submitting breast implant PMAs, explaining the scientific issues that the FDA recommends be addressed as part of their applications. The guidance document reflects the FDA's current thinking about new scientific information that the agency, manufacturers, and the clinical community have gained over the last 10 years, including information learned at the October 2003 advisory panel meeting. Consistent with the FDA's good guidance practices, the agency has asked for public comments on the breast implant guidance. The guidance is not intended for implementation until it is finalized.

"Current testing doesn't reflect reality," says Michael A. Choti, M.D., an associate professor of surgery and oncology at the Johns Hopkins University School of Medicine in Baltimore, and also an FDA advisory panel member. The implants, he says, are extremely durable when tested outside the body. "You can virtually run a truck over them and they'll hold up. But the question is, what happens when implanted long-term in a woman's body?"

The FDA's draft guidance document says that two to three years of follow-up data may not be enough to allow the agency to evaluate the safety and effectiveness of breast implants. The agency recommends the use of tests that can predict clinical outcomes, such as how long breast implants will last before rupturing in the body, as well as tests that explain how and why the breast implants rupture. In addition, the agency recommends that more data be gathered regarding the rate of rupture over time, as well as the health consequences of rupture.

Breast Implant Risks

In 1999, the Institute of Medicine (IOM) issued a report on a review of information related to health effects associated with silicone breast implants, both gel-filled and saline-filled, in humans. An important goal of the IOM was to provide women with detailed information about the potential risks of silicone breast implants.

One risk is capsular contracture, which is a tightening and squeezing of the scar tissue that naturally forms around the implant. This contracture may result in hardening of the breast tissue, rippling of the skin, and changes in breast shape. It also may cause pain, which, if severe, can require surgery to remove the scar tissue or replace the implant.

In addition, a rupture can occur at any time. While saline-filled breast implants leak only salt water when they rupture, the health effects of leaking silicone gel-filled implants remain controversial. Women sense a change more easily when saline-filled breast implants rupture. But the silicone gel-filled implants are more likely to maintain their shape after they rupture, which can make it more difficult to detect a break.

Called "silent ruptures," these breaks involving silicone gel implants may occur without a visible change. And a woman may not feel any sensation, says Sahar M. Dawisha, M.D., a medical officer in CDRII who has reviewed data submitted by implant manufacturers. Magnetic resonance imaging (MRI) with equipment specifically designed for imaging the breast may be used for evaluating women with suspected rupture of their silicone gel-filled implant. The FDA considers MRI to be the best method at this time. There are no standards on how often to screen for silent rupture with MRI, and the costs of this procedure must be considered when choosing a silicone gel-filled breast implant. Physicians usually recommend removal of the implant if it has ruptured, regardless of whether it is saline-filled or silicone gel-filled.

Another potential complication of implant surgery is nerve damage, which can cause some women to experience a loss or increase in sensation in their nipples and breast tissue. These symptoms may disappear eventually, but can be permanent in some cases. It is unclear at this time whether insufficient milk production to breast-feed—another reported problem—is due to damaged nerves or to other reasons.

Women should know that, regardless of the type of implant, it is likely they will need to have one or more additional surgeries (reoperations) over the course of their lives, because of complications from breast implants. Reasons for reoperations include any of the potential complications, such as capsular contracture, wrinkling, asymmetry, rupture, or implant malposition.

The IOM committee also found that women with silicone breast implants are no more likely than women without implants to develop the life-threatening systemic illnesses that some people have claimed might be related to the implants.

Questions to Ask a Surgeon About Breast Reconstruction

- What are all my options for breast reconstruction?
- What are the risks and complications of each type of breast reconstruction surgery and how common are they?
- What if my cancer recurs or occurs in the other breast?
- Will reconstruction interfere with my cancer treatment?
- How many steps are there in each procedure? What are they?
- How much experience do you have with each procedure?
- What is the estimated total cost of each procedure?
- How long will it take to complete my reconstruction?
- Do you have before-and-after photos I can look at for each procedure and what results are reasonable for me?
- What will my scars look like?
- What kind of changes in my reconstructed breast can I expect over time?
- What kind of changes in my implanted breast can I expect with pregnancy?
- What are my options if I am dissatisfied with the cosmetic outcome of my implanted breast?
- How much pain or discomfort will I feel and for how long?
- How long will I be in the hospital? Will I need blood transfusions, and can I donate my own blood?
- When will I be able to resume my normal activities?

Source: FDA

But many women disagree. They have reported health problems related to their immune systems or neurological symptoms that they believe are caused by ruptured or intact breast implants. And some women who have received breast implants claim they weren't fully informed of the risks.

Lynda Roth, who was diagnosed with breast cancer in 1990, says she was forced to make a quick decision, based on very little information, about getting breast implants following a mastectomy.

"I trusted what my highly respected doctors were telling me was true," says the 63-year-old social worker in central Colorado. "You're in shock, you think you're going to die, so what kind of informed decision can you possibly make about what you want your breasts to look like if you're lucky enough to survive?"

Roth did survive—both breast cancer and two silicone breast implants gone bad. But the ruptured devices, she believes, caused her to lose her good health, her job, and eventually her health insurance over the next 11 years. "I found out the hard way," she says. "There were many risks with the implants that I didn't know about."

Other women are pleased with their implants. Clara Filion underwent reconstruction in 1993 after having a breast removal that included the lymph nodes under the arm {modified radical mastectomy) due to cancer. The 67 year old Bedias, Texas, resident says she's thrilled with the outcome of her saline filled implant, as well as with her surgeon, even though her original implant will need replacing soon due to scar tissue—a local complication that Filion says she always knew could occur, Filion has experienced no other complications related to the implant in 11 years.

Other Considerations

"My doctor told me that these implants would go with me to my grave," says 44-year-old Patty Faussett of Henderson, Nev., who chose to augment her breasts with saline breast implants in 1997, after years of breastfeeding distorted their shape.

Faussett had her implants removed a year after implantation because she believes they caused a mixed bag of health problems, including disturbed vision, heart palpitations, muscle twitching, and an autoimmune thyroid disease. She says, "The risks were much greater than my surgeon led me to believe."

Experts caution that breast implants do not last a lifetime. Women should be prepared for long term follow up and additional surgeries to treat complications. They also should be prepared for the accompanying additional costs. One of the biggest problems Faussett says she hears from women in her breast implant support group is that "most don't plan for the money it takes to fix what goes wrong."

In addition, women should be aware that hard pressure on the breast (compression) during mammography may cause implant rupture. Breast implants also can interfere with finding breast cancer during mammography. Doctors say the implant can hide breast tissue and, as a result, hide lesions as well. Extensive scarring and calcium deposits in tissue surrounding an implant can mimic the appearance of cancer, making the deposits difficult to distinguish from tumors on a mammogram.

Another consideration is the choice of a surgeon. Patient advocates, professional groups, and others agree that it's important to choose a plastic surgeon who has been trained in breast implant surgery and who has performed it successfully on many women.

After switching to a new, firmer silicone gel-filled implant through a clinical study only a year after experiencing rippling with her saline implants, Kathy Bracy says it's important that women who are considering breast implants do their homework.

"I love my breast implants, but I also spent six months researching the devices, which included picking the best doctor for me," says Bracy, a 38- year-old self-employed bookkeeper from Tampa, Fla. "It's not necessarily the product, but who is doing the surgery." The key to breast implant satisfaction, she says, is to "find a doctor who is willing to answer all your questions and take all your concerns seriously. And the relationship with your doctor doesn't end after the surgery."

Experts also advise women to have realistic expectations about breast implants. There is no guarantee that the results will match those of other women. Overall health, age, chest structure, the shape and position of the breast and nipple, skin texture, the tendency to bleed, prior breast surgeries, and the surgical team's skill and experience all figure into the outcome of breast implant surgeries.

The Teen Scene

In addition to safety issues, there is concern about the growing use of breast implants among teen-agers. Health officials worry that teen-agers and their parents may not realize the relative permanence of the changes caused by the devices. They also want to be sure that teens are physically ready—that is, they're finished developing —and that they are psychologically mature enough to handle the outcome of surgery.

"I didn't know my breasts were still growing when I signed up for the surgery," admits Kacey Long, who got saline-filled breast implants in July 2001, when she was 19. Prior to her surgery, the college student from Ennis, Texas, was a 34B—a breast size she thought would be with her for life.

Teen-agers who are dissatisfied with their bodies see breast implants as a harmless—and, according to Long, "fun"—thing to do to improve their self-image. Long says she felt that her body was too "bottom heavy" for her breasts and wanted to "even out" her figure. "But I never thought about my implants being dangerous," she says. A friend's mother worked for a plastic surgeon for 12 years and told Long she knew of no problems with patients who had gotten the implants. "I really thought that I had inside information, and that these devices were completely safe and maintenance-free."

Following implantation, Long went to a 34D. But complications convinced her to have the implants removed a short time later. "I had shooting pains in my arms, excruciating pain in every joint, bone, and muscle of my body, I was exhausted all the time, had no energy, lost my hair, and had pains in my chest, heart, and ribs. I had trouble remembering things and thinking clearly, and the list goes on," she says. "Before the implants, all I had was allergies."

Many of the changes to the breast that occur with an implant cannot be undone. If a teen chooses to have her implants removed, she may experience dimpling, puckering, wrinkling, or other cosmetic changes.

Three years later, Long's breasts measure 36C—one size larger than before she was implanted—suggesting that her own breasts continued to develop even after the implants were removed. "When you're making a decision that can impact your life at 19," Long advises other young women, "you need to research the subject like you're 50 years old."

Ongoing clinical studies for unapproved saline-filled and silicone gel-filled breast implants do not allow for those younger than 18 to receive the implants for augmentation purposes. Some of these clinical studies even limit reconstruction and revision uses to women 18 and over.

Consumers can get a copy of the "FDA Breast Implant Consumer Handbook 2004," which provides in-depth information on both saline and silicone breast implants, by visiting www.fda.gov/cdrh/breastimplants/, or by writing to: FDA, Office of Device Evaluation, Division of General, Restorative, and Neurological Devices, 9200 Corporate Blvd., HEZ-410, Rockville, MD 20850.

From *FDA Consumer*, September/October 2004, pp. 33-37. Published 2004 by the U.S. Food and Drug Administration. www.fda.gov/cdrh/breastimplants/

How to Ease Your Pain

Here's what you need to know to get safe relief.

The withdrawal in late September 2004 of the painkilling drug rofecoxib (*Vioxx*) because of increased heart-attack risk—plus subsequent concerns raised about celecoxib (*Celebrex*), naproxen (*Aleve, Naprosyn*), and valdecoxib (*Bextra*)—left millions of Americans scrambling for a safe and effective way to control their pain. But it's not just users of those drugs who face that predicament.

Virtually all prescription and nonprescription pain relievers pose some risks, even when used properly. Many people multiply the risks by overusing such drugs. And even high doses may not quell the pain if the doctor or patient chooses the wrong drug. Indeed, studies suggest that roughly half of people with chronic or recurrent pain fail to get adequate relief despite drug therapy.

"Over-the-counter acetaminophen is often a good first choice for relieving chronic pain."

That's a huge amount of needless suffering. "Even when pain can't be completely eliminated, we now have numerous ways to rein it in so it doesn't interfere with your daily life," says Morris Levin, M.D., a pain-control expert at the Dartmouth-Hitchcock Medical Center in Hanover, N.H.

The key is knowing when and how to use nonprescription drugs, such as acetaminophen (*Tylenol*) or ibuprofen (*Advil, Motrin IB*), and, when prescription drugs are needed, being aware of the choices your doctor should consider. While the withdrawal of rofecoxib and concerns about its cousins celecoxib (*Celebrex*) and valdecoxib (*Bextra*) have made picking prescription drugs more difficult, there are several other good options, provided you and your doctor can overcome certain misconceptions.

For example, too many people refuse to consider opioids, such as codeine, because of excessive concerns about addiction. Others fail to consider drugs not normally considered painkillers, such as certain antidepressants and anticonvulsants, despite growing evidence that they're effective against some types of pain. Equally important, proper pain management means knowing which nondrug measures can sometimes relieve pain and even treat the underlying cause.

The accompanying table, "Targeted Pain Relief," describes proven or possible treatments for several common kinds of pain.

Below we describe the proper use of over-the-counter (OTC) pain relievers and advise when to see a doctor for prescription drugs or other options.

Acute Pain: Rate It And Treat It

For occasional or sudden pain (from common headaches, menstrual cramps, or injuries, for example), appropriate treatment starts with assessing the pain's severity. The best way is to grade your pain along a scale from 0 (no pain) to 10 (the worst pain you've ever had).

For mild-to-moderate pain, rated 5 or less, nonprescription drugs usually suffice. Though some evidence suggests that nonsteroidal anti-inflammatory drugs (NSAIDs), such as ibuprofen and, to a lesser extent, ketoprofen (*Orudis KT*) and naproxen (*Aleve*), may provide slightly faster and greater relief than aspirin or acetaminophen, all are often adequate. But certain individuals may want to choose or avoid specific pain relievers:

- Avoid aspirin if you're breast-feeding, since aspirin might cause bleeding or other problems in the baby.
- Avoid acetaminophen if you're a heavy drinker or have liver disease; even modest doses can harm the liver in such cases.
- Choose acetaminophen if you have hypertension, heart failure, ulcers, or kidney disease, which may be worsened by the other drugs. Also stick with acetaminophen if you take a daily aspirin to protect your heart. Additional aspirin might cause bleeding, while ibuprofen and possibly other NSAIDs have been shown to undermine aspirin's coronary benefits. And pick acetaminophen if you're pregnant, since the other drugs may harm the fetus and prolong labor.

If your pain is relatively severe (rated 6 or more) or persists despite the recommended doses of nonprescription medication, it's important to see your doctor for several reasons. Treating yourself by boosting the doses increases the risks, particularly with acetaminophen, since more than 4 grams a day—the daily maximum for adults—can damage the liver. And the drug you've chosen may not work against your type of pain, regardless of the dosage. Moreover, it's essential to stop acute, severe pain early because it becomes harder to control as it worsens.

Prescription NSAIDs, some of them stronger versions of the corresponding OTC drug, may yield additional relief. However,

Targeted pain relief

Most people should treat each kind of pain listed below by trying lifestyle changes and the first treatment option. If those don't help, talk with your doctor about other options. You could also consider alternative therapies, though the evidence is usually weaker and the possible benefits smaller.

Condition	Lifestyle measures	First choice	Second choice	Alternative therapies	Cautions
Osteo-arthritis	• Lose excess weight and do low-impact exercise.	• Acetaminophen (*Tylenol*). • Capsaicin cream (*Capsin, Zostrix*).	• Ibuprofen (*Advil*). Combine with stomach-protecting drugs such as misoprostol (*Cytotec*) or omeprazole (*Prilosec, Prilosec OTC*) if you've had ulcers or gastrointestinal bleeding or have signs of GI reactions to ibuprofen.	• Glucosamine and chondroitin supplements. • Relaxation techniques, such as biofeedback, guided imagery, progressive muscle relaxation, or massage.	• Acetaminophen can harm liver when used in high doses or by heavy drinkers or liver patients. • Ibuprofen and related drugs in high doses or with extended use can cause ulcers and stomach bleeding, increase blood pressure, trigger asthma attacks, and worsen kidney problems and heart failure.
Rheumatoid arthritis	• Low-impact exercise. • Avoid triggers, such as stress, infection, and insufficient sleep.	• Ibuprofen. Combine with stomach-protecting drug such as misoprostol or omeprazole if you've had ulcers or gastrointestinal bleeding. • Capsaicin cream.	• Corticosteroids, such as prednisone (*Deltasone*), for short-term relief of acute pain. • New immunosuppressants, such as adalimumab (*Humira*), etanercept (*Enbrel*), or infliximab (*Remicade*). • Older drugs, such as gold (*Solganal*) or methotrexate (*Rheumatrex*).	• Fish oil or gamma-linolenic acid, though risks (including upset stomach, diarrhea, and increased risk of bleeding) may outweigh slight benefit.	• Steroids can cause weight gain, bruising, thin bones, cataracts, and diabetes. • Immunosuppressants can increase chance of infection. • Older drugs cost less but are riskier and less effective.
Headache	• Identify possible triggers (such as red wine, chocolate, or stress) or underlying causes (such as sleep apnea, sinus infection, or caffeine withdrawal) and try to avoid or control them.	• Acetaminophen, aspirin, or ibuprofen.	• One or more first-choice drugs combined with caffeine (*Anacin, Excedrin Migraine*). • Triptans, such as sumatriptan (*Imitrex*) or zolmitriptan (*Zomig*), for migraines. Nasal sumatriptan works fastest but is more expensive. • Ergot alkaloids, such as dihydroergotamine (*Migranal Nasal Spray*) or ergotamine (*Ergomar*).	• Relaxation techniques. • The herb feverfew (products contain variable amounts of possible active ingredient). • Botulinum toxin (*Botox*) (requires up to 30 injections, must be repeated every few months, and isn't reimbursible).	• Triptans and caffeine drugs more likely to cause "rebound" headaches as drug wears off. • Triptans can cause flushing, dizziness, tightness in chest; can't be used if you have heart disease. • Ergot alkaloids cost less but are less effective. Can cause nausea, vomiting, diarrhea, and muscle cramps.
Back pain	• Apply cold pack for first day or two, then heating pad; resume gentle exercise as soon as possible. • Strengthen muscles in the abdomen and back to prevent pain.	• Aspirin. • Ibuprofen. Combine with stomach-protecting drugs such as misoprostol or omeprazole, or take acetaminophen, if you've had ulcers or gastrointestinal bleeding. • Capsaicin cream.	• For acute, severe pain, possibly opioids, such as oxycodone (*Oxycontin*) or fentanyl (*Duragesic*); muscle relaxants, such as cyclobenzaprine (*Flexeril*) or methocarbamol (*Carbacot, Robaxin*); or, for pinched nerve, steroid injections. • For chronic pain, tricyclic antidepressants, such as amitriptyline, or possibly surgery.	• Hands-on care, including chiropracty, massage, or physical therapy. • Botulinum (*Botox*) injections.	• Opioids, muscle relaxants, and tricyclic antidepressants can cause sedation, dizziness, confusion, urinary retention, and other problems, especially in older people.
Muscle or joint injury	• Rest, ice, compression, and elevation for first 24-48 hours or until inflammation subsides, then heat. • Resume gentle activity as soon as possible.	• Acetaminophen, aspirin, or ibuprofen.	• Physical therapy for chronic muscle pain and possibly surgery.	• Massage • Acupuncture.	• Acetaminophen can harm liver when used in high doses or by heavy drinkers or liver patients. • Ibuprofen and related drugs in high doses or with extended use can cause ulcers and stomach bleeding, increase blood pressure, trigger asthma attacks, and worsen kidney problems and heart failure.
Irritable bowel syndrome (IBS)	• Drink more fluids, limit triggering foods, and eat more high-fiber foods (except beans and cabbage, which can cause gas). • Regular physical activity.	• For IBS with constipation, high-fiber supplements or, for short-term use, nonprescription laxatives such as docusate (*Colace, Sof-lax*). • For IBS with diarrhea, OTC loperamide (*Imodium A-D*).	• For IBS with constipation, tegaserod (*Zelnorm*). • For IBS with diarrhea, diphenoxylate (*Lomotil*); cholestyramine (*Questran*); antispasmodics, such as hyoscyamine (*Levsin*); combination products, such as *Donnatal*; or tricyclic antidepressants.	• Relaxation techniques, especially stress management.	• Tegaserod for short-term use only; can cause severe diarrhea and intestinal problems. See doctor immediately if rectal bleeding, bloody diarrhea, or new or worse abdominal pain develops. • Frequent laxative use can worsen constipation.
Neuropathy (from diabetes, shingles, fibromyalgia, other causes)	• Treat underlying condition, such as diabetes.	• Tricyclic antidepressants; anticonvulsants, such as gabapentin (*Neurontin*); lidocaine patch (*Lidoderm*); or capsaicin cream.	• Nerve-block injections or surgery, especially for face and head pain caused by nerve damage. • Psychotherapy to develop pain-management strategies.	• Relaxation techniques. • Acupuncture.	• Consider seeking referral to pain clinic if pain persists.

the risks generally increase along with the benefits as the dosage rises. A better approach to severe, acute pain is often a prescription opioid, such as codeine or hydrocodone. With proper dosing, you can remain reasonably alert, and short-term treatment carries little risk of addiction.

Drugs that pair an opioid with acetaminophen, aspirin, or ibuprofen may be an even better choice: They provide greater relief, since the two ingredients work in different ways, and they reduce the risk of side effects because the combination permits smaller doses of each one.

Chronic Pain: Limit The Risks

You should also see your physician if you've taken a nonprescription analgesic regularly for more than about 10 days, regardless of the pain's severity. Drug risks rise with prolonged use, and your doctor may be able to recommend a better treatment. Tell him or her how severe the pain is and what it feels like—a steady ache, a sharp pain, or a burning or shooting sensation, for example—because different types respond to different drugs.

People with osteoarthritis or other chronic pain should first try the nondrug measures described in the accompanying table that may reduce or even eliminate the need for medication. If those steps don't help, their physician may first recommend a nonprescription drug. Acetaminophen is a good initial choice because even frequent, prolonged use is reasonably safe if you stick with the recommended doses and have no increased risk of liver damage.

However, many people with arthritis or other chronic pain need greater relief, which NSAIDs may provide. In theory, celecoxib (*Celebrex*) and valdecoxib (*Bextra*), like their banished cousin rofecoxib (*Vioxx*), may be less likely to cause gastrointestinal bleeding than the other, older NSAIDs. But some research has raised concerns about celecoxib and valdecoxib, too. For now, at least, our medical consultants advise people with elevated cardiovascular risk to avoid those drugs; other people should take them with considerable caution and only after careful consultation with their physician.

One alternative is ibuprofen, since some research suggests it may be gentler on the stomach than most of the NSAIDs unrelated to *Vioxx*. Those who've had ulcers or bleeding or who have any gastrointestinal reactions to ibuprofen should consider taking it with a stomach protecting drug, such as misoprostol (*Cytotec*) or omeprazole (*Prilosec, Prilosec OTC*). And try to use the pills just to treat flare-ups, not continually to prevent them.

If NSAIDs don't control chronic pain, opioids may, though the risk of addiction with frequent use generally makes them a last resort. A better choice is often an antidepressant such as amitriptyline or an anticonvulsant such as gabapentin (*Neurontin*). They can substantially relieve the burning or shooting pain from certain common neurologic disorders, such as diabetic nerve damage, apparently by interfering with certain brain chemicals.

People with unresolved chronic pain despite treatment should ask for a referral to a pain clinic. Such facilities take a multidisciplinary approach, with neurologists, anesthesiologists, psychiatrists, and other specialists collaborating on a treatment plan that eases pain, avoids drug dependency, and helps people resume a normal life.

What You Can Do

- For our latest recommendations on pain-relieving drugs, go to our new health-letter Web site.
- For short-term relief of mild to moderate pain, use nonprescription drugs, such as acetaminophen or ibuprofen; for severe pain, see your doctor, who may prescribe an opioid.
- For chronic pain, try nondrug steps when possible and see your doctor, who may prescribe a treatment described in the accompanying table.
- Avoid celecoxib and valdecoxib if you have increased cardiovascular risk; if you don't, use those drugs with considerable caution. Consider taking ibuprofen plus a stomach-protecting medication if you need an NSAID but have elevated gastrointestinal risk.

Deep into Sleep

While researchers probe sleep's functions, sleep itself is becoming a lost art.

CRAIG LAMBERT

Not long ago, a psychiatrist in private practice telephoned associate professor of psychiatry Robert Stickgold, a cognitive neuroscientist specializing in sleep research. He asked whether Stickgold knew of any reason not to prescribe modafinil, a new wakefulness-promoting drug, to a Harvard undergraduate facing a lot of academic work in exam period.

The question resonated on several levels. Used as an aid to prolonged study, modafinil is tantamount to a "performance-enhancing" drug—one of those controversial, and often illegal, boosters used by some athletes. In contrast to wakefulness-producing stimulants like amphetamines, modafinil (medically indicated for narcolepsy and tiredness secondary to multiple sclerosis and depression) does not seem to impair judgment or produce jitters. "There's no buzz, no crash, and it's not clear that the body tries to make up the lost sleep," reports Stickgold. "That said, all sleeping medications more or less derange your normal sleep patterns. They do not produce normal sleep." Even so, the U.S. military is sinking millions of dollars into research on modafinil, trying to see if they can keep soldiers awake and on duty—in Iraq, for example—for 80 out of 88 hours: two 40-hour shifts separated by eight hours of sleep.

"No—no reason at all not to," Stickgold told the psychiatrist. "Not unless you think sleep *does* something."

When people make the unlikely claim that they get by on four hours of sleep per night, Stickgold often asks if they worry about what they are losing. "You get a blank look," he says. "They think that sleep is wasted time." But sleep is not merely "down time" between episodes of being alive. Within an evolutionary framework, the simple fact that we spend about a third of our lives asleep suggests that sleep is more than a necessary evil. Much transpires while we are asleep, and the question is no longer *whether* sleep does something, but exactly *what* it does. Lack of sleep may be related to obesity, diabetes, immune-system dysfunction, and many illnesses, as well as to safety issues such as car accidents and medical errors, plus impaired job performance and productivity in many other activities.

Although the modern era of sleep research started in the 1950s with the discovery of REM (Rapid Eye Movement) sleep, the field remained, well, somnolent until recently. Even 20 years ago, "The dominant paradigm in sleep research was

that 'Sleep cures sleepiness,'" says Stickgold. Since then, researchers have developed a far more complex picture of what happens while we snooze. The annual meetings in sleep medicine, which only this year became a recognized medical specialty, now draw 5,000 participants. Harvard has long been a leader in the area. The Medical School's Division of Sleep Medicine, founded in 1997 and chaired by Baldino professor of sleep medicine Charles Czeisler, has 61 faculty affiliates. The division aims to foster collaborative research into sleep, sleep disorders, and circadian biology, to educate physicians and the lay public, to influence public policy, and to set new standards of clinical practice, aiming, as its website (**www.hms.harvard.edu/sleep**) declares, to create "a model program in sleep and circadian biology."

A Culture of "Sleep Bulimia"

Imagine going on a camping trip without flashlights or lanterns. As the sun sets at the end of the day, daylight gradually gives way to darkness, and once the campfire burns down, you will probably go to sleep. At sunrise, there's a similar gradient in reverse; from the beginning of time, human beings have been entrained to these cycles of light and dark.

Homo sapiens is not a nocturnal animal; we don't have good night vision and are not especially effective in darkness. Yet in an instant on the evolutionary time scale, Edison's invention of the light bulb, and his opening of the first round-the-clock

Number of Hours Slept per Night on Weekdays (past two weeks)

	1998	2001	2002	2005
Less than 6 hours	12%	13%	15%	16%
6 to 7.9 hours	51	49	53	55
8 or more hours	35	38	30	2
Mean (# of hours)	NA	7.0	6.9	6.8

Source: National Sleep Foundation

power plant on Pearl Street in Manhattan in 1882, shifted our time-and-light environment in the nocturnal direction. At the snap of a switch, a whole range of nighttime activity opened up, and today we live in a 24-hour world that is always available for work or play. Television and telephones never shut down; the Internet allows you to shop, gamble, work, or flirt at 3 A.M.; businesses stay open ever-longer hours; tens of millions of travelers cross multiple time zones each year, worldwide; and with the growth of global commerce and communication, Wall Street traders may need to rise early or stay up late to keep abreast of developments on Japan's Nikkei exchange or at the Deutsche Bundesbank.

Consequently most of us now sleep less than people did a century ago, or even 50 years ago. The National Sleep Foundation's 2005 poll showed adult Americans averaging 6.8 hours of sleep on weeknights—more than an hour less than they need, Czeisler says. Not only how *much* sleep, but *when* people sleep has changed. In the United States, six to eight million shift workers toil regularly at night, disrupting sleep patterns in ways that are not necessarily amenable to adaptation. Many people get only five hours per night during the week and then try to catch up by logging nine hours nightly on weekends. "You can make up for *acute* sleep deprivation," says David P. White, McGinness professor of sleep medicine and director of the sleep disorders program at Brigham and Women's Hospital. "But we don't know what happens when people are chronically sleep-deprived over years."

"We are living in the middle of history's greatest experiment in sleep deprivation and we are all a part of that experiment," says Stickgold. "It's not inconceivable to me that we will discover that there are major social, economic, and health consequences to that experiment. Sleep deprivation doesn't have any good side effects."

All animals sleep. Fish that need to keep swimming to breathe sleep with half their brains while the other half keeps them moving. It is uncertain whether fruit flies actually sleep ("We can't put electrodes in their brains," says White), but they seem at least to rest, because for extended periods they do not move. When researchers stopped fruit flies from resting by swatting at them, the flies took even longer rest periods. When lab technicians added caffeine to the water that the flies drank, they stayed active longer—and also rested longer after the drug wore of, evidence that the caffeine had disrupted their resting patterns.

Sleeping well helps keep you alive longer. Among humans, death from all causes is lowest among adults who get seven to eight hours of sleep nightly, and significantly higher among those who sleep less than seven or more than nine hours. ("Those who sleep more than nine hours have something wrong with them that may be causing the heavy sleep, and leads to their demise," White notes. "It is not the sleep itself that is harmful.")

Sleep is essential to normal biological function. "The immune system doesn't work well if we don't sleep," says White. "Most think sleep serves some neurological process to maintain homeostasis in the brain." Rats totally deprived of sleep die in 17 to 20 days: their hair starts falling out, and they become hypermetabolic, burning lots of calories while just standing still.

There once was a fair amount of research on total sleep deprivation, like that which killed the rats. Doctors would keep humans awake for 48, 72, or even 96 hours, and watch their performance deteriorate while their mental states devolved into psychosis. For several reasons, such studies rarely happen any more ("Why study something that doesn't exist?" asks White) and researchers now concentrate on sleep *restriction* studies.

In this context, it is important to distinguish between acute and chronic sleep deprivation. Someone who misses an entire night of sleep but then gets adequate sleep on the following three days "will recover most of his or her normal ability to function," Czeisler says. "But someone restricted to only five hours of nightly sleep for weeks builds up a cumulative sleep deficit. In the first place, their performance will be as impaired as if they had been up all night. Secondly, it will take two to three weeks of extra nightly sleep before they return to baseline performance. Chronic sleep deprivation's impact takes much longer to build up, and it also takes much longer to recover." The body is eager to restore the balance; Harvard undergraduates, a high-achieving, sleep-deprived population, frequently go home for Christmas vacation and pretty much sleep for the first week. Stickgold notes that "When you live on four hours a night, you forget what it's like to really be awake."

"When you live on four hours a night, you forget what it's like to really be awake."

Sleep researcher Eve van Cauter at the University of Chicago exposed sleep-deprived students (allowed only four hours per night for six nights) to flu vaccine; their immune systems produced only half the normal number of antibodies in response to the viral challenge. Levels of cortisol (a hormone associated with stress) rose, and the sympathetic nervous system became active, raising heart rates and blood pressure. The subjects also showed insulin resistance, a pre-diabetic condition that affects glucose tolerance and produces weight gain. "[When] restricted to four hours [of sleep] a night, within a couple of weeks, you could make an 18-year-old look like a 60-year-old in terms of their ability to metabolize glucose," Czeisler notes. "The sleep-deprived metabolic syndrome might increase carbohydrate cravings and the craving for junk food."

Van Cauter also showed that sleep-deprived subjects had reduced levels of leptin, a molecule secreted by fat cells that acts in the brain to inhibit appetite. "During nights of sleep deprivation, you feel that your eating goes wacky," says Stickgold. "Up at 2 A.M., working on a paper, a steak or pasta is not very attractive. You'll grab the candy bar instead. It probably has to do with the glucose regulation going off. It could be that a good chunk of our epidemic of obesity is actually an epidemic of sleep deprivation."

Furthermore, "Many children in our society don't get adequate amounts of sleep," Czeisler says. "Contrary to what one might expect, it's common to see irritability and hyperactivity in sleep-deprived children. Is it really surprising that we treat them with wake-promoting drugs like Ritalin?" Schools and athletic programs press children to stay awake longer, and

Unsound Sleep

The National Sleep Foundation's 2005 survey found that 75 percent of American adults experience symptoms of a sleep problem at least a few nights per week. Sleep clinics like Sleep Health Centers, a for-profit enterprise whose medical director, David P. White, supervises six sites with 32 beds in the Boston area, investigate many of the 84 types of sleep disorder that clinicians have identified.White, McGinness professor of sleep medicine, who directs the sleep disorders program at Brigham and Women's Hospital, explains that there are three main categories of sleep disorder: insomnias; disorders that make patients sleepy during the day, like narcolepsy or sleep apnea; and parasomnias, which include sleepwalking, sleep-talking, and REM behavior disorder.

Chronic insomnia may affect 10 percent of the population, but some Gallup polls indicate that as many as 40 percent have trouble sleeping on two or three nights per week. "Depression and anxiety states are the biggest cause of insomnia," White says. Besides treating the underlying problems and practicing good "sleep hygiene" (e.g., going to bed at a regular time, having no clock in the bedroom), one intervention is, paradoxically, sleep restriction. "A lot of insomniacs spend more and more time in bed—up to 14 hours a day. That's counterproductive," White says. "So you restrict them to the amount of time they can sleep: perhaps from 11 P.M. until 3 A.M. Get them to sleep well during that time and then build up from there."

In narcolepsy, which affects one in 2,000 people, components of REM sleep—being asleep, having muscular paralysis or weakness, and dreaming—affect people during waking hours. Research on narcoleptic Doberman dogs and genetically altered mice showed that animals unable to produce a protein called hypocretin were narcoleptic. The spinal fluid of humans who suffer from narcolepsy contains little or no hypocretin; hence treatment of narcolepsy may involve ways to enhance its production or replace it.

The most common problem that sleep clinics see is obstructive sleep apnea. "We're seeing an epidemic of sleep apnea," says Charles Czeisler, Baldino professor of sleep medicine. "It's related to overweight, and is especially prevalent in certain regions." Older, obese men are at higher risk. Sleep apnea affects individuals who may have a narrower passage of the upper throat; during sleep, muscles around this passage relax and close the passage partially or completely, stopping the flow of air into the lungs. This results in loud snoring, labored breathing, and even the cessation of breathing (apnea) for periods of more than 10 seconds. "It's important to breathe in the right amounts of oxygen and breathe out carbon dioxide, to keep the levels right," explains White, who trained in pulmonary medicine. "The mechanisms that control this don't work as well during sleep." Losing weight can help; in severe cases, sufferers may sleep wearing a special "continuous positive airway pressure" mask that keeps the passage open.

Parasomnias are a less common form of sleep disorder. In sleepwalking, something rouses the sleeper from deep (stage 3 or 4) sleep, and in a state somewhere between deep sleep and wakefulness, he or she can walk about or even drive a car for a period of 10 to 15 minutes. REM behavior disorder, which can be associated with degenerative brain disease, may last only seconds, but can be dangerous. "In REM sleep, all skeletal muscles are paralyzed, so that you can't act out your dreams," White explains. "But with REM behavior disorder, people can move."

some children may be chronically sleep-deprived. Czeisler once took his daughter to a swim-team practice that ran from eight to nine o'clock at night, and told the coaches that this was too late an hour for children. "They looked at me like I was from another planet," he recalls. "They said, 'This is when we can get the pool.'"

Stickgold compares sleep deprivation to eating disorders. "Twenty years ago, bulimics probably thought they had the best of all worlds," he says. "They could eat all they wanted and never gain weight. Now we know that they were and are doing major damage to their bodies and suffering major psychological damage. We live in a world of sleep bulimia, where we binge on weekends and purge during the week."

"When you live on four hours a night, you forget what it's like to really be awake."

The Fatigue Tax

Lack of sleep impairs performance on a wide variety of tasks. A single all-nighter can triple reaction time and vastly increase lapses of attention. Sleep researcher David Dinges at the University of Pennsylvania studied such lapses using a "psycho-motor vigilance task" on pools of subjects who had slept four, six, or eight hours nightly for two weeks. The researchers measured subjects' speed of reaction to a computer screen where, at random intervals within a defined 10-minute period, the display would begin counting up in milliseconds from 000 to one second. The task was first, to notice that the count had started, and second, to stop it as quickly as possible by hitting a key. It wasn't so much that the sleep-deprived subjects were slower, but that they had far more total lapses, letting the entire second go by without responding. Those on four hours a night had more lapses than those sleeping six, who in turn had more lapses than subjects sleeping eight hours per night. "The number of lapses went up and up for the whole two weeks," says David White, "and they hadn't plateaued at the end of the two-week study!"

There's fairly large individual variation in susceptibility to the cognitive effects of sleep deprivation: in one of Charles Czeisler's studies, somewhere between a quarter and a third of the subjects who stayed awake all night contributed two-thirds of the lapses of attention. "Some are more resistant to the impact of a single night of sleep loss," he says. "But they all fall apart after two nights without sleep." In a sleep-deprived state, says White,

"Most of us can perform at a fairly low level. And a lot can run around sleep-deprived without it being obvious. But truck drivers, neurosurgeons, nuclear-plant workers—after six or eight hours, they have to put a second crew on and give them a break." Very few people are really immune to sleep deprivation: in Dinges's study, only one of 48 subjects had the same performance after two weeks of four hours' nightly sleep as on day one.

"Your ability to do critical thinking takes a massive hit—you're knocking out the frontal-cortex functions."

Students often wonder whether to pull an all-nighter before an exam. Will the extra studying time outweigh the exhaustion? Robert Stickgold, who has studied sleep's role in cognition for the past 10 years, reports that it depends on the exam. "If you are just trying to remember simple facts—listing all the kings of England, say—cramming all night works," he explains. "That's because it's a different memory system, the declarative memory system. But if you expect to be hit with a question like 'Relate the French Revolution to the Industrial Revolution,' where you have to synthesize connections between facts, then missing that night of sleep can be disastrous. Your ability to do critical thinking takes a massive hit—just as with alcohol, you're knocking out the frontal-cortex functions.

"It's a version of 'sleeping on a problem,'" Stickgold continues. "If you can't recall a phone number, you don't say, 'Let me sleep on it.' But if you can't decide whether to take a better-paying job located halfway across the country—where you have all the information and just have to weigh it—you say, 'Let me sleep on it.' You don't say, 'Give me 24 hours.' We realize that it's not just time; we understand at a gut level that the brain is doing this integration of information as we sleep, all by itself."

Not only mental and emotional clarification, but the improvement of motor skills can occur while asleep. "Suppose you are trying to learn a passage in a Chopin piano étude, and you just can't get it," says Stickgold. "You walk away and the next day, the first try, you've got it perfectly. We see this with musicians, and with gymnasts. There's something about learning motor-activity patterns, complex movements: they seem to get better by themselves, overnight."

Stickgold's colleague Matthew Walker, an instructor in psychiatry, studied a simple motor task: typing the sequence "41324" as rapidly and accurately as possible. After 12 minutes of training, subjects improved their speed by 50 to 60 percent, but then reached a plateau. Those who trained in the morning and came back for another trial the same evening showed no improvement. But those who trained in the evening and returned for a retest the following morning were 15 to 20 percent faster and 30 to 50 percent more accurate. "Twenty percent improvement—what's that?" asks Stickgold, rhetorically. "Well, it's taking a four-minute mile down to three minutes and 10 seconds, or raising a five-foot high jump to six feet."

Bodily Rituals

So sleep is essential, but exactly why we go to sleep remains a mystery. Professor of psychiatry Robert McCarley, based at the VA Boston Healthcare System, has linked sleep to the brain neurochemical adenosine. Adenosine binds with phosphorus to create adenosine triphosphate (ATP), a substance that cells break down to generate energy. McCarley and colleagues inserted microcatheters into cat brains while keeping the cats awake for up to six hours—a long time for a cat. They found that rising adenosine levels in the basal forebrain put the cat to sleep; then, in the sleeping cat, adenosine levels fall again. In both cats and humans, the basal forebrain includes cells important for wakefulness, and adenosine turns these cells off, triggering sleep.

Like cats, when we are awake and active, we burn ATP, which breaks down to adenosine. Over time, adenosine levels build up, causing pressure for sleep. During sleep, many of the body's cells are less active and hence burn less ATP, so adenosine levels fall again, setting the stage for wakefulness.

A drug like caffeine, however, partially blocks adenosine receptors, so the brain doesn't perceive the actual adenosine level, and we don't get tired. In a world that values wakefulness and productivity over rest and recovery, caffeine has become, in dollar amounts, the second-largest commodity (after oil) traded in the world. Some consumers require ever-greater jolts—one 24-ounce Starbucks beverage packs a walloping 1,000-plus milligrams of caffeine. (A commonly used figure for one cup of coffee is 100 milligrams.)

The lab run by Putnam professor of neurology Clifford Saper has done related research, refining the location and functions of the "sleep switch," a group of nerve cells in the hypothalamus that turns of the brain's waking systems; conversely, the waking systems can turn of the sleep switch. "When you have a switch where either side can turn of the other, it's what electrical engineers call a 'flip-flop,' " Saper explains. "It likes to be in one state or the other. So we fall asleep, or wake up, quite quickly. Otherwise we'd be half asleep or half awake all the time, with only brief periods of being fully awake or asleep. But we're not—we are either awake or asleep."

The adenosine cycle at least partly explains the homeostatic drive for sleep—the longer we are awake, the greater our fatigue, and pressure to sleep builds up progressively. But circadian rhythms also profoundly affect sleep and wakefulness. Circadian cycles (from *circa,* meaning "about," and *dies,* a "day") are internal periodic rhythms that control many things like body temperature, hormone levels, sleep and wakefulness, digestion, and excretion. "The circadian cycles go way back in evolutionary time," Charles Czeisler says. "They are probably older than sleep."

Since the 1970s, Czeisler has established himself as one of the world's leading authorities on circadian cycles and the chronobiology of sleep and wakefulness. He has done groundbreaking work in the sleep laboratory at Brigham and Women's Hospital, where a special wing on one floor is shielded not only from sunlight, but from all external time cues. There, researchers can do exotic things like simulate the 708-hour lunar day or conditions on the International Space Station, where the sun

Freud's Guesswork on Dreams

One of Sigmund Freud's great complaints about his mistreatment in life was that although he won a literary award for his famous book *The Interpretation of Dreams* (1900), it never received a scientific award. A century later, his peers' judgment has been vindicated. Freud's unscientific theory of dreams-based on self-analysis and a cherry-picked group of clinical anecdotes-has been demolished by the discoveries of sleep medicine. "I came into the field so far post-Freudian that Freud felt like someone with a goofy theory two centuries back," says Robert Stickgold, associate professor of psychiatry, who has studied dreams in sleep studies for years, often in collaboration with professor of psychiatry J. Allan Hobson. "The Greeks tried to explain thunder and lightning by creating gods; Freud tried to explain dreams by creating demons like the id and repressed desires," says Stickgold. "In general, Freud's dream theories have been remarkably resistant to scientific confirmation. He made a lot of observations that are quite prescient, but his attempt to build a model to explain them is completely wrong and there is no piece of it that holds up."

For example, Freud thought we dream to keep ourselves from being awakened. "That's absolutely false," says Stickgold. "Freud thought that as we sleep, with constraints on the id reduced, all these nasty Victorian desires well up, and if they were allowed to come into the conscious mind, they would be so distressing that the sleeper would wake up. So dreaming is all about disguising and transforming these desires to make them more acceptable to the conscious mind. Freud probably was assuming that people dream one or two times a night, for a few minutes-most people think that, since that's what we remember on waking. But since the 1960s, it's been clear that we dream most of the night-six hours out of eight hours of sleep. During the Rapid Eye Movement (REM) phases of sleep, which make up 15 to 20 percent of sleep time, we do have our most intense dreaming activity, but we dream in other sleep phases, too. If dreaming is all about repressed childhood desires, does everybody have the same amount of them?"

Another core tenet of Freud's dream theory is that a dream is the fulfillment of a wish. Stickgold reflects on this by describing a study using the game Tetris, a kind of geometrical puzzle. Subjects were taught to play the game, and in a sleep lab that night, 60 to 75 percent of them saw images from Tetris in their dreams. "Someone asked Mark Solms, a brilliant psychoanalyst who is trying to create a new field called neuropsychoanalysis-an oxymoron if I ever heard one-about the Tetris dream imagery. He said, 'Those are probably dreams about competition and winning'-in other words, wish fulfillments. But nobody dreamed about winning the game or competing!" Stickgold also wonders about a mother with a son in Iraq who has nightmares about her child being killed. "Maybe a Freudian can interpret that as wish-fulfillment," he says. "But I would take that as perverse, and blind adherence to an outdated model. Any dream can be interpreted as wish fulfillment, but there's no evidence that it is. In fact, there's tons of evidence against it."

Entering into the interpretation of dreams "gets very messy," Stickgold says. "If I could give the same dream to 10 analysts and they all said, 'This is about a wish for immortality,' then I could say, 'OK, at least they all agree on the same interpretation.' But they can't even do that."

rises and sets every 90 minutes. (Czeisler leads a sleep and chronobiology team that, under the auspices of NASA, researches human factors involved in space travel.)

Exotic light environments like space challenge human biology, partly because people differ from other mammals, which take short catnaps and rat naps throughout the day and night. In contrast, we have one bout of consolidated (unbroken) sleep, and one of consolidated waking, per day (or, in siesta cultures, two of each). In addition, "There is a very narrow window [in the daily cycle] in which we are able to maintain consolidated sleep," Czeisler says, "and the window gets narrower and narrower as we get older."

The origins of humans' consolidated sleep take us to the beginnings of terrestrial life, since even prokaryotes—one-celled organisms like bacteria, lacking a nucleus—have built-in 24-hour rhythms. It is not surprising that these biological clocks are so universal, as they reflect the entrainment of all living things to the primeval 24-hour cycles of light and darkness created by the rotation of Earth.

"The light and dark cycle is the most powerful synchronizer of the internal circadian clock that keeps us in sync with the 24-hour day," Czeisler says. As late as 1978, when he published a paper demonstrating this effect, many still believed that "social interaction was the most important factor in synchronizing physiological cycles—that we had evolved beyond light," he says. "But much of our subsequent research shows that our daily cycles are more like those of cockroaches than we want to believe. We are very sensitive to light."

Light strongly affects the suprachiasmatic nucleus (SCN), a biological clock in the anterior region of the hypothalamus that directs circadian cycles. All cells have internal clocks—even cells in a tissue culture run on 24-hour cycles. "They all oscillate like violins and cellos, but the SCN is the conductor that synchronizes them all together, "Czeisler explains.

While the homeostatic pressure to sleep starts growing the moment we awaken, the SCN calls a different tune. Late in the afternoon, its circadian signal for wakefulness kicks in. "The circadian system is set up in a beautiful way to override the homeostatic drive for sleep," Czeisler says. The circadian pacemaker's signal continues to increase into the night, offsetting the build-up of homeostatic pressure and allowing us to stay awake well into the evening and so achieve our human pattern of consolidated sleep and wakefulness. (There is often a dip in the late afternoon, when the homeostatic drive has been building for hours but the circadian signal hasn't yet kicked in; Czeisler calls this "a great time for a nap.") The evolutionary benefit of consolidated sleep and wakefulness is a subject of speculation; Czeisler says that long bouts of wakefulness may enable us to "take advantage of our greater intellectual capacity by focusing our energy and concentration. Frequent catnaps would interrupt that."

"We don't know what happens when people are chronically sleep-deprived over years."
—David White, McGinness professor of sleep medicine at the Sleep Health Center in Newton, Massachusetts

The circadian pacemaker's push for wakefulness peaks between about 8 and 10 P.M., which makes it very difficult for someone on a typical schedule to fall asleep then. "The period from two to three hours before one's regular bedtime, we call a 'wake maintenance zone,' " Czeisler says. But about an hour before bedtime, the pineal gland steps up its secretion of the hormone melatonin, which quiets the output from the SCN and hence paves the way for sleep.

Some years ago, melatonin supplements became popular as a natural sleeping pill, but as Czeisler's research has proven, light is a more powerful influence on the biological clock than melatonin. Mangelsdorf professor of natural sciences J. Woodland Hastings has shown that even a split-second of light exposure can shift the circadian cycle of a single-celled organism by a full hour. Light interferes with sleep, at least partly because it inhibits melatonin secretion and thus resets the biological clock. For this reason, those seeking a sound sleep should probably keep their bedroom as dark as possible and by all means avoid midnight trips to brightly lit bathrooms or kitchens; blue light, with its shorter wavelength—and its resemblance to the sunlit sky—has the most powerful resetting effect.

Light resets the pacemaker even in the case of some completely blind people, who generally lose circadian entrainment and suffer recurrent insomnia. "The eye has two functions, just as the ear does, with hearing and balance," says Czeisler. "The eye has vision, and also circadian photoreception." A subset of about 1,000 photosensitive retinal ganglion cells connects by a direct neural pathway to the SCN; these cells are sometimes active even in those who are blind to light. Exposure to bright light will decrease melatonin levels in some blind persons, and this subset, unlike other blind people, generally do not suffer from insomnia and are biologically entrained to the 24-hour day.

Disastrous Exhaustion

The human species, or much of it, anyway, apparently is trying to become simultaneously nocturnal and diurnal. Society has been squeezing the window for restful sleep ever narrower. (Czeisler likes to quote colleague Thomas Roth of the Henry Ford Sleep Disorders Center in Detroit, on the minimal-sleep end of the spectrum. "The percentage of the population who

need less than five hours of sleep per night, rounded to a whole number," says Roth, "is zero.")

Czeisler has conducted several studies of medical interns, an institutionally sleep-deprived population who provide a hugely disproportionate fraction of the nation's healthcare services. Interns work famously long 80- and even 100-hour weeks; every other shift is typically 30 hours in duration. "On this kind of schedule, virtually everyone is impaired," he says. "Being awake more than 24 hours impairs performance as much as having a blood-alcohol level of 0.1 percent—which is legally drunk."

In addition to both acute and chronic sleep deprivation, interns sleep and wake in patterns that misalign with circadian cycles—being asked, for example, to perform with full alertness at 4 A.M. A fourth factor is that the human brain is "cold" and essentially impaired during the first half-hour after awakening—even more impaired, says Czeisler, than after 70 hours of sleeplessness. "It's a colossally bad idea to have an intern woken up by a nurse saying, 'The patient is doing badly—what shall we do?' "he says. "They might order 10 times the appropriate dose of the wrong med."

The intensity and growing technological advance of medical care only enhance the probability of errors under such conditions. Christopher Landrigan, assistant professor of pediatrics, led a study that compared interns working traditional schedules with those on an alternate schedule of fewer weekly hours and no extended (e.g., 30-hour) shifts in intensive-care units. The doctors on the tiring traditional schedule made 36 percent more serious medical errors, including 57 percent more nonintercepted serious errors, and made 5.6 times as many serious diagnostic errors.

"Being awake more than 24 hours impairs performance as much as having a blood-alcohol level of 0.1 percent—which is legally drunk."

Some Harvard-affiliated teaching hospitals, like Brigham and Women's, where Czeisler works, are taking the lead in substantially reducing work hours for physicians and surgeons in training. Yet no rules limit the work hours of medical students (including those at Harvard Medical School), and at the national level, little has changed for interns and residents. Not long ago, the Accreditation Council of Graduate Medical Education, faced with the threat of federal regulation, enacted new rules limiting extended shifts to 30 hours (before the new rules, they averaged 32 hours), and capped work weeks at 80 hours (beforehand, the average was 72 hours)—with exceptions allowable up to 90 hours. "The new, self-imposed rules largely serve to reinforce the status quo," Czeisler says. "They haven't brought about fundamental change, and haven't changed the length of a typical extended shift, which is still four times as long as a normal workday. And those marathon shifts occur every other shift, all year, several years in a row during residency training."

The risks don't end when the doctors leave work. Research fellow in medicine Laura Barger led another group in a nationwide survey of interns that showed them having more than double the risk of a motor-vehicle crash when driving home after an extended shift. (They aren't alone: 60 percent of American adults drove while drowsy in the past year.)

The moral of much sleep research is startlingly simple. Your mother was right: You'll get sick, become fat, and won't work as well if you don't get a good night's sleep. So make time for rest and recovery. Stickgold likes to compare two hypothetical people, one sleeping eight hours, the other four. The latter person is awake 20 hours a day, compared to 16 hours for the first. "But if the person on four hours is just 20 percent less efficient while awake, then in 20 hours of waking he or she will get only 16 hours of work done, so it's a wash," he says. "Except that they are living on four hours of sleep a night. They're not gaining anything, but are losing a huge amount: you'll see it in their health, their social interactions, their ability to learn and think clearly. And I cannot believe they are not losing at least 20 percent in their efficiency."

Yet instead of encouraging restorative rest, many of our institutions are heading in the opposite direction. This fall, for example, Harvard will begin keeping Lamont Library open 24 hours a day, in response to student demand, and Harvard Dining Services has for several years offered midnight snacks. "These are the wrong solutions," says Stickgold. "This is like the Boston Police Department getting tired of drunk drivers killing people and setting up coffee urns outside of bars. At Harvard there is no limit on the amount of work students are assigned; you can take four courses and have three professors say, 'This is your most important course and it should take the bulk of your time.' Students are dropping to four hours of sleep a night, and the University sees it has to do something about it. But the way you deal with students overloaded with work is not by having dorms serve snacks at midnight and keeping the library open all night. Instead, you can cut back by one-third the amount of work you assign, and do that in every course without serious detriment."

Such are the prescriptions of sleep researchers, which differ radically from those of the society and the economy. The findings of the sleep labs filter only slowly into the mainstream, especially in areas like medical internships, where enormous financial pressures favor the status quo. Even at Harvard Medical School, in a four-year curriculum, only one semester hour is devoted to sleep medicine. For a sleep disorder like narcolepsy, the average time between symptom onset and diagnosis is seven years; for sleep apnea, four years. "Physicians aren't being trained to recognize sleep disorders," Czeisler says.

When all else fails, there is always the option of common sense. Sleep is quite possibly the most important factor in health, and neither caffeine nor sleeping pills nor adrenaline can substitute for it. "As it looks more and more like some of these processes occur exclusively during sleep and can't be reproduced while we are awake, the consequences of losing them look more and more terrifying," says Stickgold. "And that's the experiment we are all in the middle of, right now."

CRAIG A. LAMBERT '69, Ph.D. '78, is deputy editor of this *Harvard Magazine*.

UNIT 10

Contemporary Health Hazards

Unit Selections

Key Points to Consider

- Why are diseases such as mumps making a comeback?

- Who is most at risk for contracting avian flu?

- What health risks followed Hurricane Katrina?

Student Website

www.mhcls.com/online

Internet References

Further information regarding these websites may be found in this book's preface or online.

Centers for Disease Control: Flu
http://www.cdc.gov/flu

National Sleep Foundation
http://www.sleepfoundation.org

Center for the Study of Autism
http://www.autism.org

Food and Drug Administration Mad Cow Disease Page
http://www.fda.gov/oc/opacom/hottopics/bse.html

Environmental Protection Agency
http://www.epa.gov

This unit examines a variety of health hazards that Americans must face on a daily basis and includes topics ranging from environmental health issues to newly emerging or reemerging infectious illnesses. During the 1970s and 1980s Americans became deeply concerned about environmental changes in our air, water, and food. While some improvements have been observed in these areas, much remains to be done as new areas of concern continue to emerge. In the 2005 hurricane season, several notable storms affected the United States including Hurricane Katrina which left the residents of the Gulf Coast with a range of environmental health hazards. In "In Katrina's Wake," John Manuel discusses the health concerns faced by residents of the Gulf Coast following Hurricane Katrina. These include lack of potable water, untreated sewage, chemical spills, insect infestations, unsafe food, growth of toxic mold, and other sources of hazardous waste.

Newly recognized diseases such as Avian Flu, Severe Acute Respiratory Syndrome (SARS), AIDS, West Nile Virus, and Mad Cow Disease may have environmental relationships. Another disease with possible environmental relationships is autism, though doctors truly don't know the exact cause. They do know, however, that autism cases continue to rise which may be due to better diagnoses or to an increase in whatever it is that is causing this vexing brain disorder that now affects one in 166 children in the United States.

While emerging diseases such as Avian Flu make headlines, other vintage viruses are making a comeback. Mumps and whooping cough are both reemerging and affecting populations such as college students who tend to live in close quarters in college dormitories.

While this unit focuses on exogenous factors that influence our state of health, it is important to remember that health is a dynamic state representing the degree of harmony or balance that exists between endogenous and exogenous factors. This concept of balance applies to the environment as well. Due to the intimate relationship that exists between people, animals, and their environment, it is impossible to promote the concept of wellness without also safeguarding the quality of our environment, both physical and social.

Avian Flu: The Uncertain Threat

Denise Grady and Gina Kolata

1. How Serious Is the Risk?

Over the last year, it has been impossible to watch TV or read a newspaper without encountering dire reports about bird flu and the possibility of a pandemic, a worldwide epidemic. First Asia, then Europe, now Africa: like enemy troops moving into place for an attack, the bird flu virus known as A(H5N1) has been steadily advancing. The latest country to report human cases is Azerbaijan, where five of seven people have died. The virus has not reached the Americas, but it seems only a matter of time before it turns up in birds here.

Even so, a human pandemic caused by A(H5N1) is by no means inevitable. Many researchers doubt it will ever happen. The virus does not infect people easily, and those who do contract it almost never spread it to other humans. Bird flu is what the name implies: mostly an avian disease. It has infected tens of millions of birds but fewer than 200 people, and nearly all of them have caught it from birds.

But when A(H5N1) does get into people, it can be deadly. It has killed more than half of its known human victims—an extraordinarily high rate. Equally alarming is that many who died were healthy, not the frail or sickly types of patients usually thought to be at risk of death from influenza.

The apparent lethality of A(H5N1), combined with its inexorable spread, are what have made scientists take it seriously. Concern also heightened with the recent discovery that the 1918 flu pandemic was apparently caused by a bird flu that jumped directly into humans.

In addition, A(H5N1) belongs to a group of influenza viruses known as Type A, which are the only ones that have caused pandemics. All those viruses were originally bird flus. And given the timing of the past pandemics—1918, 1957, 1968—some researchers think the world is overdue for another. It could be any Type A, but right now (A)H5N1 is the most obvious.

The virus lacks just one trait that could turn it into a pandemic: transmissibility, the ability to spread easily from person to person. If the virus acquires that ability, a pandemic could erupt.

Everything hangs on transmissibility. But it is impossible to predict whether A(H5N1) will become contagious among people. The virus has been changing genetically, and researchers fear that changes could make it more transmissible, or that A(H5N1) could mix with a human flu virus in a person, swap genetic material and come out contagious.

But most bird flu viruses do not jump species to people. Some experts say that since A(H5N1) has been around for at least 10 years and the shift has not occurred, it is unlikely to happen. Others refuse to take that bet.

The A(H5N1) strains circulating now are quite different from the A(H5N1) strain detected in Hong Kong in 1997, which killed 6 of 18 human victims. Over time, A(H5N1) seems to have developed the ability to infect more and more species of birds, and has found its way into mammals—specifically, cats that have eaten infected birds.

The actual number of human cases may well exceed the number that have been reported, and may include mild cases from which victims recovered without even seeing a doctor. If that is true, the real death rate could be lower. But no one knows whether mild cases occur, or whether some people are immune to the virus and never get sick at all.

In the absence of more information, health officials must act on what they see—an illness that apparently kills half its victims.

2. Q. How will we know if the virus starts spreading from person to person and becomes a pandemic?

A. If there is a pandemic, it would be everywhere, not in just one city or one country. To detect such an event as early as possible there is an international surveillance system, involving more than 150 countries, that searches for signs that a new flu strain is taking hold in humans.

One hallmark of a pandemic flu would be an unusual pattern of illnesses—lots of cases, possibly cases that are more severe than normal and, possibly, flu infections outside the normal flu season.

Ordinary human flu viruses, for reasons that are not entirely understood, circulate only in winter. But pandemics can occur at any time. A pandemic would also involve a flu virus that was new to humans, meaning that no one would have immunity from previous infections.

3. Q. If bird flu reaches the United States, where is it likely to show up first?

A. Although health officials expect bird flu to reach the United States, it is impossible to predict where it may show up first, in part because there are several routes it could take.

If it is carried by migrating birds, then it may appear first in Alaska or elsewhere along the West Coast.

But if the virus lurks in a bird being smuggled into the United States as part of the illegal trade in exotic birds, it could land in any international airport. Bird smuggling is a genuine problem: in 2004, a man was caught at an airport in Belgium illegally transporting eagles from Thailand, stuffed into tubes in his carry-on luggage.

The birds turned out to be infected with A(H5N1), and they and several hundred other birds in a quarantine area at the airport had to be destroyed.

In theory, an infected human could also bring bird flu into the United States, and that person could fly into just about any international airport and go unnoticed if the virus had yet to produce any symptoms.

4. Q. Does bird flu affect all birds?

A. No one knows the full story. Scientists say A(H5N1) is unusual because it can infect and kill a wide variety of birds, unlike a vast majority of bird flus, which are usually found in wild birds, not domestic fowl, and which cause few symptoms.

Some researchers suspect that wild ducks, or perhaps other wild birds, are impervious to A(H5N1), and may be the Typhoid Marys of bird flu—getting the virus, spreading it to other birds but never becoming ill themselves. No one has good evidence of this yet, but that may be because the way scientists discovered A(H5N1) infections was by finding birds that had gotten the flu and died.

As virologists like to point out, dead birds don't fly. So migratory birds cannot spread the virus if they are dying shortly after being infected. That is why some researchers say that if wild birds are spreading the A(H5N1) virus, it must be a bird species that can be infected but does not become ill.

5. Q. When people die from avian flu contracted from birds, what kills them?

A. Like victims of severe pneumonia, many patients die because their lungs give out. The disease usually starts with a fever, fatigue, headache and aches and pains, like a typical case of the flu. But within a few days it can turn into pneumonia, and the patients' lungs are damaged and fill with fluid.

In a few cases, children infected with A(H5N1) died of encephalitis, apparently because the virus attacked the brain. A number of people have also had severe diarrhea—not usually a flu symptom—meaning that this virus may attack the intestines as well. Studies in cats suggest that in mammals the virus attacks other organs, too, including the heart, liver and adrenal glands.

But more detailed information about deaths in people is not available because very few autopsies have been done. In some countries, like Vietnam, where many of the deaths occurred, autopsies are frowned upon. Researchers say they may glean useful information from autopsies, but fear that pressing for them would alienate the public in some areas.

6. Q. When experts refer to bird flu as A(H5N1), what does that mean?

A.

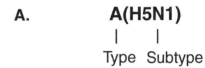

Types There are three types of flu virus.

| **A** Can mutate rapidly and cause severe disease and pandemics; infects birds and some mammals. | **B** Causes sporadic outbreaks of respiratory disease less severe than Type A; infects humans only. | **C** Common but usually causes no symptoms or mild ones; infects humans only. |

Subtypes There are more than 100 subtypes of influenza A, each distinguished by two protein spikes on it surface.

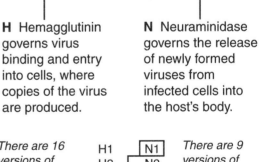

H Hemagglutinin governs virus binding and entry into cells, where copies of the virus are produced.

N Neuraminidase governs the release of newly formed viruses from infected cells into the host's body.

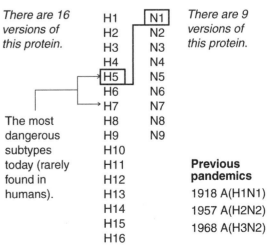

There are 16 versions of this protein.

There are 9 versions of this protein.

H1	N1
H2	N2
H3	N3
H4	N4
H5	N5
H6	N6
H7	N7
H8	N8
H9	N9
H10	
H11	
H12	
H13	
H14	
H15	
H16	

The most dangerous subtypes today (rarely found in humans).

Previous pandemics
1918 A(H1N1)
1957 A(H2N2)
1968 A(H3N2)

7. Q. If I got bird flu, how would I know?

A. There is no reason to suspect the disease unless you may have been exposed to it. Since the virus has not reached North America, doctors do not look for bird flu in people unless they have traveled to affected regions or have been exposed to sick or dead birds.

The early stages of the illness in people are the same as those of ordinary flu: fever, headache, fatigue, aches and pains. But within a few days, people with bird flu often start getting worse instead of better; difficulty breathing is what takes many to the hospital.

In any case, patients with flulike symptoms that turn severe or involve breathing trouble are in urgent need of medical care.

8. Q. Can I be tested for avian flu?

A. There is no rapid test for bird flu. There is a rapid test for Type A influenza viruses, the group that A(H5N1) belongs to, but the test is only moderately reliable, and it is not specific for A(H5N1).

State health departments and some research laboratories can perform genetic testing for A(H5N1) and give results within a few hours, but they do not have the capacity to perform widespread testing.

Because of the limited availability of testing and the extremely low probability of A(H5N1) in people in the United States, the test is recommended only for patients strongly suspected of having bird flu, like travelers with flulike symptoms who were exposed to infected birds.

9. Q. Do any medicines treat or prevent bird flu?

A. Two prescription drugs, Tamiflu and Relenza, may reduce the severity of the disease if they are taken within a day or two after the symptoms begin. But Relenza, a powder that must be inhaled, can irritate the lungs and is not recommended for people with asthma or other chronic lung diseases.

Both drugs work by blocking an enzyme—neuraminidase, the "N" part of A(H5N1)—that the virus needs to escape from one cell to infect another. But just how effective these medicines are against A(H5N1) is not known, nor is it clear whether the usual doses are enough. Also unknown is whether the drugs will help if taken later in the course of the disease.

Although government laboratories and other research groups are trying to develop vaccines to prevent A(H5N1) disease in people, none are available yet.

10. Q. If there is an epidemic of flu in humans, how can I protect myself?

A. If there is a vaccine available, that would be the best option. But if there is no vaccine it may be hard to avoid being infected. Flu pandemics spread quickly, even to isolated regions. The 1918 flu reached Alaskan villages where the only way visitors could arrive was by dog sled.

The vaccines produced every year to prevent seasonal flu are unlikely to be of any use in warding off a pandemic strain. But a flu shot could provide at least some peace of mind, by preventing the false alarm that could come from catching a case of garden-variety flu.

Similarly, people over 65 and others with chronic health problems should consult their doctors about whether they should be vaccinated against pneumococcal pneumonia, a dangerous illness that can set in on top of the flu. Again, that vaccine will not stop bird flu, but it may prevent complications.

Some health officials have recommended stockpiling two to three months' worth of food, fuel and water in case a pandemic interferes with food distribution or staffing levels at public utilities, or people are advised to stay home.

Many health experts have advised against stockpiling Tamiflu or Relenza, the prescription-only antiviral drugs that may work against bird flu. Doctors say the drugs are in short supply and hoarding may keep them out of reach of people who genuinely need them.

Also, they say, self-prescribing may lead to waste of the drugs or misuses that spur the growth of drug-resistant viruses. But people may not trust the government to distribute these drugs, and may want their own supplies.

Doctors say people can take precautions like avoiding crowds, washing their hands frequently and staying away from those who are sick.

Masks may help, but only if they are a type called N-95, which has to be carefully fitted. So far, masks and gloves have been recommended only for people taking care of sick patients.

Avoiding the flu can be hard because it is not always possible to spot carriers. Many people get and spread flu viruses and but never know they are infected.

11. Q. Is the government prepared for a bird flu pandemic?

A. No. The nation does not have an approved flu vaccine for people or enough antiviral drugs or respirators for all who would need them. The best protection in any flu pandemic will come from a vaccine, but scientists cannot tell ahead of time what strain the vaccine should protect against.

Efforts are under way to make a vaccine for A(H5N1). But the virus could mutate in a way that makes experimental vaccines ineffective, requiring more than one vaccine.

Moreover, there is no assurance that the next pandemic will even involve A(H5N1). It may involve a different strain of bird flu, and an A(H5N1) vaccine would not work for it. Recent efforts to develop a sort of universal flu vaccine that would work across strains have failed.

For now, the hope is to spot a pandemic early and quickly make a vaccine. Investigators are developing new and better ways to make vaccines—a bird flu, for example, cannot be grown in fertilized eggs like other flu viruses because it kills the chicken embryos—but these new methods must first be approved by the Food and Drug Administration.

Preparations also include government plans to stockpile drugs to protect people who were exposed to the flu and to reduce the severity of the disease in those who are ill. But the one antiviral drug that everyone wants to buy and stockpile, Oseltamivir, also sold by Roche as Tamiflu, is in short supply.

In retrospect, scientists say, maybe the nation should have started preparing sooner. But until the current bird flu appeared, there was little interest in such expensive and extensive preparations.

Antivirals the federal government plans to have in the National Strategic Stockpile

By the end of 2006	By the end of 2008
26 million treatment courses	81 million treatment courses
22 million courses of Tamiflu and 4 milllion courses of Relenza	6 million reserved for containing an outbreak; the remaining 75 million is enough to treat one quarter of the population

12. Q. If bird flu reaches the United States, will it be safe to eat poultry or to be around birds or other animals?

A. Poultry is safe to eat when it is cooked thoroughly, meaning that the meat is no longer pink and has reached a temperature of 180 degrees Fahrenheit. The risk is not from cooked meat—cooking kills viruses. Instead, it is from infected birds that are still alive or have recently died. So the person who killed an infected chicken, butchered it or put it in the pot would be at greater risk than the one who ate it.

It's not clear how long the virus lives on a dead bird, but it is unlikely to survive more than a couple of days. And it seems unlikely that infected chicken will find its way to supermarkets.

If the bird flu strikes poultry farms, the farmers will know there is a problem. Before they die, the birds develop major hemorrhages, with blood streaming from their cloacas and beaks. When the flu gets to a poultry farm, farmers have to destroy their flocks, and poultry from infected farms cannot be sold for meat.

As for contact with healthy birds or animals, there is no need to panic. The A(H5N1) virus is a nasty one. If chickens or other animals became infected they would get sick and die, and you would know the virus was present.

But animals can carry many diseases besides influenza, and whenever you are around animals it is a good idea to wash your hands afterward. Because cats in Europe have caught A(H5N1), apparently from eating infected birds, health officials there advise keeping pet cats indoors, but no such recommendation has been made in the United States.

For now, officials at the Centers for Disease Control and Prevention say it is safe to have bird feeders, and they note that even if the virus does arrive here, the kinds of birds that perch at feeders are far less likely to carry A(H5N1) than are aquatic birds like ducks and geese.

13. Q. Is it safe to buy imported feather pillows, down coats or comforters and clothing or jewelry with feathers?

A. Imported feathers may not be safe. There is a risk to handling products made with feathers from countries with outbreaks of bird flu, according to the Centers for Disease Control and Prevention.

Feathers from those countries are banned in the United States unless they have been processed to destroy viruses.

'Vintage' Bugs Return

Mumps? Whooping cough? Rickets? What year is it?

MARY CARMICHAEL

Growing up in Peoria, Ill., in the 1950s, Lance Rodewald caught "measles and mumps and probably German measles," and though he doesn't remember suffering through any of them, his wife, Patricia, assures him they were all "absolutely miserable" experiences. She knows because she had them, too. Infectious diseases were a midcentury rite of passage. But as Rodewald grew up, he watched those childhood terrors retreat. Doctors started vaccinating widely in the '60s and '70s, and by the time he was old enough to have kids of his own, it seemed the only common illness left for American parents to worry about was chickenpox.

Scientists developed a vaccine for that as well. But even after his kids made it safely to adolescence, Rodewald, 52, didn't assume that the era of infectious disease in kids in the United States was over. As a pediatrician and director of the Centers for Disease Control's National Immunization Program, he had looked at the data—and seen that "all these diseases are just a plane ride away."

Or, in the case of the mumps, which is now tearing through the heartland for the first time in decades, nine plane rides away. That's how many connecting flights it took for just two infected airline passengers, one flying out of Arizona, the other from Iowa, to apparently kick-start a new eight-state epidemic that has so far sickened 1,165 people. The outbreak serves as a grim reminder that vaccines aren't perfect and that despite modern medicine's advances, germs commonly associated with the early 20th century are still very much in the world. Right now several of the mustiest-sounding diseases—whooping cough, anyone?—are spiking again. "When fewer people start getting diagnosed, there's a premature declaration of victory," says Kenneth Castro, of the CDC. "Then we let our guard down, and the diseases come back and bite us."

Public-health officials certainly weren't expecting to get "bitten" by mumps this year. Although the virus has been circulating in British kids since 2000, it hadn't caused much trouble in the United States since an outbreak in Kansas 18 years ago. The Midwest is the epicenter again, but the victims are primarily college students, not children. Once a childhood disease, the virus has now taken hold in university towns. That's partly because crowded dorms and cafeterias are breeding grounds for germs that are spread by sneezing and coughing. But there's also a factor unique to this generation of college students. In the late '80s, the measles/mumps/rubella vaccine was upgraded from one dose to two, and some of the last kids to get the less effective single-dose vaccine are in college now. Others haven't had any doses at all because some parents, fearing a purported link to autism, did not have their kids vaccinated. And even those who've had both doses aren't fully protected: the vaccine is 90, not 100, percent effective.

"Vaccine fatigue," as clinicians call it, may also explain the recent resurgence of another rare disease, whooping cough, or pertussis. Docs introduced a vaccine in the '40s, and by the '70s the disease was practically eradicated, with only a thousand or so cases per year. But as the disease's profile dwindled, parents were less careful about getting their kids the four to five necessary booster shots. Numbers started rising again in the '80s and '90s. In 2004, the most recent year for which there is full data, there were 25,800 cases. Rodewald hopes that a new adolescent booster vaccine introduced in June will put those numbers back on a downward trend.

As if they didn't have their hands full with mumps and whooping cough, doctors are also starting to worry about other blasts from the past. National statistics haven't been collected, but many papers in the medical literature argue that rickets—a vitamin deficiency long thought to be a relic of the 19th century—is increasing among African-American and Hispanic kids, particularly in the North. Doctors blame it on everything from an increase in breast-feeding (breast milk doesn't contain much vitamin D) to the overuse of sunscreen (the body needs ultraviolet light to produce the vitamin). Another vintage ailment, scarlet fever, the scourge of "Little Women" and "The Velveteen Rabbit," though easily treatable with antibiotics now, also endures. It infects hundreds of kids each year, but pediatricians will usually say those kids have "a symptom of strep throat," not scarlet fever, if only so as not to scare the parents. Finally, though tuberculosis is at a record low, a nasty drug-resistant strain has emerged. Seems like old times.

Agencies Work to Corral Mad Cow Disease

LINDA BREN

When he entered his lab on Dec. 23, 2003, Allen Jenny, D.V.M., knew right away that something was wrong. He recalls the solemn expression on the face of a fellow scientist, who said, "I've got a slide to show you." Jenny, a U.S. Department of Agriculture (USDA) pathologist, peered through the microscope. What he saw was a bright red stain seeping into the gray matter of a slice of brain tissue—a telltale sign of bovine spongiform encephalopathy (BSE), otherwise known as mad cow disease.

"Are you sure it's a cow?" Jenny asked, a logical question in light of the fact that the National Veterinary Services Laboratory in Ames, Iowa, also tests sheep, deer, and other animals for mad cow-like diseases.

Yes, it was a cow, and this first diagnosis of BSE in the United States launched an emergency investigation that involved two countries—the United States and Canada—and regulatory changes by two U.S. government agencies to further bolster their effective safeguards to protect public health and livestock.

Emergency Response

After U.S. authorities announced on the same day that a single dairy cow in Washington state was infected with the fatal brain-wasting disease, BSE, the Food and Drug Administration and the USDA took immediate action. While the USDA went to work to trace the origin of the cow and to initiate a recall of its meat, the FDA made sure that other portions of the cow, including the infectious brain and spinal cord, didn't get into animal feed or other FDA-regulated products. It is believed that BSE spreads when cows eat feed containing remnants of infected cattle. The FDA, which regulates animal feed, has banned the use of these remnants in feed for cattle and other ruminants, such as sheep and goats, since 1997. Canada implemented a similar ban at the same time.

USDA investigators and Canadian health officials found the herd the infected cow originally came from, identified her former herd mates, and then traced many of them to the herds they were later sent to.

"BSE does not spread from cow-to-cow contact," says Stephen F. Sundlof, D.V.M., Ph.D., director of the FDA's Center for Veterinary Medicine. "But we wanted to find these cows because they may have shared a common feed source when they were young," he says, and might also be infected.

An exhaustive search uncovered no other infected cows.

By the time the BSE investigation was completed in February 2004, the USDA had examined the identification tags and other devices on 75,000 cattle in three states—Washington, Oregon, and Idaho—and had humanely slaughtered 255 adult cattle and tested them for BSE.

Previously, in May 2003, Canadian authorities had reported finding the first native BSE cow in North America. Records indicated that this cow and the one found in Washington were more than six years old. "We now have very good evidence that both of these animals were born prior to the feed ban" in the United States and Canada, says Ron DeHaven, chief veterinarian at the USDA.

New Safeguards

Beginning as far back as 1989, the FDA and the USDA had set up a series of safeguards to protect against the spread of BSE. The two agencies have continually evaluated these safeguards and other possible measures to protect public health. After finding the BSE-infected cow in Washington, the agencies introduced some additional measures to further safeguard human and animal health. [Photos Omitted]

The FDA and the USDA work in complementary roles to protect the food supply, and both have regulatory responsibilities. The FDA's responsibility in the human food area generally covers all domestic and imported food except meat, poultry, and frozen, dried, and liquid eggs, which are under the authority of the USDA. But the FDA does regulate certain foods that contain a small amount of meat, such as soups, gravies, and pizza with meat topping. In addition, the FDA regulates animal feed. The USDA also protects and improves the health of the nation's animals by preventing, controlling, and eliminating animal diseases.

Agriculture Secretary Ann M. Veneman announced the USDA's additional measures to protect against BSE on Dec. 30,

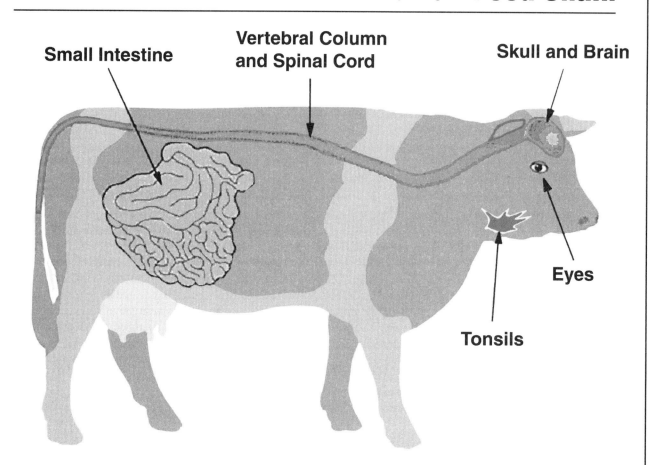

Cow Parts Banned From the Human Food Chain

Small Intestine

Vertebral Column and Spinal Cord

Skull and Brain

Eyes

Tonsils

Parts of cattle at high risk for harboring the infectious agent for bovine spongiform encephalopathy (BSE), or mad cow disease, include the skull, brain, eyes, vertebral column, and spinal cord of cows at least 30 months of age. The tonsils and a portion of the small intestine of all cattle also may contain the agent. Federal agencies protect public health by prohibiting these cow parts in the human food supply.

Infographic: FDA/Michael Ermarth

2003. These measures include prohibiting all material from non-ambulatory cattle in human food, removing certain cattle tissues from the human food chain, and banning certain nervous system tissues in meat products obtained by an industrial technology to cut meat from bones called advanced meat recovery.

On Jan. 26, 2004, Health and Human Services Secretary Tommy G. Thompson announced the FDA's new measures, including banning certain additional materials from animal feed. "These actions will make strong public health protections against BSE even stronger," said Thompson.

Previous Safeguards

The recent measures to protect against BSE add strength to the federal government's already effective series of safeguards, or "firewalls." If one firewall fails, multiple backup safeguards are in place to continue protecting the public.

The first firewall is the USDA's 1989 ban on importing live ruminants and subsequent USDA and FDA import controls over most ruminant products from countries with BSE or considered to be at risk for BSE.

USDA's Additional Safeguards

On Dec. 30, 2003, the USDA announced additional measures to bolster safeguards against mad cow disease:

- Banning all material from cattle that cannot walk ("downer" cattle) from human food.
- Holding all products from cattle tested for BSE until tests are confirmed negative.
- Prohibiting from human food certain "high-risk" organs and tissues from cattle older than 30 months, and the small intestine from cattle of all ages.
- Prohibiting the use of certain materials in advanced meat recovery, an industrial technology that scrapes muscle tissue away from the bone of beef carcasses. This ban will ensure that spinal cord and other high-risk tissues are not included in products for human use.
- Prohibiting air-injection stunning. This is a method of humanely stunning cattle during slaughter, but it poses the possibility that brain tissue, at high risk for BSE, could contaminate cow parts that become food or people or animals.

The second firewall, the USDA's surveillance program to look for BSE in cows, began in 1990. It was through this program that the BSE-infected cow in Washington was found. The USDA has tested more than 20,000 cows for BSE in each of the last two years, and plans on significantly increasing its testing to test every animal in the high-risk cattle population in 2004 and 2005.

Despite this rigorous surveillance program, some people have called for testing all slaughtered cows. But many of these cows are young and the BSE agent doesn't usually show up in animals until after 30 months of age, says DeHaven. "This is a disease with a very long incubation period—typically three to eight years," he says. "To suggest that we would test all animals regardless of age at slaughter is not consistent with the science and what we know about the disease."

"Animals may get exposed at a very young age," says Linda Detwiler, D.V.M., adjunct professor at the University of Maryland. "During the incubation period, the BSE agent replicates in certain tissues of the body and usually after three years makes its way to the brain." The tests used today can detect the infection only in the brain—not in other tissues or blood, so BSE cannot be diagnosed in very young animals, says Detwiler. "The animal may be infected, but it just can't be detected."

Detwiler uses the analogy of looking for a human disease, such as Mzheimer's, to explain the rationale for the current BSE surveillance system. "If you didn't know that Mzheimer's was in the United States, what population would you concentrate on to be able to find it?" asks Detwiler. "Would you start taking brain biopsies from teen-agers, middle-aged, or older people? Testing older folks with dementias increases your chance of finding the disease."

The FDA's 1997 feed rule, which bans most protein from mammals in ruminant animal feed, is the third BSE firewall. In 2001, the Harvard Center for Risk Analysis concluded that the feed rule provided the nation's major protection against BSE becoming established in the United States. In August 2003, Harvard reaffirmed the findings of its initial study and concluded that if infected animals or feed material entered the United States from Canada, the risk of spreading extensively within U.S. herds was extremely low.

The fourth firewall is the additional protective measures recently taken by the FDA and the USDA, and the fifth firewall is the emergency response plan that the agencies initiated immediately after finding the BSE-positive cow in Washington state.

Some critics have suggested that the federal government take further actions, such as tightening slaughter controls and feed regulations, similar to practices used by European governments in their efforts to combat BSE. "You shouldn't equate the actions that the Europeans had to take with the actions that we need to take because the situation in the two continents was very different when BSE was discovered in each continent," says Murray Lumpkin, M.D., the FDA's deputy commissioner for special programs. "In Europe, BSE was at an epidemic stage in their cattle population with ultimately thousands of cases identified. So they had to put in place measures not only to keep BSE from spreading but to contain an epidemic. Based on their experience, we put many BSE firewalls in place before we had any evidence of disease in this country."

Feed Ban Enforcement

Since the feed rule went into effect in 1997, FDA and state inspectors have conducted more than 26,000 inspections involving more than 13,000 firms that handle animal feed.

'Regulations are only as good as your enforcement activities.'

"Regulations are only as good as your enforcement activities," says Sundlof. When violations are found, the firm must quickly address them and undergo a prompt follow-up inspection. Depending on the nature of the violation, a firm's products could be recalled, it could receive an FDA warning letter that demands a response from the firm about how it will correct the violations, or it could find itself in court. Renderers, feed mills, and protein blenders that process materials prohibited for ruminants are inspected at least annually, and more frequently if they are not in compliance with the rule, says Sundlof.

From 1997 to the end of 2003, 47 feed firms had recalled a total of 280 feed products, the FDA had issued 63 warning letters, and the court had ordered one permanent injunction against a feed company. The recall track record is improving: Only 12 of the 280 recalls occurred during 2003.

Sundlof says a strong education program on the feed rule for industry and inspectors has contributed to the high rate of compliance, which has climbed from 75 percent when inspections first began in 1997 to more than 99 percent today.

"The compliance rate is the highest of any FDA compliance program in all of the categories of products that we regulate," says Acting Commissioner of Food and Drugs Dr. Lester M. Crawford. "It is probably the most effective regulatory program that FDA has had in its 100-year history."

All of the firms involved in the investigation of the BSE-infected cow in Washington were in compliance with the FDA's feed rule.

The agency is stepping up its inspections of feed facilities to further ensure compliance. The FDA, along with state agencies, plans to conduct 6,600 inspections in 2004, several hundred more than the previous year.

Protecting Foods and Cosmetics

Protecting the food supply from BSE includes ensuring not only the safety of meat, but also of milk and other foods, including dietary supplements, which may contain ingredients from cows.

There is no scientific evidence that milk and dairy products pose any risk for transmitting BSE to humans, and people should not be concerned about consuming milk and milk products, says the FDA's Center for Food Safety and Applied Nutrition.

Other cow-derived foods, such as gelatin, are also protected from BSE through FDA regulations and guidance to manufacturers. And since 1992, the FDA has advised dietary supplement manufacturers and distributors to take steps to ensure that supplement ingredients come from BSE-free herds. The agency also has directed manufacturers of soaps, lipsticks, and other cosmetics that may contain fat or other ingredients from cows to use only ingredients from BSE-free cattle.

Protecting the Blood Supply

Until recently, the possibility of getting the human form of mad cow disease, called variant Creutzfeldt-Jakob disease (vCJD), through tainted blood was only a theory. But in December 2003, authorities in the United Kingdom announced the death of an adult from vCID whom they believe was infected by a blood transfusion during surgery seven and a half years earlier. The blood had been donated by a young, apparently healthy person in 1996, who died three years later from vCJD.

"We've taken the theoretical risk of blood-borne infection seriously for years, even before the U.K. transfusion case appeared," says David Asher, M.D., head of an FDA laboratory that studies contaminants in blood and tissues. Although there are no rapid, reliable tests to screen the blood supply for vCJD, the FDA has worked with blood centers since 1999 to exclude blood donations by people who lived in the U.K. during a high-risk period for BSE. In 2002, the agency added exclusions of people who might have been exposed to BSE while living elsewhere in Europe.

Protecting Medical Products

Certain cattle parts are used to produce a variety of medical products regulated by the FDA, including some blood products, drugs, devices, vaccines, and human cell- and tissue-based products. For example, some oral medications contain amino acids from cow tissues. Vaccines may be made by growing viruses in cell cultures using a highly diluted cow blood product called fetal bovine serum. And diseased heart valves in people may be replaced with medical devices made from tissues surrounding the heart of a cow.

In regulating these and other medical products, the FDA has advised manufacturers to use cow materials only from BSE-free herds and has recommended that non-animal materials be used in their products whenever possible. Human medical products—whether they're devices or biologics or drugs—have pre-approval requirements, says Lumpkin. When companies come to the FDA for approval, "we work with them on their manufacturing processes, what materials go into the products, and where those materials come from," he says.

The FDA continues to evaluate its regulations and guidances and seeks advice from experts outside the agency to help keep pace with the evolving science relating to transmissible spongiform encephalopathies (TSEs), the family of degenerative diseases of the nervous system that includes BSE and vCJD.

One forum for soliciting independent opinions is the TSE Advisory Committee, a group of scientists and medical experts who met most recently in Silver Spring, Md., in February 2004. In this two-day public meeting, the committee discussed additional measures that the agency might take to further minimize the risk of getting a TSE disease from FDA-regulated medical products. The agency will consider the recommendations of this committee in its regulatory decision-making to keep medical products safe.

Better BSE Science

No one knows for certain what causes BSE, but the leading scientific theory is that an abnormal form of a protein called a prion is responsible. All humans and other mammals have prion proteins in their cells that are harmless in their normal form, but become potentially damaging when they fold into a different shape, clump together, and accumulate in brain tissue. In BSE, abnormal prions are believed to enter the bodies of mammals when they eat tissues contaminated with these prions.

Researchers worldwide are studying how prions cause BSE and other TSEs and how to block the conversion of normal prion protein to the abnormal form, which may lead to methods to prevent or treat these deadly diseases.

Other areas of research focus on developing tests to diagnose TSEs in humans and animals and developing methods to detect the abnormal prions in animal feed and human food. Scientists are trying to find ways to detect BSE in live cattle, since current tests can detect it only by examining brain tissue after death.

Diagnosis of the human form of BSE, vCJD, is also confirmed by looking at brain tissue. In humans, this tissue may be collected through a biopsy while the person is ill or collected after the person has died.

Probable cases can be diagnosed in living people based on their symptoms and the results of either a tonsil biopsy or two non-invasive tests of the brain, electroencephalogram and magnetic resonance imaging. The tonsil biopsy is invasive and re-

CJD and vCJD: Two Different Diseases

As of February 2004, 156 cases of the human form of mad cow disease, known as variant Creutzfeldt-Jakob disease (vCJD), have been reported worldwide, according to the Centers for Disease Control and Prevention (CDC). But there has never been a case of vCJD contracted in the United States. One resident of Florida was diagnosed in 2002 with a probable case of vCJD, but it is believed she acquired it in the United Kingdom, where she lived for more than 12 years during an epidemic of bovine spongiform encephalopathy (BSE), or mad cow disease. It is believed that the vCJD victims got the human variant by eating beef products that came from BSE-infected cattle.

The classic form of CJD has been found in the United States. Unlike the variant, the classic form is not known to be food-related. "CJD and vCJD are best thought of as two different diseases," says Lawrence Schonberger, M.D., M.P.H., epidemiologist and assistant director of the CDC's National Center for Infectious Diseases. "CJD was around long before the emergence of BSE in cattle." Both diseases are brain disorders, but the patterns of the brain lesions they leave are distinct.

Variant CJD is found in younger patients and the length of illness is longer. There is no treatment for either disease, and they always result in death. The average age for death of vCJD is under 30 years versus the mid- to late 60s for classic CJD.

Neither vCJD nor CJD is spread through direct contact with others with the infection. The classic form of CJD may be inherited (familial), transmitted by infectious surgical instruments or tissues (iatrogenic), or occur among people with no known environmental risk factors (sporadic). The sporadic form generally occurs at a rate of about 1 case per million people per year, and familial and iatrogenic cases are even rarer, according to the CDC.

quires anesthetizing the patient, says Lawrence Schonberger, M.D., M.P.H., epidemiologist and assistant director of the Centers for Disease Control and Prevention's National Center for Infectious Diseases. "What we're really looking for is a urine or blood test," he says, and research continues to identify less invasive tests.

FDA researchers are developing tests to detect the prohibited proteins in animal feed for cows. These tests will help the agency enforce the feed ban, allowing samples of feed from processing facilities to be checked to ensure that they do not contain the protein that may carry the BSE agent.

FDA scientists are also evaluating decontamination techniques to try to rid TSE agents from surgical instruments, hospital rooms, and other areas where patients and health care workers may be accidentally exposed. Using an evaluation method they developed, FDA scientists have found that conventional decontamination procedures, such as heating with steam augmented by soaking in solutions of lye or using chlorine bleach, "are extremely effective in removing most of the infectivity," says Asher. "This is contrary to the mythology that boiling, heating, or other sterilization doesn't kill the agent," he says. "They don't remove 100 percent of infectivity under worst-case circumstances, but they are successful in removing huge amounts of infective material."

From *FDA Consumer*, May/June 2004, pp. 29-35. Published 2004 by the U.S. Food and Drug Administration. www.fda.gov/oc/opacom/hottopics/bse.html

In Katrina's Wake

JOHN MANUEL

Hurricane Katrina has been called the most devastating natural environmental calamity in U.S. history. Visitors to the scene say the destruction is worse than anyone can imagine. Scientists also say that some perceived health threats have been overblown and others understated. Months after Katrina roared into the Gulf Coast, the environmental health implications of the storm are still being assessed.

Katrina presented residents of the Gulf Coast with a bewildering array of environmental health hazards. Aside from standing floodwater, hazards included a lack of potable water, sewage treatment, and electricity; chemical spills; swarms of insects (with anecodotal accounts of vermin and hungry domestic dogs); food contamination; disrupted transportation; mountains of debris; buildings damaged and destroyed; rampant mold growth; tainted fish and shellfish populations; and many potential sources of hazardous waste. Some impacts, such as deaths from drowning and injuries from cleaning up debris, have been relatively easy to determine. Others, such as post-traumatic stress disorder from the loss of homes and loved ones, may never be fully quantified.

In the weeks following the storm, federal agencies such as the NIEHS, the Centers for Disease Control and Prevention (CDC), and the Environmental Protection Agency (EPA), as well as state environmental and public health agencies, sent scientists to the region to begin assessing the environmental and human health impact of the disaster. Much of what they found was presented on October 20 at a meeting of the National Academies Institute of Medicine's Roundtable on Environmental Health Sciences, Research, and Medicine (commonly known as the EHSRT), supported by the NIEHS, the CDC, the EPA, Exxon-Mobile Corporation, the American Chemistry Council, and the Brita Water Research Institute. Still more information continues to emerge today. And much simply remains to be seen.

Katrina Hits

Katrina, rated as a Category 4 hurricane on the Saffir-Simpson scale, made landfall near New Orleans on 29 August 2005. Wind damage extended as far as 150 miles inland. Heavy rain battered the area, and the storm surge—measuring as high as 30 feet and sweeping several miles inland—breached several levees intended to protect New Orleans from the waters of Lake Pontchartrain. Water poured through the breaks in the days fol-

lowing the storm, covering approximately 80% of the city with water as deep as three meters. The American Red Cross estimates that more than 354,000 homes along the Gulf Coast were destroyed or damaged beyond repair by Katrina and, a month later, Hurricane Rita. Hundreds of small manufacturers or businesses using chemicals or fuels also were impacted.

Flooding, wind, and waves caused major damage to buildings and infrastructure whose integrity is key to the environmental health of the local citizenry. The EPA estimated that more than 200 sewage treatment plants in Louisiana, Mississippi, and Alabama were affected, with almost all the plants around New Orleans knocked out of action. Loss of power meant lift stations (which pump sewage uphill) could not work, causing sewage to overflow into houses and streets.

The region struck by Katrina and Rita is home to a large number of oil refineries and chemical plants. Prior to Katrina, the EPA had identified nearly 400 sites in the affected area as possibly needing cleanup because of their potential impact on human health. Following the storm, the U.S. Coast Guard reported numerous oil spills from refineries and tank farms in South Louisiana. A story in the September 30 Boston Globe reported that Katrina damaged 140 oil and gas platforms in the Gulf of Mexico, 43 seriously, including some that floated away or sank.

Across the Gulf Coast, more than 1.5 million people evacuated as the storm approached. More than 100,000 stayed behind in New Orleans, unwilling or unable to leave. As New Orleans flooded, thousands waded through chest-deep floodwaters to reach shelters or higher ground. Thousands more remained trapped in homes, hospitals, and nursing homes. Conditions in shelters rapidly became unsanitary. Many people were exposed to the elements for five days or more, living with little or no food, drinking water, or medicine. As of December 5, the death toll was reported at 1,071 in Louisiana, 228 in Mississippi, 14 in Florida, 2 in Alabama, and 2 in Georgia.

First Response

Numerous federal, state, and local agencies, as well as private individuals and relief groups, swung into action in the wake of the storm. Troops from the U.S. Army, Coast Guard, and National Guard as well as state and local officials and private citizens rescued those they could. The Federal Emergency Management Agency (FEMA) was assigned the lead in disaster relief planning and administration, including provision of emergency food and shelter and contracting for debris removal. The Department of Health and Human Services (DHHS) declared a public health emergency in the Gulf states and directed the CDC to take appropriate action. The CDC deployed more than 600 professionals into the disaster zone, including specialists in public health nursing, occupational safety and health, laboratory science, medicine, epidemiology, sanitation, environmental health, disease surveillance, public information, and health risk communication.

The CDC also joined with the EPA to set up a joint task force to conduct an environmental health needs and habitability assessment to identify critical public health issues for the reinhabitation of New Orleans. This city was unique among the areas hit in that it was the only one left with standing water. Major urban areas in Mississippi and Alabama, while devastated, did not remain flooded.

In advance of the storm's arrival, the EPA had predeployed teams to the area, with the mission of guiding debris disposal, assisting in the restoration of drinking and wastewater treatment systems, and containing hazardous waste spills. Immediately after the storm, these teams used their 60 watercraft to help search-and-rescue efforts, rescuing about 800 people, according to EPA administrator Stephen Johnson. Five days after the storm, the EPA began testing floodwaters in New Orleans for biological and chemical contamination.

In coordination with the Louisiana Department of Environmental Quality (LDEQ), the EPA analyzed floodwaters for more than 100 hazardous pollutants such as volatile and semivolatile organic compounds, metals, pesticides, herbicides, and polychlorinated biphenyls. They also tested for biological agents such as *Escherichia coli*. Their testing revealed "greatly elevated" levels of *E. coli*, as much as ten times higher than EPA's recommended levels for contact. According to the EPA, agency scientists found levels of lead and arsenic at some sites in excess of drinking water standards—a potential threat given the possibility of hand-to-mouth exposure. The EPA posted these and other findings on its Hurricane Response 2005 website (**http://www.epa.gov/katrina/**), created after the storm.

Shortly after the hurricane struck, the U.S. Coast Guard began working with the EPA, the Louisiana state government, and private industries to identify and recover spilled oil along the coast. The team identified 6 major, 4 medium, and 134 minor spills totaling 8 million gallons. One of the most notorious spills occurred at the Murphy Oil Company plant, which dumped more than 25,000 barrels of oil into the streets of Chalmette and Meraux, Louisiana. As of December 7, the Coast Guard reported the recovery of 3.8 million gallons, with another 1.7 million evaporated, 2.4 million dispersed, and 100,000 onshore.

Meanwhile, the NIEHS was joining with Duke University Medical Center, the NIH, and the CDC to provide assistance with relief and recovery operations along the Gulf Coast, as well as working at home to establish a website on environmental health issues related to Katrina.

Floodwater Hazards

Kevin Stephens is director of the New Orleans Department of Health. He was in charge of interpreting the EPA data and advising citizens and responders about the health hazards presented by the floodwaters. "I struggled every day to determine what [the data] meant and what to tell our health workers and the public," he says. "What does 'not an immediate health hazard' mean when you have people wading through the water? What does 'not in excess of drinking water standards' mean? Is it a danger if you get your hands wet and touch your mouth?" Journalists claimed the floodwaters were a "toxic gumbo" of dangerous chemicals and microbes, raising fears that any contact was a health threaten.

These concerns prompted a team of scientists led by John Pardue, director of the Louisiana Water Resources Research Institute at Louisiana State University (LSU), to conduct its own study of the New Orleans floodwaters. The report, published 15 November 2005 in *Environmental Science & Technology*, stated categorically that, contrary to claims in the media, the floodwater was not a "toxic soup."

"Chemical oxygen demand and fecal coliform bacteria were elevated in surface floodwater, but typical of stormwater runoff in the region," the report said. "Lead, arsenic, and in some cases chromium exceeded drinking water standards, but with the exception of some elevated lead concentrations were generally typical of stormwater." The LSU study also found only low concentrations (less than 1%) of benzene, toluene, and ethylbenzene even in places where there was a visible oil sheen. "Collectively, these data indicate that Katrina floodwater is similar to normal stormwater runoff, but with somewhat elevated lead and VOC concentrations," the report concluded.

However, the LSU study was limited to two areas within the city of New Orleans, and the authors warned that conditions could be different elsewhere, particularly in Lake Pontchartrain, where floodwaters were being pumped. LSU and the University of Colorado are currently conducting studies of Lake Pontchartrain looking for a wide range of pathogens. The Colorado team is measuring aerosols created by pumping floodwater into the lake, while the LSU team is analyzing the lake water itself.

More Water Hazards

Still other threats were posed by water. As of December 9, the EPA reported that 99% of the waste treatment and water supply systems were back online, but some had been out of operation for weeks. At the October 20 EHSRT, Howard Frumkin, director of the National Center for Environmental Health and Agency for Toxic Substances and Disease Registry (NCEH/ATSDR), said that despite the percentage of sewage treatment plants already online at that point, the danger wasn't over. "We have no guarantees that sewage being flushed is getting to treatment plants," he said. "Raw sewage is going into the Mississippi River."

Though most water supply systems may be functioning again, the safety of distribution lines that were flooded can't yet be ensured either. "There are possible changes in pipe ecology due to the intrusion of contaminants," said Frumkin. "And we have additional concerns for homes on wells." Louisiana officials speaking at the roundtable said there are dozens of community water systems and tens of thousands of private wells that need to be tested for contamination.

Standing water poses a different threat, serving as a breeding ground for bacteria and mosquitoes. Even prior to Katrina, Louisiana had the highest number of reported cases of West Nile virus (66) of any state in the union, according to the CDC. West Nile virus can be transmitted to humans via mosquito bites, and the warm, wet weather following the storm was ideal for breeding of mosquitoes. The U.S. Air Force sprayed areas of standing water with pesticides to kill mosquito larvae. The CDC reported on its Update on CDC's Response to Hurricanes website that postspraying surveillance at ten sites found a 91% reduction in total mosquito density compared to prespraying surveillance results.

The Gulf Coast is also known for the presence of the bacterium *Vibrio vulnificus*. This relative of the pathogen that causes cholera thrives in brackish waters in warmer times of the year. Humans may become infected by eating contaminated seafood or through open wounds exposed to water. While not harmful to individuals in good health, it can be fatal to those with liver damage. Health officials at the roundtable reported counting 22 cases of illness induced by *V. vulnificus* following the storm, including 5 deaths.

In late September, the EPA launched the Ocean Survey Vessel *Bold* to conduct water quality testing in the river channels and nearshore waters of the Mississippi Delta. The agency monitored 20 areas to determine whether fecal pollution from flooded communities had spread into these waters. All 20 monitoring stations showed that, at the time, the water was safe for primary contact, including swimming. The EPA said on its website, however, that the data "should not be used to assess the safety of consuming raw or undercooked molluscan shellfish."

In the wake of the storm, Louisiana, Mississippi, and Alabama closed their shellfishing waters until testing could be done. On December 8, the three states issued a joint press release saying that fish and shellfish samples collected and analyzed since the hurricanes "show no reason for concern about the consumption of Gulf seafood." Louisiana and Alabama subsequently reopened their waters, while Mississippi's oyster reefs remain closed pending additional studies.

Toxicants in Sediment and Air

Health officials also anticipated a threat from contaminated sediment in the days and weeks following the storm. As floodwaters were pumped out of inundated areas, a dark sludge was found coating buildings, land, and pavement. *E. coli* was detected at elevated levels in many sediment samples taken from around New Orleans, implying the presence of fecal bacteria. The EPA has no standards for determining human health risks from *E. coli* in sediment, but warned people to limit exposure, and if exposed, to wash skin with soap and water.

The EPA was concerned, too, about the region's Superfund sites, which include former dump sites of pesticides and dioxins. The EPA identified 54 Superfund sites in the affected area. Officials worried that at least some of these sites might have been compromised, releasing toxic chemicals into the land or water. Johnson reported at the EHSRT that as of October 20, the EPA had visually inspected all of the sites and sampled many. As of December 5, the EPA's posted test results for these sites indicated that none were compromised in a way that would present a human health hazard.

Elsewhere, as late as November 20, chemical testing of sediment samples in Louisiana's Orleans and St. Bernard Parishes indicated the continued presence of petroleum. However, the EPA's website states that exposures of emergency responders at these levels are not expected to cause adverse health effects as long as the proper personal protective equipment is worn, such as gloves and safety glasses. Volatile and semivolatile organic compounds, pesticides, and metals including aluminum were found, but at levels below what the ATSDR and CDC consider to be immediately hazardous to human health. However, the site continues, "EPA and ATSDR/CDC continue to recommend that residents avoid all contact with sediment deposited by floodwater, where possible, due to potential concerns associated with long-term skin contact."

The Natural Resources Defense Council (NRDC) and a host of local environmental groups paint a darker picture of the contamination situation. In a December 1 press release, the NRDC stated that tests it had conducted revealed "dangerously high levels" of industrial chemicals and heavy metals in the sediment covering much of New Orleans. For example, tests found arsenic levels in some neighborhoods that exceeded EPA safety limits by a factor of 30.

"We found arsenic and other cancer causing contaminants in sediment all across the entire city," said Monique Hardin, codirector of the New Orleans–based Advocates for Human Rights, at an NRDC press briefing. "We also found hot spots where there were some nasty surprises, such as banned pesticides." The groups urged the EPA to begin cleaning up or removing contaminated topsoil across the city and to conduct further testing in certain neighborhoods.

The NRDC also challenged the EPA's assertion that the flooded Superfund sites posed no threat. The December 1 press release stated that NRDC's own assessment of one of these sites, the New Orleans Agricultural Street Landfill Superfund Site, showed "visible leachate emerging from the site and spreading across the street and onto a local senior center's property. Sediment testing at this site found contamination as much as 20 times higher than the EPA soil cleanup standards for four [polycyclic aromatic hydrocarbons]."

LDEQ toxicologist Tom Harris responded in press reports that the NRDC's findings were fundamentally flawed because arsenic levels are naturally above the EPA's residential standard in Louisiana and elsewhere. "I have never personally seen soil samples come back below the residential screening level for arsenic," Harris told PlanetArk World Environmental News on December 5. "It's a naturally occurring [element] you can find everywhere." The state of Louisiana and the EPA continue to perform testing of sediment to determine when to give an all-clear to residents with respect to exposure to sediment.

The EPA has also addressed concerns about air quality in the Gulf region. According to Johnson, most of the agency's stationary air quality monitors were knocked out by Katrina. The EPA reinstalled the stationary monitors and employed their Airborne Spectral Photometrics Environmental Collection Technology to undertake airborne monitoring. The EPA also employed two Trace Atmospheric Gas Analyzer buses, self-contained mobile laboratories capable of continuous real-time sampling and analysis.

Air samples were tested for volatile priority pollutants such as benzene, toluene, and xylene, which are commonly found in gasoline, as well as other industrial solvents. The screening results indicated that chemical concentrations in most areas were below the ATSDR health guidelines of concern. The EPA stated on its website, "The low level of volatile pollutants is not surprising as contaminants may be bound in sediment. Monitoring data directly around Murphy Oil spill reveal some slightly elevated levels of benzene and toluene that are associated with petroleum release. Long-term exposure (a year or longer) at the levels measured would be required for health effects to be a concern."

Air may also play a role in an illness known as "shelter cough," or "Katrina cough." Shelter cough is presumed to be an allergic reaction to some particulate matter in the air, according to Stephens. However, despite the presence of shelter cough and earlier concerns about a wave of infectious diseases in the wake of Katrina, acute respiratory illness have made up only 8.7% of diagnoses between August 29 and September 24, according to the October 7 *Morbidity and Mortality Weekly Report*. "We have no evidence of infectious disease outbreaks," Stephens said at the EHSRT.

A Mountain of Debris

The amount of debris generated by Katrina is by all accounts staggering. FEMA estimates there are 39.9 million cubic yards of debris in Mississippi alone. Mark Williams, administrator of solid waste policy, planning, and grants at the Mississippi Department of Environmental Quality (MDEQ), says that state has enough space for the initial removal of debris to staging areas, but not for long-term deposition in landfills.

Jimmy Guidry, medical director of Louisiana's Department of Health and Hospitals, says Louisiana, too, lacks sufficient landfill space for all the debris: "We have more than three hundred thousand refrigerators that need to be disposed of. All these have freon in them." Guidry said at the roundtable that the Louisiana Department of Environmental Quality has approved dozens of temporary debris disposal sites, which will have to be carefully monitored.

Appliances can be recycled for metal content. Televisions and household computers pose a different problem. A single computer monitor contains 4.5 pounds of lead, and computer processing units contain trace metals that can leach out of unlined landfills.

As much as one-third of the debris is vegetative matter that can be burned or chipped for compost. The rest must be recycled or landfilled. Williams says burning of vegetative debris

has been allowed in Mississippi for some months and is now largely complete. He adds, "EPA in conjunction with MDEQ has done some monitoring in the area [of controlled burns], which has indicated some elevated levels of formaldehyde and acrolein in certain areas." In the interest of minimizing air pollution, the EPA and MDEQ allowed only clean vegetative debris to be burned and strongly encouraged the use of air curtain destructors and other combustion units in the early stages of cleanup.

Williams says another daunting challenge was disposing of thousand of tons of food— chicken, fish, and beef—rotting in warehouses on the docks. Officials from Mississippi's Natural Resources Conservation Service said more than 6 million dead animals—poultry and livestock—had to be removed from farms in the affected area. Now officials are dealing with wastes in homes, including such items as propane tanks, household pesticides, and asbestos from roofing, insulation, and other home sources. The waste is taken to staging areas where hazardous waste is pulled out for disposal by the EPA. As of October 31, the EPA had collected an estimated 1 million pounds of household hazardous waste in Louisiana (the agency did not report on collections in other states).

Injury Protection

One of the major concerns officials have with regard to the handling and disposal of debris is the safety of workers. "We have a large number of workers coming to the Gulf seeking employment, and many of them are not properly trained and protected," says Max Kiefer, assistant director of emergency preparedness and response for the National Institute for Occupational Safety and Health (NIOSH). High-risk occupations include debris removal, levee rebuilding, residential refurbishment, and infrastructure rebuilding.

NIOSH is trying to keep workers apprised of health hazards. "We have assessed exposure to silica and metals during levee rebuilding, debris removal, and tasks involving the sediment," Kiefer said at the roundtable. "We also worried that people were wearing protective gear that may induce heat stress. After assessing certain tasks, we were able to downgrade our gear recommendations in light of that. Psychological stress on responders has been significant. But by far the biggest issue has been injuries—lacerations, falls, and trips." NIOSH is providing guidance for responders and providers on the CDC hurricane response website.

Private citizens also face significant risk of injury during cleanup. Officials talk of a "second wave" of injury following a natural disaster as citizens undertake to remove debris and repair buildings themselves. Will Service, the industrial hygiene coordinator with the North Carolina Office of Public Health Preparedness and Response, worked in a mobile hospital in Waveland, Mississippi, in the days following the storm. "We saw a lot of injuries from things like chain saws used during cleanup," Service says. "People are tired, their thinking isn't clear. They're doing things they don't normally do."

Illnesses and injuries associated with Katrina are being tracked by the CDC, with updates posted regularly on its website. Confirming what public health officials warned about a second wave of injuries, the most common diagnosis (26.2%) in reporting hospitals and clinics from September 8 to October 4 was injury. The major cause of injury was falling, followed closely by vehicle crash–related injuries (likely related to missing or nonfunctioning traffic signs and signals). Cutting and piercing injuries ranked third.

Coming Home to Hazards

Mold growth in houses damaged by Katrina is of enormous concern to health and housing officials. Estimates of the number of homes suffering water damage range in the hundreds of thousands. Claudette Reichel, an LSU professor of education and housing specialist, says that virtually every home that sustained flood damage will experience mold growth. "Houses that people were not allowed back into for weeks will all have mold, and that mold will have had time to multiply, spread, and get really thick," she says. Says Frumkin, "The magnitude of mold exposure in the Gulf region will in many instances greatly exceed anything we have seen before, adding to the concern and uncertainty regarding health effects."

How or even whether mold causes human health problems is disputed by public health professionals, but most acknowledge a connection. "It is a very difficult science, because there is no clear-cut dose–response threshold," Reichel says. "It is highly dependent upon the type of mold, whether the mold is producing a mycotoxin, the susceptibility of the patient, and the amount of exposure."

The CDC states that people who are sensitive to mold may experience stuffy nose, irritated eyes, or wheezing. People allergic to mold may have difficulty in breathing. People with weak immune systems may develop lung infections.

Health and housing officials advise homeowners and renters to throw out any furnishings, insulation, and bedding that may have gotten wet, to clean walls and floors with soap and water, to ventilate, and then to close up and dehumidify the home.

The CDC also reported a spike in post- Katrina carbon monoxide poisoning in the Gulf Coast in the October 7 *Morbidity and Mortality Weekly Report*. From August 29 to September 24, a total of 51 cases of carbon monoxide poisoning, including 5 deaths, were reported in Alabama, Louisiana, and Mississippi. After the hurricanes, many residents used gasoline-powered portable generators to provide electricity to their homes and businesses. These devices produce carbon monoxide, which can build up to fatal levels if run inside a living space or garage.

A number of other health issues loom as residents begin returning to New Orleans, where health care services aren't widely available, sewer and water services are still spotty, and structural inspections aren't complete. Residents have asked city officials for a health assessment to address their concerns about oil spills, mold contamination, and the possible long-term health effects related to mold and chemical exposures. "We are developing an assessment tool for this purpose, and we anticipate that it will be developed for the beginning of [2006]," says Stephens.

Many health care professionals worry that mental health may be the most serious longterm health issue resulting from Katrina. Hundreds of thousands of people across the Gulf region have had their homes destroyed. Thousands are still living in shelters. Many have no jobs, no health insurance, and no job prospects. "We are seeing a lot of symptoms of post-traumatic stress disorder," says Marty Allen, a psychologist with the Mississippi Department of Mental Health. "The trauma was not just the day of the storm. People are still being traumatized by living in tents, not having jobs, and having to walk for miles just to get food and water."

Lessons Learned?

What lessons have been learned from Katrina with respect to environmental health? Debate about how to protect Gulf Coast citizens from hurricanes and storm surge was ongoing before the storm and will continue with renewed intensity.

In Mississippi, Governor Haley Barbour enlisted the Chicago-based Congress for New Urbanism to come up with recommendations for rebuilding the Gulf Coast. The Congress sponsored a week-long Mississippi Renewal Forum in October attended by some of the nation's leading architects, engineers, and urban planners. Working with local leaders, the teams produced reports for 11 coastal towns impacted by the storm. Recommendations include improving the connectivity between towns by moving the CSX freight line north and transforming the abandoned right-of- way into a boulevard for cars and transit, connecting the Gulf region towns with highspeed rail, realigning and revising U.S. 90 to become a pedestrian-friendly "beach boulevard," and creating a Gulf Coast bikeway.

A similar process is under way in Louisiana under the auspices of the Louisiana Recovery Authority created by Governor Kathleen Blanco. The authority is developing short-, medium-, and long-range plans to guide the rebuilding of Louisiana in the wake of the hurricanes. At the authority's request, the American Association of Architects, in collaboration with the American Planning Association, presented the Louisiana Recovery and Rebuilding Conference on November 10–12. The authority has developed a 100-day plan that includes completion of an environmental evaluation of damages caused by the hurricanes and development of recommendations for how to proceed with reconstruction.

Discussion will center on how to protect New Orleans from further flooding and whether certain low-lying parts of the city should even be reoccupied. Such decisions will be made in the months and years to come. Meanwhile, environmental and public health officials have drawn some conclusions about how to better respond to events like Katrina.

Officials at the EHSRT agreed that communication in advance and in the wake of natural and man-made disasters is key. Fears and rumors of disease ran rampant in the days following Katrina. Citizens, the media, and even public health officials did not know which factors presented a genuine health threat and which did not. Federal agencies conducted testing and provided data, but people often did not know how to interpret those data with respect to the kinds of exposures they were encountering.

"The public health community must be actively involved and articulate key health issues," said Kellogg Schwab, an assistant professor at Johns Hopkins Bloomberg School of Public Health. "We must keep the message simple and focused. We must develop effective strategies to provide targeted timely results. We must provide concise and accurate public health information and advice."

Officials also agreed that responders must be properly trained and deployed, provided with proper protective gear and an effective communications system (land lines and cell phones were inoperative in much of the area for weeks after Katrina). Health officials must be able to assess the particular kinds of exposures that people have been subjected to and respond accordingly.

"Your response strategy for exposure varies with each event," said Paul Lioy, deputy director of the Environmental and Occupational Health Sciences Institute at Rutgers University. "The World Trade Center [collapse] was an instantaneous acute air exposure event like we'd never experienced. Katrina for the most part involved an acute water exposure event, but the exposure was over a longer period of time."

Lioy pointed out the need for a national review of the kind of standards and guidelines necessary to ensure that the correct information is given out to the public about immediate hazards versus long-term exposures and risks. "Comparison to general drinking water or ambient air quality standards are not sufficient for guiding the public or public officials during an acute exposure event," he said.

Most of all, roundtable participants agreed, Katrina represents a chance for officials across all levels of government to do things better—evacuation planning, urban design, communication, environmental monitoring, and involvement of citizenry, particularly minority and low-income residents. John McLachlan, director of the Tulane/Xavier Center for Bioenvironmental Research, said that preparing for disasters like Katrina requires the involvement of virtually every academic discipline. To that end, Tulane and Xavier are creating a Katrina Environmental Research and Restoration Network (KERRN) of researchers who share data and ideas across disciplinary, geographical, and institutional lines. Paraphrasing one of his colleagues, McLachlan stated, "This is the mother of all multidisciplinary problems."

From *Environmental Health Perspectives,* January 2006. Published by National Institute of Environmental Health Sciences. www.ehponline.org

Index

Index

Test Your Knowledge Form

We encourage you to photocopy and use this page as a tool to assess how the articles in *Annual Editions* expand on the information in your textbook. By reflecting on the articles you will gain enhanced text information. You can also access this useful form on a product's book support Web site at *http://www.mhcls.com/online/*.

NAME: DATE:

_____

TITLE AND NUMBER OF ARTICLE:

_____

BRIEFLY STATE THE MAIN IDEA OF THIS ARTICLE:

_____

LIST THREE IMPORTANT FACTS THAT THE AUTHOR USES TO SUPPORT THE MAIN IDEA:

_____

WHAT INFORMATION OR IDEAS DISCUSSED IN THIS ARTICLE ARE ALSO DISCUSSED IN YOUR TEXTBOOK OR OTHER READINGS THAT YOU HAVE DONE? LIST THE TEXTBOOK CHAPTERS AND PAGE NUMBERS:

_____

LIST ANY EXAMPLES OF BIAS OR FAULTY REASONING THAT YOU FOUND IN THE ARTICLE:

_____

LIST ANY NEW TERMS/CONCEPTS THAT WERE DISCUSSED IN THE ARTICLE, AND WRITE A SHORT DEFINITION:

We Want Your Advice

ANNUAL EDITIONS revisions depend on two major opinion sources: one is our Advisory Board, listed in the front of this volume, which works with us in scanning the thousands of articles published in the public press each year; the other is you—the person actually using the book. Please help us and the users of the next edition by completing the prepaid article rating form on this page and returning it to us. Thank you for your help!

ANNUAL EDITIONS: Health 07/08

ARTICLE RATING FORM

Here is an opportunity for you to have direct input into the next revision of this volume.
We would like you to rate each of the articles listed below, using the following scale:

1. **Excellent: should definitely be retained**
2. **Above average: should probably be retained**
3. **Below average: should probably be deleted**
4. **Poor: should definitely be deleted**

Your ratings will play a vital part in the next revision.
Please mail this prepaid form to us as soon as possible.
Thanks for your help!

RATING	ARTICLE	RATING	ARTICLE
	1. The Perils of Higher Education		24. Strategies to Reduce Medication Errors
	2. Is Health Promotion Relevant Across Cultures and the Socioeconomic Spectrum?		25. The Price of Pain
	3. Putting a Premium on Health		26. You, Me, and Porn Make Three
	4. Fix Your Worst Health Habits-Fast		27. Sex Ed for the Stroller Set
	5. Love Is Real Medicine		28. It's Just Mechanics
	6. Enough to Make You Sick?		29. Promiscuous Plague
	7. Are You OK?		30. 'Diabesity,' a Crisis in an Expanding Country
	8. Attention Deficit Disorder: Old Questions, New Answers		31. The Battle Within: Our Anti-Inflammation Diet
	9. Dealing with Demons		32. Why We Are Still Losing the Winnable Cancer War
	10. Too Young to be Stressed		33. How AIDS Changed America
	11. Diet and Genes		34. The Puzzling Origins of AIDS
	12. When It Pays to Buy Organic		35. Pharmacist Refusals: A Threat to Women's Health
	13. The Future of Foods?		36. A High Dose of Tech
	14. What Does Science Say You Should Eat?		37. Medicine's Turf Wars
	15. Food News Blues		38. Putting a Value on Health
	16. Exercise Abuse: Too Much of a Good Thing		39. Dentists Frown at Overuse of Whiteners
	17. The Female Triad		40. Making an Informed Decision about Breast Implants
	18. How Sleep Affects Your Weight		41. How to Ease Your Pain
	19. Fat Chance		42. Deep into Sleep
	20. Why We're Losing the War Against Obesity		43. Avian Flu: How Serious Is the Risk?
	21. Rx for Fraud		44. 'Vintage' Bugs Return: Mumps? Whooping Cough? Rickets? What Year Is It?
	22. Drinking Too Much: Too Young		45. Agencies Work to Corral Mad Cow Disease
	23. Just Say No Again: The Old Failures of New and Improved Anti-Drug Education		46. In Katrina's Wake

(Continued on next page)

ANNUAL EDITIONS: HEALTH 07/08

BUSINESS REPLY MAIL
FIRST CLASS MAIL PERMIT NO. 551 DUBUQUE IA

POSTAGE WILL BE PAID BY ADDRESEE

McGraw-Hill Contemporary Learning Series
2460 KERPER BLVD
DUBUQUE, IA 52001-9902

NO POSTAGE
NECESSARY
IF MAILED
IN THE
UNITED STATES

‐ ‐

ABOUT YOU

Name   Date
_____   _____

Are you a teacher? ☐   A student? ☐
Your school's name
_____

Department
_____

Address   City   State   Zip
_____

School telephone #
_____

YOUR COMMENTS ARE IMPORTANT TO US!

Please fill in the following information:
For which course did you use this book?
_____

Did you use a text with this ANNUAL EDITION? ☐ yes ☐ no
What was the title of the text?
_____

What are your general reactions to the *Annual Editions* concept?
_____

Have you read any pertinent articles recently that you think should be included in the next edition? Explain.
_____

Are there any articles that you feel should be replaced in the next edition? Why?
_____

Are there any World Wide Web sites that you feel should be included in the next edition? Please annotate.
_____

May we contact you for editorial input? ☐ yes ☐ no
May we quote your comments? ☐ yes ☐ no